The Measure of Canadian Society

Carleton Library Series No. 144

The Measure of Canadian Society

Education, Equality and Opportunity

John Porter

Introduced by Wallace Clement and with an annotated bibliography of writings about John Porter and his work by Richard C. Helmes-Hayes.

Carleton University Press
Ottawa, Canada
1987

Canadian Cataloguing in Publication Data

Porter, John, 1921-1979.
　The measure of Canadian society : education,
equality and opportunity

(The Carleton library ; 144)
Includes bibliographical references and index.
ISBN 0-88629-065-1

　1. Equality—Canada. 2. Education—Canada.
3. Canada—Social conditions—1971-　. I. Title.
II. Series.

HN107.P67 1987　　971.064　　C87-090285-7

Distributed by: Oxford University Press Canada,
　　　　　　　70 Wynford Drive,
　　　　　　　DON MILLS, Ontario, Canada,
　　　　　　　M3C 1J9.
　　　　　　　(416) 441-2941

Printed and bound in Canada.

ISBN 0-88629-065-1

To Marion

THE CARLETON LIBRARY SERIES

A series of original works, new collections, and reprints of source material relating to Canada, issued under the supervision of the Editorial Board, Carleton Library Series, Carleton University Press Inc., Ottawa, Canada.

Acknowledgments
Carleton University Press gratefully acknowledges the support extended to its publishing programme by the Canada Council and the Ontario Arts Council.

Contents

Acknowledgments

The essay "Research Biography of a Macrosociological Study: *The Vertical Mosaic*" was originally published in *Macrosociology: Research and Theory*, James S. Coleman, Amitai Etzioni, and John Porter (Boston: Allyn and Bacon, 1970), pp. 149-181.

The essay "The Human Community" was originally published in *The Canadians: 1867-1967*, eds. J.M.S. Careless and R. Craig Brown (Toronto: Macmillan of Canada, 1967), pp. 385-410.

The essay "The Future of Upward Mobility" was originally published in the *American Sociological Review*, vol. 33, February 1968, pp. 5-19. A substantial number of the original notes have been deleted.

The essay "Canadian Character in the Twentieth Century" was originally published in *Annals* of the American Academy of Political and Social Science, vol. 370, March 1967, pp. 49-56.

The essay "Ethnic Pluralism in Canadian Perspective" was originally published in *Ethnicity: Theory and Experience*, eds. Nathan Glazer and Daniel Patrick Moynihan (Cambridge: Harvard University Press, 1975), pp. 267-304.

The essay "Melting Pot or Mosaic: Revolution or Reversion?" was originally published in *Revolution versus Evolution*, ed. Richard A. Preston (Durham, N.C.: Duke University Press, 1979).

The essay "Postindustrialism, Postnationalism, and Postsecondary Education" was originally published in *Canadian Public Administration*, vol. 14, Spring 1971, pp. 32-50.

The essay "Power and Freedom in Canadian Democracy" was originally published in *Social Purpose for Canada*, ed. Michael Oliver (Toronto: University of Toronto Press, 1961), pp. 27-56.

Foreword

THE MEASURE OF JOHN PORTER*

Wallace Clement

John Porter died on June 15, 1979 of heart failure, only weeks after submitting the manuscript for *The Measure of Canadian Society* to the original publisher. John said he wished to dedicate the book to his wife, Marion, because he felt it might be his last major work. His health had been precarious for the previous two decades, having suffered two major heart attacks during the 1960s. Those who knew him during the decade of the 1970s saw an apparently healthy man, handsome in appearance and vigorous while working at his cottage or walking in the woods. John had an attractive personality. Around the university he was sure of himself and confident in his contribution. Although somewhat retiring in public gatherings, he was effective in getting his views across. In private he was charming but challenging as he strove for excellence in himself and others.

Carleton University was John's intellectual home. He had a major part in building it as an institution and his influence remains significant. For this reason it is particularly fitting that the Carleton University Press re-issue *The Measure of Canadian Society*. The book had a rocky start. It was released by Gage Publishing at a difficult time in Canadian publishing and did not get the exposure that it deserved, finally going out of print in the mid-1980s. With the support of the Dean of Social Sciences, the Department of Sociology and Anthropology, and the John Porter Fund, the book is again available.

This re-issue of *The Measure of Canadian Society* retains all John Porter's original material. In the original I had contributed a Foreword and Appendix on 'The Writings of John Porter' (at the request of Gage Publishing and Marion Porter). Carleton University Press has asked me to expand the Foreword into the present introductory essay. In addition, the 'Writings' have been updated and an additional Appendix 'Writings About John Porter' has been added, compiled by Richard Helmes-Hayes (who is currently researching an intellectual biography of John Porter as a post-doctoral project). Proceeds fom the sale of the book will return to the John Porter Fund at Carleton University to be used to assist scholarly publishing and a graduate student bursary.

Shortly before his death, John Porter had completed the selection, editing, and introductions for the ten papers collected in this volume. These pieces are what he regarded as his most significant ''reflective pieces'' and complement his more systematic research published as *The Vertical Mosaic: An Analysis of Social Class and Power in Canada*, *Does Money Matter: Prospects for Higher Education* (a more scholarly version appearing as *Stations and Callings: Making It Through Ontario's Schools*) and the posthumously published *Ascription and Achievement: Studies in Mobility and Status Attainment in Canada*. These publications earn John Porter the right to be called Canada's pre-eminent sociologist.

The fact that John Porter became an academic relatively late in life and lived only to the age of fifty-seven, overcoming major illnesses in between, makes his contribution all the more outstanding. Born in Canada to a working-class family, he moved to England at the age of fifteen where he worked at odd jobs and became a journalist before joining the Canadian Army. After his military days he received a university education. His brief formal education was, as he writes in the first essay of this volume, the formative influence in his academic life. During these years he consolidated the principles, values, and ideas which were to guide his career. His central concern, as the Prologue to this volume makes evident, was overcoming inequality.

This concern became expressed following his return to Canada in 1949, when he then began teaching at Carleton College. In 1952 he embarked on the research for what was to become Canadian sociology's single most renowned scholarly work — *The Vertical Mosaic*. The values and many issues which guided this work are masterfully outlined in his ''Research Biography,'' reprinted here; but, as anyone familiar with the book will know, this background, as enlightening as it is, cannot substitute for the original. *The Vertical Mosaic* merits attentive reading over twenty years after its publication.

Before the publication of *The Vertical Mosaic*, John Porter wrote what I regard as his strongest piece, ''Power and Freedom in Canadian Democracy,'' the earliest article (originally published in 1961) he chose to include in this selection. The reader will find contained within that essay the central dilemmas, contradictions, and insights which informed all of his work. They will also find, as in the Prologue (which is likely the final piece he wrote), a frankness and honesty about his own values and his view of the limits of sociology. The final paper included here, which must rank among his most valuable, is a damning indictment of the educational system and advanced industrial society generally. He saw as his task the explanation and evaluation of societal events and directions. As he often said of sociologists, ''we ought to try to explain society to itself.'' From this task he never faltered. To this end he was an active researcher and shrewd observer of Canadian society.

Indignant is a word which well describes John Porter's intellectual stance. He was angry about the human waste he saw in advanced industrial societies. Their lack of justice, he felt, impeded the development of human potential. Inequalities were to be abhorred and alternative means to organize societies were to be sought. A complacent man does not write *The Vertical Mosaic* or the articles appearing in this volume. Although he acknowledged that change too often occurred at "glacial" speed, he continued to press for progressive changes and to attempt to persuade others of the injustice he felt characterized the existing order.

Personally, John was a quiet man, secure in himself yet almost shy. It was not easy for him to perform publicly. He generally disliked lecturing to crowds and was not always at ease even in large seminars. His medium was the written word, where he was eloquent, and individual contact, where he was incisive. He could penetrate an argument quickly and see patterns in data that eluded others. He could follow and devastate an argument with a brief, cutting comment or just as quickly provide a key insight and direction to an entire research project. He worked with a clear image of Canadian society and could readily situate a piece of evidence or an entire argument into that image, thus enabling him to make insightful comments and observations. It is this skill which is so evident in the essays included in the present volume.

The John Porter in this collection — particularly in the Prologue, the final paper, and the introductions to each of the papers — will be one many readers will not have encountered since *The Vertical Mosaic*. During the intervening years he had been engaged primarily in detailed empirical investigations of education and mobility while publishing his more reflective pieces in places inaccessible to the general public. I believe many people will be pleasantly surprised by what they find. Others will react angrily, as they often have, to Porter's arguments.

John Porter was a complex man. This complexity came from his broad knowledge and experience and, most of all, from the difficult issues he addressed. Casual readers of his work could easily miss the dilemmas and debates underlying his writings. This collection will reveal to many for the first time some reasons for this complexity. Even though I knew him personally for seven years and read nearly all the papers before, it was not until reading them as a collection, accompanied by his commentary, that many of his deep-rooted concerns became clearly evident. Those who saw a great leap from *The Vertical Mosaic* to "The Future of Upward Mobility" (included here), will see an equally great leap to the final paper in this volume, "Education, Equality, and the Just Society." They will also find continuity and an explanation for the shifts.

While I have never agreed with all of his arguments, I always respected his manner of thought and insight. Porter tackled problems in an impressive manner. In his selection of issues to investigate, in the way he constructed arguments, and in his use of data he was a master.

He was not always right but he always asked significant questions and came to conclusions that furnished innovative insights. Porter held his convictions strongly and was willing to defend them but not to the point of being dogmatic. He was willing to listen to counter positions and, in light of contrary evidence, to change his opinions. Such a case is evident in this collection concerning the upward mobility afforded by so-called post-industrial societies, as can be seen by contrasting his papers on "The Future of Upward Mobility" (1968) and "Education, Equality, and the Just Society" (1977). As he cautions in the Prologue, "our explanations will be always limited, tentative, and time-bound." The advance of understanding must, in large measure, be a process of debate which offers evidence and counter-evidence to arrive at convincing positions and conclusions.

Porter was always influenced, if not convinced, by marxian analysis. For him, many marxists were either too dogmatic or too abstract. As he notes in the introduction to "Power and Freedom in Canadian Democracy," his concerns included but were not limited to those of marxism:

> How this seemingly inexorable process of bureaucratization and alienation might be halted and at the same time high levels of productivity maintained is a fundamental question for the next stage of societal development which some call post-industrial. The renouncing of capitalist modes of production may be necessary but can by no means be sufficient.

He was convinced only by those who made concrete empirical analyses which made sense of society. Insight and evidence always impressed him, whatever the source.

Frankness about changes in his views is apparent in his introduction to "The Future of Upward Mobility" where he re-evaluates his 1968 optimism about education as an instrument of equality and about the progressive quality of "post-industrial societies," especially regarding their upgrading of skill requirements. Similarly, in his introduction to "Power and Freedom in Canadian Democracy" he remarks that "I would probably want also to modify my views about how the changing occupational structure which has come with industrialism really provides upward mobility." This is very significant in light of the time and energy he devoted to the study of occupational mobility. In "Education, Equality, and the Just Society" he concludes that "Public education's false promise was that it would be one of the chief instruments to achieve social equality." Education was, of course, a central pillar in his search for equality of opportunity. Porter was always frank about his errors of judgment. Rather than attempt to disguise them he frequently shared them with his students as examples to learn from and avoid. This is a sign of a man more interested in his society than himself.

Porter provides in the Prologue a firm direction for those engaged in studies of inequality; he reminds us of the importance of our own values, about the limits of sociology, and about the desirability of developing a macrosociology which is both explanatory and evaluative. Foremost, he reminds us of the requirement for solid empirical research guided by these concerns. His statement is particularly strong in its condemnation of "value-free" abstract empiricists: "Some social scientists believe themselves to be neutral when in fact they have become neuterized by employing statistical accounting procedures as their major tools in the service of existing bureaucracies and power centres." The line he draws is a thin one, particularly for someone like himself who was attempting social policy changes. For this reason he especially valued academic freedom and stressed the need for the university to have autonomy (but not detachment) from the state and corporate worlds. Academics should be free, he felt, to critically evaluate their societies. This freedom, moreover, should be exercised.

At various times Porter considered revising *The Vertical Mosaic* with an extensive introduction covering three major trends with which he had failed to deal in the early 1960s; French- Canadian nationalism, the rise of foreign control of the economy, and the women's movement. Unfortunately none of these issues receives extensive analysis in this collection. There are, however, some indications of a new macrosociology of Canada he intended to write. It would not only have included these "new" issues but others as well. He had planned to apply for a Killam Award to spend time living in various parts of Canada, in part to re-evaluate his position on regional differences. It would, however, have been much more. The tone of Porter's proposed macrosociology would, I imagine, have been much like his concluding paper in this collection. It would have been reflective, self-critical, evaluative, insightful, and apt. It would have been filled with philosophical questions of justice, equality, and fairness. It would have attempted to design means to maximize human development and freedom — the potential of humankind. While we may lament the fact that these writings were never completed, we should be thankful for the fullness of his life and the richness of the understanding he left; particularly this collection completed so late in his career.

His work deserves to be studied carefully and as a whole. Although there is a central theme of equality, there is also a clear development, refinement, and maturity. He was not caught, as some had feared, in a downward spiral of technocratic exercises. He was working toward a more sophisticated understanding of what we are and he hoped to discover something about what we could be. This collection is a major step in that direction. The reflective man who wrote it should be a model for all who are interested in understanding and improving society.

Porter's Search for Equality

John Porter was born in Vancouver, British Columbia on the 12th of November, 1921, and left Canada in 1937, remaining abroad for what he called "twelve formative years." As a teenager he worked at odd jobs and eventually as a reporter for the *Daily Sketch*, a Kemsley (now Thompson) Newspaper, in London. He joined the Canadian Army in 1941 as a private, rising by his release in 1946 to captain, having spent the war in the Canadian Intelligence Corps in Italy, North Africa, and North-West Europe. His class origins had prevented him from receiving much formal education; his father "did some clerical work but had no inclination to do anything very much," and John never graduated from high school. The war, however, gave him the chance to enter university through a veterans' program. He entered the London School of Economics and Political Science, graduating with a B.Sc. in 1949. Porter's military service allowed him to enter the London School of Economics at a vibrant time in that institution's history. As Frank Vallee has said:

> In the postwar period when John was an undergraduate there, LSE was dominated by a spirit of optimism about the chances of reconstructing a world that was badly out of joint. Social democracy was the prevailing ideology, a kind of socialism without revolution which had been advocated by two generations of Fabian scholars and writers. A vital role in the socio-economic reconstruction was to be assumed by the sociologist through his research, the ideal form of which Porter later described as 'rational enquiry guided by humanistic values.' This research was to have a direct bearing on social policy and its findings stated in language which laymen could understand. Very special attention was to be devoted to exposing those inequities which derived from structural faults in distribution of power and life-chances.[1]

Travelling on a Department of Veterans Affairs' grant and intending to write some journalistic articles, Porter returned to Canada in 1949, after what he described as 'twelve formative years' abroad. He stopped in Ottawa to look up an army friend. Paul Fox invited him to become a teacher of Political Science at Carleton, where he remained, aside from a brief sojourn at the University of Toronto in 1968-69, until his death. Through his experience abroad, he had gained something of an 'outsider's' perspective, a built-in comparative approach. This influence is apparent in his greatest publication, *The Vertical Mosaic*, which was completed in 1963 and published in 1965.

Particularly during his later years, Porter again spent considerable time outside the country. He was a Canadian Fellow to the International Institute for Labour Studies in Geneva in 1966-67; he held the Canadian Chair at Harvard in 1974-75, and took his 1975-76 sabbatical in Paris. He found these periods abroad to be intellectually stimulating, giving him a distinct vantage point from which to view Canada and the opportunity to be exposed to outside influences. By this point he had achieved an international reputation, having received the prestigious MacIver Award of the American Sociological Association in 1966 for *The Vertical Mosaic*, the same year he finally received a D.Sc. from the London School of Economics (having submitted *The Vertical Mosaic* as his thesis).

Many young social science scholars must find it confusing that John Porter could have had such an overwhelming presence in Canadian scholarship. What was it that made *The Vertical Mosaic* so prominent? My interpretation is that this work was a statement of the times. Not only was it enormous in its scope, rich in detail and suggestive in its analysis, it also encapsulated many of the important issues of the day. For the first time in the Canadian social sciences there existed a statement of where we were socially. It continues to be a baseline from which many contemporary researchers begin. Since *The Vertical Mosaic*, of course, many other statements have appeared, but it was the opening volley in the explosion of Canadian social science.

Because he addressed so many issues in *The Vertical Mosaic*, contemporary reviewers seem to want him to have done everything. They seem to forget the paucity of existing literature and data, and the fact that most of the material used was subjected to analysis for the first time. Since its publication, Canadian social science has blossomed, in no small measure due to *The Vertical Mosaic*. Even ten years after its publication critical reviews were being written, often without sufficient regard to the historical conditions of its writing.[2] When first published in 1965, *The Vertical Mosaic* was welcomed by the Canadian left (broadly defined) and during the student movement of the late sixties was often used as the basis for radical analysis. Into the 1970s, as a more theoretically sophisticated (but less activist) left developed and became re-acquainted with marxism, Porter was subjected to much criticism. Much of this criticism he reacted to as mere "carping" rather than "constructive" empirical research designed to expose or eradicate inequalities.[3] Toward the end of his life, Porter adopted some of the criticisms of his work but only after its shortcomings had been demonstrated empirically to his satisfaction. At that point he incorporated some of the insights of the left into his analysis.

Although *The Vertical Mosaic* opens with the disclaimer that "no one volume can present a total picture of a modern society," it may safely be said that Porter did, to the extent possible, present a thorough overview of contemporary Canada. There are, of course, significant gaps — the study is weak historically; it does not adequately situate Canada internationally; the analysis of Quebec and other regions is limited; real (as opposed to statistical) classes are dismissed. Its strengths, particularly for its time, compensate for these shortcomings.

The analysis of power in its various expressions is likely the most comprehensive done anywhere; its treatment of education, ethnicity, migration and income and particularly the inequalities associated with them — were a *tour de force* in Canadian social science. Those engaged in empirical research tend to appreciate Porter's work more than those who work primarily at the theoretical level (or do little research at all). The methodological problems, sources of data, and access to information were all formidable barriers to solid research and to the application of theory. He marshalled amazing empirical detail and did so in a way informed by theory if not in a way that "tested" or "generated" theory. His work was drawn together thematically — the master theme being inequality.

The most consistent aspect in Porter's work was his concern with issues of vital concern to the whole of Canadian society, such as inequality. Particularly during his later years he spent a great deal of time thinking about concepts like "justice" — what it meant, how it could be achieved, etc. These were his concerns, his value premises, which he never hesitated to put forward. Porter's philosophical roots were in the British social democratic tradition of Harold Laski, R.H. Tawney and T.H. Marshall but his values, as will be argued later, were those usually flaunted as "American" ideals.

The Vertical Mosaic, while essentially an exercise in sophisticated description, was also a prescriptive. Porter attempted to identify what was in order to evaluate what could be. Rather than develop a theory of class he chose to bring to light inequalities characteristic of the contemporary class structure. It was his judgement that the priority was empirical rather than theoretical. He envisioned himself as establishing a base from which he and others could work. It was not intended, as he never tired of reiterating, as "the last word" — although he was not too modest to claim it as "the first" comprehensive statement.

He outlined in some detail the intellectual forces integral to his early research in a "Research Biography." There he reflected on his consciously "eclectic" use of theory, an eclecticism which continued throughout his career. The strongest and most concise statement of the value concerns and theoretical dilemmas informing his democratic socialism was articulated in "Power and Freedom." His final pronouncement on the values of social scientists appears in his Prologue to *The Measure of Canadian Society*, and in his previously unpublished paper on "Education, Equality, and the Just Society", all of which appear in this collection. Together these papers consolidate the essential concerns of his work. As he said in his Introduction to the "Research Biography":

"My research and social action interests since [*The Vertical Mosaic*] was published have all been extensions of it, particularly those parts which are most relevant to social change in Canada as it is at present on the threshold of post-industrialism: the search for highly- qualified manpower, social mobility, educational opportunity, and the planning of post-secondary education."[4]

In his final collection of essays he amended his position on post-industrialism and the centrality of educational reform.

The Preface to *The Vertical Mosaic* clearly states Porter's value position regarding equality and specifies the type of equality he means. It is equality of opportunity — the removal of barriers which prevent the "most able" from attaining "top positions." This promotion of "meritocracy" is desirable, he argues, "on both ethical and practical grounds." He sees the "creative role of politics" as the means to achieve this goal and the educational system as the principal mechanism. At times he wandered into the territory of inequality of condition by identifying structural sources of inequality but opportunity was his most basic focus, at least until his final years when he returned to the structural features of society.

Porter's is what may be referred to as a "meritocratic critique" of inequality in contrast to an "egalitarian critique".[5] Never, however, does he shy away from the issue of values. In a little known piece called the "Limits of Sociology," written in 1973, he addressed some of these issues and it is worth reproducing his conclusion at length:

> Important as measurement is to the clarification of ethical problems, measurement alone is not enough, for it leads to the free-floating findings which, lacking an anchor in a clear philosophical position, can be used to support contrary points of view. Perhaps that is a limitation of sociology, but in the search for equality it is difficult to avoid ethical considerations because equality is a moral problem. This difficulty is aggravated by the very legitimate need to measure, without which social sciences cannot make their contribution, but measurement reduces important ethical ideas to very mechanical procedures and limited scopes. It is all the more important, therefore, to capture findings within a clearly defined ethical framework; otherwise someone will come along and seize them for his own ideological purposes.[6]

The author of this statement is a man aware of "ideological warfare," of the ethics and morality of research. It is also the statement of a humanitarian who sees the need to develop human qualities and develop a more equitable society.

The particular form of equality Porter strove for was that often used to characterize "American" values in which the ideals of altruism and equality of opportunity dominate. Shortly after the publication of *The Vertical Mosaic* he was quoted as saying, "In my optimistic moments. . .I think the best thing for Canada would be greater Americanization — the more American values we get the more we can become genuinely North American."[7] It may be argued that the egalitarianism produced by these values is *egalite de droit* (formal or legal equality) but not *egalite de fait* (practical or economic equality). Equality before the law and equality of opportunity, particularly through access to education and mobility through the occupational structure, were the forms of equality Porter sought throughout most of his career and thought were possible to achieve. Canadians, unlike "Americans," he thought, were impeded in their development because they lacked values appropriate to advanced industrial societies. He opposed all "ascriptive" inequality — particularly ethnicity and inter-generational advantages transferred through education and occupational mobility.

Capitalism, as a way of organizing a society's productive capacities, was viewed by Porter as a source of grave inequalities. He argued that "Individual property rights meant that those who owned the instruments of production controlled their use and access to them. In many respects the new urban proletariat of the industrial revolution was less free than the feudal serf who had at least some legally defined claims against his master."[8] At times he denounced capitalism and its "lack of conscience" which "can only be explained in terms of habituation to the capitalist ethos and the complex attitudes which legitimates predatory behaviour. . . . The exploitive, predatory and restrictive character of capitalist institutions rests on a morality defined by those at the apex of our institutional hierarchies."[9] The irony of these statements is that he simultaneously called on Canadians to become more like the "Americans" who lived in the most advanced capitalist society of all! Thus capitalism is a progressive system, yet it severely limits human potential and its barriers must be transcended.

For Porter, socialism was not free from many of the problems plaguing capitalism. A common problem was that of bureaucracy:

> Bureaucracy provides socialist theory with a built-in contradiction. Socialism, which seeks to release men from productive drudgery, envisages larger productive units, more intricate co-ordination between these units, and more extensive planning of the total social effort, none of which can be achieved without a very great increase in administrative machinery.[10]

It is this problem which made elites so important to Porter's analysis. In his view there would always be elites of some kind. You cannot "do away with power." The point was one of "transforming it in some fashion to serve justice and equality."[11] The only way was to somehow inject more humanitarian values into those at the top. He concentrated on "opening up" or making accessible power positions within existing institutions. This problem became a preoccupation for the rest of his life.

Post-industrialism and Mobility Studies

From this stage in Porter's argument it is necessary to make a rather large leap. It is a leap from ''industrial'' to ''post-industrial'' societies. These changes were brought about by the new demands of science and technology which required freeing people from the bonds of an earlier stage of capitalism through a demand for talent. ''Post-industrial'' societies would require a new kind of labour force, new sets of values appropriate to the times, and would provide the productive capacity required to meet the society's material demands. The problem of power retreats into the background for Porter as the imperatives of science and technology take hold and re-shape the society. A new problematic emerges:

> With the great expansion in the number of occupations as well as the emergence of new occupations that come with the post-industrial culture of science and technology, it is necessary for all societies at this stage of development to solve their recruiting problems.[12]

The first statement of this new problematic appeared in Porter's 1966 MacIver Award Lecture where he began to address the problem of the ''recruitment of highly qualified professional workers'' because of the new ''culture based on science and technology.'' With this change there is ''unfilled room at the top of our emerging occupational structures.''[13] This would be handled through greater social planning, particularly planning associated with the educational system where training would take place and new values instilled. Porter's contention was that industrial societies were moving in the direction of greater potential for the ''good society'' whereby greater parts of the society could share more equally in the benefits. His goal was to eradicate barriers — specifically mobility barriers — which prevented people from sharing in the newly created ''good life'' and which, for the society, wasted the talents of its people. The measure of egalitarianism in Porter's work is not clear. The focus, however, is on ascriptive barriers to achievement. While there is an analysis of inequality, there is not one of exploitation, of the structural relations between classes. There is a sense that we have to be motivated by the imperatives of science and technology, which are creating new possibilities. The problem is one of *barriers* which simultaneously prevent people from equally sharing in the possibility of benefits and wastes the potential talents at the society's disposal. It is, in a word, the classic problem of ''meritocracy,'' a word Porter chose to use.

For Porter the problem of barriers superseded the problem of power, although they were related to the extent that elites upheld self-serving values. Exclusion practices meant a waste of talent. If recruitment were widened, society's institutions would become more innovative and hence more productive. This position was evident in *The Vertical Mosaic* but became the dominant problematic of his later work. In *The Vertical Mosaic*, as in his later work, Porter argued that industrialization was a means for overcoming some forms of inequality but at the same time the overcoming of these inequalities was necessary for the full benefits of industrialization to be realized:

> The egalitarian ideology holds that individuals should be able to move through this hierarchy of skill classes according to their inclinations and abilities. Such an ideology reinforces the needs of an industrial economic system. A society with a rigid class structure of occupational inheritance could not become heavily industrialized. On the other hand the industrial society which has the greatest flexibility is the one in which the egalitarian ideology has affected the educational system to the extent that education is available equally to all, and careers are truly open to the talented.
>
> At some point in social development industrialization with its attendant egalitarian ideology comes into conflict with the structure of class.[14]

Thus Porter contended that "the correct values for the mobility needs of the industrialized society are those of achievement and universalism."[15] Barriers to these values are offered by "subcultural values and norms — of class, ethnicity and religion [which are not] appropriate for post-industrialism."[16] These barriers inhibit the development of society and are, at the same time, a major source of injustice. If societies were to adopt a "universalism-achievement orientation" then their institutions would be more creative because talent would be more effectively used and the principles of meritocracy would be achieved. Thus the lack of "mobility values" creates "dysfunctions" for societal development. He argued, "If one were to locate within industrial social structures the areas where these dysfunctions can be best elucidated they would be class systems, particularly working-class culture, the family as a socializing agency, and education systems."[17] This explains his concentrated research in the areas of intergenerational mobility, ethnicity, and education, each mediated by the family, in the years following *The Vertical Mosaic*.

Porter's first major undertaking after *The Vertical Mosaic* was on occupational prestige classifications, but it ran into serious technical problems.[18] Eventually it led into an even larger scale national project on occupational mobility, entitled *Ascription and Achievement: Studies in Mobility and Status Attainment in Canada*, involving five coresearchers. The final study was only written in draft form before Porter's death. Porter's two papers for this study were "Ethnic Origin and Occupational Attainment" (co-authored with Peter C. Pineo) and "Canada: The Societal Context of Occupational Allocation."

Education

Porter was opposed to any form of inequality which limited the development of a society's talent, whether it be class, gender or ethnicity. The core institution for overcoming inequality was the educational system. This required, in his view, changes in access to education and in the content of education itself. In his own case, only the Second World War provided the necessary conditions for access to a university education; likely the fact that his own formal educational career was in large part an historical accident was a factor in his deliberations.

The major area of public policy upon which Porter pronounced was education. He undertook a massive study of this subject and published, along with Marion Porter and Bernard Blishen, a policy report entitled *Does Money Matter? Prospects for Higher Education*, which contributed to the debate on educational reform. A longer, scholarly analysis of this data is entitled *Stations and Callings: Making It Through Ontario's Schools*. The major finding of this research was that "educational and occupational horizons of Ontario high school students are bounded by the class structure of the society in which they live; that associated with that class structure, there is a wastage of bright young people from the educational process; and that girls, particularly lower class girls, see themselves destined for the labour force and excluded from the learning force."[19] The report evaluates student assistance plans and the effects of family resources on students' educational prospects.

The study does not limit itself to the educational system *per se* but locates it within a broader social context. The authors say, "We are not so naive as to think . . . that educational reform alone is going to make for a society of equality."[20] This introduces the "what comes first" problem. Education is itself part of a larger structure of inequality but, in Porter's view, is the key institution for overcoming many inequalities. This was a problem of which he was acutely aware, arguing "equality in education cannot be truly achieved without moving toward a more equal society, and that could come about . . . through greatly reduced income differentials or a much more progressive tax system."[21] As far as education itself was concerned, the major reforms considered were the abolition of tuition fees and the provision of maintenance grants to students, but these would only be effective in the context of broader social reforms. Such reforms as progressive taxation and reducing income equality aside, however, means that abolishing tuition and providing student maintenance grants would have to be 'postponed' since it is the children of the privileged who most benefit from post-secondary education. These were longstanding problems for Porter, as he wrote in 1961:

the fact remains that educational systems reflect the values of the dominant institutions within the society, and their influence in bringing about the desired psychological changes is thereby reduced. To achieve some measure of social change it may be necessary to find ways of changing the institutional structure before changing modes of thought.[22]

Porter offered no simple solutions for what he regarded as a complex subject. More than most researchers he was acutely aware of the way institutions such as education were biased by the interests of the powerful. He found it difficult, however, to abandon the possibility of educational reform because it was integral to his vision of positive social change. In his critical essay on "Education, Equality and the Just Society," written near the end of his life, he began to have serious reservations about the centrality of education to accomplishing these changes:

The crucial point is that education has failed to equalize. Perhaps it was naive to think that it might have or that educational reform alone was sufficient to deal with the basic structure of inequality, which in its consequence is much more pervasive and deep rooted than we think.[23]

Ethnicity, Quebec and Regionalism

Paralleling the attention Porter devoted to education was his concern with ethnicity. As he made clear in *The Vertical Mosaic*, ethnicity acted as a major barrier within Canada to the achievement of equality. While he weighed the pros and cons of ethnic sub-cultures he concluded that they were serious impediments in Canada's development. His statements were strong, as the following indicates:

"What price culture?" As cultures converge through science and technology, cultural differentiation, in the sense in which we have usually meant it, will end. In fact, we may have reached the point where culture has become a myth, in the sense of a belief in a non-existent world which might become a reality. The more culture becomes a myth, the less can it become a working concept of social science. . . . In the contemporary society of change, culture can act as an impediment to social development, because it emphasizes yesterday's, rather than tomorrow's, ways of life.[24]

Thus he argued that, "considering as alternatives the ethnic stratification that results from the reduction of ethnicity as a salient feature of modern society I have chosen an assimilationist position."[25] This was an unpopular position, given the revival of ethnicity being experienced in Canada from the late 1960s onwards and the official state policy of multiculturalism. Regardless of its controversial qualities, he clearly articulated the reasons for his position, noting that ethnicity "emphasizes descent group identification and endogamy . . . [thus] it runs the risk of believed-in biological differences becoming the basis of invidious judgements about groups of people . . . Moreover, where ethnicity is salient there is often an association between ethnic differences and social class and inequality."[26] Not only does ethnicity interfere with the search for equality, Porter argued, "it has also served as a form of class control of the major power structures by charter ethnic groups who remain over-represented in the elite structures."[27]

Ethnicity, in the way Porter analysed it, was a barrier to the mobility of individuals within the class structure. The problem, as he argued, was that ethnicity was often an impediment to mobility because the values it promoted were contrary to those required for achievement within the dominant culture. Thus, if the salience of ethnic values were reduced and substituted with other values, there would be a freeing of the talent required by "post-industrial" societies. As it was, ethnicity was an instrument of social control by the powerful and a barrier to mobility.

Although Porter had less to say on the subject than others, he did not regard the Quebecois as he did "other ethnics." In 1961 he argued that the "French desire for cultural separation can be justified both psychologically and socially."[28] Later he argued that French culture could not withstand the onslaught of "modernization" but felt "there need not be a loss of language. If bilingualism can increase, and that requires a great effort on the part of the English, this distinctive dualism of Canada will remain."[29] His own actions were in this direction. At almost fifty years of age, Porter sought to improve his French and spent a great deal of time working at it. He valued the retention of the French language. He also recognized the two-nation reality of Canadian society. As he wrote me in 1976 concerning my study of class,

> What are you going to do about French? It seems to me we have now reached the point in Canada where Fr and Eng Canada can be treated as two separate societies and one or the other left out. The Fr always leave the Eng out since they consider Quebec unto itself. Now they no longer mind if Quebec is left out of macroanalysis of "Canada" which they see almost as another country. That becomes increasingly the reality of course.[30]

I certainly would have welcomed more of his views on Quebec in more developed form. I am not aware of any specific writings on the subject but expect it would have been addressed in his proposed macro-sociology of Canada (to be discussed below). His general position, however, was that Canada was entering a "post-industrial" stage of development where science and technology would dominate, leaving little room for particularistic cultures to survive; within this development he did feel that there was room for bilingualism and for Quebec to have greater independence.

In advocating this position, however, Porter continued to support stronger central powers, if not vis-a-vis Quebec, then at least for the rest of Canada. He contended that "lessening of federal power particularly in a wide range of social policy can be seen as a loss of the ability to establish national goals."[31] He wished to see, for example, a greater federal presence in the educational system as a means of standardizing and upgrading this institution.

He had little favour for regional analyses, contending that the differences within Canada were less geographically-based than class-based. He argued, "It is difficult to know how, other than in the statistical sense, provinces can be 'poor'. People are poor, and some of their poverty could be caused by protected privilege and regressive policies within provinces which in no way change through equalization transfers. To equalize provincial averages in some resource need not affect within- province distributions."[32] He also maintained:

> If one attempts to define communities by transaction flows, Montreal, Toronto and Vancouver are probably more closely linked and provide mutual identities than do these metropolises with their respective hinter-lands. Hardrock and coal miners and pulp workers moving through Canada's single industry towns might have a regional identity which geographically spans the country.[33]

I suspect that his opinion of regionalism was much like that of ethnicity. It spawned values inappropriate to the needs of "post-industrial" society by emphasizing particularistic rather than universalistic values, thus acting as possible barriers to mobility and, in this case, to national goals. Toward the end of his life he was prepared to re-evaluate his views on regionalism and toward this end was preparing to apply for a Killam Award to live in various regions of the country.

Class

In his analysis of class, Porter was more intent on demarcating ranks and strata than on analysing relationships between classes. Inequalities based on class are real in his studies but they are grouped or ordered by artificial lines drawn by application of various criteria, not by "legally recognized" relationships as was the case for estates or castes.[34] In Part I of *The Vertical Mosaic* on "The Structure of Class," no class resistance or struggle appears, no agents of change in the working class since, he argued, we are in a "post-Marxian industrial world." Porter contended that "in the nineteenth century it may have been the case that two groups classified by the criterion of owning or not owning property were sociological groups, but in the present day such classes are statistical categories and nothing more."[35] For him class is a ranking of occupations, income, and education; it is a "spectrum" of socio-economic status led by a wealthy and powerful elite. This conception of class was very much a product of the dominant social sciences in the 1960s.

The fundamental reason for the shift from conflicting to statistical classes, Porter contends, is the advance of industrialization. There has been a proliferation of occupations and a reduction in overt exploitation. "For the proletariat, the work world has not been one of increasing drudgery, nor one requiring an increasingly low level of skill, making workers a vast class of 'proles'. The skills that modern industry requires have become more and more varied and complex so that unskilled occupations have formed a much larger proportion."[36] Generally, throughout this work, he understates the amount of class conflict in society, arguing in the early 1960s that "the idea of the general strike has almost completely disappeared from union ideology."[37] He also had a low expectation at that time of unionization or resistance from "the white-collar group,"[38] expecting them to grow dramatically within the occupational structure but offering little possibility for unionization or resistance. His stress was on the weakness and fragmentation of labour and the relatively low and stagnating rates of unionization. There were some obvious truths to his observations but for the most part he underestimated the struggles that would emerge from the new working class, particularly among state workers, for union recognition and wages. The upgrading of skills assumed with application of science and technology did not turn out to have the projected effects, as will be illustrated shortly.

Much of what Porter wrote in *The Vertical Mosaic* can be read as informing analyses of class cleavages, but most is not analysed by him in this way. The chapter on "Class, Mobility and Migration," for example, provides information on the making of a working class through detachment from the land and particular immigration policies, but primarily it is an analysis of imported education and skills creating a "mobility trap" for native-born Canadians and an ethnically stratified society. Instead of class, Porter uses the concept of elite as a substitute saying, "What we have instead of a class of capitalists is a smaller and probably more cohesive group — an elite within the private sector of the economy."[39] This leaves an obvious analytical gap for all those outside the elite, particularly the working class and petite bourgeoisie but also smaller capitalists. The "class" quality of the elite does not, however, provide an explanation for social change. This requires an analysis of class transformations. Porter did not ignore classes but he did deny them as real forces in contemporary society.

As has emerged as a consistent theme throughout his work, Porter's contention was that a fundamental change was taking place in industrial societies. The problems of capitalist societies would not hold in post-industrial ones:

> The radical-conservative polarity based on class may have been appropriate in the development of a modern industrial society. It led to welfare policies of redistribution and hence legitimated capitalist systems. It also led to policies to maintain levels of demand for the output of the economy. But high evaluation of working-class culture as something of benefit to be preserved becomes increasingly less appropriate to the society based on science and technology.[40]

His analysis was based on a fundamental belief that progressive changes were taking place which would represent a movement beyond classes in the classical sense.

There is some evidence, however, that late in his life he began to re-evaluate some of the premises of this belief. It is worthwhile establishing some of these assumptions, as evident in *The Vertical Mosaic*, and comparing them with his more recent remarks. He argued that "It would be fairly safe to generalize that as industrialization proceeds the shape of the class structure changes from triangular to diamond or beehive . . . [using] the criterion of occupational skill."[41] Further, he said, "it can reasonably be assumed that the increasing proportion of blue collar workers in manufacturing had higher levels of skills at the end of the sixty years [1901-1961] than at the beginning."[42] Porter's analysis of post-industrialism places great stake in the decline of unskilled and the rise of semi-skilled and skilled workers. The 'upgrading' of skills was accepted by Porter, as by most observers, as a matter of faith, concomitant with industrialization. They equated the decline of backbreaking labour with greater skill but failed to examine the content of the rising 'semi-skilled' category and the changes among the 'skilled'.

In light of these assumptions, Porter's comments on Harry Braverman's influential *Labor and Monopoly Capital*, which makes the opposite points Porter had made earlier about class, are informative. Porter was particularly impressed by Braverman's critique of census and occupational classifications, saying "his analysis of the methodology of the prevailing official [classifications], more than any other part of the book calls into question the notion of an upgraded labour force. All of these things add up to a tremendously powerful critique of how we have looked at work."[43] Additional evidence of a change in Porter's position near the end of his life comes from his introductory commentary on his "Power and Freedom" article contained in the present collection where he remarks, "I would probably want also to modify my views about how the changing occupational structure which has come with industrialism really provides upward mobility."[44]

Porter's Reflections

As Porter continued to pursue the concerns evident in *The Vertical Mosaic*, he was led to the subjects of education, occupational mobility, and ethnicity. He embarked on detailed empirical investigations to more fully understand the patterns he had uncovered. More than seeking understanding, he was attempting to influence the direction of change by doing social policy analysis. The main example of this was *Does Money Matter? Prospects for Higher Education* with Marion Porter and Bernard Blishen. In the present volume Porter makes some critical comments about his own work and the direction of the discipline. As he had been from the beginning, he was conscious of his values and reflective about the way they influenced his research. During the later years the philosophical side of equality — the concepts of justice and fairness — captivated his thoughts and caused him to re-evaluate some of his earlier arguments. His aim, which unfortunately was never realized, was to translate these philosophical issues into means to evaluate society and inform a new macrosociology he wished to develop.

Both Marion Porter and Peter C. Pineo have pointed out that John's massive surveys of prestige, education, and occupational mobility, undertaken after *The Vertical Mosaic*, were all close replications of U.S. studies.[45] This is ironic for one who is regarded as the foremost builder of a distinctive Canadian sociology. Each of the three surveys were undertaken collaboratively, had findings which were 'not surprising,' and were clearly geared to testing very specific propositions. Although it is difficult to say definitely, I think the studies were not ends-in-themselves for Porter but a means toward building even a grander macrosociology than that of *The Vertical Mosaic*.

James Heap has charged Porter with pursuing a 'strategy of respectability' after *The Vertical Mosaic*, contending that "Porter's muted radicalism can be understood as an attempt to be both left and right, 'simultaneously respectable and polemical'."[46] Can the 'left' not be 'respectable' (whatever that means)? If, as I take it to mean, respectable is something or someone worthy of esteem or having some quality of excellence, then certainly Porter aimed (as should all) for 'respectability'. He never hesitated to be polemical, at least in the milder meaning of that word (controversial), if not in the stronger meaning (doctrinaire). Any esteem Porter sought was for the quality of the work done, not by doctoring his conclusions to please the powerful. His 'restraint' and 'tentativeness' were confined to the strength of conclusions which could be drawn from the quality of data available. When data warranted, he did not hesitate to draw a 'radical' conclusion.

There is a sense, however, in which the education and mobility surveys were based on a false assumption about post-industrial societies and the demands they would make for highly qualified labour power. Education was, in Porter's view, an important means through which broader inequalities could be addressed, as well as a mechanism for expanding society's talent pool. Toward the end of his career, as Marion Porter points out, he began to have serious reservations about the ameliorative qualities of education. Similarly he re-considered the assumptions underlying the mobility studies he participated in but remained open to strong arguments, even if they contradicted his earlier assumptions. This is clear in his comment on Braverman's *Labor and Monopoly Capital*:

> The book was an articulate reminder of facts we did know but were prepared to overlook, and I use 'we' here in the sense of the whole gamut of followers of conventional social science, of the post-Second World War period. I think we were prepared to overlook this evidence because of our overconcern for economic growth as the raison d'etre of industrialization . . . the basic assumptions underlying analyses of these father-son occupational data [on mobility], on which I have been engaged myself, is that the overall effects of industrialization have been beneficial and progressive. Social scientists, of course, bear this burden of oversight, or guilt depending upon how severe one considers the offence to be.[4]

Even late in his career Porter was willing to consider arguments and evidence which contradicted assumptions basic to his mode of analysis. The failure to examine the class content of occupational changes has proven to be a major flaw of many statistical treatments of class, Porter's work included. To his credit, he did not pursue a 'strategy of respectability' but took these challenges seriously and, I would argue, sought to incorporate them into his planned research.

John Porter's search for equality was a never-ending one. At the end of his life there was still a vibrance to his work, a feeling that he still had another great book in mind. He wrote in 1970, in the Introduction to his "Research Biography," that "Much more material is now available than formerly to undertake another macroanalysis of Canada in transition or to revisit the 'mosaic'. That would be an attractive possibility if time and energies allow."[48] In 1974 he wrote to me from Harvard that "course preparation I have found irksome and heavy, but I hope what I am doing will ultimately develop into a macrosociology — although the pay off is far ahead."[49] Again in 1976 he wrote, saying "When I can get out from under my present grant obligations I have every intention of doing another macro-book on Canada."[50] It is my impression that John was dissatisfied — or perhaps more accurately impatient — with his later studies of education and intergenerational mobility. They were massive research projects involving enormous grants and much complex collaboration. As I saw them, they were for John a means to an end, the necessary homework for a more important project, but they took much more time and energy than he had planned. They were only coming to a conclusion at the time of his death. There are, however, a few clues about what he intended to accomplish.

Porter's macrosociology after *The Vertical Mosaic* contained a strong comparative focus,[51] arguing the desirability of understanding 'types' of societies. Although he was hopeful about the promise of such studies he was aware of their pitfalls and critical of the rigor they had exhibited to date. One of the general concepts he continually returned to in later life was that of 'citizenship rights':

> What distinguishes a modern industrial society from earlier types is that, because of greater productive capacity, it can implement all the rights of citizenship according to the principles of justice. . . . John Rawls' *Theory of Justice* which is perhaps the best contemporary attempt to develop a socialist ethic, suggests that, while liberty has primacy in modern industrial society, it could well not have it in an underdeveloped one where the development of economic resources must have primacy. Modern industrial societies, then are a type with their own capacity to achieve social welfare, to implement citizenship and achieve equality and justice in the here and now.[52]

Porter was working with the concept of justice and how it could be translated not only into legal and political rights but social rights as well. Thus he considered the best way to develop a 'socialist ethic' would be through the concrete application of specific enforceable rights available to each individual. These rights, which he felt advanced industrial societies were capable of fulfilling, included such things as a decent standard of living for all, equal access to education and equal access to all occupations. It is evident that the macrosociology he had in mind would not be a mere description. As he said, macrosociology

> should be capable of both explanation *and* evaluation, that is we should be able, on the one hand to understand how a society in its totality works and how it got to be where it is, and on the other hand we should be able to judge whether or not it is moving in a desirable direction, that is in the direction of maximizing human welfare. . . . If we are not concerned with questions of value then sociology will return to that condition of aimless empiricism and labourious webs of theory spinning towards which recent criticism has been directed, or it will return to that condition where its major premises are those of the *status quo*.[53]

Central to this projected work was the notion of citizenship rights, originally derived from T.H. Marshall's idea in *Citizenship and Social Class* that citizenship should include 'legal, political and social rights'. Moreover, it was to include John Rawls' notions from *A Theory of Justice* to complement the liberties of citizenship rights. A rare glimpse into his intended research is available in his own words:

[t]he type of model which I have in mind would enable us to trace how variations over time in major elements of social structure, the components of a societal system, as independent variables would produce certain outcomes notably the distributive system that is the degree of equality, and the process of mobilization and concensus formation that is the degree of political participation generated largely by conflicts between major social divisions with a society (1975:3).[54]

Although there is some dispute about Porter's devotion to theory, I think he did use theory extensively and creatively and was attempting, especially in his later years, to build a macrosociological theory incorporating the concepts of justice, fairness, and equality. It would not be theory for its own sake but theory with an end. That end would be a means of evaluating the direction of society and acting as a basis for guided social change. He was a man who never ceased to amaze me with the range of his understanding and knowledge, so I would not have been surprised if his planned macrosociology had lived up to his expectations.

My favourite story about John is something that happened in 1974. I was taking a course with Leo Panitch at Carleton who introduced me to the work of Antonio Gramsci. I poured through the *Prison Notebooks*,[55] finding them a source of great revelation. Since it had only been translated from Italian in 1971, few English readers were aware of this work. I decided to share my finding with John and approached him with great glee (and not a little smugness) to reveal this 'new' source of knowledge. I was greeted by his telling me that he had been exposed to Gramsci's work during his wartime stay in Italy and, indeed, back in England had considered translating Gramsci before being drawn into the research for *The Vertical Mosaic*. Never again would I underestimate John Porter.

John Porter was someone you had to respect; not only did he allow disagreement, he encouraged it. He was tolerant of differing viewpoints, but only if you did your homework ('get the facts straight') and could sustain the logic of your position. He had little time for the merely opinionated or superficial. His accomplishments were many and his life a full measure. Few can ever hope to contribute as much as he did. We should be thankful for the fullness of his life and the contributions he made. We are richer for them. We will be better researchers, better teachers, and, most important for those of us fortunate enough to have known him, better people.

*   This Introductory Essay is based upon the original Foreword, an article called "Searching for Equality: The Sociology of John Porter" in the *Canadian Journal of Political and Social Theory* (4:2, 1980) and another article called "John Porter and the Development of Sociology in Canada" in the *Canadian Review of Sociology and Anthropology* (18:5, 1981). I would like to thank Marion Porter, Dennis Olsen and Richard Helmes-Hayes for comments on this paper as well as Daiva Stasiulis and Michael Gnarowski from Carleton University Press for their assistance. John Harp, Chair of the Sociology and Anthropology Department, and Dennis Forcese, Dean of Social Sciences, at Carleton University have assisted in making the re-issue of this book possible.

NOTES

1. Frank Vallee, "Obituary: John Porter (1921-1979)," in *Society/Société* 4:1 (September) 1979, 14.

2. See Edwin R. Black, "The Fractured Mosaic: John Porter Revisited," in *Canadian Public Administration* 17 (Winter), 1974; James Heap, *Everybody's Canada: The Vertical Mosaic Reviewed and Re-examined*, Toronto: Burns and MacEachern, 1974; Harvey Rich, "*The Vertical Mosaic* Revisited: Toward a Macrosociology of Canada," in *Journal of Canadian Studies* 11:1 (February) 1976.

3. See John Porter, "Foreword" to *The Canadian Corporate Elite: An Analysis of Economic Power* by Wallace Clement, Toronto: McClelland and Stewart, 1975.

4. John Porter, Introduction to "Research Biography of a Macrosociological Study: *The Vertical Mosaic*," in *Macrosociology: Research and Theory*, James Coleman, Amitai Etzioni and John Porter, Boston: Allyn and Bacon Inc., 1970, p. 148.

5. See Clement, *Canadian Corporate Elite*, pp. xxv, 1-8.

6. John Porter, "The Limits of Sociology," in *Contemporary Sociology* 2:5 (September) 1973, 467; also, see Prologue to *The Measure of Canadian Society*, pp. 1-5.

7. *Toronto Daily Star*, 31 December 1965.

8. John Porter, "Power and Freedom in Canadian Democracy," in *Social Purpose for Canada*, ed. M. Oliver, Toronto: University of Toronto Press, 1961, p. 30. This collection, see Chapter 9.

9. *Ibid.*, pp. 37-38.

10. *Ibid.*, p. 42.

11. John Porter, "Notes as Commentator" for "Macrosociological Issues in Canadian Sociology" session, Canadian Sociology and Anthropology meetings, Edmonton (May) 1975, p. 10.

12. John Porter, "Evaluation and Status: Some Theoretical Perspectives," unpublished paper, Department of Sociology and Anthropology, Carleton University, Ottawa, n.d., p. 15.

13. John Porter, "The Future of Upward Mobility," in *American Sociological Review* 33:1 (February) 1968, 5. This collection, see Chapter 3.

14. John Porter, *The Vertical Mosaic: An Analysis of Social Class and Power in Canada*, Toronto: University of Toronto Press, 1965, pp. 166-167.

15. John Porter, "Mobility, Stratification and Highly Qualified Manpower," Cornell Conference on Human Mobility, Cornell University (October) 1968, p. 12.

16. *Ibid.*, pp. 13-14.

17. Porter, "Future of Upward Mobility," p. 11.

18. See Peter C. Pineo and John Porter, "Occupational Prestige in Canada," in *Canadian Review of Sociology and Anthropology* 4:1 (February) 1967, 24-28.

19. Marion R. Porter, John Porter and Bernard R. Blishen, *Does Money Matter? Prospects for Higher Education*, Toronto: York Institute for Behavioural Research, 1973, p. x.

20. *Ibid.*, p. xiii.

21. *Ibid.*, p. 202.

22. Porter, "Power and Freedom," p. 52.

23. John Porter, "Education, Equality and the Just Society" in *Measure of Canadian Society*, p. 260.

24. John Porter, "Bilingualism and the Myths of Culture," in *Canadian Review of Sociology and Anthropology* 6:2(May) 1969, 118.

25. John Porter, "Canada: Dilemmas and Contradictions of a Multi-Ethnic Society," in *Sociology Canada: Readings*, ed. C. Beattie and S. Crysdale, Toronto: Butterworths, 1974, p. 13.

26. John Porter, "Ethnic Pluralism in Canadian Perspective," in *Ethnicity: Theory and Experience*, ed. N. Glazer and D.P. Moynihan, Cambridge: Harvard University Press, 1975, p. 288.

27. *Ibid.*, p. 294.

28. Porter, "Power and Freedom," p. 35.

29. Porter, "Ethnic Pluralism," p. 276.

30. John Porter, personal correspondence, 28 October 1976, Carleton University, Ottawa.

31. Porter, "Ethnic Pluralism," p. 272.

32. John Porter, Introduction to "Mr. Trudeau and Federalism," in *Measure of Canadian Society*, p. 164.

33. Porter, "Notes as Commentator," p. 6.

34. See Porter, *Vertical Mosaic*, pp. 7-8.

35. *Ibid.*, p. 20.

36. *Ibid.*

37. *Ibid.*, p. 26.

38. See *Ibid.*, pp. 309-310.

39. *Ibid.*, p. 23.

40. Porter, "Future of Upward Mobility," p. 16.

41. Porter, *Vertical Mosaic*, p. 148.

42. *Ibid.*, p. 150.

43. John Porter, "Comments by John Porter," Symposium on Braverman, *Alternate Routes: A Critical Review* 2 (1978), 25.

44. John Porter, Introduction to "Power and Freedom in Canadian Democracy," in *Measure of Canadian Society*, p. 209.

45. See Marion Porter, "John Porter and Education" and Peter C. Pineo, "Prestige and Mobility," *Canadian Review of Sociology and Anthropology* 18:5 (December) 1981.

46. Heap, *Everybody's Canada*, p. 101.

47. Porter, "Comments," p. 25. See Marion Porter's Note 45.

48. Porter, Introduction to "Research Biography," p. 148.

49. John Porter, personal correspondence, 22 March 1974, Harvard University, Cambridge, Massachusetts.

50. John Porter, personal correspondence, 14 July 1976, Lake Constan, Ontario.

51. See John Porter, "Some Observations on Comparative Studies," International Institute for Labour Studies: *Bulletin* 3 (November) 1967, pp. 82-104.

52. Porter, "Notes as Commentator," pp. 3-4. See John Rawls, *A Theory of Justice*. Cambridge: Harvard University Press, 1971.

53. *Ibid.*, p. 2.

54. *Ibid.*, p. 3.

55. See Antonio Gramsci, *Selections from the Prison Notebooks*, New York: International Publishers, 1971.

Prologue

John Porter

Most of my work as a sociologist in Canada, as reflected in the papers brought together in this volume, has been concerned with some aspect of social inequality. I have sought to expose inequality in some of its many forms, such as access to education or the relations between ethnic groups, because I think that condition as it continues to exist in Canada is insupportable.

I am not sure how one comes to adopt a particular stance to social affairs—conservative, liberal, or radical. Perhaps it is one's personal experience of extreme hardship or excessive comfort, but the causal direction of such an hypothesis would be difficult to state when we see so many liberals and radicals coming from the more privileged classes, and so many reactionaries from among the threatened and the poor. Backgrounds are as often deserted as embodied in one's philosophy.

More important than a background of poverty or riches in the explanation of how personal attitudes to inequality are formed might be the elegant analyses and eloquent arguments by which some interpreters are able to bring the hazy and inscrutable flux of events into an image that makes sense to us. Once the picture is available, however abstracted or impressionistic, we are able to express our approval or disapproval of things as we see them. I was recruited early in my intellectual development to the liberal egalitarian position and the first essay in this volume tells something of the circumstances.

We continue to live in a country and a world where few have much and many have little, but that is a condition not widely disapproved. Thus, the idea of equality in its liberal or more radical forms does not necessarily win out even in our epoch of welfare states, reverse discrimination, and human rights commissions.

It is remarkable that two influential books, John Rawls' *A Theory of Justice* and Robert Nozick's *Anarchy, State and Utopia*, published close together in the 1970s, should come to quite opposite conclusions on the equality-inequality debate, with Rawls seeking to specify the severely constrained conditions under which inequality might exist, and Nozick with his theory of justice in holdings which would allow fortunes justly acquired to be transmitted to the next generation. In these intellectual skirmishes which are as old as human philosophy, what can be persuasion for one can be dissuasion for another.

Although many would like to avoid the issue, social scientists have to choose sides and to fashion their work with a clear idea of what their values are. Some may think there is a neutral position on every issue of great social importance which can be analysed objectively, but that is the position of the bureaucrat rather than the intellectual, and almost always a position taken from a power base with a prior commitment to the status quo. Some social scientists believe themselves to be neutral when in fact they have become neuterized by employing statistical accounting procedures as their major tools in the service of existing bureaucracies and power centres.

To me, the major task of social science is to abstract from the confused flow of events perspectives which clarify and which permit some judgment about a society in the light of moral principles. The natural sciences have provided us with a considerable command over nature, not all of which by any means has been for human benefit, but because of their high status, to say nothing of the financial support they have received, they have provided models which many social scientists have sought to emulate. I find it difficult to imagine the social sciences pursuing, in the modalities of the experimental sciences, objectives of explanation that might give command over society parallel to that which the natural sciences have over nature. For one thing, explanation implies a deterministic system in which we become helpless observers of events, but it also implies, paradoxically, that there can be some command over society as our knowledge of it increases, and that raises the question of knowledge for what, in the hands of whom?

The difficulty is in part resolved for us by the condition that our explanations will be always limited, tentative, and time-bound. The most we can hope for are broad explanatory sketches and evaluative frameworks which fall far short of telling the whole story of reality but which are convincing enough, or more convincing than others, that they engage our critical attention and lead us to conclude that we wish to make some changes.

In providing such perspectives on social reality, carefully designed and executed empirical research with all the tools available to the social investigator makes an essential contribution. There now exists a substantial school which rejects this empirical research, this positivism, on the grounds that most of it has served the interests of those in power in society. That, of course, is simply to say that it is the interpretative frameworks of the powerful which have been best filled in by these methods. Research methodologies, as I suggested earlier, are, like accounting procedures, relatively neutral. It is a matter of the purposes to which research is put. We can be devoted to an aimless pursuit of "explanation," or we can be concerned with the presentation of things as they appear to be and as others are likely to find them if they repeated the process with the same methods. It is pointless to argue as some do in the social sciences that however clear the focus or how often replicated the procedures, the view is still biassed, and, therefore, the picture is unreal and useless.

We conduct research with careful design and controls in order to provide evidence that might enlighten publics and policy makers, spark debate about whether what we find is desirable, satisfactory, or reprehensible in the light of some standards that we have, and, depending on the outcome of that, help to mobilize forces of change.

I would like then to work towards a macrosociology that is capable of both explanation *and* evaluation, that is, we should be able on the one hand to understand—as limited as that understanding may be—how a society in its totality works and how it got to be where it is, and on the other hand we should be able to judge whether or not it is moving in the direction of maximizing human welfare. I think it is possible to combine within the same framework both explanatory and judgmental modes of analysis although it is not possible here to elaborate on what is necessary to provide such a sociology. We need to know how the great society in Graham Wallas' sense can also be the good society.

If we are not concerned with questions of value, sociology will never emerge from the aimless empiricism and laborious webs of theory-spinning towards which recent criticism has been directed, or it will remain in that condition in which its hidden major premises are those of the status quo.

The guiding judgmental principle, it seems to me, for an evaluative sociology derives from the concept of citizenship as it has been developed by T.H. Marshall. Citizenship has evolved historically at different times and rates in western societies with the extension of legal, political, and social rights. Social indicators can be developed to measure their distribution. In some of the essays in this volume I have tried to relate Marshall's concept of citizenship to contemporary discussions of equality.

I think most of the papers brought together in this volume are linked not only by the binding, but also by this concern for equality. They contain little empirical research, that being more properly left to research monographs, but some are reflective pieces, often critical, about the state of affairs in Canadian society. Some of them were written for audiences outside Canada and have appeared in scattered publications or books, and there seemed some point in bringing them together. For each one I have written a brief introductory comment which should help to put them in some temporal or intellectual context.

It might be worth considering briefly what the future is likely to be for studies of inequality. No doubt the subject will continue to inspire the complex and abstract theorizing so attractive to academic intellectuals. Not only has the work of Rawls and Nozick been keenly debated, but so, too, has the neo-Marxism which has come to North America from Europe.

Arguments about theories should not allow us to neglect our empirical research. The evidence that advanced industrial societies have, since the Second World War and the advent of the welfare state, moved toward greater equality is mixed. No doubt the welfare state has had some ameliorating effects by reducing the gross inequalities that existed. Some would argue that the role of the welfare state is to ameliorate sufficiently to legitimate the considerable inequalities that remain. During the 1970s western capitalism had reached a critical point of slow growth giving the state an increasingly ambiguous task of intervention to maintain or re-establish climates favorable for capitalist enterprise. In this context has arisen the new conservatism, calling for reduced government expenditures from the level of about four-tenths of gross national products which they now dispose of.

The new conservatism is both economic and political; it warns us of an inescapable trade-off between equality and economic efficiency and equality and political liberty, since the redistributive objectives which equality requires can be reached only through increased state encroachment and control.

For social scientists, as opposed to philosophers who will keep the abstract debates alive, the task ahead, I think, will be one of improving our means of measuring inequality in the light of changing social institutions and mores. For example, in the past it has always been thought appropriate in examining inequality of condition to take the traditional family, where the father is the main income earner and the mother stays home, as the unit of analysis. Now mothers increasingly work outside the home for pay and their income is regarded as part of the family income, an assumption in the analysis of income distribution which could have the effect of reducing inequality or bringing many families above the poverty line. But many wives and mothers work to be independent of their husbands, or so one can interpret present normative trends. If married women are treated as statistically independent, as the emerging mores would suggest, then the distribution of income would be different than if they were regarded as family members. Similar unit-of-analysis problems exist with young workers and pensioners. Thus a good deal of thought is necessary to bring concepts and measurements into line with changing social values, particularly since the evidence we seek is to help us in making judgments about where as a society we are going. In a general vein it might be said that the inequality between the sexes intersects other structures of inequality—say, power and privilege—so greater sex equality can effect changes in others, but we need some new analytical tools to measure properly the processes.

In recent years we have become much more sophisticated in our analysis of inequality of income and resources by disaggregating the various components of income and wealth such as income from work, transfer payments of various kinds, and unearned income. As a result we are beginning to develop a much clearer picture than formerly of the way in which these various income sources affect resource distribution.

To move to the political domain where the inequality of resources to bring influence to bear on elites and decision makers is considerable, we need in Canada more studies of which groups have access to elites and which are excluded. There has not been sufficient attention paid in Canada to interest or lobby groups and how they affect the legislative and bureaucratic decision-making process. Electoral reform, as important as that has been, is not enough to ensure equality in the political arena because the politics of pressure begin where the politics of persuasion leave off.

In Canada we have seen the emergence of two forms of communalism, the costs of which we have not properly assessed. One is ethnic communalism and the other regional. Both have arisen because of the structure of inequality peculiar to Canadian society, but ironically they could impede politics directed to social and economic equality. Moreover, regions become jealous of their advantages and claim eminent domain in their resources as regional rather than national citizens. At least their political elites behave that way, as they have tilted the balance of federalism heavily in the direction of the provinces. One consequence of communalism is that equality is judged in terms of groups rather than individuals, and that is poor judgment, for behind group averages—however equal they may be—there can lie great inequalities between individuals, or whatever fundamental unit of analysis we might employ.

Studies are soon to appear which will help to uncover the processes by which individuals of both sexes attain their levels of education and occupational position, and how those of different social background have differential chances of exploiting the opportunities that exist. Whether or not we ought to be satisfied with equality of opportunity and let inequality of condition continue, analyses of both are essential to get the proper measure of any society.

1

Research Biography of a Macrosociological Study:

The Vertical Mosaic

In the decade since the 1970s, sociologists have become increasingly interested in the study of total societies, an enterprise to which they have given the inelegant label of "macrosociology." In the United States, the country from which so much of the discipline in its contemporary form has spread, most of the rapid growth of sociology that followed the Second World War was made up of the analyses of families, neighborhoods, small towns, work places, delinquent gangs and other fragments of the wider society. With few exceptions, there were no broad interpretations of the totality of American society by sociologists, although from time to time they would make ample use of de Tocqueville's Democracy in America. *In fact, American sociology had rejected its European paternal ancestors, Comte, Marx, Spencer, Durkheim, and Weber, and their interpretations of broad historical change. Sociologists insisted instead on investigating what they called "middle range" problems more amenable to scientific inquiry, verification or falsification of hypotheses and the accumulation of a body of knowledge. The broad sweeps were contaminated with historicism: much safer with the new scientism.*

Perhaps the new interest in total societies rather than fragments of them as objects of study came in the United States with the great protest movements of the late 1960s, the Vietnam war, America's involvement in the developing and decolonized world and new transnational organizations like the multinational firms. Ideological conflicts about what kinds of social systems were most desirable in terms of general human welfare awakened American social scientists from their "celebrationist" somnolence and their dream of the "end of ideology." New critical appraisals were demanded, new assessments of what America was about.

In Canada, which was to feel the impact of American sociology as it was to feel other cultural effects of continentalism, there was very little sociology of any kind, unlike the indigenous schools of history, for example. The Americanization of Canadian sociology did not occur without resistance. The repulse almost succeeded, in part because sociology had never attained academic respectability in the face of the hostility of the more entrenched disciplines of political economy and history. There was also the stout determination of two of the early pioneers of Canadian sociology, Carl Dawson and S.D. Clark, to create a sociology that would have meaning within the context of Canadian social development. Even the distinguished American, Everett Hughes, who was to have such an important early influence on sociology in Canada, was not a typical American sociologist.

Although I always admired American sociologists for their methodological skills, I was never particularly attracted to the kinds of problems to which they were bringing their skills. The first piece in this volume, "Research Biography of a Macrosociological Study: The Vertical Mosaic," *gives some reasons why in the 1950s I turned to much more fundamental problems and the examination of basic elements of Canadian social structure. The "biography" was written in response to an invitation to contribute, along with some leading American sociologists, to a volume of papers on macrosociology. Not all the contributors came through with their contributions. The book, published in the United States,* Macrosociology: Research and Theory, *ended up with only two other contributors, James S. Coleman and Amitai Etzioni. The three papers bore little connection with each other, and the book probably deserved the obscurity from which it never emerged. I doubt that it circulated very widely in Canada.*

I have chosen to introduce the book with this piece because it gives an account of my early intellectual development, why I embarked on the long research program that The Vertical Mosaic* *required, and how I went about it. As it originally appeared, it had a brief introduction which read:*

The Vertical Mosaic: An Analysis of Social Class and Power in Canada, *published in 1965, was an attempt to interpret Canadian social structure from the global or total society viewpoint.*

In 1966 the book received the American Sociological Association's MacIver Award for its ". . .comprehensive analysis of stratification in Canadian society and contribution to macrosociology." When the participants in the session on macrosociology at the 1967 A.S.A. meetings in San Francisco decided to publish some papers in what has become

---

* *University of Toronto Press, 1965.*

the present volume, the suggestion apparently arose that it might be a good idea to include one in which the author of a macro-study would give an account of how he actually conducted it. I received an invitation from Amitai Etzioni inviting me to write an essay which ". . .could be either quite informal, somewhat in the vein of those included in the book Sociologists at Work, *or a much more formal treatment of the methodological problems, but all illustrated from your own personal experience and work. This should allow many other sociologists to benefit from your experience."*

It is not for me to say whether or not that purpose has been achieved, but it has been very interesting for me to review my own orientations to the discipline of sociology. My research and social action interests since the book was published have all been extensions of it, particularly those parts which are most relevant to social change in Canada, as it is at present on the threshold of postindustrialism: the search for highly-qualified manpower, social mobility, educational opportunity, and the planning of postsecondary education. It is gratifying for me also that many other investigators of Canadian society and social policy makers have found The Vertical Mosaic *a helpful point of orientation. For Americans, affluent as they are in social science productivity, it might seem odd that one book could generate so much interest, but it came at a time when there was a paucity of sociological materials about Canada and at a time when Canadians were experiencing great problems of national identity and coherence. Much more material is now available than formerly to undertake another macro-analysis of Canada in transition or to revisit the "mosaic." That would be an attractive possibility if time and energies allow.*

The genesis of a major research enterprise can often be traced back to early academic socialization. Several of the contributors to those revealing chronicles, *Sociologists at Work*,[1] remark how their research interests were directed by exposure to particular experiences and ideas early in their academic training and intellectual development. They observe, also, how important was their contact in their graduate school years with great teachers and leaders in the discipline.

It is a matter of regret to me that I never attended one of *les grandes écoles* of the North American academic system, but I do consider myself fortunate in having been an undergraduate immediately after the Second World War at the London School of Economics and Political Science at surely what must have been its most superb period. On reflection it seems to me that the traditions of L.S.E. established by Sidney and Beatrice Webb were most salient at that time. The relationship between the social sciences and social policy was exemplified in the work of Lord Beveridge, the architect of postwar social security, who had been the School's Director until 1937. R.H. Tawney, H.L. Beales, Karl Mannheim, Lionel Robbins, F.A. Hayek, Harold Laski, Morris Ginsberg, T.H. Marshall, and Raymond Firth were among the stars. K.R. Popper had just published his influential *The Open Society and Its Enemies*. He was tremendously impressive in his lectures on logic and scientific method. Edward Shils had recently come from Chicago, and through a seminar in sociological research put sociology students into contact with the developing empirical work in the United States.

The war years were a watershed between the age when social forces were pretty much left to themselves to confer benefit or distress as they might on those who lived in industrial societies, or in their colonies, and the period of optimism when it was felt that the social environment could be controlled, that depressions could be made a thing of the past, and distributive justice was a matter of social engineering. It was Mannheim's "age of reconstruction," and in England as confirmation of that fact a Labour government had been elected with a huge majority for the first time since the enfranchisement of the working classes in the late nineteenth century. It was the beginning, too, of decolonization, and, for Great Britain, the dissolution of an Empire. Someone has remarked that the new colonial elites of the disintegrating Empire were trained either at the Royal Military College at Sandhurst or the London School of Economics. It was the time, also, when Israel emerged and when Ernest Bevin at the Foreign Office, as someone put it at the time, was learning "the importance of being Anthony."

Previous to this time the London School of Economics had no student residences, but after the war a small men's residence called Passfield Hall after Lord Passfield (Sidney Webb) was opened. It accommodated around sixty people who must have been chosen on the basis of national quotas because we were like a miniature United Nations. The discussions were intense, and, as with all university groups, ranged over the major issues of the day. We did not much care how our universities were governed, but rather our enthusiasms were about social equality at home, and the end of colonialism abroad and, at a time before tourists could go unashamedly to Spain, the removal of the final remnants of fascism in Europe. Many of us called ourselves democratic socialists, but the careers of some have subsequently proven socialist inclinations to have been weak. My own links were with the Labour party in Great Britain and the social democratic parties of Europe. It is not surprising that one should emerge from such a socialization process with a global orientation to societies and highly sensitive to the problems which social stratification creates for people as individuals and for societies as collectivities.

In the autumn of 1949, I returned to my native Canada after an absence of twelve years, five of which had been spent in the Canadian Army during the war. My visit to Canada was to have been a short one. Because I planned to write some articles on Canada for English publications, I began to take notes about what I saw. I was particularly struck by the relative positions of the French and British in Canada. I wrote about ". . .cheap French-Canadian labor constituting the proletariat of Ottawa, the Canadian capital, and servicing in laundries, stores, and restaurants a predominantly English bureaucracy." These remarks were a presage of one of the major themes of *The Vertical Mosaic*.

My stay in Canada was longer than I had intended. I was offered a job teaching at what was then Carleton College in Ottawa. It was very new and very small. During the next two years I was able to travel across the country and learn something of its great variations. Back in London in the summer of 1951, I was discussing a thesis topic with Morris Ginsberg, and outlining to him my interest both in Canada and in social stratification. Finally he suggested something on the structure of property and wealth in Canada. I was attracted to this idea, but I pointed out that it was not easy to obtain the necessary data in Canada. I doubted, working solo, that a good job could be done in less than ten years, and that since I was interested in an academic career it was a long time to work on a thesis. He was a distinguished scholar in the old tradition with little concern for quick returns in research projects. and was not, therefore, too sympathetic to my problem and simply remarked that if a study was worthwhile it did not matter very much if it took a long time.

I returned to Canada and in the summer of 1952 began to explore sources of data for a study of the structure of property. This was the first stage, an analysis of economic stratification, of what was to become a much more extensive study of power and class in Canadian society. As I reflect on my own intellectual concerns of this period, I realize that I was much more interested in the global view of societies, their operation and historical development, than in smaller social units. Again, this was a consequence of studying sociology at the London School of Economics at that time, where importance was attached by Ginsberg and others to the work of L.T. Hobhouse. I was attracted to Hobhouse's principle of social development, that a community develops as it grows in scale, efficiency, freedom, and mutuality: efficiency toward an end, freedom and scope for thought, mutuality in a service toward an end in which each participates. "Social development corresponds in its concrete entirety to the requirements of rational ethics. . . . Good is the principle of organic harmony in things."[2] Hobhouse was a grand theorist of social evolution and he saw emerging in the process the principle of reason and progress. To him, the relationship between social values and social science was close. He was firmly convinced of the need for an empirical social science and believed one could be developed which was closely linked to ethical principles, or at least addressed itself to ethical problems. I was surprised to find in North America how relatively unknown were the works of Hobhouse, and as modern systematic theory was being developed by Parsons and others, I was struck by how many affinities there were between Hobhouse and contemporary writers. Sometime I would like to trace these affinities, particularly now that comparative and evolutionary perspectives have once more acquired scientific respectability. In view of all the influences in those immediate postwar years, it is not surprising that ideas of social development, the global orientation, and a concern for ethical principles in social life became a dominant part of my outlook.

We now refer to this global orientation as macrosociology, and the present resurgence of interest in it may reflect a new concern of sociologists for the quality of social life and in the conditions of progress. Certainly the major problems of contemporary societies, poverty, opportunity, urbanization, and so forth are the problems of achieving "organic harmony" and can only be understood as global or macrosystem problems. The problems of societies on the road to development are similarly global. Questions of social planning and the construction of social indicators are linked to the new interest in macroanalysis. This global or macro-orientation requires a time dimension rather than the static or "moment in time" orientation of equilibrium theory. The macrosystem is a dynamic one in which the time dimension is as important as any other system boundary. That is why the macrosystem can be viewed as one in evolution, and the appropriate macrodata to trace out this evolution are to be found in time-series and ultimately expressed in complex mathematical models.

I had no intention at the beginning of my research of undertaking the large-scale study that *The Vertical Mosaic* became. One thing led to another, however, and as the work proceeded, I began to contemplate, with some foolhardiness and no little arrogance, that I might write an interpretation of Canada as a modern democracy. The United States had had its grand interpreters, de Tocqueville, Lord Bryce, and Laski—all of them outsiders to that country. Lord Bryce had included Canada in his *Modern Democracies*[3] and Goldwin Smith[4] and later André Siegfried,[5] also outsiders, had written about Canada—I felt I had something of the outsider's objective gaze by having lived abroad for twelve formative years.

ECONOMIC STRATIFICATION

I overcame my more grandiose fantasies and got down to the study of economic stratification in Canada. More specifically, I began to collect material relating to the distribution of property and the distribution of income. It is economists who most often compile the relevant data on the size distribution of income, the structure of national wealth, and the concentration of economic power. I approached the subject with what appeared to me to be two excellent models as guides to the kind of thing which I hoped to do. One was H. Campion's *Public and Private Property in Great Britain*[6] and the other, A.A. Berle's and G.C. Means' *The Modern Corporation and Private Property*.[7] Both of these books, it seemed to me at the time (1952–53), revealed the anatomy of inequality and the concentration of economic power in two major industrial societies. I have always thought it wise in social research to make the most use of the work and conceptualizing already available. Not only does this help in creating a cumulative effect which is important in the development of science, but it also serves the purpose of comparative analysis which can still be regarded as the method *par excellence* of sociology. No doubt since macrosociology deals with systems from a global point of view, its main contributions will come from comparative studies.

In the foreword to Campion's book, Professor Jewkes raised the basic moral problem created by the economic inequalities of the 1930s:

> Must we be prepared to tolerate, so long as we have a system of private enterprise, the apparent paradox that although men were equal politically, they must inevitably remain as unequal economically as they are now? Was there no answer to those who argued that liberty for the individual created by the machinery of democracy was a shadow whilst the substance, economic power, was vested in the hands of the few?[8]

In his examination of the changing distribution of income and of public and private property, Campion was able to show the enormous inequalities of wealth. He estimated, "One per cent of the persons aged 25 and over in England and Wales owned 55 per cent of the total property in private hands in 1936.""[9] His was a trend analysis in which he concluded that property distribution was only slightly more equal in 1936 than in 1911. Of course, this work on income distribution has been superseded by more recent but equally gloomy investigations,[10] but at that time Campion's study was rather basic macrodata relevant to economic stratification in Great Britain, which I hoped to replicate for Canada.

Ownership and Control

Berle and Means had studied what they called the "corporate revolution" or the transformation of a major proportion of the industrial wealth of the United States from individual ownership to ownership by the large publicly financed corporations. Theirs was also a trend analysis of the changing social institution of property, the organization of which has ". . . played a constant part in the balance of powers which go to make up the life of any era."[11] Their now well-known findings showed two major changes: the concentration of economic power and the separation of ownership from control. In respect of the first, they estimated that two hundred of the largest non-banking corporations (as measured by gross assets) controlled 49.2 per cent of all corporate wealth, 38 per cent of all business wealth, and 22 per cent of the entire national wealth in 1930. In respect of the second major change, they found that over half of all the corporate wealth represented by the assets of these 200 giants was under management control, and that only 6 per cent of it was controlled by a group of individuals owning more than one-half of the stock.[12] This was basic macrodata relevant to the organization of a society's productive instruments, of its economy. I wished to use this work also as a guide to economic power and stratification in Canada.

To my surprise, as I explored possible sources, I found that these questions had been ignored by Canadian economists, a fact which was itself a reflection of the Canadian value system, for how much was the principle of equality valued in a society in which the roots of inequality in the economic system had never been examined? I decided that I would start with the concentration of economic power rather than the distribution of income. One problem at the outset was the very great protection which Canadian companies enjoyed by the then existing provincial and federal companies acts. In the granting of incorporation, and in the regulations governing the operation of stock exchanges, only the minimum disclosures were required. It is doubtful that any other major industrial society permitted corporations to operate in such complete anonymity and protection. If Canadian corporations, as a few of them did, listed their stock on American exchanges then much more information, as required by the Securities Exchange Commission, was available. Moreover, many Canadian firms are wholly-owned subsidiaries of American parent firms, with their accounts consolidated with their American parents. Consequently, they became "private companies" under Canadian legislation with very little information about them.

My principal sources for the study of concentration were the annual industry reports of the Dominion Bureau of Statistics, details of company reports as they appeared in *The Financial Post Corporation Service, Moody's Industrials, The Stock Exchange Year Book*, and various directories of directors and reports of commissions of inquiry held in Canada from time to time. Fortunately, the Dominion Bureau of Statistics had prepared in 1950 a list of all the manufacturing establishments employing more than 500 hands in 1948. Also I was able to secure from D.B.S. the aggregate gross value of production of all these establishments. I decided to use the gross value of production of the large corporations rather than their gross assets as the measure of concentration. The Statistics Act would not allow the disclosure of any one establishment's value of production but it was possible to obtain aggregate figures. By working through this list I was able to group various establishments into their main firms and to consolidate parents and subsidiaries. After a long and laborious process, I was able to present a relatively clear picture of concentration in the manufacturing industries. I had to resort to other methods and sources for the non-manufacturing sectors of the economy. The final step was to show the links between all the "dominant corporations" through interlocking directorships. The results I published as a paper, "The Concentration of Economic Power and the Economic Elite in Canada."[13] In time, I was able to show what I thought were interesting differences between the findings of Berle and Means in the United States and concentration in Canada, in particular the important role which ownership continued to play for both families and groups of investors if they wished to preserve their holdings from foreign take-overs.

THE POWER ELITES

I had, by this time, the names of all the directors of the "dominant" corporations, banks, and insurance companies, and these formed the basis of my next step, an analysis of the social background and origins of those whom I called the "economic elite." This concentration study took the best part of three years of my non-teaching time.

While I was working on the analysis of economic power, I gradually regained my enthusiasm for undertaking a much more extensive investigation into the entire range of power and stratification in Canada and for treating the two, not as isolated segments or aspects of social life, but as integrated in a total social system.

It is one thing to wish to study the structure of power in a modern industrial society and another to select the most appropriate theory or theories to guide in the selection and interpretation of data. Obviously Marx could not be ignored, particularly since we were still in the period before ideology had ended and when Marxian and neo-Marxian interpretations were in vogue. It seemed to me to be true that the economic processes were fundamental to any social order, that clearly economic exigencies tended to be overriding and required solutions before other developments could take place, and that economic power spills over into other areas of social life. But none of these conditions necessarily meant economic determinism in the Marxian sense, nor did they automatically lead to a primacy of the economic in social affairs.

I decided that for theoretical orientation, I would be eclectic. It was not my intention to test any particular hypothesis linked to a specific theoretical system. Rather my task was analytical and descriptive, and it was therefore prudent to use those general structural categories, such as stratification and kinship, most widely employed in sociology and anthropology. Kinship and family units, for example, are significant in the analysis of stratification, as has frequently been pointed out. Total family income, therefore, is sociologically more relevant for a description or profile of income stratification and the distribution of life chances than individual income. Similarly, the concept of institutional system or major subsystem is an important analytical device. Perhaps anthropologists have been more successful than sociologists in employing these structural concepts in the empirical analysis of total societies. Community studies such as those of Middletown and Yankee City were global in their approach. The large-scale modern industrial society is more differentiated than the primitive society or the modern community by itself, but the fundamental social activities and system imperatives are the same. Thus, since these major analytical categories had been in use for a long time, it did not seem to me to be necessary to introduce an esoteric vocabulary of my own neologisms.

Because modern societies are highly differentiated, the analysis of them as total social systems would involve breaking them up into major parts or subsystems such as the economic, the political, the governmental bureaucracy, the military, and what I called the ideological system. At this point, I adopted a simple functionalist view that each of the subsystems contributed to the whole, that they were dynamically interrelated and that there should be a degree of integration between them.

Since I had decided to be eclectic, I was able to draw on both macro- and micro-theories. For example, I found Homans'[14] theory on the relationship between frequency of interaction and positive feelings helpful in interpreting the solidarity of the small collegial groups which made up the institutional elites. Among the macro-theorists, both Mosca and Pareto provided significant orientations particularly in respect of power. The work of these men, so very close to each other in time and place, constituted a severe criticism of nineteenth-century liberal theory. They put in most convincing terms the inevitability of minority rule and the absurdity of some of the notions of participatory democracy in large-scale systems. An important element in Mosca's scheme is the concept of social forces which appear in the process of social development and differentiation and seek representation in the ruling class. The society is most stable, Mosca theorized, in which a balance of social forces is represented in its ruling class.

Mosca, in his notion of the political formula, and Pareto in his doctrine of derivations, threw much light on the role of ideas and sophistry in the structure of power. (What fun Pareto would have had with the current "credibility gap"!) From these concepts and from Weber's concept of legitimacy, I developed my own idea of an integrated ideological subsystem consisting of religious, educational, scientific, mass media, and popular culture activities.

It was while I was trying to bring together the elements of theories which seemed to me to be most appropriate for the analysis of stratification and power, that I read Raymond Aron's two papers on "Social Structure and Ruling Class."[15] Aron's approach was for me a confirmation that I was going in the right direction. He attempted to synthesize some of the ideas of Marx and Pareto, a problem which he reduced to the question: What is the relation between social differentiation and political hierarchy in modern societies? In these papers on postwar France his aim was to combine ". . . the analysis of social structure with the

analysis of elite structure."[16] A few more quotations from Aron
will illustrate the influence of his ideas on my final scheme. (I also
quote because I think what he has said is an important
contribution to macrosociology.)

> . . . analysis of the economic structure, the social structure, the struc-
> ture of power within the elite, and, it should be added, the structure
> of the constitutional system; all these elements are of equal impor-
> tance in any theory of sociology which wishes to understand society
> as a whole.[17]

Later he adds, ". . . one of the most characteristic features of any
society's structure is the structure of the elite, that is, the relationship between the groups exercising power, the degree of unity or
division between these groups, the system of recruiting the elite
and the ease or difficulty of entering it."[18] The elite groups which
Aron identified as being important in postwar France were the
leaders of industry, the political leaders, and the leaders of the
masses, that is, politicized trade union leaders, and government
bureaucrats.

I decided, by adding some Mosca and Weber, to elaborate
Aron's Pareto-Marx synthesis into a scheme for the study of
power in Canada. I accepted the "anti-democratic" view of the
minority rule school. Moreover, what they had said was consistent
with much of what was being written about authoritarianism by
writers like Fromm and other social psychologists. The democratic personality was not yet the basic personality of modern
industrial society and, until it was, obedience, submissiveness, and
apathy would continue to characterize the posture toward power
and authority of people within large-scale social systems. I don't
think that at any time I graced this scheme, or framework, with
the word "theory," because I was not concerned to develop theory, to derive interrelated propositions, or test hypotheses. I was
analysing important aspects of a large-scale social system.

My attempts to synthesize these various elements resulted in
a paper, "Elite Groups: A Scheme for the Study of Power in
Canada,"[19] which I read in 1955 to a meeting of the Canadian
Political Science Association. In that paper I stated the following
propositions. There can be no widespread participation in the
making of major decisions in any modern society, but rather this
is done by relatively small groups. Decisions are made within a
legitimate order deriving its sense of rightness from myths, derivations, legal fictions, and so forth. I then introduced the notion of
power or decision-making and co-ordinating roles within the various institutional structures which in the process of social evolution

had become differentiated as separate antonomous systems, the economic, the political, the administrative, the defensive, and the ideological. These were separate and distinct but interrelated systems characterized by bureaucracy and hierarchy and corresponding to essential social functions. I left open which of the systems, the political or the economic, for example, was dominant as a matter for empirical investigation. Power, the right to make major decisions within each of these institutional hierarchies, rested with elite groups, small collectivities with a high degree of cross-membership. Power was collegial and shared with others within these overlapping collectivities. Thus a degree of co-ordination within institutions was achieved. Co-ordination within the total society was achieved by co-operation and competition of institutional elites at those points where they came into contact with one another. They shared power within a normative order which presupposed freedom for elites to exercise power in their own domains. Aron had made the distinction between "soviet" and "western" types of elite structures. In the western type, elites are separate and compete for power, with the result that control tends towards an equilibrium of compromise. In the "soviet" type, on the other hand, elites were ideologically unified by common membership in the Communist party. At this point, it was possible to make a value judgment that the western type was better because it resulted in a diffusion of power rather than the tendency for power to be concentrated through ideological commitment.

This value judgment provided me with an important interpretive focus. What would the evidence have to say about the degree of power concentration resulting from the coalitions, compromises, and deals between elite groups in their co-ordinating functions? What was the degree of interchangeability between elite roles and how specific were career systems to particular institutional orders? At that time I was not too concerned about the "efficiency" of the system. I had a vague idea that one of the costs of more diffused or democratic power structures was a certain loss of efficiency and a degree of muddling through because of a lower level of co-ordination than in the centralized system. Since then, of course, we have learned something of the inefficiency of the centralization of the "soviet" type, at least in the economic system.

Early in 1956 I met C. Wright Mills in Toronto, where we were both reading papers at a colloquium. *The Power Elite*[20] was at that time nearing publication. I found it interesting to compare our approaches. For him, power in the United States was monolithic and centralized in a coalition of economic, political, and military elites, a condition very close, in fact, to the "soviet" type with commitment, not to ideology, but a "higher immorality." Mills was, of course, writing about the United States at a particular point in history and, therefore, his scheme—rather than being generally applicable to power in industrial societies— was specific to an epoch in the history of the United States. I was not concerned to discover "the power elite" in Canada. I had, in any case, considerable doubts about the monolithic view of power in the United States.

Previous studies of elites had emphasized the importance of their being renewed by recruitment from outside their own narrow groups. As it was put by Mosca, better representation of social forces in the elites is likely when recruitment from outside takes place. In any case demographic factors would make for some external recruitment since elites did not reproduce themselves sufficiently to fill all the places at the top which were created with social development, differentiation, and specialization. Thus the recruitment of elites, avenues to the top, selection processes, bases of exclusion in terms of social background became major interests of the elite studies. Aron's observation that the structure of a society's elites was a characteristic feature of that society was certainly borne out as the data of the various elite groups were analysed.

The Economic Elite

With the key concept of institutional elites defined, it was necessary to identify them in an empirical social system, and then to consider the various methods by which the relevant data about them could be gathered. After my study of the concentration of economic power and interlocking directorships, I took the directors of the dominant corporations as the economic elite. Because of the question of how far down any hierarchy one should go, since there is rarely an abrupt break between elite power and nonelite power, some arbitrariness is inevitable in the final selection of any elite group. I was not studying "business leaders" in the sense that I wanted a representative sample of leaders of small and large enterprises. Rather, the economic elite were to be the senior managers and directors of the major corporations in the Canadian economy as well as those of the banks and the largest life insurance companies. I wanted a large enough group to give a reasonable statistical profile. The selection of an economic elite of nine hundred was criticized for being too large, but I was able to separate the top one hundred whose range of directorships indicated a high degree of power.

The Bureaucratic Elite

The identification of the bureaucratic elite was relatively easy since names of the senior officials in the federal government departments could be easily obtained. It was a question largely of how far down from the top one should go in each department or agency. As with all elite groups, there is always a smaller core who are more powerful than others, because of the nature of their departments, because of their reputations and personalities, and because of the informal system that operates in all bureaucratic structures. But to select out such a small group would have precluded any kind of statistical profile. I decided, somewhat arbitrarily, but also on the basis of a considerable knowledge I had built up about the federal public service after a number of years of observing it at work in Ottawa, on a group of 212 senior public servants. Subsequently, in the section on the bureaucratic elite, it was possible to deal in a narrative fashion with the "inner circle."

The Labor Elite

Trade union leaders were selected by a logic similar to that by which members of the economic elite had been determined, that is, on the basis of the concentration of power which results from the largest and most important unions having a disproportionate number of all organized workers within their ranks. Initially I took the leading officials, elected and appointed, of the forty-two unions with over 10 000 members in Canada at that time. There was an element of the reputational method involved in selecting the labor elite. I discussed at some length with union officials the complicated structure of organized labor and its relationship to international unionism. I found, for example, that it was sensible to include the leaders of very large locals, and also that some of the smaller unions had leaders who were important in the movement as a whole. I consulted officials of the Canadian Labour Congress and those of the Canadian Department of Labour who were knowledgeable about the labor movement. I followed much the same procedures with *La Confédération des Syndicats Nationaux*, the central congress of the French-speaking syndicates of Quebec. In all, after extensive comments on my list of names by a number of the labor leaders themselves, I selected 394 individuals as comprising the labor elite.

The Political Elite

Little preliminary work was necessary to arrive at a satisfactory empirical definition of the political system and its elite. The realities of the Canadian political scene, as I interpreted them, indicated that federal cabinet ministers, as the leaders of the national political system, and the premiers of the ten provinces should be in the elite. This is not the place to expand on the peculiarities of the Canadian federal system, but it did seem to me to be correct that because provincial premiers had very great influence over their cabinet colleagues and were the principal negotiators in federal-provincial relations, they should be included within the elite, but provincial ministers should not be.

I excluded from the elite all members of Parliament, the Senate, unless they were also in the Cabinet, and all members of provincial legislatures. In any modern, and particularly in a federal political system, the senior judiciary should be considered among the major decision makers. Moreover, for many of them, careers are through the political system. Thus, I included all members of the Supreme Court of Canada, the President of the Exchequer Court, and the Chief Justices of the provinces. Most of the other elite groups had been selected because of their members occupying particular positions at a given point in time. The political elite, as I had defined it, would, I felt, give too small numbers to provide a statistical profile. Rather than dilute the eliteness of the group by enlarging the number of political roles considered to be "elite," I extended the same roles backward in time and accordingly selected all those who had occupied them between 1940 and 1963. I was fortunate in being able to secure, for comparative purposes, similar data from the beginning of Confederation (1867) from a project of the Political Science Department at Carleton University.

The Ideological Elite

Because the social sciences had treated ideological systems much less adequately than they had economic or political systems, it was a little more difficult to provide the theoretical rationale for the ideological elite and to translate this rationale at the empirical level into specific power roles and their incumbents. I argued that in very large groups, such as modern nations, the problems of internal cohesion and the maintenance of social values are so great that the informal mechanisms which had been brought to light in small group studies were not sufficient. Rather, specialized social roles were necessary. In earlier historical periods, these roles were located within religious institutions, but in the secularized modern world, while religion had still some importance, it had given way, as the foundation of consensus, to other institutions and belief systems. Because of differentiation, the ideological roles had to be institutionally specialized ones. Moreover, the ideological system functions at different intellectual levels. Both the highly educated and the masses share in the consensus, but through quite different cognitive and evaluative processes and, as a consequence, are served by quite different media of value transmission.

Obviously, in any modern society, the mass media are important in providing a view of the world, in shaping social values, and in reinforcing ideology. They are the shared experience of most members of modern society. To study power within the mass media, I felt it necessary to have a picture of the concentration of control. I measured concentration as the proportion of all daily newspaper circulation accounted for by a group of metropolitan dailies in all major Canadian cities. After consolidating all these dailies into a few major publishing enterprises and chains, I was then able to show the ownership links of these publishing groups with periodicals, with the broadcasting media, and in turn, with the corporate world. The interesting facts which emerged concerned the degree of family continuity in the ownership of these media.

For the more sophisticated levels of the ideological system, I drew from such writers as Znaniecki, Mannheim, and Shils. The "intellectual elite" were the *savants*, the men of learning, the theorizers of the economic and social processes. Thus as "authorities" they help to legitimate social policy or the lack of it. Since in Canada there were very few intellectuals outside of the universities who would not have been included as editors of the mass media, it was in the academic system that these important ideological roles were to be found. The selection of such an elite posed problems of judgment on the part of the investigator much greater than was the case with other elites where functional position is at least an initial definition of elite status. It was difficult to conceive of the concentration of intellectual power.

Fortunately, there exists an honorific organization called the Royal Society of Canada which contains all the leading savants and into which leading intellectuals might at some time expect to be elected. It is an exclusive and self-selecting group. To be a Fellow of the Royal Society of Canada requires election by the already existing Fellows. Hence selection is, in effect, "reputational." Many people have criticized my using the Royal

Society as the basis of the intellectual elite, but my impression is that the criticism is much greater on the part of the non-Fellows than Fellows. It seemed to me at the time, and to others with whom I discussed the matter, to be a perfectly correct way of selecting the elite of the academic and intellectual community.

Although ideology has become increasingly secularized, church leaders still contribute an important element to consensus, particularly with the high level of religiosity of Canada. Since some religions are authoritarian and hierarchical, their elites could be defined relatively easily. For the Catholic and Anglican Churches in Canada, I took archbishops and bishops. The largest Protestant church in Canada, the United Church, is a union of Congregationalists, Methodists, and Presbyterian elements. It is not hierarchical, but is presided over by a Moderator who is elected for two years. The locus of power in the church is the permanent bureaucracy which operates the executive offices. It was these permanent bureaucrats, along with a few professors, writers, and theologians who were selected as the elite of that church.

By the methods which have been briefly outlined, the elites of the major institutional subsystems within Canadian society were located and identified. For most elite groups, the names of members were not difficult to obtain. To follow Aron's principle that the characteristic features of any society's structure was the relationship between groups exercising power, their degree of unity and division, their system of recruitment and ease of access to elites, it would be necessary to obtain a substantial array of uniform data pertaining to all members of elite groups. The type of data ideally required included social background, educational experience, career lines, membership in a range of groups and organizations such as clubs, political parties, honorific welfare positions, regulatory boards and agencies, fraternal societies, and so forth.

The Linkage Mechanisms

While social structures become differentiated, there are mechanisms making for coherence between the differentiated parts. One of these linkage mechanisms is the web of cross-membership in a variety of groups and institutions such as religious and ethnic groups, political parties, trade unions, and a wide range of associations. Although elites were functionally specific, co-ordination at the global level required points of linkage between decision-making groups. These points of linkage I thought might be found in cross-membership in institutional and associational groups. For example, important business leaders might share power with church leaders in synods, trade union leaders might have important posts in political parties, the economic elite might own the mass media, or the political elite might control them. For this reason I felt it important to gather data on these kinds of linkages. Of course, the "western model" of elite structure presupposes some absence of co-ordination and a degree of competition and conflict. These areas of conflict and competition, and the linkages of cross-membership, I tried to present in the last chapter of the book on the relations between elites.

SOURCES OF SOCIAL INFORMATION

While I was working out my general theoretical or schematic model for the study of elites, I was also collecting data on the economic elite. To do the latter, I had to make some rather basic decisions on sources and procedures. I would have very much liked to follow the methods of Taussig and Joslyn in their classic study, *American Business Leaders*,[21] which was also to become the model for the replication study of Warner and Abegglen.[22] In Canada at that time sociology was very much underdeveloped and there was little appreciation of sociological procedures which required eliciting information from individuals. Canadian business leaders would have been astounded at the thought of providing sociological information and would have viewed the whole thing as an intrusion on their private domains. In both the Taussig and Joslyn and the Warner and Abegglen studies, the researchers were established scholars in important universities, but even they required the sponsorship of a committee of business leaders. Thus I ruled out the use of a mailed questionnaire. I surmised also that the response rate would be low because I was dealing with an elite group rather than a broader category of business "leaders," and that the higher the position in the elite, the less possibility there was of the person responding. The resulting sample would thus be biassed toward the lesser elite. There was also the fact that no studies existed in Canada based on survey techniques so there was no way of estimating what a response rate might be. Moreover, there were practically no research funds available.

I therefore decided to use the standard biographical dictionaries of the "Who's Who" type. There had been a number of studies of institutional leaders based on such sources, both contemporary and historical, and from most of these sources, although the data were limited, they were uniform and accessible. Obviously these sources could provide no attitudinal data but since at this point I did not want attitudinal data, that did not worry me. Not surprisingly, the more prominent the elite members, the more biographical data were available about them. It was also possible to supplement these sources through newspaper clippings kept in the libraries of daily papers in Ottawa and Toronto. For several years I had been keeping very extensive newspaper clippings myself of materials that would be helpful and from these I was also to learn of the ongoing activities of many of the elite.

Incidentally, newspapers and periodicals are important sources of information for the analysis of modern societies on a global scale. It is necessary, of course, to select both publications and writers and to become acquainted with their individual biasses and styles of treating problems. The more reliable and prestigious journalists working in different parts of a country become a field staff of informants presenting and analysing a wide range of "system problems" contemporaneously with the sociologist as investigator. Moreover, good journalists specialize, in business, labor, science, politics, and so forth, and often become important contributors to debate and discussion within the institutions in which they work. If the sociologist can establish personal contact with such journalists, it is possible to define particular problems for them to investigate.

Much the same methods as those described for securing data on the economic elite were later used to obtain the necessary social background data for the other elite groups. For the bureaucratic elite, a limited amount of career line data was obtained from the Civil Service Commission. For the political elite, the various editions of The Parliamentary Guide[23] became the most important sources.

Social background and career line data for the labor elite could not be obtained in the same way because they had not made their way into the biographical dictionaries in sufficiently large numbers. There was no alternative to a mailed questionnaire. One was prepared with an English and French version and pre-tested with the help of people in the trade union movement. One of the costs of survey research in Canada is the need to adapt interview schedules and questionnaires to the social structure of Quebec; to print in two languages and to keep the French and English versions equivalent. By this time in my research (1958) a number of union leaders were familiar with my papers on economic concentration and the economic elite and were very favorable to a similar study of their own group. Consequently, the President of the Canadian Labour Congress provided me with a supporting letter, reproduced on Congress letterhead and urging the recipients to co-operate. A similar letter was obtained from the Director of Education of the *Confédération des Syndicats Nationaux*. No doubt the assistance of these labor leaders contributed very much to the final response rate of 70 per cent of the 394 questionnaires sent out. The use of a mailed questionnaire gave me the opportunity, if I wished, to secure attitudinal data, but I chose not to do so. For one thing, it was a bad year for industrial relations in Canada and even under normal circumstances I felt that the response rate would be much lower if attitudinal questions were asked. I was glad I made this decision because the relatively high response rate enabled me to show how, as a group, Canadian labor leaders related to the general social structure, and, as well, to provide a picture of the career system within the labor movement.

One of the important aspects of the analysis of elite groups is their intergenerational continuity. This is just another way of stating the problem of role allocation in respect of the higher leadership positions. Theoretically, one would argue that the more ascriptive criteria operate rather than achievement criteria, the less efficient is allocation in terms of talents and abilities. Power structures can operate against rational and universalistic criteria by establishing particularistic criteria, kinship, and ethnic affiliation as a principle of selection. To analyse this process of intergenerational continuity, I worked with a very wide range of biographical dictionaries going back into the nineteenth century, and from these I was able to trace a range of kinship links from one generation to the next. I also examined a great number of biographies of elite group members and histories of elite families to help understand the continuity of the upper class and the elites, and also to provide some insights into the behavior of individuals in them.

One source of data about which I had to make a decision was formal interviewing of elites. I thought it would be extremely difficult to accomplish this, particularly on the subject of power, although no doubt some, such as politicians, would be more accessible than say leading corporation directors. Occasionally I found myself in situations, private parties, conferences, political party meetings, trade union conventions, and so on, where I would meet members of the various elites. When the opportunity arose, I would talk to individuals about their work and about the power they held as major decision-makers. Reactions to my questions were varied. Some would deny firmly that they had any power. Power was something other people had—politicians, governments, trade unions, and so forth. For many, I think these denials were genuine. For others, denial was simply the way of unconsciously rejecting the idea. On the other hand, some obviously enjoyed their powerful positions and never made any effort to hide the fact. It occurred to me, as I continued these chance discussions, that elites found it as difficult to analyse their positions, either as individuals or collectively, as did members of other groups. Most had never been trained to systematic thinking about society, and were rarely moved to think about their role in the global scheme of things. They had their own particular kind of false consciousness.

Because of these perceived difficulties, limited time and resources, and the fact that I was working alone, I decided against a formal interviewing program. Whenever I had the opportunity, I continued to observe these people in action and interaction, and when possible to turn a conversation in a direction in which I was interested. Opportunities appeared in unexpected ways. For example, one very large economic development taking place in Northern Canada became the subject of a research project concerned with the social, economic, and planning problems of rapidly growing communities. I was a member of a group looking at these communities. We were accompanied by directors of the companies involved. This was a week-long expedition so that I had many opportunities to discuss some of the things which interested me (quite unrelated, of course, to the subject of our journey). At times, I was even able to set them discussing with each other how they viewed their roles as directors of large corporations. Two in particular became very interested and read and commented on drafts of manuscripts. Of course, there was no consistency in these observations. One, whose father had fitted closely Weber's model of the Protestant entrepreneur, had changed his religion from the sect-like affiliation of his father to the more aristocratic Anglican church. It never occurred to him, even though he had friends in a similar class position who had done the same thing, that the individual changes might be a part of a wider social change in the relationship between religious and economic institutions. At another time we began a discussion of the relationship between the directors of large corporations and the chief managers. I felt that by taking such opportunities for discussion as they arose, and that by exploiting the more perceptive of these elite informants, I would get some valuable insights into the problems which I was examining. I have no doubt that this method was very important in orienting me to many aspects of the work and in forming ideas about the collegial nature of elite groups, and their accessibility and knowledge about each other.

INEQUALITY AND THE CHARTER GROUPS

From these various sources of data pertaining to elite groups, I was able to show how their structure reflected the "characteristic features" of society as a whole. Notable among these features was the almost exclusive position of the British as a charter group of the system. In some of the institutional subsystems, particularly the political and the ideological, the French, the co-charter group, shared some power with the British. There was practically no representation from the non-British and non-French groups. Each of the elite groups, with the obvious exception of the Catholic hierarchy, showed a high degree of internal recruitment or recruitment from upper and middle classes, and very often through a private fee-paying school system. These features suggested a relatively low rate of mobility into the elite and a poor integration of the non-charter groups into the higher levels of the social structure. As well, the strength and continuity of the economic elite resulted in a disproportionate influence in the overall structure of power. This dominant position of the British upper-class group was unchallenged because of the relative incapacity of the political system, and the absence of any polarization in politics as well as the brevity and amateur character of political careers. This is not the place to restate at length the findings of these elite studies, but from them it was possible to give a broad interpretation of Canadian society and its values, particularly those relating to equality, opportunity, mobility, and achievement.

The Class System

As the study of elite groups was taking form, I turned increasingly to the problem of articulating the elite structure with the wider stratification system. In my planning of the stratification part of the study, I had grouped a number of items under the general heading of the social framework of inequality. These items included the inequalities in the distribution of income as the basic economic inequalities from which others, such as levels of consumption, styles of living and life chances, flowed. Because of the importance of education to social mobility, I was particularly concerned to look at the inequality of educational opportunity. Also, the exclusive charter group character of the elites alerted me to the all-important relationship between ethnicity and stratification. To deal with this latter problem, I decided to look at the history of immigration policy in Canada, and the history of the immigration and settlement of non-British, non-French ethnic origins. In fact, in my original plan, there was to be a chapter which I called "The Emergence of Canadian Class Structure," which was to provide an essentially historical perspective. Canada was a relatively new nation without a class structure with long historical roots. As my original notes said:

> I would try to locate factors in the economic and social develop-
> ment of Canada which created a particular class system. The fur
> trade, railway building and early industrial activity are seen as the
> foundations of wealth. At the same time, an ethnically-heterogene-
> ous labor force accompanied capital investment and eventually
> became sorted and sifted into a class system. In the process a variety
> of institutional adaptations took place.

Data for the study of the framework of inequality which I proposed were to come mainly from two sources: the decennial census which had existed since 1871, and a range of government surveys on a variety of subjects, including the published annual statistics of the income tax division of the Department of National Revenue. A preliminary survey of these various sources indicated that the data of many of them could be brought together or used conjointly either for a particular time or for several points in time to present a trend analysis. Data rarely come in the way that is ideally wished, but the world of social research is far from perfect. As I proceeded, I realized that there was a vast array of macrosociological materials which had never been exploited.

Income and Wealth

No one, as far as I could find out at the time, had brought together data on the size distribution of income, although the data for such a study were available from the income tax statistics. There were deficiencies in these data, of course, but I decided that if used with care and with a clear statement about their shortcomings, it was possible to provide a reasonable picture of income inequality, and to locate particular areas in the social structure where inequalities were particularly acute. The data were arranged in tables to show size distribution and also presented in the form of Lorenz curves for income from all sources as well as income from dividends, the latter giving some indication of the distribution of equity capital in the country. The concentration of equity capital was, of course, consistent with the findings on the concentration of economic power and the closely held stock in Canadian corporations.

Fortunately, it was possible to confirm and supplement this profile of inequality of income and wealth from sample surveys of non-farm family incomes and expenditures which the Dominion Bureau of Statistics conducted at various times during the 1950s. These surveys contained data relating to different forms of income by size of family, age of head, and other background characteristics, as well as information relating to different forms of assets. Other surveys dealt with family expenditures, household facilities and equipment, and the utilization of a wide range of health services. Combined, these various sources provided a global picture or profile of economic stratification.

Education

Data relating to educational inequalities were drawn mainly from a combination of census items such as the number of children in school by occupation of family head. These were distributed according to a socioeconomic scale constructed on the basis of education and income data from the 1951 census by B.R. Blishen.[24] The Dominion Bureau of Statistics also conducted two national sample surveys, in 1957 and 1962, on incomes and expenditures of university students. By obtaining the completed schedules, it was possible to recode father's occupation by the Blishen scale and thus show the relationship between class position, attendance at university, and type of degree program. A ratio of representation was calculated, based on the proportion of each class at university compared to the proportion of children aged 14 to 24 in each class, a figure which was derived from the census.

Concentration of wealth and the unequal distribution of income are found in all industrial systems so that there was nothing startling in finding these conditions in Canada. The task was one largely of showing its extent or peculiar features. The inequalities in educational experience which I found surprised me because I thought that Canada was sufficently close to the United States to have absorbed some of the values concerning the democratization of education. As I reflected on these educational findings, however, I realized that they were consistent with other features of the structure of inequality in Canadian society which were being revealed in the analysis of social class and ethnicity.

Ethnicity

Canada, like the United States, has evolved as a new society or new nation. This process in both countries has been accomplished by the migration of large numbers of people of diverse origins from Europe and elsewhere into the vast regions of North America. This highly differentiated migration has become an integral part of the evolving systems of both countries, and in particular of their stratification systems. If one pushes back the time boundary of either of these macrosocial systems, one can see newcomers being sorted out by a variety of criteria, socialized to varying degrees, and assigned to social roles primarily on ascriptive and particularistic bases. As the system develops over time, these various demographic and ethnic elements may change their character, they may become absorbed with other elements or they may retain a solidarity which differentiates them clearly as a distinct ethnic group within the system. To understand properly the relationship between ethnicity and stratification in the modern industrial system it is necessary to see how it has evolved and the direction in which it is changing. The relationship between stratification, or inequality, and ethnicity creates problems for these systems at the macro level. Consequently, their solution is at the global level of social policy.

As with the analysis of other parts of Canadian society, I was guided by what theoretical insights were to be found in the literature. I was struck by Schumpeter's brief note on why he entitled his essay "Social Classes in an Ethnically Homogeneous Environment," and his reason was ". . . not to complicate the basic features of the picture."[25] He feared the picture might be complicated by racial elements in social class, although he was careful to point out that these were not ". . . the heart of the matter, not the reason why there are social classes."[26] Although Schumpeter leaned more to Gumplowicz' theories of conquest, other writers in treating the ethnic or racial problem as it affected class structure had emphasized the social biology or social Darwinism approach that the status hierarchy reflected differences in genetic endowment. Most social theories, in as much as they tried to deal with the relationship between ethnicity and class, tended to overlook the evaluative component in that relationship. Evaluations were reinforced by pseudo-scientific theories of racial inferiority, theories which gave rise to restrictive immigration with specific categories of more or less preferred ethnic stocks. In so much of American sociology which deals with race and ethnic relations, the stratification significance of ethnic differentiation tended to be superseded by notions of culture conflict. Ethnic groups and social classes were seen as different social categories, often cross-cutting each other. Yet, where ethnic differentiation does exist it almost invariably creates or supports systems of inequality.

I tried to give some thought to the preconditions of ethnic stratification in order to better understand the data which I was assembling. It seemed to me that in most historical instances, it resulted from conquest or migration. In the case of conquest, the victors enslave their victims or relegate them to inferior statuses and forms of work. This process can be seen in the successive conquests over centuries which hardened into the classical caste system in India. It can be seen in the quasi-caste systems of Central and South America, and also in North America in the case of the indigenous Indian populations. Where, however, ethnic differentiation has arisen, as in the United States and Canada, through immigration, there has been a host or charter group that got there first and determined the conditions under which other groups might enter. These conditions ranged from unfree slave immigration to free selective immigration under which the host society made judgments about the appropriateness of various groups for particular jobs. Migration is an economic process by which one factor of production moves with the other factor—capital. The entire process is selective in which people get sorted out according to their believed-in qualities or aptitudes for different economic activities. In the United States, although a laissez passer system prevailed while the old immigration from Northern and Western Europe predominated, the new immigration from Southern and Eastern Europe gave rise to prejudices about suitability which found their way into such books as Madison Grant's *The Passing of the Great Race*[27] and ultimately into immigration restrictions based on invidious notions of quality. (We can see in our own time the building up of stratification systems through ethnic migrations. In the United States, it is the Puerto Rican and the black moving into urban areas. In England, it is the migration of the colored Commonwealth. Throughout Western Europe, it is the migration of Italian, Spanish, and Portuguese labor, most of it unskilled, and sometimes with a minimum of social and legal rights. Migrations, of both unskilled and highly skilled labor, link national societies into super-systems making the latter important objects of macroanalysis.)

Economic conditions are factors which create the inequalities of ethnic stratification. There are jobs which the host or conquering groups do not want to do or consider demeaning, servicing jobs for example. Or, it is necessary for the building up of a labor force of a particular type of economy, for example the plantation economy where labor force needs have been met most frequently through slavery or indentured labor. Or, as with the building up of the Canadian west, it was done with a more or less freely-moving migration. Over time, this marked differentiation at the period of entry can either harden into a permanent class system or change in the direction of absorption, assimilation, integration, and acculturation, as a result of which the relationships between ethnicity and class disappear. The direction being taken by a particular society can be determined by examining the distributions of the various ethnicities through the occupations of the labor force and also their distribution through elite or powerholding groups. The stratification order which exists, hardened or modified, has a subjective counterpart in the evaluations which are made about the standing or place of various ethnic groups in the population and the degrees of social distance—that is, the degree of intimacy which they are prepared to engage in with members of other groups—which prevail between people of different groups. These subjective counterparts can be determined with considerable precision.

These ideas were only vaguely formulated as I approached the matter of ethnic differentiation in Canada. From an examination of Canadian immigration policy, I was aware of the importance that the ideas of social biology had played in the evaluation of potential immigrants. I set out to analyse the various ideological influences as expressed by leading writers on the subject in Canada from the turn of the century until the Second World War. I must confess, as familiar as I was with the ideas of social Darwinism, I was shocked by some of the things that I had found: stock-breeding concepts as applied to the mixing of the "races," estimates of the inherited capacities of different nationalities to perform specific types of occupations, inherited propensities to evil, and such evaluations. They found particularly strong expression in the writings of the great Canadian humorist Stephen Leacock, who—when he was not being funny—was a Professor of Economics at McGill University. Writing in 1930, he denounced immigration policies which were bringing Eastern Europeans to Canada rather than people from the white British Commonwealth, acknowledging as far as Eastern Europeans were concerned only that "a little dose of them may even by variation, do good, like a minute dose of poison in a medicine."[28]

It occurred to me then that, in the relationship between ethnicity and immigration, the charter group (the British or the elite ethnicity in Canada) brought the other groups in on an "entrance status." It was important, I thought, to determine how, in the evolution of the society, entrance status changed into some form of structural assimilation through social mobility. This idea of tracing the upward movement of ethnic groups through the social structure I took from Elbridge Sibley's "Some Demographic Clues to Stratification,"[29] one of the few attempts to deal with the matter of class, ethnicity and immigration. Sibley argued that, since such a very large proportion of the immigration before the First World War to the United States was unskilled, it enabled the unskilled native-born in the labor force to move up from blue-collar to white-collar occupations. He further made the point that after selective immigration began and the immigrant labor was more highly qualified, the effect was a slight downward movement. Whether or not the effects of immigration on the class structure and mobility processes were quite as Sibley suggested, his analysis alerted me to a process which I thought was important.

At the empirical level, the data available for tracing these processes were both rich and poor. Poor because early immigration statistics were meagre and unreliable, and good because the Canadian census has consistently asked an origins or ethnicity question. Thus some of the research, such as tracing the ethnic distribution of the labor force from census to census, could be dealt with reasonably well. To do this required accepting certain inadequacies in the quality of the origins data. Certain difficulties also arose because the question had been asked in somewhat different ways at different censuses, and, as well, European boundaries had changed over time, but none of these objections were, in my view, sufficiently strong not to use census data to provide a general picture of the movement from entrance status to some degree of structural assimilation. Where macroanalysis involves the pushing back of the time boundary, the problem of the comparability of the statistics produced over time by administrative and data collection agencies can become most difficult.

Immigration statistics were meagre for the early period and they gave no details on the occupations or intended occupations of immigrants. Since the Second World War, the data collected by the immigration authorities have been of a high quality. Emigration statistics were non-existent, since no one in Canada seemed to have cared where its population went. Most of the emigration was to the United States and estimates of the Canadian-born in the United States could be obtained from United States sources.

Canada has had a fascinating demographic history. It has been a country of high immigration and almost equally high emigration. Much of its population growth has come from natural increase. Several Canadian demographers and historians have reconstructed these demographic movements. I was able to draw on their work as secondary sources and to provide some sociological interpretations of their findings. In the evolution of Canadian society from a predominantly rural to an industrial type, there were a variety of factors impinging on an emerging class structure. These were varying rates of population growth, high levels of immigration and emigration, and ethnic heterogeneity as the important demographic variables; the changes in occupational structure and industrial growth as the important economic variables; and from the value system, there was a heavy emphasis on particularism and ascription coming into conflict as the industrial system developed with achievement and universalism.

The particularistic orientation could be traced to the fundamental historical condition of Canadian society which produced enormous divisiveness and profound rigidity, that is, the bifurcation of the social structure into its anglophone and francophone components. The concentration of the francophone component in the geopolitical area of Quebec within which a tradition-bound Catholic hierarchy enjoyed an almost established status drove the division to deeper and more lasting proportions. This historical reality has meant differences between the francophone and anglophone subsocieties in their demographic histories, in migration rates, fertility rates, in educational systems, in urbanization, in occupational mobility, and in the shift from particularistic and ascriptive to achievement and universalistic values. Above all, there was the French ideology of nationalism and the determination to survive as a separate society in an anglophone North America. This nationalism was the foundation of the doctrine of cultural pluralism against which the ethnic diversity of the immigrant forces and the continuing ethnic differentiation of the population developed.

THE TOTAL SOCIAL SYSTEM

The elements which have just been enumerated have been the basic determinants of Canadian society as a total social system. The first part of *The Vertical Mosaic* was an attempt to assemble the relevant and available data to show the interplay of these determinants. The material was grouped into problem areas: the effect of migration on social class and mobility; the reflection of ethnic differentiation in the class structure; the effects of urbanization and off-farm migration which had been going on since the turn of the century on the formation of new strata into which the various regional, ethnic, and other elements were drawn.

In this way I sought to provide a sociological interpretation of Canada as a developing system, that is, with both an evolutionary and functional orientation. Some of the problems of adaptation were thus brought into focus. For example, Canada had relied very much at crucial points in its industrial development on the importation of skilled and professional workers and in doing so had neglected its educational systems. This importation of highly skilled labor was a counterpart of the importation of capital without which Canadian industry would never have developed. As it developed, it became increasingly foreign-owned. Thus it could be said that industrialization has been "in" Canada but not "of" Canada. The driving force of contemporary Canada has not been indigenous. I argued at the time that, by their neglect of educational systems, Canadians had deprived themselves of much of the mobility which comes with the industrial occupational system.

At the empirical level, the analysis of total social systems, particularly the modern or postmodern type, will always be a formidable undertaking, in part, because of the very complexity of these systems, but also because of the richness of the data that become available with modern information retrieval and data banks. The wealth of data throws us back on our theoretical skills, for it is by improving our theoretical guidelines that we can sort out relevant data from what often has the appearance of a garbage heap of empirical materials.

In the generation of new data, it is likely that comparative macrosociology will increasingly demand comparable statistical data to be produced, most promisingly, by international agencies. It will also require increasing concern for cross-national equivalence of research instruments. Beyond the total society are the boundaries of the super-systems into which total systems are increasingly drawn. No one is more aware than the researcher himself of the shortcomings of a particular undertaking. Among the inadequacies of *The Vertical Mosaic* I would include a lack of the enlightenment that comes from comparative analysis and a lack of consideration for Canada's integration into the super-system of North America and other western industrial societies. Perhaps now that the sociological resources in Canada are more plentiful, we can move in these more ambitious directions.

Notes

1. Phillip E. Hammond (ed.), *Sociologists at Work* (New York: Basic Books, 1964).

2. L.T. Hobhouse, *Social Development* (New York: Henry Holt and Co., 1924), pp. 88, 93.

3. James Bryce, *Modern Democracies* (New York: The Macmillan Co., 1921), Vol. 1, pp. 455–97.

4. Goldwin Smith, *Canada and the Canadian Question* (London: Macmillan, 1891).

5. André Siegfried, *Le Canada, les deux races: problèmes politiques contemporains* (Paris: Libraire Armand Colin, 1907).

6. H. Campion, *Public and Private Property in Great Britain* (London: Oxford University Press, 1939).

7. A.A. Berle and G.C. Means, *The Modern Corporation and Private Property* (New York: The Macmillan Co., 1948).

8. J. Jewkes, in foreword, *Public and Private Property in Great Britain* by H. Campion (London: Oxford University Press, 1939), xi.

9. *Ibid.*, p. 109.

10. For England, see: R.M. Titmuss, *Income Distribution and Social Change* (London: Allen & Unwin, 1962); and for the United States, see G. Kolko, *Wealth and Power in America* (New York: Frederick A. Praeger, 1962).

11. A.A. Berle and G.C. Means, *op. cit.*

12. *Ibid.*, Chapter III.

13. John Porter, "The Concentration of Economic Power and the Economic Elite in Canada," *The Canadian Journal of Economics and Political Science*, XXII (1956), pp. 199–221.

14. G.C. Homans, *The Human Group* (New York: Harcourt Brace, 1950).

15. Raymond Aron, "Social Structure and Ruling Class," *British Journal of Sociology*, I (1950), pp. 1–16 and I (1950), pp. 126–141.

16. *Ibid.*, p. 10.

17. *Ibid.*, p. 141.

18. *Ibid.*

19. John Porter, "Elite Groups: A Scheme for the Study of Power in Canada," *The Canadian Journal of Economics and Political Science*, XXI (1955), pp. 498–513.

20. C. Wright Mills, *The Power Elite* (New York: Oxford University Press, 1956).

21. F.W. Taussig and C.S. Joslyn, *American Business Leaders* (New York: The Macmillan Co. 1932).

22. W.L. Warner and James Abegglen, *Occupational Mobility in American Business and Industry* (Minneaopolis: University of Minnesota Press, 1955).

23. *The Parliamentary Guide* (Ottawa: Annually).

24. B.R. Blishen, "The Construction and Use of an Occupational Scale," *The Canadian Journal of Economics and Political Science,* XXIX (1958), pp. 419–531.

25. Joseph Schumpeter, *Imperialism and Social Classes* (New York: Meridian Books, 1955), p. 102.

26. *Ibid.*

27. Madison Grant, *The Passing of the Great Race* (New York: Charles Scribner's Sons, 1921).

28. Stephen Leacock, *Economic Prosperity in the British Empire* (Toronto: The Macmillan Co., 1930), pp. 195–96.

29. Elbridge Sibley, "Some Demographic Clues to Stratification," *American Sociological Review,* VII (1942), pp. 322–30.

2

The Human Community

1967 marked the beginning of Canada's brief celebrationist period. Our Centennial year came at about the time when the affluent waves of the postwar years were cresting. The shock of economic recession in the liberal capitalist democracies was yet to be experienced. Although the Royal Commission on Bilingualism and Biculturalism was telling us, we chose to ignore the deepening split that was eventually to break out from behind its political plastering. The celebration went on in a burst of cultural development and cultural protectionism. Theatres were built, publishers were subsidized, mass media content was monitored, and universities directed towards Canadianization.

Although not celebrationist, the following piece was written for one of the many Centennial volumes that were to appear. The inappropriate title was provided to me by those who planned the book in which it originally appeared. I have always thought (and it makes sociological sense) of communities as relatively small social units, where most know each other, find most of their relationships, live most of their lives, and where they are closely identified with locality. Large urban and industrialized societies cannot be communities in this sense, but in Canada where the rural-urban transition has been recent, and particularly marked with the population growth that followed the Second World War, there is still the nostalgic image of the small community. The Canadian population has always been highly mobile despite its early rural origins, and so the bucolic myth might serve to compensate for a lost Eden.

The paper picks up several themes that have been dominant in Canadian sociology: population trends, ethnic pluralism, and social change through the industrializing process. I try to examine these within a value perspective of equality and opportunity through education. All of these themes reappear in the later papers with some modification and further development. For example, as I show in the paper "Melting Pot or Mosaic: Revolution or Reversion?" my later enquiries have led me to the view that the concept of ethnic pluralism is not firmly rooted in Canadian history. I have also in later papers clarified what I consider to be some of the undesirable consequences of ethnic pluralism. As we learn more, things come into clearer focus. The

41

paper is reprinted more or less as it was originally published except that data from the 1971 decennial census have been brought in to show the trends as currently as possible.

Canada for more than one hundred years, like the United States for almost twice as long, has been conducting an experiment in the creation of a new society—a new nation—in the vast regions of North America. The American experiment—we must concede the word "American" to the United States—was begun with a revolution which had clearly stated aims. These goals have been repeated continually, not only in school textbooks and by Fourth of July orators, but by great leaders such as Lincoln, Wilson, and Roosevelt, who inspired the people once more to believe in and strive for "the American dream." These charter values of liberty and equality, particularly equality of opportunity, are recurring themes in American culture, and provide goals towards which society strives, and in the light of which progress can be measured.

Canada did not start with a revolution, and therefore, unlike the United States, the charter values that guide it are not clear. With its counter-revolutionary past, prolonged colonialism, and monarchical institutions, Canada has not rejected the old European forms as Americans are said to have rejected the "European father." Consequently people are judged more in terms of what they have achieved than of what they might achieve. This conservative climate has been reinforced by the efforts of Canadians to distinguish themselves from Americans. Hence Canadians have rejected republicanism as being essential to the creation of a new nation.

Canada has been described by S.M. Lipset as elitist rather than equalitarian in its values; that is, Canadian values tend to stress the superiority of those in elite or leadership positions rather than the equality of all persons because they are human beings. This tendency to value the differences of status and aristocratic modes has been reinforced by the fact that Canada has two charter groups speaking different languages. The emphasis on the differences between people rather than on their similarities as human beings has led to the "mosaic" rather than to the "melting-pot" as the basis of social integration.*

Yet Canada is a twentieth-century democracy based on an

---

* Ten years later, after further study of ethnicity in Canada, I came to question whether or not the United States and Canada were very different in this respect. See "Melting Pot or Mosaic: Revolution or Reversion?" included in this volume.

industrial economy. It is more similar to the United States than any other country in the world. Canadians as often as not compare themselves with Americans. Millions of them, in the course of time, have gone to live in the United States. It is not the task of this paper to engage in an extensive comparative analysis of the two societies, but if Canadians make any judgments about how they have done in their first century, they are likely to make them in terms of North American standards, by comparing themselves with the American experiment. The social scientist can do the same thing.

We can ask to what extent Canada has become a coherent society in the new world; to what degree has there been a democratization of its social institutions by the provision of opportunity, particularly educational opportunity, and to what extent has industrialization provided opportunities for upward social mobility. Industrialization and democratization of society are concomitant social processes. Both may be impeded by the orientation to conservative values, to traditionalism: both may be served, as in the United States, by the values inherent in revolutionary beginnings.

Canada, one hundred and ten years after Confederation, is a modern, urban, industrial society. About three-quarters of its population live in towns and cities that the official census defines as urban, that is, a centre with a population of 1000 or more. Less than one-tenth of Canadians live on farms, a small proportion considering the importance of agriculture in the past and the still-lingering ruralism in social images and popular culture. The census definition of an urban community is not very satisfactory, but there are other criteria by which Canadians can be considered city-dwellers. About one-half of the people live within the twenty-two metropolitan areas ranging in size from Montreal with 2.8 million population and Toronto with 2.6 million, to Saint John, New Brunswick, with 107 000 in 1971.

About two-thirds of all the people live in two of the ten provinces. Ontario has 36 per cent of the population and Quebec 28 per cent. The four Atlantic provinces combined have less than one-tenth of the population. Two of the Prairie Provinces, Saskatchewan and Manitoba, share between them a further one-tenth. Alberta and British Columbia, like Ontario and Quebec, are provinces of growing economic and political power and prestige in Canada's industrial epoch. Most of the ten years between 1951 and 1961 were ones of rapid economic growth, when the Canadian population increased by 30 per cent to reach 18.2 million. After 1961 the population continued to increase at a slower rate to

21.6 million in 1971. This growth was not uniform for all parts of the country. Between 1951 and 1971 Alberta's population grew by 59 per cent, British Columbia's by 68 per cent, Ontario's by 55 per cent. All the other provinces grew at a rate that was less than the country as a whole. Quebec's population grew by 42 per cent, and Saskatchewan's increase for the two decades was only 11 per cent.

Differential rates of growth between the provinces and regions of Canada have been the pattern throughout the twentieth century, except that the rapidly growing regions and provinces have changed. With the exception of the stagnation years of the 1930s when the population of Canada grew by only 10 per cent, the Atlantic provinces have grown in population at a rate far less than that of the whole country, a fact that marked the decline of those once proud and vigorous provinces to the low status of economically depressed regions.

For the rest of Canada there have been in the present century two important phases in population growth and economic boom. The first was the rapid development of the West, particularly the wheat economy in the first decade of the century, and the second was the rapid development of the industrial areas of Ontario, Quebec, and British Columbia during and after the Second World War. In the first growth period between 1901 and 1911, the population of both Saskatchewan and Alberta grew by more than 400 per cent compared to 34 per cent for the whole country. Ontario and Quebec were regions of slow rates of growth compared to the West, until the census of 1931.

Although for the first thirty years of the present century the Canadian West was growing faster than the East, the country as a whole was receding from a predominantly rural and primary producing way of life. Every census from the first in 1871 to the latest in 1971 has seen a steady decrease in the proportion of the total population—from 80 to 24 per cent—who live in rural areas. Even as the West was developing its wheat economy and the plains were filling up with Canadian, British, and European settlers, the cities of both the East and West were growing relatively more quickly than the rural population.

Canadians often think of themselves as a rural outdoor people, and both their popular and their high culture tend to emphasize this, but throughout the present century there has been an inexorable economic push towards industrialization and urbanization. The First World War was the point of no return in this process of social and economic development. It was the ordering of the economy to the needs of war that marked the Canadian lift-off to industrialization. After the stagnation of the years following the First World War, the economic requirements of the Second World War provided a powerful second-stage booster in the same direction.

The Canadian community—in so far as an industrialized society can be said to have any community features—is no longer a rural and primary producing one. Perhaps one reason the idea of ruralism remains is because of the romance and drama of some of the primary producing sectors of the economy, such as the exploitation of oil in Alberta, the extraction of iron ore in the Ungava peninsula, and the opening up of the northern territories. As these exploitations are portrayed in picture-book accounts of what Canada is like, they leave the impression that Canadians are primary producers achieving great feats in breaking through mountain and across tundra, and gouging out seaways, canals, and dams. Some Canadians are primary producers and take part in these feats, more often accomplished with foreign capital and skills than with indigenous resources. The typical Canadian worker lives in a city in housing ranging from slums to suburbs. He rides the bus or commuter train to work or drives his car along the freeways that penetrate deep into the hearts of the large cities. It is this process of urbanization that characterizes the present developing Canadian community. Consequently Canada takes on many of the features, both pleasant and unpleasant, of any industrialized "community." There are concert halls and art galleries, and in larger cities a genuine theatre. At the same time there are rates of crime, suicide, and alcoholism, which are more or less "normal" for the types of social structure that industrialization brings.

The growth of the Canadian population from 3.5 million in 1867 to 18.2 million in 1961 and to 21.6 million in 1971 has come more from natural increase than from net migration. (The natural increase is the excess of births over deaths, and net migration is the excess of immigrants over emigrants.) This is because Canada has lost almost as many people through emigration as she has gained from immigration. Nathan Keyfitz, in calculating the Canadian demographic equation of natural increase and migration, has estimated that in the one hundred years between 1851 and 1951, 19.4 million were born in Canada and 8.9 million persons of all ages died, leaving a natural increase of 10.5 million. The number of immigrants for the same period was 7.2 million, but the loss through emigration was 6.5 million, leaving a net migration of only 700 000 over a century.

The loss from emigration is striking and surely is of consequence for Canadian social structure. Canada has received large numbers of migrants for a temporary stay who have gone on to other places, most often to the United States, but also many have returned to their former homeland. At the same time large numbers of Canadian-born have left the country for the United States. There has thus been a very great moving around of the population, some coming in, some leaving, and some moving from one province to another, for interprovincial migration has always been high as economic opportunity has shifted from one region to another. Still others have moved off the farms into the cities.

The scale of these demographic movements suggests a weakness of ties within the human community of Canadian society, and as well a weakness of attachment to the physical and natural surroundings which have both beauty and drama. A coherent social structure requires close human ties, a sense of belonging, and a feeling of being different from others. These social-psychological relationships are difficult to trace in Canada. Obviously many of the people now living in Canada, both native-born and immigrant, have strong kinship links with both the United States and Europe. Whether these family ties with former homeland or possible future homeland are stronger or weaker than ties within Canada we do not know. In the absence of any extensive studies of the social consequences of these demographic movements, we can only speculate that they have a weakening effect on Canadian social life. Quite possibly they could also have a conservative effect, for by and large it is the young who migrate. They leave behind an entrenched and tradition-bound generation less desirous of change and less perceptive of the need for change. If the adventurous and bold find greater opportunities elsewhere there is a drain on the scarcest resource of any society, its human talent. This condition could be creating for Canada a very great problem of leadership at all levels of its institutions.

This peculiar demographic condition is not all that impedes the cohesion of Canadian society. In the early 1960s, as the centennial of Confederation approached, the country's great historical French-English bifurcation became increasingly pronounced and the major issue around which political power-holders and power-seekers made their moves. The lack of cohesion of which we have been speaking applies more to "English" Canada than it does to French Canada. It has been estimated that there were about 65 000 French in Canada in 1763. There are now more than six million. This growth of population is attributable almost entirely to natural increase, since immigration from France or French-speaking territories has been negligible. In addition to their natural increase within Canada the French supplied an emigration to the Unites States (these became the Franco-Americans of New England) of about 800 000 between 1830 and 1930.

French Canada has until recently been a society of high fertility. In Quebec, with its 80 per cent French-speaking population, the birth rate in 1951 was 30 per 1000 compared to 26 per 1000 in Ontario and 28 per 1000 in Canada as a whole. However, the more that French Canada assumes the characteristics of an urban, industrial society the less is the gap in the differential birth-rates. In fact, in the 1970s, Quebec has had the lowest birth rate of any province. In 1973 it was 13.8 per 1000 compared to 15.5 in Canada as a whole. The French in Canada have created a culture of their own by living predominantly within one province, and by being isolated in language from the rest of North America. This culture has been dependent upon natural increase rather than immigration for its survival.

Other parts of this French culture besides high fertility rates were being threatened by the industrialization of French-Canadian society. The traditional culture of French Canada has been outlined in a variety of sociological studies. Its recurring themes were ruralism, church-centred parochialism, authoritarianism in church and politics, and a rejection of worldly acquisition of skills and economic gain. Consequently, class lines within French Canada were clearly drawn. A small proportion of the population was educated in the humanistic, church-operated classical colleges, but masses of the people were poorly educated and lacked the skills for a modern industrial technology. (Actually the difference between English and French Canada in this respect was only one of degree, since Canada has relied very heavily on skilled immigrants.) The French, moving off farms and out of rural areas into the industrial system, became grossly over-represented in the low-status, unskilled, poor-paying jobs. Moreover, the values of the traditional culture tended to make them submissive workers in mines, mills, and factories. Their confessional trade unions lacked the militancy of their English counterparts. At the top a relatively small, educated middle and upper class supplied recruits to political and church elites who lived in contented coalition with English leaders. The political regime, authoritarian and corrupt, of Maurice Duplessis was the high tide of this French-English class relationship. In the late 1950s and 1960s the so-called quiet revolution took place that was to bring one of the most curious social contradictions of modern Canada—a society's leaders claiming to safeguard their culture by in fact rejecting it. The values upon which the quiet revolutionaries were making their appeal—equality of opportunity, political and educational democratization, laicization if not secularization of many of the activities which the Church controlled—were of an alien culture with their origins in the French and American revolutions, neither of which had much influence on French Canada. Anti-authoritarianism in politics and rationalization and efficiency in economic life were among the revolutionary values acquired from outside.

French intellectual and political leaders began to protest, with values borrowed from other cultures, the low economic status of French Canadians, and insisted that this inferior class position could be remedied if they were masters in their own house. The conflict of interests with the rest of Canada was expressed in terms of ethnic rights, the right of a "nation" to control its own destiny. But the movement could equally be interpreted as a revolt against the old culture, where French-Canadian elites ruled in coalition with the dominant English. With the election of the separatist Parti Quebecois to power in 1976 the movement towards "nationhood" gained momentum and the future of a united Canada became more precarious.

In more than 100 years then, Canada had failed to create a coherent society. The two major ethnic components of the population, the British and the French, continued to live in separate linguistic islands. In addition, many ethnic groups other than British and French, as they came into the country, were encouraged to maintain ethnic solidarity and separateness. The ethnic fragmentation of Canada has been one of the outstanding features of its social structure. If there is any Canadian ideology, if Canadians can be said to stand for anything in general (as in general Americans can be said to stand for the charter values expressed in their revolutionary beginnings), it would seem to be the doctrine of unity through diversity.

Canadians have sought to create a society made up of many mutually exclusive subsocieties which must find a way to live together within one nation state. Strength or unity through diversity may or may not be a sociologically absurd doctrine, but in Canada it has become so, as the divisiveness of ethnicity has been reinforced by the political divisiveness of the federal system. Provincialism in politics is associated in some respects with ethnic differentiation, and so by 1960, in response to this dominant ideology, the locus of political power had shifted from the central government to the provinces. The rejection of strong instruments of central government, and hence the rejection of a strong Canadianism, would seem to be an about-face from the intentions of-the original founders of the country. If Canada was to be a new nation with a new purpose it was to be one with hyphenated citizens, who were expected to keep their ties to the lands of their forefathers and to live with dual loyalties. Canada, in official documents, does not even recognize itself as a nation in the sense that "Canadian" can be an ethnic origin, despite the fact that Canada has existed longer than many modern European nations whose people are considered to have an ethnicity, and who are recorded as such when they come to Canada.

The ethnic fragmentation, the cherished mosaic, has been the most important stumbling block to a coherent society. All the ethnic groups in Canada are now minorities. The largest in 1971 were the British with 44.6 per cent of the total. In 1901 they were 57 per cent, but throughout the century their proportion has been declining. Many of the British retain in Canada the historic divisions of the British Isles, even though the majority, probably the vast majority, of them have never been near Britain. England, Scotland, or Ireland are still for large numbers of Canadians "the old country," romantic ideas of which have been kept alive through voluntary associations promoting folk cultures and ritualistic activities such as Highland games, and St. Patrick's Day and Orange parades. The transplanting of these rivalries and differences of the British Isles was an important contribution to ethnic pluralism. It is difficult to see how people whose ancestors sang "Loch Lomond," or "Saturday Night in the Old Kent Road," or "The Harp That Once Through Tara's Halls," but who themselves have been Canadian for several generations, can be culturally different. But the fictions are maintained, and the cue is given to all other groups to do the same thing.

If one considers the 45 per cent British as made up of English, Irish, and Scottish minorities, the French were the largest minority with 28.7 per cent of the population. Non-British, non-French ethnicities made up, in their great variety, 26.7 per cent of the population. They were German (6.1 per cent), Ukrainian (2.2), Dutch (2.0), Italian (3.4), Polish (1.5), native Indian and Eskimo (1.5), Jewish (1.4). The remaining 8.1 per cent of the population were of many origins, although none of them made up more than 1 per cent of the total.

When members of a society are differentiated in some way, as Canada's ethnic groups are, it usually serves some sociological function or purpose. For example, the differentiation of men and women has led in all societies to specific social roles or tasks for each sex. Sex is, however, a visible biological difference. Often quite spuriously other visible differences—skin color, for example—are taken to mean differences of other qualities such as intelligence, moral worth, and so forth. These erroneous ideas form the basis of privilege and exploitation, both of which are being broken down only very slowly on a world-wide basis in the latter part of the twentieth century.

Ethnic differences are differences in language and culture, and only to a minimal degree, as far as most of the European ethnicities are concerned, are there visible physical differences. Differentiation into ethnic groups can lead, like sex differences, to discrimination in the assignment of social roles. Some groups are believed to have particular qualities which suit them more for some social and economic activities than for others. One of the costs of cultural or ethnic pluralism seems to be that the diversity becomes structured into class arrangement, into higher and lower ethnic groups. It is not possible here to go into the extensive literature that debates the relative merits of "melting-pot" assimilation or cultural pluralism. Pluralism means the creation of subsocieties and subcultures which often develop into a class structure. This class structure may not always be inevitable, but Canadian pluralism appears to have developed that way.

Ethnic differentiation results from conquest or from migration. In the first case the conquerors subdue the conquered and put them into inferior positions, often retaining the indigenous class structure as an instrument of rule. The British conquest of Canada kept intact some of the authority structure of New France, particularly the Church. In the second case, through immigration restrictions, the host society lays down the conditions of entry, selects those to come in, and determines what they should do. The idealist would ask if it must always be so or whether the principle of equality can ever assert itself over the ethnocentricity which leads to invidious distinctions. Unlike the American value system, which has always emphasized the idea of equality of peoples within a new nation, the Canadian value system has stressed the social qualities that differentiate people rather than the human qualities that make them the same.

Canada has always had its preferred and less-preferred sources of immigrants who, as they have arrived to work, have ended up at different levels of the occupational world. The British have always provided a large number of skilled and professional immigrants. On the other hand, Ukrainian peasants were important as settlers to take on the forbidding task of opening up the western prairies, as Italian peasants were an important source of construction labor in the period after the Second World War.

It is to be expected, particularly if they do not speak one of the two "official" languages of the country and in addition have a low educational level, that newcomers would assume a low status until they, or what is more likely, their children, fitted more into the host culture. However, the entrance status of the various groups tends to harden and becomes perpetuated over generations. This condition leads to a particular distribution of the various groups in the occupational world.

In one study Bernard R. Blishen derived from census data an occupational class scale based on average earnings and average years of schooling. In this way he ranked 343 occupations in the 1951 labor force. He then sought to show how the various ethnic groups in the labor force were distributed through this occupational class scale. He discovered that the British were over-represented in the higher-level occupations and under-represented in the lower. The French, on the other hand, were under-represented in the higher-level occupations and over-represented in the lower. There were relatively fewer British as the occupational scale was descended, and there were relatively more French and more of all the other ethnic groups. Jews were the only group who followed the British pattern. They were over-represented in the top occupational levels, because of the frequency with which they were found in the learned professions. This high occupational status represented a great achievement for the Jewish group, because many of the parental generation came to Canada as very poor immigrants and worked in low-status, factory occupations. The great emphasis on learning in the Jewish culture resulted in high educational levels for the second and third generations. Such a pattern does not seem to have been the case with the other non-British, non-French groups. This distribution of Jews in professional occupations should not, however, become confused with power, because Jews very rarely get to the top positions in either the economic or political system.

With the growth of industrialization the French have consistently dropped in terms of occupational status; that is, their over-representation in low-status occupations has increased relative to all other groups with the exception of the Italians. Even in Quebec where the French made up about eight-tenths of the labor force in the 1960s the same differences in occupational levels were to be found. Thus the opportunities for advancement that came with the industrialization of Quebec were not equally distributed between the English and the French. There is little doubt that these marked differences in status levels were an important ingredient of the quiet revolution.

The relationship that is here being sketched between ethnicity and social class, as measured at least by occupational level, has been clear to any sophisticated observer. The French-English difference in the class structure has been a literary theme, and also the subject of important sociological studies such as E.C. Hughes' *French Canada in Transition*. One cannot live in Canada for long without noticing the social levels of the different groups, for among other things it leads to residential segregation, with particular groups living in isolated community-like subcultures. In large Canadian cities the British will be over-represented in high-status occupations, and certain other ethnicities, depending on the region, will service them from lower-status jobs. An interesting example is the low-status jobs occupied by the French in Ontario along the Quebec border where the French are over-represented among unskilled laborers and in restaurants, laundries, and other types of low-status service occupations.

In other regions of Canada there are similar class-like characteristics of interethnic relations, although the groups will be different because of their varying regional distribution. In 1951 about four-tenths of all those of non-British, non-French European origin lived in the Prairie Provinces and one-third in Ontario, but only one-tenth lived in Quebec and the Atlantic Provinces combined. Two-thirds of the Ukrainians and six-tenths of the Scandinavians lived on the Prairies. Manitoba, Saskatchewan, and Alberta, with about one-fifth of the Canadian population, had more than two-fifths of those of European origin in Canada. Alberta and British Columbia, with about one-seventh of the population, had almost half of those of Asian origin. More than one-half of all Italians in Canada lived in Ontario urban areas.

By the time of the 1971 census there were some changes. The proportions of Scandinavians and Ukrainians living on the Prairies had decreased, but 58 per cent of those with a Ukrainian origin and half of the Scandinavians still lived there. And by 1971 Manitoba, Saskatchewan, and Alberta had only one-sixth of the population. Alberta and British Columbia had by 1971 one-sixth of the population and they had more than half of those of Asian origin. The Italians were even more concentrated in the urban areas of Ontario. More than 60 per cent lived there.

In some respects this regionalism of ethnicity is a reflection of the different groups' attachment to agriculture. With the relative decline in the proportion of the labor force in agriculture some ethnic groups have moved out of this occupation more than others. In the 1960s the Germans, Dutch, Scandinavians, and East Europeans were over-represented in agriculture as they always have been in Canada. The British have been under-represented. The Jewish and Italian groups are almost entirely urban. It should be noted that with the dramatic fall from nineteen to twelve per cent of the male labor force in agriculture during the 1950s, no group had more than one-quarter in agriculture by 1961 or more than 16 per cent in 1971.

Canada had in 1971 an aboriginal population of 295 215

Indians and 17 550 Eskimos, making up together about two per cent of the total population. About three-quarters of all Indians lived on reserves. The Indians and their reserve system are administred by the federal government. To be an Indian for the purposes of the Indian Act, and thus to be entitled to the benefits or otherwise of the reserve system, the individual must have Indian paternity. Indian maternity and white paternity defines the individual as Métis. No one really knows how extensive this marginal group is, but some estimates are as high as 250 000. They are probably the most distressed of all Canadians. Many of them live on the edges of reserves, but are not of the reserves. Similarly they are rejected by the white community when they seek a place in the white economy. The welfare and educational benefits provided the Indians are denied the Métis, since not being Indians they are the responsibility of the provinces in which they reside. Their low level of education makes it difficult to integrate them into the industrial economy. In their social no-man's-land they were perfect objects for the war on poverty which was announced in 1965.

Government officials make great claims about what has been done for the Indians, and professional anthropologists, more often than not, are extremely critical of government policies. Many Indians themselves place a high evaluation on their own cultures, and wish to retain within the reserve system their treaty rights. This attitude is, of course, consistent with the ideology of diversity. However, no assessment could ignore the fact that native Indians are, after more than one hundred years of the system, at the very lowest end of the occupational ladder. Almost half of them, by far the largest proportion of any group, were in 1961 in low-level primary and unskilled occupations. Judged by the Blishen scale of 1951, 85 per cent were in the lowest two classes. The position of the Indians had not changed much by 1971. In the 1971 census they were by far the largest group who did not state an occupation. There were 25 per cent of them in that category compared to about 10 per cent of the total labor force. And those who did state an occupation were primarily in service, construction, fishing, and forestry occupations.

While Indians, from the time that treaties were made with them, have in the main lived in bands on reserves, the Eskimos have come into contact with white civilization much more recently. In earlier times they had only sporadic contact with fur traders or white missionaries. In the post-Second World War period of northern military installation and mineral exploitation they have increasingly been absorbed into the white man's economy, primarily as unskilled workers. Thus many of them have become transformed in a very short time from nomadic hunters to wage earners living in settled communities and sending their children to school. The Eskimos have no treaties with the government of Canada, but are full-fledged citizens, although unlike their white fellow citizens they are the object of the paternalistic policies of a remote government department in Ottawa. Many observers have suggested that such a guided democracy has had the effect of destroying a proud people's native skills of living off the hunt and surviving in the most brutal climate in all the world. It is unlikely that those who express such conservative views would ever themselves want to live such a life, dependent on the caribou for their bodies' needs and the itinerant, dog-sledding missionary for their souls'. Obviously many of the Eskimos do not prefer it. Given time the Eskimos could be integrated into Canadian life, while the reserve system could prevent the Indian from ever becoming so integrated.

Although the transition to an industrial economy has been going on throughout the present century, the change was accelerated in the period following the Second World War. The development of an industrial economy brings changes in the occupational structure of the labor force. In 1901, 40 per cent of the labor force worked in agriculture. The proportion dropped slowly until 1951 when it was 20 per cent, but by 1961 it had dropped to 11.5 per cent, and in 1971 it was 6.3 per cent. During the 1950s the off-farm migration was about 40 000 per year. In 1961 there were 481 000 occupied farms, a loss of 142 000 since 1951, and the farm labor force fell by 340 000. Saskatchewan, the centre of Canadian wheat production, felt the changes with particular force. It had lost 100 000 of its farm population in the four years preceding 1960. By 1961 only about one-third of the Saskatchewan population lived on farms. By 1971 the proportion living on farms in Saskatchewan was down to one-quarter. Although farming was of a different type in Quebec and Ontario, similar changes were taking place in the agricultural labor force and in farming as a way of life.

Across the country the number of farms declined, but the average size of farm increased from 279 to 358 acres between 1951 and 1961. The consolidation trend in farming has been continually accelerating since 1941. In 1966, 53 per cent of census farms contained less than 240 acres and in 1971, 49 per cent. As well, farming methods were becoming more scientific and more mechanical, and often involved large-scale corporate farming. With these changes farmers and farm managers required higher levels of technical and managerial skill.

Along with the decline of farming as an occupation has gone a relative decline in the importance of other primary occupations such as mining, logging, and fishing. There has been, that is, a shift out of primary producing occupations into more skilled occupations. The proportion of a society's workers engaged in occuptions such as services and commercial activities compared to those engaged in the primary occupations is often taken as a measure of economic progress. If for comparative purposes the United States is taken as the most advanced industrial society, it had in 1955 14 per cent of its work force in primary occupations and 52 per cent in tertiary occupations. At the same time Canada had 21 per cent in primary occupations and 46 per cent at the tertiary level. A similar way of looking at the labor force as it changes to an advanced industrial level is to trace the changes in the proportion of those in the goods-producing industries with those in the service-producing industries. Again on this criterion the 1950s was a watershed period for Canada. In 1951, 58 per cent of the labor force was engaged in goods-producing industries, and 42 per cent in service-producing industries. By 1963 almost the reverse situation applied. Less than half the workers (45 per cent) were producing goods while more than half (55 per cent) were producing services. The trend continued during the sixties and at the time of the 1971 census 34 per cent of the labor force were in goods-producing and 58 per cent were in service-producing industries. (Eight per cent were unspecified as a result of the self-enumeration of the questionnaire.)

Yet another way of measuring these changes is by examining the changing proportions of the labor force engaged in non-manual and in manual occupations. Between 1901 and 1971 the non-manual and service occupations rose from 23 per cent of the labor force to 50.5 per cent, while the manual occupations, including agriculture, fell from 72.2 per cent of the labor force in 1901 to 41.8 per cent in 1961 and 32.2 per cent in 1971. The agricultural occupations by themselves, as we have seen, dropped from 40.3 per cent to 6.3 per cent over the same period. Thus the manual occupations, excluding agriculture, remained almost steady, moving only from 31.9 per cent in 1901 to 31.0 per cent in 1971. Although it is difficult to measure, there is little doubt that at each of these levels the skill content of most occupations was more advanced than formerly. The non-manual white-collar occupations have grown because of the increased number of professional, managerial, and clerical personnel required as the economy becomes more industrialized. These components of the labor force were increasing at a rate greater than others.

Although it is not possible here to extend the analysis into the differences between the male and the female labor force over the period (we have had to consider the two parts of the labor force as one) it is important to realize that women have an important labor-force role in an industrial economy. There is probably a dual process here: women can acquire as easily as men many of the skills that an industrialized economy requires beyond those for which they have been traditionally trained, such as teaching, nursing, stenography, and the like. They also become important second-income earners, so that their families can enjoy the higher standards of living that industrialization brings. There seems to be in all industrial societies an increased tendency for women to enter the labor force. In 1901 in Canada only 12 per cent of women of working age were in the labor force, that is, working for pay, while in 1961 the proportion was 30 per cent and in 1971, 40 per cent. In the 1950s and '60s the female labor force was growing at a faster rate than the male. Two-thirds of the women who were working in 1971 were married. The fact that the increase in the female labor force has been greatest for women over thirty-five years of age suggests that the developing pattern is for women to return to the labor force when their major child-rearing activities are completed or have been handed over to other agencies such as the school.

It is important to consider some of the social changes that are associated with the basic changes in the economy and in the occupational structure. In very general terms, despite the nostalgia of some for the old ruralism, industrialization represents progress, particularly in terms of higher standards of living, and a more widespread appreciation of culture, lengthening of life, control of disease, reduction of the working day, and, most important of all, higher levels of education. But there are many other benefits as well. Philosophers, of course, will dispute the definition of progress in such empirical terms as here suggested, and others will point to increased rates of deviant behavior such as crime, suicide, and mental disorders as evidence that industrialization brings a toll of human casualties. It is doubtful, however, that given a choice a majority of Canadians would want to return to the kind of life that went with earlier periods of industrialization or the old ruralism.

Industrialization represents a general upgrading of the labor force which has become richer in skills than formerly because of the increasing number of skilled and professional workers. Since low birth-rates prevail in the higher occupational groups, the skilled and professional classes, even if they replace themselves, do not supply enough recruits to fill all these emerging jobs.

Consequently, new skilled and professional workers either must be recruited from formerly unskilled lower classes, or they must be imported from some other society. Industrialization makes such demands for skilled technical and professional workers that all industrial societies have had to revolutionize their educational systems. Earlier phases of industrialization brought universal secondary education. In the present phase of industrial growth, further development of the system and even its survival as an independent entity depends on the provision of tertiary-level education, including not only university but various forms of technical, subprofessional training beyond high school. It is possible, and this is in fact what Canada has done, for a society to rely so heavily on outside sources for skilled and professional workers that it can neglect, at least for a time, its own educational resources.

Industrialization, then, constitutes an opportunity for large numbers to move upwards in the class structure. This process sociologists call upward social mobility, that is, the condition in which individuals are better off or have higher status than their parents. Upward mobility is the social counterpart of the upgrading of the labor force. The educational level of the population, then, can be considered the single most crucial measure of capacity for industrial development. Educational purists are often upset at measuring the advantage of education in these practical market-place terms, but there is no basic conflict between the civilizing and humanizing effects of education and the role that education has in providing skills and technology. The long historical trend has been for these to work together to make for general social progress.

Industrialization has a further important social consequence. It cannot be fully exploited as a form of economic activity without a democratizing of the society, because it cannot rely on a system of privilege as the basis for recruitment to occupations. For example, if education is costly it becomes available mainly to those who can afford to pay for it rather than to those who could, because of their ability, make the most use of it. To survive and develop, an industrial society must search out and train its human resources, particularly in a period of intense international competition for talent. Migration statistics show that during the 1960s a tremendous transfer of skilled and professional workers took place from one country to another. To compete with other countries requires policies directed at the democratization of education. We will now try to assess Canadian achievement in the light of these requirements of industrialization and democratization.

By any measure Canadian educational systems were seriously inadequate for the great industrial development of the post-Second World War period. In 1951, at the threshold of this development, more than half of the men in the labor force (55 per cent) had no more than an elementary-school education. About one-third had some high-school, and less than a tenth had some university or other tertiary-level training. Women in the labor force were better educated than men, and this is probably because there has been a much closer link between schooling and traditional female occupations. Even in the 20- to 24-year age group of males in 1951 at least half had no more than elementary school. There was some improvement in educational levels by the time of the 1961 census, but the changes were minimal, a continuation of the slow trend of improvement of the last fifty years. There was no indication that Canadians generally or their leaders in particular were aware of the critical needs of the educational system. By 1961 the proportion of males in the labor force with elementary-school education only had dropped to 44 per cent. But for the important age group 20 to 24, who would be in the labor force for the next generation, the proportion with elementary school only was still as high as 31 per cent. This lower third had very poor prospects indeed in the complex occupational world of the 1960s and the future. It is doubtful that they even had the basic skills for retraining. A large proportion of this undereducated group were the off-farm migrants who ended up at the bottom of the new class structure that was developing in the large cities.

There was a great expansion of educational opportunities during the 1960s that was reflected in the 1971 census. At that time thirty per cent of males in the labor force had an elementary education only, but only 12.4 per cent of the 20- to 24-year age group had less than Grade 9 education.

Educational attainment, as would be expected, was not uniform for all provincial regions or groups. The percentage of the male labor force with elementary education only in 1971 was as follows: in both New Brunswick and P.E.I., 42.7 per cent; in Newfoundland, 41.1; in Quebec, Nova Scotia and Manitoba respectively, 39.2, 34.8 and 30.3; in Ontario 27.2. Alberta and British Columbia were the best-educated provinces with 23.7 and 21.5 per cent respectively having only elementary education.

There were important differences in the relationship between ethnicity and school attendance. In 1951 just half of the age group 5 to 24 years were in school. By 1971 the proportion had risen to 67.6 per cent. The ethnic distribution of those in school in this age group was striking. The Jewish group in 1961 had 84.8 per cent, a fact which further confirms the high value that Jews place on education. In descending order they were followed by Asian, 73.6 per cent; British, 72.3 per cent; and Scandinavian, 69.1 per cent. Less than the national proportion of 68.3 per cent were the Dutch with 67 per cent; German, 65.6 per cent; French, 64.1 per cent; Italian, 61.7 per cent; native Indian, 54.8 per cent. All other European groups combined, as they were for this census tabulation, had 70.1 per cent.

A 1971 census profile study by John Krolt, *Ethnic Origins of Canadians*, distinguishes between "old ethnics," those who arrived in Canada before the Second World War, and "new ethnics," those who arrived afterwards. On the whole the "new ethnics" are better educated than the "old." Thirty-seven per cent of the former compared to 25 per cent of the latter had some form of postsecondary education. When Eskimos and Indians with their very low educational levels and Jews with their exceptionally high ones are excluded the remaining "old ethnics" are remarkably homogeneous. The proportions having postsecondary, non-university education were 15.6 per cent overall, ranging from 13.1 per cent of the Italians, to 17.2 per cent of the Scandinavians. Among the "old ethnics" 9.6 per cent had some university education, ranging from 7.5 per cent of the French to 11.2 per cent of the British.

The "new ethnics" are not so homogeneous and do not necessarily have the same relative distributions as the "old ethnics." For example, "new ethnic" French have a somewhat higher educational level than "new ethnic" British. Among the "new ethnics," Italians have very low educational levels and Asians, very high. With the exception of the Italians, in all the "new ethnic" groups more than 10 per cent have had a university education.

The levels of education in Canada that have just been reviewed and the attitudes to education that must lie behind these statistics cannot be separated from another significant divisive element in Canadian society, that is, religious differences. As though ethnic diversity were not enough, religious divisions impose additional strains on unity. Moreover, religion and ethnicity are often interwoven to constitute the vital components of religio-ethnic subcultures. In 1971, 46 per cent of the population was Catholic. Catholics in Canada, as elsewhere, have always claimed the right to control education for their children, and the subject has long been a contentious issue in Canadian politics. Education falls within the jurisdiction of the provinces, and provinces vary in the extent to which separate Catholic schools are supported through taxation. Whether Catholic schools raise money on their own or receive public funds, they have always been impoverished, relative to public, tax-supported schools. If the educational rights of Catholics are a liberty they are entitled to enjoy it would seem to be a liberty denied by inadequate financial support. In Quebec, where 88 per cent of the population is Catholic, the former low educational levels did not spring from constitutional or political disadvantage but reflected the traditional values of French-Canadian society. The low occupational levels of the non-charter ethnic groups in Canada are a reflection, not only of their minority ethnic-group status, but also of the fact that many of the groups are predominantly Catholic. The problem of providing a highly skilled industrial labor force is made more difficult because many values about education are imbedded in these religio-ethnic subcultures.

The inadequacy of the educational system to meet the demands of an increasingly complex work world was counterbalanced by a heavy importation of skilled and professional workers. Between 1953 and 1963, according to the Economic Council of Canada, 80 000 professional and highly skilled workers came to Canada from outside North America. About three-fifths of these professional and skilled workers were British, a fact that shows the tendency for the occupational level of the different ethnicities in the immigrant labor force to correspond to the occupational levels of the ethnic groups already in Canada. Large numbers of unskilled workers, for example, came from Italy during the same period.

Reliance on immigration for some professions is striking. Of all the physicians and surgeons working in Canada in 1961 almost 20 per cent had immigrated in the preceding five years. For engineers the proportion was 25 per cent, for architects about 34 per cent. Calculated in a different way, between 1953 and 1963 the number of engineers entering Canada was equal to 73 per cent of the number graduated by Canadian universities. For architects it was 141 per cent, for physicians and surgeons 53 per cent. In one estimate made by the present writer about one-third of all the new professional occupations that came with the industrial expansion between 1951 and 1961 were filled from immigration, and about one-half of all the new skilled and technical manual occupations were also filled from immigration.

In spite of the expansion of educational opportunities during the 1960s, Canada continues to import large numbers of professionals. In 1973, of 92 228 immigrants admitted to Canada who entered the labor force, 27 per cent stated their intended occupation as a managerial or professional one.

Upgrading the skill levels of the labor force took place by

heavy reliance on external recruitment, since Canadian educational systems were not geared to the needs of the industrial economy. This cultural lag reflected the low evaluation of education within the society. Canadian families in the fifties were not transmitting positive attitudes and values about education to their children, and Canadian leaders were not putting the necessary emphasis on the need to stay in school. Nor were they investing enough resources in education. These conditions applied particularly to tertiary-level education. Even in the 1960s Canadian university education was more expensive to students than it was in any other comparable industrial society. In 1962–63 in Canada, the charge to students through tuition income amounted to 26 per cent of university operating costs, compared to 9.9 per cent in the United Kingdom. A large proportion of this 9.9 per cent in the United Kingdom would have been met through state awards to students. In 1957–58 in a group of 364 publicly sponsored universities and colleges in the United States the proportion of costs paid by student fees was 8 per cent. For Canadian students the annual costs for a year at university were extraordinarily high in the early 1960s, and the amount of money available for student awards was pitifully low.

During that decade, however, there was an enormous expansion of tertiary-level education in Canada. Full-time enrolments at all postsecondary institutions increased by 214 per cent, from 163 143 in 1960–61 to 513 358 in 1972–73. Improved facilities, the establishment of community colleges, and the founding of new universities resulted in an even sharper rise in expenditures. The total expenditures on postsecondary institutions, capital and operating, increased in Canada from about 33 million in 1960–61 to over $2.5 billion in 1972–73, an increase of 800 per cent. At the same time there was some effort to increase equality of educational opportunity. Tuition fees were increasingly a lower proportion of operating funds. In 1964 the federal government introduced the Canada Student Loan Plan by which loans were made to eligible students by banks, credit unions and trust companies, and guaranteed by the federal government. Interest was paid by the federal government until six months after graduation. Provinces supplemented this student assistance by making available to disadvantaged students grants based on need and family resources. In spite of these efforts university students still came disproportionately from higher income families. A survey of postsecondary students conducted by the federal Department of the Secretary of State, published in 1976, indicated that about one-third of all postsecondary students said that their fathers had incomes of over $15 000 and about one-fifth, that their fathers earned less than $6000 a year. This kind of survey of students who were present in postsecondary institutions did not give a true picture of the proportion of young people in different social classes that made use of available educational opportunity because it did not take into account all those who left the educational system before reaching the postsecondary level.

A survey of the aspirations of Ontario high school students in 1971 revealed that whether a student wanted and expected to go to university was very much related to his social class. When students were allocated to one of six social classes according to their fathers' occupation and an occupational scale developed by Bernard R. Blishen, it was found that, among Grade 12 students, 60 per cent in the highest social class and 24 per cent in the lowest expected to go to university. Among the students in the top one-third of the mental ability range, about two-thirds of the upper-middle-class students and one-third of the lower-class students expected to go to university.

Democratization of education, that is, the making of all levels and types of education available to all according to their talents, is essential to the release of a society's creative potential. The technical, scientific, and social problems of a highly advanced industrial society are so complex that no society can afford to waste its human resources but must engage in a constant search for talent. There is little doubt that had their educational systems been more developed Canadians would have experienced much more upward social mobility than they have. They would also be in a much stronger position to meet the international challenges of the mid-twentieth century.

As well as a release of their creative energies societies require leadership. Modern challenges are such that no society can afford to recruit its leadership groups on the basis of privilege. The requirement of upgrading the labor force which has been referred to earlier had its counterpart in the opening up of all the top positions to those who have the necessary ability. In the past Canada's elite groups, its top leaders in business, politics, the civil service, and the educational systems, have been recruited from a narrow base of middle- and upper-class British. At times middle- and upper-class French, particularly in politics and the Catholic Church, have shared power with the British. But the rest of Canada's ethnic groups are scarcely represented at all in the top decision-making positions. Thus the educational system should be called upon in the future not only to supply the necessary skilled and professional workers, but also to supply the very ablest at the top of all major social institutions.

Only in this way will Canada offer equal opportunities for all and make the best use of its human resources. And, in addition, if the official ideology recognizes a Canadian ethnicity, rather than only European or others, then, even though bilingualism and biculturalism should spread, the society would be more coherent and less fragmented than in the past.

3

The Future of Upward Mobility

Some would say that I would reprint the following paper only on a dare because it contains a "ghastly error" of social science prediction and analysis, namely that modern industrial societies—what I called "postmodern"—would continue the rates of growth they had experienced through to the late 1960s, and that their educational systems would fail to produce the level of highly qualified workers that were needed. The paper does, I think, reflect accurately the dominant thought of the time, that the expansion of education was necessary for the continued growth of these advanced societies. Educated workers were viewed as "human capital," and the more any industrial society had, the greater was its potential for further growth. Indeed, so great was the demand for highly qualified workers that the major industrial societies of the world were in competition with each other for trained workers. "Brain drain" was the name of the process.

My interest in the migration of highly qualified manpower (a standard expression of the time) arose because of my work in Canada which had shown how heavily we had relied on the importation of such workers to meet the demands of industrial development, and to overcome the inadequacies of our own educational systems. Canada had lagged far behind other countries at a comparable stage of development in school retention rates and postsecondary education. It was a problem I took to Europe when I spent a sabbatical leave at the International Institute for Labour Studies in Geneva.

What I discovered was that the migration of highly educated workers was a worldwide phenomenon and that generally the movement was from the less developed to the more developed societies, although there were, too, substantial exchanges between the most advanced societies. These processes led me to conclude that even with the great expansion of educational facilities the advanced societies were not producing all the skills they needed. I searched for an explanation in the class structures of these societies and the differential distribution of aspiration for education and upward occupational mobil-

ity in the large working classes these societies had created. Hence, social policy should be directed towards encouraging working-class young people to stay in school and go on to higher education. Education and occupational opportunity were closely linked, and I was among those who argued forcibly to expand educational opportunity to serve the principle of equality.

Several events took place which called into serious question the type of analysis represented by this paper. One was the reaction against the multiversity: the massive educational factory generating human capital for the industrial-military complex. That was a part of the revulsion against the Vietnam war, the remnants of European colonialism, and in the United States the continued exclusion of blacks from the opportunities that appeared abundant. In 1968, the year this paper was published, universities were exploding as revolutionary centres. Canadian students were all caught up in this movement. Whilst they would then invite me to talk about power structures and economic concentration, they showered criticism on this paper because of its apparent acceptance of the view that education alone is sufficient to serve equality and because of the failure to recognize that equality of condition was never served by a system that gave differential rewards based on education. As can be seen from the later papers on education and equality in this volume, I sought to re-examine the more optimistic view.

In the late 1960s, however, the criticism of education and the system was irrational, crude, and at times violent. Since then, with the new respectability given to Marxian frameworks of analysis some fresh insights have been gained on the relationship between education and economy that cannot be ignored.

Another great surprise unforeseen at the time of forecasting the future needs of the industrial societies for educated manpower was the great economic crisis that was to strike the capitalist economies of the 1970s. How much of that crisis can be attributed to OPEC behavior and oil politics, how much to cyclical exhaustion of rates of profit, how much to the cutting back of scientific research with the end of the war in Vietnam, how much to resource depletion and north-south conflict, how much to government overspending on the welfare state, is difficult to apportion and that is not the task here. Cumulatively, they brought about changes that created high levels of unemployment in the advanced societies and, in particular, the underemployment of educated workers who less than a decade earlier were in such great demand.

But was the predicted need for highly qualified workers such a "ghastly error"? Everyone will have his own answer to that. My own is provided in the later papers. Despite the shift in my own views on the role of public education, I think "The Future of Upward Mobility" is more than a period piece because of the way it attempts to assess how working-class cultures respond to opportunity. It is a mistake to think, as so many do, that "everybody" goes to university now and that we have oversold education. The fact is that even towards the end of the 1970s only about 14 per cent of the relevant age group goes to university in Canada and that proportion comes overwhelmingly from the more advantaged families. Of course, the university population has increased tremendously and, as pointed out in the previous paper on the human community, it does represent some extension to the less privileged, but the fact remains that the democratization of education has a long way to go. The question of "education for what?" is still with us.

The paper was written as the MacIver Award Lecture of the American Sociological Association. In 1966, the Award was given for The Vertical Mosaic.

In this paper I want to discuss the problem which the major industrial societies of the West are experiencing in the recruitment of highly qualified professional workers, the light which sociology might throw on this problem and the way in which the problem reflects on the present state of mobility theory and research. These major industrial societies are advancing into a stage of postmodernity[1] with a culture based on science and technology. They have high levels of productivity and have the potential for vastly increased productivity. They may, however, be seriously limited in their development because the occupational structure which is emerging demands more positive values about education and stronger mobility aspirations than appear to have been current in what we have been calling the modern industrial stage. I intend to be speculative about this unfilled room at the top of our emerging occupational structures, and I intend also to orient what I have to say to questions of social policy.

Economists speak of the difference between the first and second industrial revolutions, the latter being based not, as the first, on a machine technology, but on the "silent conquest of cybernation." This transformation into the postmodern cybernated society is not confined to production processes in factories. In medicine, for example, can be seen the development of biophysics and the application of electronic techniques in medical care. In his studies of the communication media Marshall McLuhan has tried to show how the environment and the human understanding of it have become transformed. We have also seen great changes in the means and speed of travel. In fact there is scarcely an area of social life for which the new culture of science and technology has no relevance.

Much of the discussion of the effects on the labor force of

these changes has concerned the displacement of workers. Although less attention has been given to the problem of manning the very much upgraded occupational structure that is emerging, this problem has not been ignored. In the United States, the nation most advanced into postmodernity, the President's Science Advisory Committee has reported, "Impending shortages of talented, highly trained scientists and engineers threaten the successful fulfilment of vital national commitments."[2]

It is becoming apparent that all large-scale industrial societies are failing to produce the full range of highly qualified manpower that is necessary for them to maintain themselves and to develop further their industrial potential and economic growth. This situation can be seen from the continuing discussion of the shortages of manpower in official studies, occupational projections, requirements of national plans (such as that in France), and in the various symposia and colloquia on the subject that are held from time to time in the major industrial societies of the West.

The migration of highly qualified manpower provides some of the most interesting evidence of the shortages in these societies. They appear to be competing for each other's trained talent as a way of making up their own deficiencies. They also recruit heavily from the less-developed societies. In absolute numbers, the United States seems to be the greatest net importer of trained manpower. The National Science Foundation's surveys of scientists and engineers from abroad provide interesting data. Altogether, between 1949 and 1964, more than 63 500 natural scientists, social scientists and engineers entered the United States labor force as immigrants from abroad. Of these, 16 000 came during the three-year period 1962–1964. This number was equivalent to 3 per cent of the domestic graduates in comparable fields over the same three years, although in 1963, for engineers, the largest component of these highly qualified immigrants, the number entering was equivalent to 12 per cent of the domestic engineering graduates of that year. The National Science Foundation has also established that, of 79 000 scientists with doctorates in the 1964 National Register of Scientific and Technical Personnel, 5000 (6 per cent) received their degree in foreign countries. Of the 61 200 for whom the master's degree was the highest, the proportion obtaining their degree abroad was only 2 per cent. These proportions suggest that the higher the qualifications, the greater the reliance on external recruitment.

It has been suggested that this importation of engineers and scientists is equivalent to the training provided by several large universities; R.M. Titmuss has estimated that the saving in educational costs for the United States is four billion dollars. A National Science Foundation report in 1962 said, "Since domestic institutions of higher education do not yet provide the country's needed annual aggregate of scientists, it would seem reasonable to assume that the American scientific community could continue to absorb foreign scientists at approximately their present rate of entry for some time to come."[3] This view was certainly borne out in subsequent years for which immigration data are available.

Medicine is another profession in which there is considerable importation to meet the shortage of physicians estimated by an American Medical Association report in 1967 at 50 000. It appears that the rate of entry has been around 1500 physicians a year, and one estimate puts the stock of foreign-trained physicians at about 20 000. Another estimate suggests that 28 per cent of the internships and 26 per cent of the residencies in United States hospitals were filled by foreign graduates, the vast majority of them coming from underdeveloped countries.

In addition to the highly qualified workers who entered the United States as immigrants, many others entered with non-immigrant status. For engineers and scientists the number was 6100 in 1964, the largest proportion being exchange visitors. As the National Science Foundation reports, "The admission of scientists and engineers to a country even if only for a short-term stay can provide some increment, however limited, to current manpower resources both in terms of numbers and of specialized skills."[4]

The spectacle of the most advanced industrial society "plundering the educational systems of Western Europe," the colorful phrase used by Mr. Quintin Hogg in the British House of Commons, has been viewed with alarm by other industrialized societies, particularly Britain and Germany, where there are great fears of losing out in the competition for highly qualified manpower. But most countries of Western Europe appear to be net importers of trained talent. Unfortunately immigration statistics for European countries are not as good as they are for the United States. In Great Britain, where there appears to be a net loss of engineers and scientists, there is a net gain of physicians. Nearly half the present junior staff in the Hospital Service have come from abroad. Britain is also a net importer of university teachers. It has been caustically noted that the new African nation of Togo has sent more physicians and scientists to France than France has sent to Togo.

At the level of highly qualified manpower which we are

considering the quality of the migrants is almost as important as the quantity. British investigators who tend to see the manpower problem almost entirely in terms of the "brain drain" have noted that nine fellows of the Royal Society emigrated from Britain to America between 1952 and 1961. Over the last ten years Britain has been losing between 15 to 20 per cent of its annual output of Ph.D.s in engineering and science, and around 8 per cent of the output of first degrees in 1965. News of shortages in the U.S. is received almost with fright and a desire to lock the doors. When the American Institute of Physics published a report early in 1967 which stated that an earlier estimate of a shortage of 20 000 physicists by 1970 in the U.S. was too low, the news was headlined in *The Times* of London, "U.S. Brain Drain to Take More Britons."

It would seem that the more industrialized the society, the greater the need to import highly qualified manpower, a problem which is solved in part by the attractiveness these societies have for highly qualified people. One investigator has said, "Every advanced nation faces a shortage of highly qualified scientists for the indefinite future. They will exert strenuous efforts to educate more scientists and to educate them better. They will tend to attract scientists from other countries. And they will have a scarcity."[5] Most of the studies concerned with the supply of highly qualified manpower are about scientists and engineers because they are essential to the transformation and maintenance of the postmodern society. In these disciplines there is clearly an international career system in which the opportunity structure goes far beyond the boundaries of one society.

Other occupations requiring high levels of skill are also increasing at a relatively greater rate than less-skilled occupations. In the labor force projections from 1965 to 1975 made by the U.S. Department of Labor, total employment is expected to increase by 22.9 per cent, but professional, technical and kindred workers are expected to increase by 48.6 per cent, managers, officials and proprietors (except farm) by 25.3 per cent, and clerical and kindred workers by 30.8 per cent. In 1965 all these major occupational groups had more than the median years of schooling of the entire civilian labor force (12.2 years). For the most rapidly expanding professional, technical and kindred workers (48.6 per cent) the median schooling was 16.3 years. In absolute numbers the U.S. labor force is expected in the decade 1965–75 to require 6.2 million workers in the two most educated of its major occupational groups, compared to the 1.7 million that were added between 1960 and 1965.

It is not difficult to see the forces making for these increases.

In the first place, organizing and producing units are likely to become larger, and based on increasingly complex procedures which require more highly trained managers with greater amounts of science and engineering in their educational backgrounds. In this postmodern society there will also be high expectations about distributive justice, thus increasing the proportions of health, welfare and recreational occupations. In the United States at present the most rapidly growing occupational sector is state and local government and it is the sector in which the anticipated growth to 1975 will be greatest. The 1966 Manpower Report of the President dealt with future needs in this way: "Growth in research and development . . . can be expected to demand ever-rising numbers of experts in many professional and technical disciplines. In addition, greater numbers of city planners, engineers, and architects will be needed to rebuild and redesign blighted areas of many of our major metropolitan centers. Talents of a wide range of social scientists will be used to redeem human resources in these cities. Many more teachers will be needed. Among other occupations due for major increases are those involving personnel necessary to implement the new medicare program and other programs developed by Federal, State and local government agencies to improve the health of the Nation's citizens."[6] The Report then goes on to say there must also be a similar increase in the number of subprofessional occupations to ensure the proper utilization of higher professional workers.

Some have argued that the demand for highly qualified manpower is associated with automation, aerospace exploration, and defence, and is therefore of limited duration and scope. If there were substantial lessening of these demands there would be a threat of professional unemployment. Such a condition is not likely to arise. Defence establishments and their associated scientific enterprises are a part of contemporary occupational structures and will continue to be so. Moreover, the social sciences have provided great possibilities for policies to control economic and social processes. Thus there has been a return to the idea of social progress, not as a freely moving evolutionary process but as a deliberate planned collective effort to improve the quality of social life. The ideological pressures for such policies are very great, as are the moral pressures to extend these benefits to the underdeveloped areas of the world. The culture of science and technology has as striking a role in this social progress as it has had for the destructiveness of war.

If I have used American data to illustrate the ever-increasing demand for highly qualified workers it is probably because they are most readily available, and, in the United States, policymakers have given more thought to the problem than have policymakers in European countries. Moreover, the United States is more advanced and the supply of highly qualified workers is a more acute problem. But in terms of future economic growth the problem is also acute elsewhere.

In Great Britain considerations of the problem have also had a relatively narrow focus on scientists and engineers, as can be seen from the continuing surveys of technological and scientific manpower. The National Plan, published in 1965, makes repeated references to shortages of skilled and professional workers and the detrimental effects these shortages will have on the plan. "In practically every industry, existing and potential shortages were reported for most of the types of skilled and highly qualified manpower. . . . Some of the forecast shortages, if not relieved, may have repercussions throughout the country."[7]

Evidence of shortages in various occupational groups turns up in curious ways. In the same issue of *The Times* of London there appeared an account of the trend in the national shortage of priests, and, as well, a story about how the British Army tries to interest sixth-form boys in the Armed Services. These latter were taken on a tour of the Royal Military College of Science and shown the Army's modern weapons. Concerning the former, the Roman Catholic Archbishop of Liverpool appealed to sixth-formers and university students "who are thinking about what they are going to do in life." He suggested that the Church could appeal by arranging visits to seminaries and by holding exhibitions. It appears that a large number of priests in Britain are borrowed from Ireland on a five-year loan period. The Anglican Church has also experienced difficulties in attracting young men. In the past both the army and the priesthood have been prestigious occupations but they now find themselves in competition with new occupations for the relatively small supply of people who have reached the top secondary-school years.

In France, labor force projections which cover the period of the Fifth Plan from 1966–1970 envisage the highest rates of growth to be among the most highly qualified professional groups, and it is anticipated that the growth rates will continue through to 1978, the last year for which projections have been made. For research personnel it has been anticipated that the increase between 1966 and 1970 would be greater than that which took place in the U.S. between 1950 and 1960. The manpower analysts have made it clear that the success of the plan depends on a sufficient supply of the most highly qualified workers. In France particularly because of the former French-speaking colonies, it is possible to recruit from outside. In 1966 *Le Centre National de la*

Recherche Scientifique had 575 foreign scientists working for it, only 18 of whom were from the United States.

The concept of a "shortage" of personnel for a particular occupation which requires a high level of training is a difficult one to define. Obviously if a country recruits extensively from abroad there is a shortage in terms of domestic supply. If projected requirements exceed the projected output of training facilities, that is another kind of shortage. There are others which are extremely difficult to quantify. One is the substitution of workers of poorer quality either in terms of training or ability. As has been noted, ". . . most of the scientific and engineering jobs that will exist, in say, 1970 will be filled by *someone*. It is doubtful, however, if national needs can be adequately met during the next decade unless such jobs are filled by people trained to the highest levels of competence in institutions that are themselves centres of excellence."[8]

There is a further kind of shortage where there is little or no recognition of the functional importance of particular kinds of jobs. An example has been the general absence of professional management in Great Britain of the kind where, as often in the United States, a person will take a postgraduate course in business or administration after a first degree in engineering. Until recently there were only two postgraduate business schools in the United Kingdom. As the National Plan said, "The most intangible and yet by far the most important factor in improving industrial efficiency is the quality of industrial management. There is now a growing interest in managerial education. . . ."[9]

Another type of hidden shortage is the failure to exploit fully a productive potential because of the shortage of qualified personnel. This is often seen as an acute problem for developing countries, but it may also be critical for the highly developed ones. The current state of medicine as a social resource is a good illustration. The discoveries of medical research are so extensive and so advanced that the problem of their utilization on a large scale becomes the lack of properly qualified physicians and subprofessional workers. Similarly, advances in social welfare are restricted because of the lack of qualified social workers. Thus current labor force statistics and projections based upon them cannot always take into account these hidden "shortages."

It becomes clear that for major industrial societies the advance into postmodernity requires extensive adaptations of their educational systems to the new occupational structures. It may be thought that the increased capital investment in plant and the increased numbers of young people now retained in educational systems indicate an adaptation which in time will be adequate. This is unlikely because it is a question not only of an increase in the number of highly qualified jobs, but as well, the increasing educational requirements of these jobs. At the level of highly qualified manpower we can expect years of educational activity to lengthen and years of labor force participation to contract. The need to lengthen training and the need for retraining will exist at most occupational levels. In the past it has been the improvement of educational attainment within occupations that has been responsible, much more than changes in the occupational structures, for the rise in the educational level of the labor force. Some part of increased enrolments can be accounted for by this increase in the educational content of jobs.

I want now to try to link what I have been saying about changes in occupational structures to some current ideas about social mobility. There would appear to be constantly improving opportunities for upward mobility, since much of the upward mobility of the past in industrial societies has come from similar changes in occupational structures. It is likely, however, that the positive prospects for mobility inherent in the emerging occupational structure will be offset by the slowness of educational systems to adjust to the culture of science and technology, and the widespread low evaluations about education and upward mobility in all western industrial nations.

Comparative studies have shown that upward mobility is a fundamental process in all industrial societies. They would probably also show great similarities in the distribution of ambition, mobility values and levels of aspiration. In fact, as one looks at research findings on this topic from various countries the similarity is so great that they, like the mobility they give rise to or restrict, are characteristic of modern industrial systems. To the extent that mobility values are not strong enough or widespread enough, modern industrialism has created a set of dysfunctions which hinders the development into postmodernity based on the culture of science and technology. We can consider also that the modern societies of the West, because of their institutional and career links, have a mutual concern in solving the problem, and indeed there have been a good number of official and private international conferences on the subject. If one were to locate within industrial social structures the areas where these dysfunctions can be best elucidated they would be class systems, particularly working-class culture, the family as a socializing agency, and educational systems. It is at points where these structures intersect that the future of social mobility will be determined.

As Lipset and Zetterberg said some time ago[10] we have a

large number of descriptive studies of social mobility, but very little theory. In fact their paper was the first serious attempt since Sorokin. Because a variation of it appears in Bendix and Lipset's larger work on the subject, and the original version appears in the new edition of *Class, Status and Power*, we may take it as an important statement. For present purposes I am concerned only with that part of the theory which has to do with what, to my mind, are questionable assumptions or doubtful hypotheses about motivation. For example, ". . .the desire to rise in status is intrinsic in all persons of lower status, and individuals and groups will attempt to improve their status and (self-evaluation) whenever they have any chance to do so."[11] This hypothesis is derived from Veblen, specifically his view that individuals have an insatiable need for more possessions which place them ultimately well beyond the average pecuniary standard of the community. The question of the source and universality of such motivational equipment is left in some doubt,[12] although it is clear from his fictional anthropology that Veblen saw it as an inherited disposition that comes into play as soon as there is an economic surplus.

Most American sociologists seem to accept the view of widespread mobility aspirations, if not for all humans at least for properly socialized Americans. Barber, for example, has said, "Even those Americans who have not themselves raised their class position . . . feel that their own and other people's children should be able to be upwardly mobile. So strong are these institutional norms, apparently, that they can withstand fairly heavy blows from actual adverse social reality."[13] Here is a recent articulation of the same view in a somewhat extreme form. "Through the mobility ethos a potential motivation of some or even many individuals becomes a compulsory life goal for all."[14] And "While practically everybody feels committed to upward mobility as a central lifegoal, a majority fails to achieve it."[15] Does the evidence really support such assertions, and if so is it overweighted with middle-class response?

These last two quotations suggest that mobility strivings are not inherited, but are learned as part of the culture of a "mobility ethos." They are acquired through socialization in the family, and, in the instrumental but also increasingly in the normative sense, through the educational system. The appropriate motivational equipment for mobility seems to be a desire to acquire material possessions, to achieve, and to postpone gratifications in favor of the irksomeness of learning. The "anxiety-laden climb" of the middle-class child is the best illustration of this process. There is no guarantee, however, that socialization agencies will function adequately to produce individuals in the right numbers and with the right intensities of motivation. On the question of the distribution of mobility aspirations and achievement values throughout the society, the American literature is ambiguous. This confusion may be the difference between theory and empirical findings.

One of the recurring questions is whether or not mobility values are part of a common value system for the whole society, or whether they are middle-class subcultural values. Sociologies may reflect their national ethos on this subject. The egalitarianism of the United States, with its legendary opportunity structure, may be responsible for American sociologists theorizing that mobility aspirations, the desire to get ahead, to be successful, to achieve high levels of consumption, pervade the entire class structure as part of a common value system. Of course the theory becomes qualified by the assertion that these common values will be weakened in some social milieux and appear as variants in others. The question is how thinned out values can be before they become something else. To use Rodman's phrase, how much "stretching"[16] can values take before they are no longer recognizable? The notion of common values about mobility has serious implications when social policies assume—something like the old instinct theory—that by providing certain opportunities where they did not previously exist, latent mobility aspirations and achievement motives will be triggered and the previously deprived will be brought into the main stream of an upwardly mobile and achievement-oriented society. Evaluation studies of manpower training schemes designed to upgrade workers' skills indicate that opportunity alone is not enough. One study noted that trainees were not prepared to make the necessary sacrifices, a condition the investigators attributed to a lack of middle-class male role models and middle-class socialization. Similarly, a study of out-of-school youth showed that those who most need further education, those who drop out of school before graduation, are the least likely to take the opportunities offered.

Much has been accounted for by this image of man as upwardly striving. Deviant behavior is traced to thwarted mobility aspirations or to status frustration.[17] In one interesting treatment of the subject much that is American serves to compensate for unfulfilled mobility drives or the failure to live up to the rigors of the "mobility ethos." Americans, it would seem, are constantly being shored up by the mass media, by religious experience, by intellectual cliques, esoteric cults, and by jazz. Even the modern view that sex is good and to be enjoyed rather than an evil to be suppressed is a collective adaptation to failure, and Americans are thought to be failures even when they retain the middle-class position from which they started. In the light of the evidence that levels of aspiration and attitudes to education vary so much by class one wonders how it could ever be claimed that, as part of the common values system, all Americans are achievement-oriented or share in a great quest for opportunity.

Middle-class investigators seem genuinely puzzled about how the lower or working classes do or should react to the realities of their class position. Evidence is presented that they are deviant, depressed or despaired and adopt a devil-may-care attitude.[18] These would be logical reactions if working-class people had indeed internalized middle-class norms, and were not blessed by any kind of "false consciousness." But could they not be participants in a working-class culture with different norms, and view their class position in - relative terms according to their membership reference groups? The reference group concept provides the most interesting possibilities for recasting theory. It has been used ingeniously by Runciman in his study of social attitudes to inequality in modern England. Of course the concept has been used in the analysis of mobility, but mainly in terms of how reference groups aid mobility through anticipatory socialization. It has scarcely been used at all to help explain low mobility aspirations. The emphasis on the former use rather than the latter is an example of what I mean in pointing out how a national ethos can affect sociology. Reference groups can be mobility-inhibiting, particularly in a society where class is reinforced by ethnicity and religion.[19] The individual is more likely to acquire his values from his membership group and more likely to judge his own position in relation to it rather than the society at large.

There is some reluctance then to accept the reality and the semi-autonomy of working- or lower-class culture. This is not to say that American sociology does not recognize class differences. Far from it. Socioeconomic status is perhaps the most extensively employed background variable in American sociology, but this usage means that behavior is taken out of its social context and a coherent picture of working-class life is difficult to put together out of a collection of discrete items from unrelated studies.

When class differences in values and motives are found there is often considerable confusion in the treatment of these findings, as Keller and Zavalloni have shown. As they point out with great logic, the amount of ambition required by lower-class young people to reach the same goal as middle-class young people must be greater because they have a relatively greater distance to go to achieve it. They might, therefore, have greater ambition if they strive for skilled occupations than have the middle class if they strive for professional occupations. Yet most of the research has assumed that the lower classes have the same distance to run, or at least do not require more effort. It is not particularly ambitious for middle-class high school students to want a college education. The desire for education cannot be used both as a middle-class norm and as a sign of higher middle-class aspirations. A further important point of their criticism, made also by Miller and Riessman, is that lower classes would give a greater priority to security rather than success. The notion of distance to be covered is a reminder of the difficult social task of transmitting adequate motives to large segments of the society.

If our theories of social mobility contain assumptions about human motives which are not empirically valid, research gets diverted into less fruitful channels. Moreover, as argued earlier, there are difficulties at the policy level. Here the concern is the way in which subcultures have strong dysfunctional elements in terms of mobility requirements of a society based on the culture of science and technology. Higher outputs from the educational systems are essential to the emerging occupational structures reviewed earlier. The educational experiences of the lower and working classes are everywhere the greatest impediment to this increased output. Although the educational systems of the United States and European countries have been very different, they have in common the characteristics of not being universal institutions available equally for all groups and classes. Despite the great development towards democratization of education in the United States, it is extraordinary how these systems have favored the middle class. In European countries the class character of education is even more marked. In all western industrial nations there have been studies to show this general relationship between class and educational experience, attitudes to work and upward mobility, and the heavy loss of able people out of the educational stream. Taken together these deficiences of western educational systems represent a staggering waste of human resources. In the past these systems have managed to get along because a relatively small band of middle-class children were committed to staying in high school and going on to university with a curricular content heavily weighted to the humanities, while the children of manual workers have learned industrial skills and have generally followed a pattern of occupational inheritance or have experienced some modest mobility.

There is no need here to review the statistics on social class and educational experience, but it is helpful to go behind the macrodata which show this relationship to appreciate fully its genesis. Occasionally we get studies which enable us to do so. It matters little what society they come from, because one of those respects in which industrial societies are very much alike is in their creation of subcultures of manual workers with similar values about education and mobility. There are two well-known English studies, one by Hoggart[20] and the other by Jackson and Marsden,[21] which take us behind the statistics. Both take us into the milieu of the working-class family. That they do it so well is in part because the authors themselves were working-class children who won grammar school places and went to university. The working class of which they write are not slum-dwelling or overly impoverished, nor are they an oppressed minority; rather they are stable manual workers. Hoggart describes with great feeling the anxieties and tensions of the working-class scholarship boy as he moves out of his working-class neighborhood and the "ethos of the hearth," the culture of the working-class home. Hoggart's account is reminiscent of the experience of immigrants in the United States who, in being melted into Americans, had to abandon the European cultures and identifications of their parents.

Jackson and Marsden write about education and the working classes in an industrial city. The working class is underrepresented in the grammar school population and it becomes increasingly underrepresented as the levels of education and achievement are ascended, a relationship which holds true for the country as a whole. They studied eighty-eight working-class children who had successfully completed their grammar school education. They also selected ten middle-class children to compare for difference in school experience and home environment. Middle-class parents often encouraged their children beyond their capacity. They understood and were able to work the school system to the advantage of their children. They were careful in the selection of a primary school to find the one which secured the best number of grammar school places. When things went wrong the family was able to interfere and maintain the child even against the school's opinion. They worked at the child's educational problems, the "eleven plus," grammar school streaming, early specialization, the sixth form, the choice of university, and finally careers. On the other hand, working-class parents chose the wrong schools, they found difficulty in getting access to educational authorities, they were generally ignorant of the system, and felt uneasy in the presence of teachers with different accents. The grammar school was alien to working-class parents.[22] Jackson and Marsden speak of the important role of the working-class mother in influencing and encouraging those of her children who do succeed in the educational system. This finding recurs in studies of other industrial working classes.

Although it is difficult to understand why mothers should be the source of educational ambition, it is less difficult to see why fathers cannot be. Fathers, of course, do not see as much of their children as do mothers. They are very much ego-involved with their own work and much more imbedded in that part of working-class culture related to the work situation—the common cause against management, threats of layoff, short time, redundancy, and so forth. Moreover, the welfare of his family is dependent on the father's work. To downgrade his work—and to persuade a son to do better is an implied downgrading—can be a considerable psychic strain. Rather the father is likely to enhance his work, and to place a higher evaluation on it than it might objectively warrant. This self-enhancing process can be seen on the macro level from occupational prestige rankings by which manual workers will rank manual occupations more highly than non-manual workers.

At the cultural level this enhancement becomes expressed by the working classes as a high evaluation of their way of life, the worthiness and dignity of manual labor as being real and true work, variations on the themes of the "blessedness of poverty," and "the salt of the earth." Relationships within the working-class community, with its social networks of mutual aid, are thought to be more genuine, more intense, more lasting, and more likely to generate virtue, than the middle-class culture, with its competition, its artificiality, its strains, its falseness and its status concerns. This belief in the quality of working-class culture has been important in the maintenance of working-class movements even against the *embourgeoisement* that is supposed to have taken place. It is also an element in the solidarity of organized labor, and has been important in the creation of dynamic politics. The radical-conservative polarity based on class may have been appropriate in the development of a modern industrial society. It led to welfare policies of redistribution and hence legitimated capitalist systems. It also led to policies to maintain levels of demand for the output of the economy. But high evaluation of working-class culture as something of benefit to be preserved becomes increasingly less appropriate to the society based on science and technology.

In their theory, Bendix and Lipset suggest that developing industrial-occupational structures will create mobility aspirations where they did not previously exist; they deal with possible political consequences in the Soviet Union and in South Africa. By contrast, the most advanced industrial societies with great possibilities for economic growth are threatened by inadequate levels of mobility aspirations. In the period of postmodernity, even for the middle class the educational demands may well be excessive.

It might be worth mentioning here that downward mobility out of the middle and upper classes is another aspect of the manpower problem. Occupational mobility studies have for a long time wrung out of their data that mobility which results from changes in occupational structures, and sometimes also from demographic factors. What is left constitutes true social mobility or interchange between classes. When rates of true social mobility are compared over time we have some knowledge of whether social classes are becoming more or less rigid. These studies assume that less rigidity in class structure, by this measure, is good and functionally appropriate to an industrial society because it reflects the primacy of achievement over ascriptive criteria, but this model of true social mobility is static and closed and unrelated to economic development. The developing labor force requires more than interchange between classes. It recruits for jobs that never existed before, and for a constantly expanding and more highly qualified occupational world. Too much social mobility or interchange between classes may be cause for alarm, because it may reflect, among other things, inadequate aspirations on the part of the middle class.

If serious efforts are to be made to draft working-class children for the long and grinding educational experience the postmodern economy requires, policies will have to be devised to deal with the acute and complex problems of motivation. The provision of opportunity through training schemes and the democratization of education may not be enough. The solution may require a conscious attack on a set of outmoded values, providing policymakers with certain moral problems, so well put by two American sociologists: "Do we attempt to make the middle-class style a model for all to follow? Or do we adopt a rigid cultural relativity position that the lower class has a right to its way of life regardless of the social effects? Or do we attempt to develop what appear to be the most positive elements from the point of view of society and the individuals involved, of the styles of life closest to them?"[23] There is no ready answer to the moral question, but we may have to accept further intrusions into the realm of the family through social policy. For there is also a moral problem in not providing working- and lower-class children with a chance to move up.

I have been speaking of working-class culture as common to all industrial societies. Perhaps there are differences between

European societies and the United States in the values and motives of the working-class subculture, but I think also there are many cross-cultural similarities. Perhaps there are different sociologies rather than sociological differences. There appears now to be a renewed interest in the United States in the sociology of the working class as an entity in itself, and not simply as a contrast with the middle class concerning how they answer questions about childrearing or occupational values.

Although it is difficult to document with any precision because of its subtlety, one gets the impression that in Britain sociology has emphasized the positive values of working-class culture. Why should working-class children be educated out of this good world into the hazards, the competitiveness, the impersonality and the truncated kin groups of upwardly mobile middle-class society. The psychic costs can be high, as Hoggart suggests. Moreover it uproots and makes the upwardly mobile working-class child suffer the strains of assimilating an alien culture; he becomes a marginal man trying to pass for what he is not. Here is another theme reminiscent of one in American sociology, i.e., the need to preserve ethnic cultures to mediate between the individual and the mass. These cultures are receptive, warm, protecting and fulfilling, and, no doubt, life can be lived with satisfaction in the ethnic or the working-class community. The trouble is that theories of democracy and equality come along to break down these subcultures and highly complex economies evolve which, if they are to be maintained and developed, may not be able to depend on what has been called "optional mobility," without at least a social policy directed towards influencing the options.

The crucial role of education in social mobility and the provision of the highly qualified manpower required for the postmodern type of society needs no elaboration. It is important, however, to recognize that educational systems do not adapt easily. They are often thought of as a servicing part of a society producing a supply of trained people for the economy, or as producing education to be consumed for its own sake. If the demand for trained people increases, government policy, it is thought, can step up the output, but each stepping up is not easy because educational systems have developed an institutional autonomy of their own. There can be very serious lags and dysfunctions arising out of present educational arrangements. I want to indicate briefly what some of these are.

The first is the slowness with which democratization takes place. This process of democratization, i.e., the opening up of educational institutions at all levels to those who can make use of them, is more advanced in the United States than in other western countries. The reason is that an ideology of equality has combined with economic necessity to improve the educational level of the labor force. But, behind the numbers of school attendance, how democratized is American education, particularly in terms of the quality that is necessary for the mobility task set by the new occupational structure? As Bowles has observed, "The good elementary and secondary schools that helped make American cities good places to live are now in the suburbs where the middle classes and particularly the professional classes live."[24] He also observes that the city schools that once were the means of upward mobility are now the synonym for segregation.

In western European countries the process of democratization is only very slowly taking place against the resistance of tradition, class, and power, but the movement from elitism to egalitarianism can be seen. An important aspect of this reform is the comprehensive school to replace a system of selective schools into which children are put at an early age. Another reform is the abandoning of early commitment to a particular educational program in favor of a common program, and cycles of orientation, a reform which improves the possibility of linking talents and interests to training.

Despite the past failure of these European systems the meritocratic principle is still widely revered. The idea of the sanctity of education, which can only be acquired by a few blessedly endowed with the appropriate qualities, dies hard. Many cling to the "pool of ability" notion, even though there is increasing evidence that the pool is limited more by the pedagogical machinery by which it is pumped than by human genetics. Furthermore, the expansion of educational facilities brings out the fear that to educate more is to cheapen the quality. A recent UNESCO survey of the educational systems of twelve countries concludes that the comprehensive system can bring a large number of students up to a high level of performance. The superior performance of thirteen-year-olds in selective schools over those in comprehensive schools disappears when they reach eighteen.

The tradition of the curriculum also provides resistances to change, particularly in societies where high prestige has been given to humanistic learning. This Brahmanistic outlook prefers dead languages and conventional history, the less exact and undemanding disciplines where the criteria of excellence are subjective. Here the exact sciences and mathematics are thought to be a barbarian's breakfast. The struggle between the "two cultures" is as much a generational conflict as it is a struggle between tradition and modernity. Curricular traditions are entrenched in the minds of teachers, school administrators, and staffs of departments of education, a generation, in the large, poorly trained in mathematics and science and believing it right and proper to be so. In the United States, it is scientists themselves rather than teachers who have been responsible for the reforms in secondary school mathematics and science. The teaching of these exacting disciplines—and they are likely to become increasingly exacting and require even stronger motivation and effort to master—on the scale required, is probably one of the weakest points in American education.

There are many other elements in the western educational systems which make them function inadequately in terms of the manpower needs of the postmodern society. The different educational experiences of males and females, for example, is characteristic of them all. Only 3 per cent of physicists in the United States are women, as are only 8 per cent of all registered scientific manpower. Another example is the way in which the teaching profession is organized in some countries, creating vested interests which can interfere with the implementation of needed changes. However, it is not possible to explore all these in one paper.

In conclusion, I might briefly summarize. The occupational trends which have come about with industrialization will accelerate in a period of postmodernity, creating a new wave of opportunities in all western industrial societies, now becoming increasingly integrated. We have the prospect, however, of the opportunities going in search of the opportunity-minded. I have tried to argue that the modern period of industrialization has created low levels of motivation, working-class culture, educationally deprived areas, and outmoded educational arrangements and curricular content for societies based on the culture of science and technology. Cumulatively these dysfunctions constitute a major manpower problem for these societies taken separately, or as a set of societies drawing on common reserves of human resources.

Notes

1. The terms "postindustrial society," "postcapitalist society," and "postbourgeois society" have been in currency for some time. They refer mainly to the diminution of class conflict and the "end of ideology" in political systems. For a discussion of the origins of these terms, see S.M. Lipset, "The Changing Class Structure and Contemporary European Politics," *Daedalus*, 93 (Winter, 1964), p. 296. Despite what may be said about coining new words I think postmodern is consistent with the other "post" terms and refers to their counterparts in the educational systems, the content of learning and occupational structures. It is the fault of sociology rather than the English language that the term "modern" has been used as a label for a model of advanced, developed, or complex industrial societies. These societies have not stopped evolving, but are changing very rapidly.

2. *Meeting Manpower Needs in Science and Technology*, A Report of The President's Science Advisory Council, Washington, D.C.: White House, 1962, p. 1.

3. National Science Foundation, *Scientific Manpower from Abroad*, United States Scientists and Engineers of Foreign Birth and Training, Washington, D.C.: Superintendent of Documents, United States Government Printing Office, NSF 62–24, p. 32.

4. National Science Foundation, *Scientists and Engineers from Abroad*, 1962–1964, Washington, D.C.: Superintendent of Documents, United States Government Printing Office, NSF 67–3, p. xi.

5. Charles V. Kidd, "The Growth of Science and the Distribution of Scientists Among Nations," *Impact of Science on Society*, 14 (1964), p. 6.

6. United States Department of Labor, *Manpower Report of the President and a Report on Manpower Requirements, Resources, Utilization and Training*, Washington, D.C.: Superintendent of Documents, United States Government Printing Office, p. 44.

7. United Kingdom, Department of Economic Affairs, *The National Plan*, London: Cmnd. 2764, Her Majesty's Stationery Office, 1965, pp. 401–41. See also W. Beckerman *et al.*, *The British Economy in 1975*, London: Cambridge University Press, 1965, p. 25.

8. Organization for Economic Cooperation and Development, *Higher Education and the Demand for Scientific Manpower in the United States*, Paris, 1963, p. 80. Italics in original.

9. *The National Plan*, p. 53.

10. S.M. Lipset and Hans L. Zetterberg, "A Theory of Social Mobility," International Sociological Association, *Transactions of the Third World Congress of Sociology*, III, pp. 155–177.

11. S.M. Lipset and R. Bendix, *Social Mobility in Industrial Society*, Berkeley and Los Angeles: University of California Press, 1959, p. 73.

12. The authors suggest that motivation arising from norms pressuring for mobility might supplement the motivations to rise derived from ego-needs, and that societies will vary in the intensity of norms stressing mobility. "A Theory of Social Mobility," in R. Bendix and S.M. Lipset, *Class, Status and Power*, London: Routledge and Kegan Paul, 1967, p. 566. See also *Social Mobility in Industrial Society*, pp. 60–64. Obviously the theory needs elaboration. My concern is the assumption about a widespread desire for mobility.

13. Bernard Barber, *Social Stratification*, New York: Harcourt, Brace, 1957, p. 345.

14. Thomas Luckman and Peter L. Berger, "Social Mobility and Personal Identity," *European Journal of Sociology*, 5 (1964), p. 340.

15. *Ibid.*

16. Hyman Rodman, "The Lower-Class Value Stretch," *Social Forces*, 42 (December, 1963).

17. There has developed an extensive continuity of research and discussion on the relationship between the cultural goal of success and the socially structured access to it since Merton's original paper, "Social Structure and Anomie," Robert K. Merton, *Social Theory and Social Structure*, New York: The Free Press, 1957, pp. 131–194.

18. Merton's original formulation of a relationship between lower-class mobility or success strivings, social impediments to achievement and deviant behavior has guided a good deal of research. In his later discussion of the relationship his hypothesis has been clarified. *Social Theory and Social Structure*, p. 174, *passim*.

19. In their treatment of the subject, Merton and Rossi recognize this possibility; they suggest that, where stratification systems are rigid, ". . . then the individuals within each stratum will be less likely to take the situation of the other strata as a context for appraisal of their own lot," Robert K. Merton and Alice K. Rossi, "Reference Group Theory and Social Mobility," in Bendix and Lipset, *op. cit.*, pp. 510–515. The stratification systems of modern industrial societies may have that degree of rigidity which makes the individual's own class rather than the classes above him the more likely reference group.

20. Richard Hoggart, *The Uses of Literacy*, London: Penguin Books, 1958, Chapter 10.

21. Brian Jackson and Denis Marsden, *Education and the Working Class*, London: Routledge and Kegan Paul, 1962.

22. There is a body of literature in the United States dealing with the same problem, starting with A.B. Hollingshead, *Elmtown's Youth*, New York: John Wiley, 1949. In the present controversy in England over the extension of the comprehensive school it is argued by conservatives that there should be different types of secondary schools, so that parents can have a choice for their children. Given the differences between class cultures there is little doubt that parental choice would perpetuate the class character of the present selective and differentiated system. Thus what may be an expression of freedom for the middle-class parent can become a restriction of freedom for the working-class child.

23. S.M. Miller and Frank Riessman, "The Working-Class Subculture: A New View," in Arthur B. Shostak and William Goinberg, editors, *Blue-Collar World: Studies of the American Workers*, Englewood Cliffs: Prentice-Hall, 1964, pp. 35–36.

24. Frank Bowles, "American Higher Education in 1990," *Minerva*, 5 (Winter, 1967), p. 236.

4

Canadian Character in the Twentieth Century

Closely linked to the concept of culture, which, as I have suggested in the two papers on ethnicity in Canada, creates more confusion in discussion than clarity, is the idea of national character. The belief that a people have a soul, a spirit, a collective mind, or geist that marks them off from other groups is as old as history. The singular characters that peoples are thought to possess have been attributed to many factors and are believed to find their expression in modal forms of behavior and in material and expressive artifacts like tools, houses, crafts, graphic arts and literature. In the modern period of social science, the distinguished anthropologist, Ruth Benedict, brought together the two ideas of social character and culture in her famous book, Patterns of Culture.

Perhaps the most frequently cited creator of national character is the geographical environment in which the society or group finds itself as when Aristotle said, "Nations inhabiting cold places are full of spirit, but somewhat deficient in intelligence and skill. . ." or when Montesquieu made the observation that "Democracy can never flourish where the orange grows." In Canada, Margaret Atwood writes of "Nature as Monster" as a major theme in this country's literature.

I have always thought that when it comes to nations continental· in scope, compared to the small homogeneous societies that anthropologists study, the analyses of national character could rarely reach beyond the stereotypic and the impressionistic. In fact, I often used views of national character as evidence of unreason leading to hostility, illustrated by a prejudice when someone says such and such behavior is typically American, German, Chinese, or Russian. There is a similar danger with today's preoccupation with culture as a way of differentiating peoples. It is interesting that during the Second World War the study of national character achieved further respectability because it was thought that we might learn something that would help us better to defeat our enemies. During the fragile peace of the Cold

War we made no effort to see if there were ways through studying their character that we might love them better.

It was with some hesitation and scepticism, then, that I agreed to join a group of social scientists from other countries in making a contribution to the state of the art of national character analysis to be published in the Annals *of the American Academy of Political and Social Science. The volume,* National Character in the Perspective of the Social Sciences, *appeared in March, 1967. The title of my piece, "Canadian Character in the Twentieth Century," was not mine but given to me by the editor, but I suspect the only one that would make sense for Canada in any case, since Canada is a largely twentieth-century nation, and the paper was written at the time Canada was cranking up for its Centennial celebrations.*

In the paper I make the point that apart from the field of literary criticism there was a paucity of information upon which to draw to construct a plausible Canadian character. The social sciences have developed a great deal in the intervening decade, and were one to take on the task again one could mine the deposits of the data banks for attitudes to everything under the sun. I do not know that much that is different would emerge. Although she sparked a controversy, I found Margaret Atwood's Survival *the best analysis of the representative images of Canadians as she draws these images from her reviews of Canadian literature. She provides many more insights from literary themes than could be drawn from overly sophisticated statistical analyses of public opinion polls. Unfortunately, in the search for our national character, if such there is, we cannot be sure that Canadian literature is so widely read that it can be said to reflect a state of the "national mind," subject as that mind is to so much foreign "brainwashing" from abroad.*

However, survival is a dominant theme in the country's political life, too, and that fact impinges on us all whatever our favorite reading might be. The concern for survival as a political entity places a premium on the practices of the past, favors compromise and things as they are. Play it safe and the chances of survival are greater. And so I think my conclusion in this paper, that we Canadians are a conservative people, would remain as the working hypothesis for any study of national character in our country.

Superficially, Canada seems much like the United States. Canadians use the same products, appear to go to the same kind of schools, largely read the same periodicals, and watch the same television programs. On the whole, Europeans do not distinguish between Canadians and Americans. Yet, in spite of the magnetism of the United States, Canadians have succeeded in maintaining a distinct political identity. Are there, then, qualities in the Canadian character which make them different from Americans?

French and English

Of all modern nations Canada is perhaps the most difficult in which to search for a distinct national character. There are many reasons for this. In the first place the country is broken into two major linguistic and cultural blocs which maintain a high degree of exclusiveness from each other. In addition to this major English-French division, one quarter of the population is neither English nor French in origin or tradition, but lives in varying degrees of assimilation, mainly to the English part of the population. The retention of strong European ethnic affiliations is deeply imbedded in the Canadian value system. This strong emphasis on ethnic pluralism, which seems to have increased during the twentieth century, has stood in the way of creating a coherent social structure supported by a commonly held set of values and beliefs, a consensus, that is, about what Canada is and what it means to be Canadian. A national consensus is, surely, an important element in any national character. All societies are differentiated, but when differences rather than similarities are emphasized, social structure lacks coherence.

French-English dualism in Canadian life has been considered its most important characteristic throughout its history. Lord Durham spoke in his famous report over one hundred years ago of two nations warring in the bosom of a single state. In 1965, the Royal Commission on Bilingualism and Biculturalism, in a preliminary report based on public hearings held across Canada on the subject of French-English relations, wrote that Canada was "passing through the greatest crisis in its history," a crisis which "if it should persist and gather momentum could destroy Canada."[1] The ever-present hostility and jealousy between the two groups, expressed perhaps more by institutional leaders than by large segments of the population, have resulted in great emphasis on the retention of things as they are, and have, no doubt, contributed to the conservatism of Canadian life.

In the twentieth century, with large-scale immigration from continental Europe, the dualism became pluralism, as various groups were encouraged to retain their European identities within a Canadian "mosaic." Perhaps because of its place in the British Empire and, after 1931, in the British Commonwealth, there never has been in Canada, as in the United States, a strong commitment to the creation of a new nation, a new ethnicity. Nor has there been, in the schools of English Canada at least, the presentation of Canadian history as the unfolding of a great human experiment. Hence, children have not been exposed to strong doses of national sentiment. To be Canadian is not likely to evoke a set of feelings or images about belonging to a particular group with a clear beginning, a set of charter values, a history, and an imagined destiny. Undoubtedly, most Canadians will have some private or ethnic-group views about these things, but it is unlikely that, as a people, they will have an *idée fixe* about their society. There seem to be no overwhelmingly dominant cultural goals such as the pursuit of happiness, progress, equality, or opportunity. There is certainly no rejection of the "European father" that Geoffrey Gorer saw as a dominant element in American character.[2]

Older British Canadians may feel strong links with Britain's imperialistic past or take pride in its monarchical and aristocratic institutions. Younger British Canadians, on the other hand, judging impressionistically from contemporary university students, prefer to see Canada with a clear Canadian identity rather than the present dualistic or pluralistic fragmentation. They may even harbor republican sentiments. Some younger Canadians would like to see their country more American in its values, a condition which would place greater emphasis on equality of opportunity through, for example, the democratization of education. The superior position of the British in Canadian society and even, perhaps, of English as the main language is gradually being eroded through inexorable demographic changes, if not through distinct policies to help equalize the position of the French and the French language. Throughout the present century the proportion of the population which is British has been declining steadily from 57 per cent in 1901 to 43.8 per cent in 1961. In 1961 the British made up 58 per cent of the over 65s but only 41 per cent of the under 15s. The French had only 21.6 per cent of the over 65s, but 33.4 per cent of the under 15s.[3] Thus, while the British are at present strong in the age cohorts from which elites are drawn, they will become increasingly less so.

It would be in keeping with the prevailing attitudes about Canadian dualism to treat the French and English groups separately and to show how each—as separate nations, as the French have recently been insisting that they are—have their own peculiar character. Yet, two large groups cannot have lived together in a system of ordered relationships for two hundred years without affecting each other's way of life in some respects. There may be an analogy in this situation to the conflict-habituated marriage, where husband and wife manage to survive an antagonistic union and where the antagonistic relationship in time affects their personalities. Perhaps both groups have a deeply rooted conservatism which has placed them only marginally within the influence of North American values.

Population Growth

A second reason why it is difficult to generalize about Canadian national character is Canada's demographic history which, in the absence of comparative studies, appears to be peculiar and inimical to the growth of strong collective sentiments or a common personality system. Where population growth oscillates between very rapid and very slow rates, and sometimes becomes static, where emigration is always high and where immigration depends on the fortunes of the economic cycle, the question arises whether there can be any stable group which holds the collective sentiments of the nation. A strongly held set of beliefs or a basic personality structure would seem to require a relatively stable population or one with relatively stable rates of growth over some considerable time. Shared culture and shared habits are broken up, or never get established, where demographic trends are erratic. There is clearly a difference in this respect between older, established societies in Europe and those which have been created by populating vast vacant regions. Canada and Australia might make an interesting comparison. Both have depended on immigration for economic development at particular times, but it is very unlikely that Australia has been subject to population loss through emigration, as has Canada. European societies, with their long histories and firmly rooted traditions, can experience considerable emigration, and even the frontier surgery of generations of peacemakers, without losing traditional values and behavior patterns.

Between 1851 and 1951 Canada lost almost as many people through emigration as it gained from immigration. An estimated 7.1 million arrived during this period, and an estimated 6.6 million left.[4] Between 1951 and 1961 (the decennial census years) immigration has been estimated at about 1.5 million and emigration at .6 million.[5] These numbers may not seem large, but for a country whose population grew from 2.5 million in 1851 to 18 million in 1961, they represent a sizable proportion of the population, particularly when it is considered that in the present century it has been the non-French part of the population which has participated in the migration process. Thus, at any time, many people in Canada have been either newcomers or potential migrants. This demographic condition should be looked at in the light of the doctrine of ethnic pluralism and the toned-down sentiments about a Canadian identity. Under these circumstances neither the newcomers nor their children will be socialized to specifically Canadian values. Nor will there be any particular normative pressures on the potential migrants to stay. If this particular interpretation has any validity, it is difficult to see how a coherent set of traditions, values, and behavior can emerge.

There is also a vagueness with respect to national symbols. Until 1965 Canada had no national flag or any exclusively Canadian national anthem. The creation of the first truly national symbol, a flag, came only after a very bitter and prolonged political squabble. The absence or weakness of national symbols puzzles many newcomers, particularly those from non-British territories, who want to make a home for themselves and who look for a national symbol system for orientation and a sense of having arrived in a new home.

It is possible that the emigration from Canada reinforces the conservatism of Canadian life. The evidence suggests that it is the younger age groups who move out. The quality that is lost in this way is not known. Are they the most able, the most adaptable, those with the most initiative, those with the most leadership potential, or are they the failures, the weaklings lured by what they feel is an easier life to the south? If they are the former, then the conservative mold of Canadian society becomes more firmly set. In addition to international migration, there has been a high degree of internal migration. Here, too, the older generation stays behind to exercise a conservative influence at the level of regional and community power.

The Social Sciences in Canada

In Canada, the slow development of the social sciences, particularly psychology, anthropology, and sociology, has meant the absence of accumulated data from which an account of national character or a profile of values might be derived. There are, for example, no studies based on national sample surveys eliciting attitudes and values about any subject. It is true that there are public opinion polls on various questions, but these have never been subjected to systematic analysis which might provide an account of psychological tendencies such as conservatism, traditionalism, authoritarianism, and so forth. Nor are there satisfactory studies producing attitudinal or other psychological data for special populations such as young people, manual workers, or elites. This lack of knowledge applies also to the major socializing agencies, the family and the school. Childrearing and educational practices have long been considered important in the formation of basic personality, but there is very little known about whether childhood and school experiences are different in Canada from those in the United States. The state of the social sciences in Canada is illustrated by the fact that, until recently, only a few Canadian universities had sociology departments, a further example of the Canadian conservative orientation. Knowledge from the social sciences can lead to mastery over the social environment, and this mastery and control implies, in turn, change from past social arrangements, a development which the conservative views with apprehension. Conservatism is reflected in the high status of the humanities in Canadian universities, and the view, still expressed with some frequency, that an education in the classics, history, or belles lettres is a better preparation for leadership roles than training in the social sciences.

High and Popular Culture

National character can be reflected also in the symbolic and expressive materials of the arts and letters and popular culture. These can provide the "representative images," the "archetypes," and the "preferred fantasies" of the society in which they are produced. For Canada these cultural materials either do not exist or are not very helpful. There is, for example, no national cinematic industry producing for popular consumption. Even such a Canadian-controlled medium as the Canadian Broadcasting Corporation (CBC) has not produced from Canadian history fictionalized or actual folk heroes who have caught the public imagination. Canadian poetry and fiction are neither widely known nor widely read in Canada, probably because they are produced by and for a relatively small group of university-associated writers. However, this small body of indigenous literature has been analysed by Canadian literary critics for the themes which they contain. Canadian poets have been found to express a melancholy, a feeling of resignation to misery, isolation, and the feeling that man is "encompassed by forces beyond his ability to control which strike out repeatedly and blindly to destroy him."[6] The assessment of Canadian fiction is similar.

> The representative figure of Canadian fiction is not the innocent Adam, nor yet the Adam of the fortunate fall who is triumphant even in defeat at the hands of the alien tribe—as for example are Melville's Billy Budd or the Joads in Steinbeck's *The Grapes of Wrath*. Nor is he, like Dorothea Brooke in George Eliot's

Middlemarch, the figure made strong and capable of extended life by voluntary renunciation.

These are positive; our archetype is negative.[7]

This critic goes on to say:

> In our literature, heroic action remains possible, but becomes so deeply tinged with futility that withdrawal becomes a more characteristic response than commitment. The representative images are those of denial and defeat rather than fulfillment and victory.[8]

Moreover, Canadian literary themes have little social reference. Plots do not deal with the clash of social forces, social progress, social equality, or the achieving of upward social mobility. Rather, they tend to be, R.L. McDougall has pointed out, concerned with personal values, personal relationships and private worlds—worlds of gloom and despair at that.[9]

It is very tempting to trace these cultural themes of negativism, lack of commitment, withdrawal from social issues, and a feeling of resignation, through the social development of Canada: periods of economic stagnation, the ever-present crisis in English-French relations, religious bickering, and the constant efforts by some to retain a Canada that will not be absorbed by the overwhelming power of its neighbor to the south. The last is frequently expressed as a fear of being "swallowed up," an image that might be a clue to a collective Canadian anxiety. It is interesting that, in the mid-1960s, at the end of twenty years of enormous economic growth, when Canada achieved a standard of living—at least according to the statistical measures used—second only to the United States, and at a time when Canada was approaching its centenary, there should be an open season, not for rejoicing, but for lamenting the state of national affairs. One of the most widely read and widely discussed books published at this time was George Grant's *Lament for a Nation*,[10] with its subtitle, "The Defeat of Canadian Nationalism." Grant wrote: "To lament is to cry out at the death or the dying of something loved. This lament mourns the end of Canada as a sovereign state." How constant is his theme with those which have been found in Canadian literature by the critics! Grant is poetic in his anguish. "We find ourselves like fish left on the shores of a drying lake."[11] For this philosopher, the tragedy is Canada's failure to create a society of tradition and order which would be clearly differentiated from the homogenized industrial culture of the United States. As one perceptive reviewer has written:

> To Grant, the "Good Society" is apparently one in which there is a
> high order of control over action, control in the sense of being deter-
> mined by a belief in certain immutable truths . . . . His "Lament" is
> a decrying of experimentation and flexibility in human affairs.[12]

Despair at the failure of the conservative experiment in North
America is an interesting convergence of two elements in the Canadian character.

The Canadian Political System

It is also tempting to trace in Canadian institutions another quality which critics have found in Canadian literature, that is, the
lack of social relevance, the lack of commitment to and ambiguity
about social ends and purposes. In modern nations, national goals
and values are expressed and debated by political parties and
political leaders. The political system operates to mobilize the
social effort toward the achievement of social goals. The core values of modern nations can be expressed collectively through their
politics. In the 1960s, with minority government rule, the federal
polity seems almost to have collapsed with progressive disman-
tling of federal power in favor of the provinces. It is a system
which Canadians have come to call "co-operative federalism," but
it becomes increasingly less federal and less co-operative.

This lack of a dynamic polity can be traced to the lack of
commitment of the two major political parties which have governed Canada since its beginning in 1867, a beginning which was
not revolutionary, nor marked by a resounding charter instrument
such as a declaration of rights. Any commitment there may be on
the part of Canadian political leaders is likely to be commitment
to the status quo. There is an almost pathological reluctance to
assume leadership functions. In part, this reluctance can be traced
to the assumed fragility of Canadian society. National unity is
best safeguarded by not disturbing the present; and nothing, it is
thought, would be more likely to imperil national unity than parties with some clear social goals. The Liberal party has been in
office for more than two-thirds of the time in this century. No one
has expressed this lack of commitment, this ambiguity, more than
Mackenzie King, who was the Liberal party, for all intents and
purposes, for thirty years. J.W. Pickersgill, himself a Liberal cabinet minister and editor of King's diaries, wrote: "Mackenzie King
genuinely believed and frequently said that the real secret of political leadership was more in what was prevented than what was

accomplished."[13] Ideology did not end in Canada. It simply did not begin.

The Cultural Impact of the United States

Tempting as it is to show how literary themes are a reflection of Canada's social and political history, the exercise can be misleading, because Canadian literature can have meaning for only a very small proportion of the population. Canadians are overwhelmingly and enthusiastically consumers of United States culture, both popular and high. Because such a large proportion of the population lives so close to the border, United States radio and television are available and more likely to be listened to and watched than are Canadian programs. The Canadian Broadcasting Corporation was created to counteract the attraction from the south and to provide, through this new medium, some sense of national unity. Until broadcasting policy changed in 1958, the CBC played a unifying function as no other agency did, but it has had to become increasingly commercial with the result that its programming has become much more like that of the United States networks and, in fact, has a large content of United States origin. With the development of a second privately owned television network in the 1960s, the exposure to United States popular culture has been even greater. As with broadcasting, the printed media— from women's homemaking magazines, pulp romances, children's comics, and girlie magazines to the literary and intellectual periodicals—contribute substantially to Canadian values and the view of the world held by Canadians. In sharing common mass media, Canadians and Americans share a common exposure to advertising and hence common standards of taste and common items of consumption. If the Canadian item is not an exact replica produced by a Canadian subsidiary, then it is not greatly unlike the United States prototype. There is no real evidence to suggest that economic integration and cultural inundation are resented or resisted by the vast majority of Canadians. They seem to have come very close to accepting the status which George Grant has called the "branch plant" society. If such is the case, Canadians may be in the process of becoming more American, and it could only be a matter of time before the American egalitarian values of the United States would have a permanent effect on Canadian conservatism. In the meantime, no doubt, there will remain some who will always wish for a Canada truly different in character from that of the United States. Poets will continue to despair and philosophers to lament.

Despite the difficulties presented by the existence of strong ethnic pluralism, migration, cultural contamination from the United States, and the general absence of satisfactory data, there have been many attempts to outline the qualities of the Canadian character. Among the sociologists who have contributed to this picture are S.D. Clark,[14] Dennis Wrong,[15] and the late Kaspar Naegele.[16] Their observations have been comprehensively reviewed and elaborated by S.M. Lipset.[17] Canadians, he has concluded, are conservative, authoritarian, oriented to tradition, hierarchy, and elitism in the sense of showing deference to those in high status. Canadian values have been shaped by a distinct anti-revolutionary past which contrasts with the strong egalitarianism of the United States, with its emphasis on opportunity and personal achievement as the basis of social rewards.

It would be difficult to disagree with Lipset. The slow manner of democratizing educational systems is one example of how Canada diverges from the egalitarian model. In Canada in 1961 only 6 per cent of the male labor force aged 25 to 34 years had university degrees, compared to 14.7 per cent in the United States.[18] Canada has been far behind other countries in developing tertiary levels of education and removing financial barriers to them. This low evaluation of education has meant that in order to maintain a rate of industrial development, skilled and professional workers have had to be imported from abroad. Thus, imported capital and imported skills have helped to make modern Canada, a fact which suggests that industrialization is in, but not of Canada, or at least that the values necessary to support industrialization are not as strong in Canada as in the United States. Egalitarian values, particularly applied to education, are essential to high levels of industrialization, because they serve the search for talent that every industrial society must make.

The French and English Again

We might now return to the question raised at the beginning, whether the conservative mold is characteristic of both English and French Canada so that it might be considered the element common to both their cultures. Certainly there has been no shortage of interpretations of Catholic French Canada as authoritarian and traditional, with great obstacles to overcome before becoming democratic.[19] English Canadians know very little of the undemocratic and authoritarian character of some of their institutions, or, if they do, they are resigned to them as being necessary compromises within the Canadian polity. The English Canadians' commitment to religious values is wholly as strong as the French Canadians'. While there is no established church in English Canada, there is an establishment of religiosity which puts churchmen in particularly strong positions of influence and power. The "drum ecclesiastical" is still heard throughout the land, ecumenically stronger than before and oddly predominant in a scientific and secular epoch.

French Canadian education has, quite rightly, been criticized as being inadequate for a modern industrial society, but the non-French parts of Canada's educational systems have also proved inadequate to provide the necessary trained manpower or equality of opportunity.[20] Both groups have been content to educate a relatively small middle class in a humanistic style. French Canada has been said to be oriented to ruralism, but the mythology of rural virtues has been strong everywhere in Canada and has been taken, among other things, to support rural overrepresentation in legislatures, with no Supreme Court to suggest that democratic values require changes. In the last Canadian general election in 1965, the constituency boundaries were still, after fifteen years of unprecedented off-farm migration and urban growth, based on the 1951 census.

English and French Canadians are more alike in their conservatism, traditionalism, religiosity, authoritarianism, and elitist values than the spokesmen of either group are prepared to admit. They have been drawn together in a mutual defence of these cultural elements in North America, and some of the more articulate of them look out on a world of social change, including the Americanization of their own society, with much the same ambivalence and fear. Conservatism is, of course, a general quality of all social structure, because behavior patterns are habitual, but in modern industrial societies there is also, in the interests of adaptability, a readiness for change, a readiness which may be stronger in elites than in the mass of the population. In Canada this conservatism characterizes elites as well as the mass of the population and pervades most of its institutions to a greater degree than in the United States.

In all the present concern for biculturalism we might raise the question of whether if, after all, there is not a single culture in Canada in which the core values are conservative, and on the matter of lesser values the French and the English are subcultural variants. One can only plead again the almost total absence of data with which to provide profiles of major or minor value patterns. It is not possible to tell in this centenary year whether the French and the English will together follow the egalitarian model of the United States, or whether their conservatism will continue to assert itself.

Notes

1. *A Preliminary Report of the Royal Commission on Bilingualism and Biculturalism* (Ottawa, 1965), p. 13.

2. Geoffrey Gorer, *The American People* (New York: W.W. Norton, 1948).

3. *Census of Canada, 1961*, Vol. 1.2.

4. Nathan Keyfitz, "The Growth of the Canadian Population," *Population Studies*, IV (June 1950).

5. John Porter, *The Vertical Mosaic* (Toronto: University of Toronto Press, 1965), p. 31.

6. Robert L. McDougall, "The Dodo and the Cruising Auk," *Canadian Literature*, No. 18 (Autumn 1963), p. 9. Professor McDougall is discussing the views of Professor Northrop Frye on Canadian poets.

7. *Ibid.*, p. 10.

8. *Ibid.*

9. *Ibid*, p. 13.

10. George Grant, *Lament for a Nation* (Toronto: McClelland and Stewart, 1965).

11. *Ibid.*, p. 4.

12. Robert Blumstock, "Anglo-Saxon Lament," *The Canadian Review of Sociology and Anthropology*, Vol. 3, No. 2 (May 1966), p. 101.

13. J.W. Pickersgill, *The Mackenzie King Record* Vol. I (Toronto: University of Toronto Press, 1960), p. 10.

14. S.D. Clark, *The Developing Canadian Community* (Toronto: University of Toronto Press, 1962).

15. Dennis Wrong, *American and Canadian Viewpoints* (Washington, D.C.: American Council on Education, 1955).

16. Kaspar D. Naegele, "Canadian Society: Some Reflections," in B.R. Blishen *et al., Canadian Society* (Toronto: Macmillan of Canada, 1961).

17. S.M. Lipset, "Revolution and Counter-Revolution: The United States and Canada" (Berkeley: Institute of International Studies, University of California, undated).

18. Economic Council of Canada, *Second Annual Report* (Ottawa, 1965).

19. See, e.g., Pierre Elliott Trudeau, "Some Obstacles to Democracy in Quebec," *Canadian Journal of Economics and Political Science*, Vol. 24, No. 3 (August 1958).

20. John Porter, *The Vertical Mosaic*, chap. vi.

5

Ethnic Pluralism in Canadian Perspective

Because its population is made up of indigenous Indian and Inuit and people whose ancestors have come from other diverse linguistic and cultural backgrounds from around the world, Canada is said to be an ethnically plural society. In more popular speech and in the terminology of government policies, we are "multicultural."

Many other national societies, old and new, are also ethnically varied. In fact, it is rather difficult to find a modern nation that is ethnically pure in the sense that its entire population shares a common descent, cultural, linguistic, or biological. For reasons which are explained in the following paper on Canadian perspectives on ethnic pluralism, the 1970s brought to most of these ethnically plural societies a new consciousness about ethnicity, language, and culture. It became the fashion for groups to celebrate their ethnic origins and for individuals to search for their roots.

For many, the revival of ethnicity was a good thing since it could be a means of breaking up large centralized and powerful nation states. Regionalization, decentralization, and fragmentation to community seemed to be desirable social goals, although paradoxically at the same time a movement was at work to build large political aggregates such as the European Community.

In 1972 two American sociologists, Nathan Glazer and Daniel Patrick Moynihan, who had written a good deal on the subject of ethnic groups in the United States including the very successful Beyond the Melting Pot,* *convened a conference in Brookline, Massachusetts, under the auspices of the Ford Foundation and the American Academy of Arts and Sciences. The conference brought together social scientists from many countries where ethnic diversity was a feature of social structure, and who had made some study of it. The conference analysed the reasons for and the consequences of the new ethnic consciousness. The paper which follows was initially prepared for*

---

* The M.I.T. Press, Cambridge, Mass., second edition, 1970.

*that conference and subsequently revised in the light of it and percep-
tive editorial comments of Nathan Glazer. It appeared in the book
editied by Glazer and Moynihan,* Ethnicity: Theory and
Experience.*

*I was asked to do the paper on Canada, no doubt, because eth-
nicity and its bearing on inequality was a major theme of* The Vertical Mosaic, *as indeed the title implies. The paper reviews the ethnic
structure of Canadian society and its relationship to the binationalism
which was the founding principle of Confederation; the difficulty of
imposing on that historic condition a quite different notion of multiculturalism; and some of the dangers and dilemmas of retaining ethnicity as a salient feature of any society. In fact, in the later section of
the paper I come to reject it altogether because in the long run ethnicity only makes sense if we also seek to perpetuate endogamous
descent groups. The great value now placed on this primordial identity
is reminiscent of the German romantic movement with its emphasis on
volkgeist.*

*Culture has also become a loosely used "in" word linked to eth-
nicity because ethnic groups are frequently charged with historic mis-
sions to be the exclusive guardians of cultures either through living
them or simply celebrating them from time to time. And so culture
takes on a mystique as the expression of a* volk.

*While there might be some psycho-social benefits to be derived
from the return to community, the movement also contains dangers
because it can generate hostilities as well as shift loyalties from the
larger national entities. It runs counter to any emerging concept of
the unity of mankind within a conceivable rational order and directed
towards a common good, as Morris Ginsberg put it many years ago.
Loyalties to the larger national systems are important because they
are the principal instruments by which some measures of a stable
international order can be maintained and humanity as a whole can
be served. In the transnational order which has emerged since the
Second World War, we have seen something of the sense of common
purpose and obligation develop which makes the unity of mankind in
a contracting world a much more attainable objective than earlier in
history.*

*Such views at present are not popular because of the conservative
trend along which we are projecting ourselves into the 1980s. The
revival of ethnicity can be understood in the many societies in which it
finds expression, but its sheer existence does not make it, to the liberal, morally compelling. It is important to be aware of the dangers and
to put up some warning signals.*

---

* *Harvard University Press, Cambridge, Mass., 1975.*

Canada, like the United States and many other societies around the world, has been experiencing a revival of ethnicity. The reasons for this world phenomenon are many and complex. In part it can be traced to the post-Second World War decolonization which was so often bitterly fought over, as in Algeria, for example, where a heightened consciousness of racial and ethnic differences, beyond the visibility of color, was a part of the demand for independence and self-determination. In eastern Europe, socialist societies were allegedly suppressing the national cultures that lay within their borders, a situation which émigrés sought to counteract by enlisting their fellow countrymen and sometimes the descendants of previous generations in a national movement in exile. The escalation of the Vietnam war was interpreted in many parts of the world as the United States taking over from the retreating European powers the role of white domination through force in the affairs of the world.

In the United States a highly visible deprived minority was not sharing in the affluence that the society was supposed to have produced. In Canada, similarly, the French had been denied much of the opportunity and had carried a good deal of the cost in less education and lower paid jobs—lower, that is, than some immigrant groups that were coming in near the bottom—of Canada's take-off as an industrial society. The demand by some intellectuals in French Canada that something be done about this inequality led to the establishment in 1963 of the Royal Commission on Bilingualism and Biculturalism.

Canada was caught up in a global movement and although all the examples of the world-wide revival of ethnicity can best be understood within their own local and historical contexts, they have, through modern communications and common intellectual leadership, become mutually supportive. Fanon becomes widely read in Quebec and Wounded Knee takes on symbolic significance far beyond South Dakota.

One feature of this ethnic revival common to the two modern societies of North America is, then, the depressed status of a large minority group, but there are three important respects in which the Canadian situation differs from that in the United States. In Canada the deprived ethnic group that is large enough to have a political impact is white and hence ethnicity does not have the wide visibility that it has across the border. However, there is the barrier of language which can operate as effectively as color differences to reduce friendly interaction between groups. If people from two groups cannot communicate, as is the case in Canada where the French and English have been effectively out of communication with each other, then the language division is as real as that of color.

The long-standing hostility of so many of the English in Canada to learning French is analogous to the hostility toward blackness that has marked black-white relations. In both cases the psychological elements are deeply layered, all the more so because Anglophones in Canada, like whites in the United States, are the dominant majority in both numbers and power. Occasionally the psychological tensions of color may be invoked by referring to the French as "les nègres blancs d'Amérique."[1]

Such symbolism, however dramatic, is scarcely appropriate because of the second major difference between these two plural societies of North America. That difference is that some French Canadians have enjoyed high status and power in collaboration with English-speaking Canadians and foreign investors, largely United States corporations. Canada has had three French prime ministers and two French governors general as titular head of state. Moreover, in Quebec the French have power. There has never been an English *premier ministre* of Quebec. This seeming contradiction between being a large deprived minority within Canada and having representatives in the structure of power can be explained in terms of the class structure of French Canada which until recently has been premodern, with a narrow band of classically educated elites and members of the learned professions at the top, and a mass of poorly educated at the bottom who increasingly left a rural way of life for the industrialized cities. It was an American and an "adopted" Canadian, E.C. Hughes, who first drew attention to this phenomenon in his *French Canada in Transition*, or as its French title says, *Rencontre de deux mondes*.[2]

By and large the French elites of church and state have been prepared to collaborate in the federal state, although in doing so they have exacted a price which has given a particular shape to Canadian federalism and has generally served the interests of the class from which they came rather than the interests of Quebec society as a whole. The strongest of the intellectual critics will argue that the French elites of Quebec have aided its colonization by English-speaking Canadians and Americans.[3] Whether or not one agrees with such strictures there is little to be said against the notion, whatever the behavior of their elites, that French Canadians within the global context of Canadian society, until recently, were an "ethnic class" of deprived status.[4]

The third and perhaps the most important difference between Canada and the United States in the sphere of ethnicity is that French Canadians, concentrated as they are in Quebec where about 80 per cent of them live, have territory or a homeland which was conquered. That historical and immensely symbolic fact makes some sense and gives an impetus to a separatist movement for an eventual French-speaking state of Quebec as the visionary solution to the deprived status that the French as an ethnic class have experienced. It should be remembered also that the French are a large minority within Canadian society, comprising about three-tenths of the population, a demographic fact that makes such a solution as the "equal partnership" recommendations by the Royal Commission on Bilingualism and Biculturalism a possible resolution of the current tensions. But the same demographic fact of numbers combined with the concentration in "homeland" makes the separatist solution also possible.

French-English Relations: an Assessment

The wide-ranging examination from 1963 to 1968 of French-English relations by the Bilingualism Commission took place over the same period as official and unofficial inquiries were being made in the United States on the condition of non-white minorities and of increasing violence in interethnic relations. Even though in Canada violence has been minimal, the Royal Commission found the future of the society itself in question and suggested that with or without violence, Canada had a far greater problem in the solution of its interethnic tensions than had any other modern society.

In a preliminary report in 1965 the Commission had said, "Canada, without being conscious of the fact, is passing through the greatest crisis in its history."[5] This view was reiterated in the first of several volumes of its *Report*. Canada was facing a national crisis, a time when, the Commission said, "Decisions must be taken and developments must occur leading either to its break-up, or a new set of conditions for its future existence."[6] For all the violence in the United States, or to take another modern society, for all the suppression in South Africa, it is doubtful that similar commissions would come to such gloomy conclusions about the future of their societies.

It is not my intention exhaustively to review here the relations between the English and the French in Canada. They have involved varying degrees of hostility and co-operation since the English conquest of 1759 and have been the major preoccupation of Canadian history, politics, and sociological investigation for over two hundred years. With my rather optimistic observations about French-English relations since the Royal Commission's report and a brief discussion of Canada's non-English, non-French groups I intend rather to serve the more general purpose of critically examining the revival of ethnicity in modern societies.

In response to the recommendations of the Royal Commission for "equal partnership" and "institutional bilingualism," the federal government embarked on a series of policies to improve the position of the French and the French language in those agencies and institutions within its jurisdiction.[7] Bilingualism within the federal public service improved. The French became better represented than formerly within the higher levels of the bureaucracy. Ottawa began slowly taking on the aspect of a bilingual national capital.[8] Much money was spent on language training and grants were made to provincial governments to improve their provision of second language education. The federal government saw itself as constitutionally responsible for safeguarding the two official languages even though language, because it is the principal means of cultural expression, would normally be considered a provincial responsibility.

Since the Royal Commission's sombre accounts it is becoming increasingly likely that an adaptive and flexible federal system can come about. Perhaps this is possible because on the matter of political and constitutional solutions concerning the French and Quebec within Confederation, the Royal Commission literally gave up the ghost and failed to complete its job. The evolving Canadian federalism of the last few years is not without its problems for nation building, but neither is it confined to a rigid blueprint.

According to some Anglo-Canadians the concessions made to Quebec particularly in social welfare legislation appear to come close to providing a special status for that province. Somewhat the reverse has happened, however. As an outcome of ingenious diplomacy on the part of the federal and provincial bureaucrats and politicians, all the other provinces are becoming more like Quebec, the final and ironic outcome of the insistence of the French that Quebec was not a province *comme les autres*. The lessening of federal power particularly in a wide range of social policy can be seen as a loss of the ability to establish national goals and as a process of decentralization.

Much of the change can be attributed to French political leaders and an intellectually strengthened provincial bureaucracy in Quebec who were determined to do something about the deprived status of the French. They were more conscious of the need for social and educational reforms than were earlier elites. Thus, as in the past, the French have continued to exercise great power in the shaping of Canadian federalism. Other provincial political leaders and bureaucrats are enjoying the enhanced power that Quebec has won for the provinces as the federal government has become enfeebled in a wide range of important economic and social issues. The alternative of a special status for Quebec within the federal system is scarcely considered any more outside the context of complete separation. Special status is anathema to the present federal leadership under Mr. Pierre Trudeau, as indeed is separation.

The October 1973 provincial election in Quebec was an important test of the type of federalism that has been developing. The results indicate that a majority of those in Quebec favor *la fédéralisme rentable* combined with *la souveraineté culturelle,* slogans of the Liberal party which won 54 per cent of the popular vote and 102 of the 110 seats in the National Assembly. However, in the same election the separatist Parti Quebecois increased its proportion of the popular vote from 24 per cent in 1970 to 30 per cent in 1973.[9] Since the other parties running were all federalist— that is, wanting to work within Confederation—the 30 per cent for the Parti Quebecois can be taken as a good measure of those who would like to create a separate French state. As yet no extensive analysis has appeared, but it is taken as self-evident that the separatist supporters were almost all French and heavily representative of the young. The less sanguine might, therefore, still consider the future of Canada in question. There are also some doubts about the legitimacy of an electoral system which gives a party 30 per cent of the votes, but only 9 per cent of the seats.

Whatever directions "diplomatic" or "executive" federalism[10] and constitutional bargaining may take over the next decade, the future of French-English relations really lies within the provinces, particularly in Quebec where 19 per cent of the population are non-French-speaking, in New Brunswick where 34 per cent of the population speak French, and in Ontario where though overall only 6 per cent are French-speaking, in some parts of northern Ontario almost half the population is French-speaking and in some counties in the St. Lawrence-Ottawa River triangle the proportion that is French-speaking is over 80 per cent. The absolute number of French-speaking people in Ontario is much greater than in any other province outside Quebec.[11]

Areas in which provincial government policies will be crucial for the improvement in French-English relations are education, language training, the provision of governmental services in French and English where both groups live in sizable numbers, and extending French as the language of work in Quebec.

It is not possible here to provide a province by province balance sheet on French-English relations. We might instead look at the country's two major and neighboring provinces, Quebec and Ontario. It is in the development within these provinces that the future of Canada may well be settled.

In Quebec it is clear that English-speaking parents (and French for that matter) will always be able to have their children educated in English. Quebec will never become unilingual in education. No party seeks to remove this right from the English minority. However, one of the most seriously discussed issues in the 1973 provincial election was the existing legislation permitting immigrant parents to educate their children in either English or French. Immigrant parents, such as Italian and Portuguese, have shown a strong preference for having their children go to English-speaking schools because of the greater opportunities that an education in English provides in North America. The French on the other hand, highly sensitive to their own falling fertility rates and substantially unable to recruit immigrants from the French-speaking world, foresee a gradual decreasing use of French in the province. In the last election all political parties recognized this threat, and the re-elected Liberal government promised to review the legislation.

Among the most striking of the documentations of the Royal Commission on Bilingualism and Biculturalism was the use of the French language in the industries of Quebec, large segments of which are owned by American or Anglo-Canadian corporations. The pattern was familiar: French blue-collar workers, bilingual foremen, and a large over-representation of unilingual Anglophones in managerial and higher occupational levels of the private sector. French who did achieve these levels because of their professional education in fields such as law, accounting, and public relations were most often required to work in English. The upper levels of the work world were essentially English-speaking, imposing a requirement of written and oral bilingualism on the French but not on the English Canadians or Americans. This condition was strongly resented by the younger French. They were being turned out in increasing numbers from a reformed educational system where their upward mobility in their home province might be blocked because their English was not adequate, and their own language was downgraded or never used by a "foreign" management.

The Royal Commission recommended that in private industry in Quebec the objective should be French as the language of work at all levels and that the Quebec government should set up a task force to discover means of achieving such an end.[12] The Quebec government did set up a special commission under the chairmanship of Jean-Denis Gendron. After four years of examining the problem the Gendron Commission recommended that French become the provincial *official language* and French and English be provincial *national languages*.[13] There is widespread recognition on the part of the government and political parties that French cannot be made the language of work at all levels by lightning legislation.

By the end of 1973 there was still no official government policy on language of work. There was, however, a set of basic guidelines pressing firms in the direction of bilingualism. French should be the language in internal oral communication and all oral and written communication with customers, suppliers, and government agencies. Many firms have responded positively to this pressure and have set up French instruction programs for managerial personnel at all levels. The situation is complex, not only because of the ingrained habits of the past, but also because Quebec appeals to foreign investment and does not want to scare it away. That is why the tone of the language at work problem exemplified by the Gendron Commission is moderate, encouraging gradual change. Not all French nationalists are moderate however. This is particularly true of Montreal where the proportion of French speakers (66 per cent) is lower than in the rest of the province and the demographic forces of Anglicization are most strong.[14]

With the democratization of education and an increased emphasis on science and technology in curricula, the prospects for the improvement in the occupational opportunities for the French are very good. Upward mobility and participation in an increasingly transnational and postindustrial world will, however, lead to a further erosion of traditional culture begun with the earlier industrialization of Quebec which transformed the rural *habitant* into an urban proletarian. The French face the dilemma of modernization or of maintaining a traditional culture. But there need not be a loss of language. If bilingualism can increase, and that requires a great effort on the part of the English, this distinctive dualism of Canada will remain, if not across the entire country at least in Quebec, where French and English have lived long together. The undesirable relationship of elite collaboration and low occupational status for the majority of the French is becoming gradually transformed, not rapidly enough for some, but at least in the direction of a more equal partnership.

Ontario, the province which is the very heart of Anglo-Canadian traditions, pride, privilege, and power, has taken very positive steps, particularly in education, to improve the position of its large French-speaking minority in response to the Royal Commission's report, and to some militancy on the part of Franco-Ontarians. Until new legislation took effect in 1969, children from French-speaking families suffered a variety of handicaps in obtaining instruction in their own language. Educational attainment levels were low except for those whose families could afford to pay fees for private Catholic French-speaking schools. The legislation of 1969 transferred these fee-paying schools to the system of provincially supported local boards of education. The legislation also provided that when ten or more French-speaking parents submitted a written request to have French instruction for their children, local school boards were to provide it. Thus schools are English-speaking, bilingual, and French-speaking. The process of introducing bilingual schools has led to community conflicts but most of them have been successfully mediated.

Educational opportunity for Ontario's French in their own language is a major change. On the other hand extensive new programs to teach French to English-speaking students have been much less successful. French instruction is not compulsory. In 1972 the proportion of Ontario secondary school English students that were taking courses in French was only 37 per cent.[15] It would seem, therefore, that much of the strong resistance to learning French on the part of English-speaking Canadians continues.

The teaching of French in anglophone Canada has been described as a continuing catastrophe. If that is so the future of a bilingual Canada remains very much in question. What will probably happen is that enough bilingual Anglophones will be found to work with bilingual Francophones within federal institutions, and there will be a gradual movement toward more French spoken at work throughout Quebec. In the rest of the country bilingualism will decline the greater the distance from Quebec and Ottawa. An increase in bilingualism can make a workable system which might result in positive and beneficial French-English relations in Canada.

The future of French-English relations will also depend, of course, on factors outside provincial control, particularly economic conditions, for which the federal government has a major responsibility, and also on the visibility and vitality of ethnicity, nationalism, and tribalism in the world at large, which, as I pointed out at the beginning, was an important element in moving French-Canadian nationalism in a more active and even militant direction.

Canada's Other Ethnic Groups: a View from the Census

Interethnic relations in Canada are not confined to the French and English. Canada has always drawn and continues to draw its population from diverse sources. Some indication of this diversity can be seen from the following table. The first point to be noted is the decreasing proportion of those of British origin since the beginning of the present century. The second is the relatively stable proportion represented by the French. The drop to 28.7 per cent in 1971 reflects the fact that the lowest fertility rates in Canada are now in Quebec, making for one of the most interesting reversals of reproductive behavior to be found, a fact which many French Canadians view with alarm.[16]

Ethnic Origin of the Canadian Population 1901-1971 [a]

Origin	1901	1921	1941	1961	1971
British	57.0	55.4	49.7	43.8	44.6
French	30.7	27.9	30.3	30.4	28.7
German	5.8	3.4	4.0	5.8	6.1
Italian	0.2	0.8	1.0	2.5	3.4
Dutch	0.6	1.3	1.9	2.4	1.9
Polish	0.1	0.6	1.5	1.8	1.4
Scandinavian	0.6	1.9	2.1	2.1	1.8
Ukrainian	0.1	1.2	2.7	2.6	2.2
Indian and Eskimo	2.4	1.3	1.1	1.2	1.3
Other	2.5	6.2	5.7	7.4	8.6
Total	100.0	100.0	100.0	100.0	100.0

Source: Report of the Royal Commission on Bilingualism and Biculturalism, Book IV, 248.
[a] Newfoundland was excluded from the Canadian census until 1951.

The table also indicates that no other ethnic group comes close in size to the British or the French although in total they come to somewhere between one-quarter and one-third of the population of Canada. The ethnic categories shown in the table are those of the 1971 census. The 1961 census used twenty-eight categories, many of which are contained under "Other" in the table. These included in 1961, for example, Icelandic, Lithuanian, Roumanian, and Japanese, each with 0.2 per cent of the population.[17] Thus the non-British, non-French component of the Canadian population is extremely diverse.

At this point it is important to note that all the distributions of ethnic origins shown in the table are artifacts of the census itself and result from the questions from which the data are derived.

Ethnic "origin" has been asked for in a variety of ways in different censuses, and the instructions to census enumerators have also varied, adding a further artifactual element to the distributions.

In 1961 the question was "To what ethnic or cultural group did you or your ancestor (on the male side) belong on coming to this continent?" Two important facts are clear from the census treatment of ethnicity. One is that one's ethnic origin was to be patrilineally traced, and second, except for native Indians and Eskimos, there was no recognition in any census tabulations of Canadian or American ethnic origin. Thus for census purposes both those born in Canada and immigrants had to have a non-North American ethnicity. For the first time, in the 1951 census, if all the techniques in their manuals failed them, enumerators were allowed to write in "Canadian" or "American" if the person absolutely insisted. The same was also permitted in 1961. In that year according to an administrative report on the census only 118 185 persons reported their origin as "Canadian," 15 786 as "American," and 70 163 as "Unknown." These numbers combined make up slightly more than 1 per cent of the population, about the same as in 1951.[18] These insistent and uncertain people were lost in the residual "Other" category in all census tabulations.

In 1971 the ethnic question was asked in the same way, but for the first time the census was self-enumerated. Neither Canadian nor American was among the response categories provided. The only possibility was "Other-Specify." The 1971 census form also included a question on citizenship, the main purpose of which was to enable those persons who wished to identify themselves as Canadian to do so, since Canadian was not a valid answer to questions on language or ethnicity. The conscientious self-enumerator, who would like to feel above all that he was Canadian, might have been satisfied by being able to say, two questions before he came to the ethnicity one, that he was a Canadian citizen.[19] His instruction booklet was clear on what the census officials wanted for the ethnic question. It read, "Ethnic or cultural group refers to descent (through the father's side) and should not be confused with citizenship. Canadians belong to many ethnic or cultural groups."[20] The patrilineal emphasis which has existed throughout becomes sociologically absurd where there have been exogamous marriages, because of the important role the mother plays in the socialization of children, and in language learning.

Why the ethnic origin concept took the form it has—that is, non-North American and exclusively patrilineal—is rather obscure, but it can probably be traced to the basic duality of Canadian society. Censuses before the Confederation of 1867 classified the population as "French origin," "not of French origin," and "Indian." The successive censuses after Confederation have not been consistent. The earlier ones defined origin according to the birthplace of the individual or of his paternal ancestor before coming to North America. Two major wars in the twentieth century have broken up international boundaries, making it rather absurd to relate ethnic origin to political entities, and there has been a gradual evolution toward a cultural and linguistic definition of ethnic group. Discussions of the 1931 census placed a great emphasis on "racial" differences and their importance to Canada because of the extensive European migration to Canada after the opening up of the West in the 1890s. There was a suggestion in the official comments on the 1931 census that, as the "races" fused, there would no longer be any need to differentiate between them, indicating some orientation at that time to a "melting pot" concept. Because of the discrediting of the concept of race during and after the Second World War a 1941 census monograph on ethnic origins was not published until 1965![21]

A trenchant critique of Canadian origin statistics was made by Norman Ryder in 1955.[22] He suggested that if the origin question were to have any sociological or cultural meaning it should be asked in terms of language. If the important socio-political question of assimilation to either French or English was to be reasonably answered, the question should be about the language first learned by the individual and by his parents. Two generations of English or French as mother tongue would give some indication of assimilation.

The 1971 census asked not only a mother-tongue question but also one on the language most often spoken at home. The assimilation to English has been very marked. While the English-speaking ethnic origin constituted 45 per cent of the population, English as the language most often spoken in the home was 65 per cent. While the non-English, non-French ethnicities made up 28 per cent of the population, only about 12 per cent had the same mother tongue as their ethnic origin, and only about 6 per cent spoke their ethnic origin language most often in the home. Thus if ethnicity and culture are based on language a considerable process of assimilation has gone on. The French ethnic origin showed a minor language loss, with 28 per cent of the population reporting French ethnic origin and 25 per cent as speaking French in the home.[23]

Despite the historical variations, the focus on patrilineal descent, non-recognition of Canadian or American origin, and other inadequacies in the census statistics, it has proved impossible to eliminate the question or change its form, as indeed the federal government sought to do for the 1961 census, when John Die-fenbaker was prime minister and spoke out strongly against hyphenated Canadians. The French were insistent on its retention because it provides them with some measure of their survival and their claims for co-charter group status within Canada, a status which can scarcely be denied. Organizations of the other ethnic groups have also demanded its retention because it gave grounds to their claim that Canada is a cultural mosaic rather than the so-called American melting pot.

A comparison of the history of the censuses in Canada and the United States would tell in a fascinating way how the two countries have attempted to treat ethnicity in the course of nation building. Melting pot and mosaic are almost stereotypical terms to describe the divergent ways in which these two new nations have tried to deal with ethnicity, but they do reflect the two opposed orientations, clearly to be seen in the policies and instructions surrounding the two censuses from the last century.[24] We know now that the lives of ethnic groups are not responsive to the intentions of the policymakers and the bureaucratic organizations that take the censuses. Melting pot and mosaic are not such extreme opposites as the terms would imply because in the United States, ethnicity, in the sense of awareness of European national origins of ancestors, is still very much alive while in Canada many reject European ancestry and identify with the country where they were born.

The Organization of Ethnic Groups

If the Canadian census gives an artifactual quality to the ethnic structure of Canadian society a different impression is gained from ethnic organizations which are very much alive, ably led and responding predictably to the widespread ethnic revival. With the demands in Quebec for a reconstruction of Canadian society, the other ethnic organizations also made demands to be heard and, when the Royal Commission on Bilingualism and Biculturalism was established, the government of Canada felt compelled to include in the Commission's terms of reference "The contribution made by the other ethnic groups to the cultural enrichment of Canada and the measures that should be taken to safeguard that contribution." Two of the ten commissioners were members of these other ethnic groups and an entire volume of the Commission's *Report* was devoted to the matter of the other ethnic groups.

Government policymakers, as do politicians who seek their electoral support, like to view these diverse non-British, non-

French ethnicities as a "third element" despite the fact that, as I have said, they were listed in the 1961 census as 28 ethnicities ranging from 5.6 per cent of the population to 0.2 per cent.

Despite this fragmentation, the so-called third element has its own spokesmen such as Senator Paul Yuzyk who, in a paper presented to the Canadian Association of Slavists in 1965 entitled "Canada: A Multi-Cultural Nation," said, "The third element ethnic groups now numbering approximately five million persons, are co-builders of the West and other parts of Canada, along with the British and French Canadians and are just as permanent a part of the Canadian scene. . . . As co-founders they should be co-partners who would be guaranteed the right to perpetuate their mother tongues and cultures."[25] He called for the government, and government agencies such as the Canadian Broadcasting Corporation, actively to promote all other cultures. This was not only a right belonging to these groups, but the policy had other merits as well. He quoted approvingly an American sociologist, Charles Hobart, working in Canada as saying, "Multiculturalism beats the melting pot idea all to Hell." At about the same time, at a Toronto conference on "national unity" a spokesman for other ethnic groups talked about the disunity that would result from emphasizing the English and the French elements in Canada to the neglect of the others and suggested that there should be an "estates-general" to explore ways of preserving non-English and non-French cultures in Canada.[26] Views such as these were typical of many forcefully articulated before the Royal Commission on Bilingualism and Biculturalism.

Ethnic group leaders were given much encouragement by the last volume[27] of the Commission's *Report* which was devoted to the other ethnic groups, and since then there has been a great deal of promotion of the idea of "multiculturalism." Although one gets the impression that most of the commissioners would have preferred to have confined their attention to French-English relations the spokesmen on the Commission for the other ethnic groups were firm, leading in one case to a strong dissenting opinion to the Commission's views in the first volume of the *Report* that English and French should be the only two official languages.[28]

Multiculturalism within a Bilingual Framework

In October 1971 Mr. Trudeau, the prime minister, announced in the House of Commons a new policy which he called "multiculturalism within a bilingual framework" and which he considered "the most suitable means of assuring the cultural freedom of

Canadians."[29] The government had already taken a number of steps mentioned earlier, such as the Official Languages Act of 1969, to make French and English equal as official languages within the federal jurisdiction, to promote the teaching of both the official languages, and to introduce bilingualism into the Public Service.

Canada was becoming caught up in the ethnic revival. The government was attempting to maintain a difficult balance between the hostility of many in Quebec to any formal recognition of the other groups and the electoral support that would be forthcoming from a program to promote multiculturalism. French critics of the new policy argued that it was an about-turn from the earlier position, on the basis of which the Commission had been set up, that is, that Canada should be a truly bilingual and bicultural society based on the central ideas of two founding peoples, two societies, and two dominant cultures. Some argued that it was impossible to talk of multiculturalism without multilingualism because culture could not be detached from language. If that were true then the official bilingualism that was developing at the federal level, and in some provinces, would be endangered by demands that other languages be recognized. Moreover, multiculturalism in some provinces would be more likely to promote a bilingualism in the form of Anglo-Ukrainian or Franco-Italian rather than English-French bilingualism, which had basic sociological and historical links and which was so important for the future of Canada as a viable society.[30] Indeed, it has always been assumed that immigrants to Canada would assimilate to either the French or the English communities. If that was no longer to be so, French Canadians would interpret it as a threat to their own survival. As I mentioned earlier, lowering French fertility rates and English-speaking school attendance by immigrant children gave substance to these French fears.

The multicultural pronouncement has many critics also among English-speaking Canadians, particularly those who see the only hope for Canada to lie in a policy of biculturalism and bilingualism based on the two collectivities which they represent,[31] and seems to contradict the view of the Commission which had written, "To the degree that the demands of certain ethnic groups make awareness of the fundamental duality of the country more difficult, to that extent they aggravate the state of crisis in Canada. Above all, they provide new arguments for the partisans of a 'One Canada.' "[32]

The Canadian government took quite the opposite view to the common sense one that strong ethnic loyalties, because they are little nationalisms, would be divisive. Mr. Trudeau, in fact, argued that multiculturalism would be integrative. He said Canada would become "a special place, and a stronger place as well. Each of the many fibres contributes it own qualities and Canada gains strength from the combination. We become less like others; we become less susceptible to cultural, social, or political envelopment by others."[33]

All major political leaders outside of Quebec support some policy of multiculturalism. Robert Stanfield, the federal leader of the Opposition, referring to the government's program as "grudging acceptance," went on to say, "If we really believe that Canadian pluralism should be encouraged, and not merely tolerated, government should work together with the various ethnic groups to help them survive, not simply as folklore, but as a living contributing element of the Canadian cultural mosaic."[34]

On the subject some achieve new heights of rhetoric. Mr. John Yaremko, the Ontario Provincial Secretary and Minister of Citizenship, in announcing a 1972 multicultural conference *Heritage Ontario* said:

> No other part of the globe, no other country, can claim a more culturally diversified society than we have here in this Province . . . But does everyone really grasp that Ontario has more Canadians of German origin than Bonn, more of Italian origin than Florence, that Toronto has more Canadians of Greek origin than Sparta, that we have in our midst, fifty-four ethno-cultural groups, speaking a total of seventy-two languages? . . . Just as a hundred years ago the Canadian identity was moulded in the crucible of nationalism, it is now being tempered by the dynamics of multiculturalism.

Mr. Yaremko also touched upon another cause of the current revival of ethnicity and that is the large non-British component of postwar immigration. He then went on to make the common mistake of seeing this component, made up of people from such a variety of countries, as in some way being homogeneous:

> There are generally speaking four demographic groups among us— Indians, Anglo- and Franco-Ontarian, and members of the third element . . . One effect of the post-war boom in third element immigration has been to bolster ethno-cultural groups, some of which have been here through four generations. The Government has welcomed and encouraged this immigration. We have recognized and helped foster all our constituent cultural communities. Is it then any wonder that these communities have heightened expectations in many areas?[35]

In the bolstering of ethno-cultural groups, as Mr. Yaremko

puts it, the postwar immigrants have played an important leadership role because of their long association with nationalist political struggles in their European homelands. They have continued their activities, often ideological as well as national, aimed at keeping alive in Canada the culture they believe is being obliterated abroad. This leadership has managed in some cases to shift the focus of activity of their national organizations from the problem of integration within Canadian society to the problem of cultural survival either in Europe or in Canada as a locus for cultures in exile.

The official Canadian government policy of "multiculturalism within a bilingual framework" has as its goal the encouraging of non-British, non-French ethnic cultures. A multicultural program, established in the Citizenship Branch of the Department of the Secretary of State, was to study such aspects of multiculturalism as broadcasting in third languages, the role of the ethnic press, and language training in third languages. The most important part of the program, though, was the giving of grants to ethnic organizations to help them preserve their culture. Initially the program was modest. One and one-half million dollars were allocated for grants in the first year, but by 1973 the budget had increased to 10 million dollars, and a cabinet minister was appointed whose exclusive responsibility was multiculturalism.

The grants are given to viable ethnic organizations for specific projects. For example, among the 400 grants that were given in the first year of the program was $1500 to the Canadian Arab Association in Montreal to teach Arab folklore and dancing, and $5000 to the Mennonite community in Waterloo to celebrate the Amish quincentennial.[36]

The "Guidelines for Submissions for Grants under the Multicultural Programme" emphasize the "multicultural" goal of the program in the Canadian context.[37] The criteria considered for granting funds to a specific project include whether it is "designed to share a cultural heritage with other Canadians," whether it will "promote an awareness of Canada's cultural diversity," and whether it will "assist immigrants to become full participants in Canadian society."

A problem is that many ethnic organizations are more interested in promoting their cultures within their own ethnic communities than in sharing cultures with other Canadians. Because of that, the program could become a multi-unicultural one. In October 1973 the federal government sponsored the first national conference on multiculturalism in Ottawa to which 400 delegates went from across the country. In his speech to delegates Dr. Stanley Haidasz, the minister responsible for multiculturalism, said,[38]

"Those who think multiculturalism is a cynical form of tokenism or a sop to keep some ethno-cultural groups happy" should know that multiculturalism is a permanent government policy.

Non-English, non-French ethnicity, then, continues to be a salient feature of Canadian social structure. Whether it will eventually be integrative or divisive, in that the emphasis on Canada's multiethnicity will intensify French nationalism, must be left to time. For those who view the ethnic revival as something good because it represents something deep and primordial and genuinely human, Canada must appear as an attractive place to live. However, it is my intention to raise some serious doubts about this revival of ethnicity, not only for Canada, but for other advanced societies and perhaps developing ones as well.

Some Questions about the Revival of Ethnicity

In some respects the revival is regressive. Because it emphasizes descent group identification and endogamy, important principles of ethnic group survival, it runs the risk of believed-in biological differences becoming the basis of invidious judgments about groups of people, a matter to which we will return later. Moreover, where ethnicity is salient there is often an association between ethnic differences and social class and inequality. That is why much of the discussion of the relations between ethnic groups concerns equality, equality of legal rights, political rights, and in the more recent period, social rights such as education, jobs, good health, and equality of opportunity. Class inequality becomes obscured and more difficult to analyse where there is ethnic heterogeneity in the social structure. This may reflect some inadequacy in the sociological theories of class, almost all of which assume ethnic homogeneity.

Some scholars contest the view that when ethnic differentiation is an important organizing principle of social life it must also result in ethnic groups forming a hierarchy of inequality, creating what has come to be called ethnic stratification. One writer, Donald L. Noel, raises that question in developing a theory of the origins of ethnic stratifications and answers it in this way: "Distinct ethnic groups can interact and form a stable pattern of relations without super-subordination."[39] The "classical example" he gives is of the Tungus and Cossacks of northwestern Siberia from an anthropological study of 1938. This at least suggests that ethnic differentiation without some hierarchical features is rare. Certainly the degree and strength of hierarchy depend upon many factors, and there have been many studies of the conditions under which super- and subordination exist in plural or multiethnic societies.[40]

My own view is that ethnic saliency or differentiation in social structure always creates a high risk of ethnic stratification. To understand the interplay between ethnic inequalities and class inequalities it is important to look at how ethnic differentiation in a society comes about. Multiethnic societies are created through conquest or migration. Where there is conquest, the conquerors take over the high status activities—even if these are confined to exercising power as dominant minorities—and relegate the conquered populations to inferior statuses.

Migration of peoples from one part of the world to another has been much more important than conquest in the creation of multiethnic societies, at least in the modern historical period, but it too creates relationships of subordination of some groups to others. There was, first of all, unfree migration by which slaves have been transported for plantation economies, for cotton and cane. There was also the constrained migration of indentured labor, which was a common practice of the European powers in their colonial empires, and many of their former colonies, which are now developing countries, have the roots of their ethnic diversity in these processes. European powers also often forced together various tribal groups of great cultural differences into administrative units convenient for their own purposes. Now that most of the colonies have achieved independence from their European creators many of them are subject to severe strains. These conflicts are between ethnic groups and most of them are about which one should rule, who should have privilege and who should have the good jobs. One has only to mention the Congo, Nigeria, and Pakistan to remember the violence with which these disputes are settled.

New nations developed mainly by Europeans in sparsely populated regions such as the United States, Canada, Australia, and South Africa first forced the aboriginal groups to the base of the stratification structure. Ethnic differentiation then arose through immigration which was free, or relatively free, if the economic and political factors in some of the countries of origin which prompted it are considered. It was only relatively free also because the receiving societies were dominated by people who got there first and from their position of early "entrance status" determined the conditions under which the other groups might enter.

Migration is an economic process, the movement of labor with capital. The host society regulates the movement with varying degrees of rigidity by making invidious judgments about the appropriateness of people of particular origins for particular jobs.

This selective process, by which people were sorted out according to the qualities or aptitudes that were thought to suit them for different economic activities, was intensified in the twentieth century as the North American societies became more industrialized. Even the laissez-passer system by which Europeans came into the United States, or leapfrogged through Canada, was abandoned, and the legal restrictions which were ultimately imposed in both Canada and the United States were racist in that they had as their objective the maintenance of the existing ethnic composition, based on the dominance of British and northern European groups.

Along with this mixing up of the peoples of the world through empire and economic expansion went an ideology of racism, masquerading as a pseudo-science of race differences, which attempted to demonstrate that some groups were inherently superior to others and that it was more than a coincidence that those who were ranked highest controlled the economic processes of the society.[41]

More recently we have seen the further differentiation of stratification systems as a result of new ethnic migrations, in the United States Puerto Ricans, in England immigrants from the colored Commonwealth, in France Algerians. Throughout western Europe Italian, Spanish, and Portuguese laborers have entered the social structure, generally as unskilled labor and sometimes, unless protected by Common Market agreements, with few legal rights.[42]

In Canada this historical relationship between migration and economic or class position has been reinforced by the heavy immigration since 1945, despite recent changes in immigration regulations designed to reduce the preferential position of the British and others most like them.[43] Immigrants from Britain and the United States continue to be heavily over-represented in the higher professional, managerial, and white-collar occupational levels, while those from Portuagal and Greece are taking over from Italians at the lower levels of the immigrant labor force. Caribbean and Asian countries are now appearing as a new source of immigrants to Canada and will, because of early controls on immigration of Chinese and Japanese, and the previously small black population, make color a newly visible element in the structure of ethnic stratification.

All multiethnic societies have to deal with the problems of legal, political, and social rights which stem from the inequality between their component ethnic groups. They vary so widely with respect to basic features of economic development and political culture that it is questionable whether it is very instructive to pursue an understanding of interethnic relations, or the management of them, through comparative analysis. However, the temptation to construct another typology, even though others already exist, is difficult to avoid.[44]

Consider four sets of dichotomies. There are old and new nations; there are developed and underdeveloped ones; there are those built up through migration or "pasted" together in the process of decolonization; there are those in which the ethnic units have territory and those in which they are dispersed. How societies deal with problems of ethnic inequality will depend to a great extent on where they fall within this set of dichotomies.

Much of the recent sociological discussion of interethnic relations concerns the stability of multiethnic societies which are on the road to development and whose basic institutions and culture are premodern. The stability and development of the Third World is without doubt a desirable objective, but any solutions to its ethnic problems are not likely to be very helpful in the discussion of employment quotas in the United States or policies of multiculturalism for Canada. The ethnic identity of a Hutu or an Ibo must surely be of such profoundly different psychological quality and social consequence from that, say, of an Italian American or a Ukrainian Canadian that the subjective states involved are scarcely of the same order. It is questionable whether both can be considered "primordial."

A premodern tribal culture, in which a people consider it legitimate to dominate by brutal means rivals whom some act of history has placed in a common political state, is a vastly different situation from a society with legally safeguarded rights and freedoms and a history of liberty. Thus minority rights have very different meanings in different multiethnic societies, but because modern communications contribute to the world phenomenon of ethnic revival, these differences are overlooked. Ethnicity may be genuinely primordial and essential to individual survival in a former African colony made into an artificial political unit, but in a society on the threshold of postindustrialism it could, with its great emphasis on the particularistic, be considered atavistic if it were to become a salient organizing principle of social life.

Comparison is, however, useful between societies which can be located in similar positions with respect to the previously mentioned dichotomies. Canada and the United States, for example, are both new nations built up through migration and have "democratic" political cultures. Generally this political culture has been liberal in the sense which Parsons has recently used in tracing the secularization that followed the democratic revolutions with their slogans of liberty, equality, and fraternity.[45] Among these liberal values was the notion that the ethnic stratification which resulted from immigration was temporary and would not harden into a permanent class system.

Most liberal social scientists viewing this phenomenon of ethnic stratification assumed that over time processes which they called absorption, assimilation, and acculturation would eliminate this relationship between national or ethnic origin and economic condition and they advocated policies that would lead to such a result. Moreover, educational institutions, more so in the United States than in Canada, were geared to provide some equality of opportunity for all young people. The emphasis was on individual achievement and in the context of a new nation with universalistic standards of judgment it meant forgetting ancestry and attempting to establish society of equality where ethnic origin did not matter. Some fears were expressed, of course, that these liberal assimilationist values would require a large measure of Anglo-conformity on the part of "non-Anglo" groups. In a large measure these fears were probably justified, but it could also be said that what was being advocated was conformity to the values of societies leading in the modernizing process.

If universalistic standards and achievement values were important for the mobility offered by the occupational structure of a modernizing society, then liberal assimilationist policies served to provide opportunity for those of all ethnic origins. The revival of ethnicity and the consequent labeling could mean an emphasis on the contrary values of particularism and ascriptive criteria which would be less conducive than imperfectly applied universalistic standards to equality of opportunity and mobility in the two major North American societies.

Mobility means movement up more than the occupational system. It also means movement into higher levels of political and economic power structures. Hence, as ethnicity has operated in the past as a selective device to sort and sift people within the occupational structure it has also served as a form of class control of the major power structures by charter ethnic groups who remain overrepresented in the elite structures.

Thus the United States and Canada, both societies within the western liberal tradition with ethnicity as a salient feature, seem to be faced with a dilemma; on the one hand if they value and emphasize ethnicity, mobility and opportunity are endangered, on the other hand if they emphasize mobility and opportunity, it will be at the cost of submerging cultural identity.

The dilemma is stated in the hypothesis of Frank Vallee, in his study of French Canadian communities outside of Quebec, communities which are like ethnic groups anywhere in Canada in that they are spatially dispersed and without territory. His hypothesis is as follows:

> The more a minority group turns in upon itself and concentrates on making its position strong, the more it costs its members in terms of their chances to make their way as individuals in the larger system . . . Among ethnic minority groups which strive to maintain language and other distinctions, motivation to aspire to high-ranking social and economic positions in the larger system will be weak, unless, of course, it is characteristic of the ethnic groups to put a special stress on educational and vocational achievement.[46]

The last observation applies especially to Jews, but generally Vallee argues that any collectivity has limited resources and energies and cannot spend them on maintaining ethnic specific institutions and at the same time prepare its members for achievement in the larger society of which it is a part. The choice is no doubt a cruel one, particularly so because it cuts across the generations, introducing a contradiction between the parents' rights and choices with those their children might prefer. Nonetheless, the present drift seems to be against the liberal assimilationist views, now pejoratively referred to as being overly rational, secular, and universalistic.[47]

For some, the revival of ethnicity has come about precisely because of the failure of universalistic and achievement values to take hold, and thus create a society of equality of opportunity and condition. Ethnic stratification has been a feature of both the United States and Canada. Consequently there has been a shift to achieving equality through a system of organized minorities demanding rights and making claims qua minorities, and away from human rights legislation, fair employment practices legislation and the like, which were a product of the liberal value system and which were to provide individuals—not groups or collectivities—with rights, enforceable in the courts, against discrimination.

It is no doubt understandable that because of the failure of these instruments, fashioned as they were for the individual, minorities have had to organize to obtain some measure of distributive justice when deprivation remained concentrated within particular groups. The increasing demands of deprived groups and the accumulating evidence of their deprivation have brought certain policy responses by dominant majorities as represented by governments and other power groups. These policy responses have produced a new terminology: affirmative action, positive discrimination, preferential hiring and benign quotas. The new instruments, focussed as they are on groups, and providing what might be called group rights, for example, to proportional representation within all institutional hierarchies, constitute a radical departure from a society organized on the principles of individual achievement and universalistic judgments, even if these were often honored as much in the breach as in the observance, to one organized on group claims to representation on the basis of particular, rather than universal, qualities.

It is interesting in this respect that the Universal Declaration of Human Rights, which encouraged a good deal of the postwar human rights legislation, nowhere mentions group rights, but speaks entirely in terms of the rights of individual human beings. It is not possible, in Canada at least, to find the concept of group rights embodied in jurisprudence except perhaps for the so-called aboriginal rights and treaty rights of native Indians.

When the evidence is very clear that discrimination and deprivation bear so heavily on ethnic minorities, it seems logical to correct the condition through positive discrimination in which institutions, corporations, universities, and the like, are required to maintain quotas throughout their hierarchical structures to make them representative with respect to minorities. These processes have gone much further in the United States than in Canada, where they are largely confined to federal government attempts to improve the position of the French in the federal public service, and of native people—the most wretchedly deprived of all—in areas where the federal government awards contracts. However, in response to recommendations of the Royal Commission on the Status of Women (1970) similar policies of positive discrimination for this deprived "minority" are beginning to appear.[48]

Positive discrimination brings a new problem in disturbing existing relationships between ethnic and other minorities within occupational structures that have been accepted and institutionalized in the course of their historical development. In Canada, an English-speaking person reacts against appointments and promotions which favor the French, as an eastern European "ethnic" in the United States would to positive discrimination in favor of non-whites, or a man against such discrimination in favor of a woman. Whatever its benefits, and however much its purposes can be understood, positive discrimination brings these institutionalized differences in power and privilege between the majority and minorities well into view and gives a new saliency to minority and perhaps pseudo-minority group membership, and intensifies hostility and rivalry. The individual, in order to make his claims, will have to determine to which group he belongs, and one can visualize a somewhat complex passbook arrangement. Membership could crosscut in several ways, making it necessary to calculate the maximum advantage for preferential employment and career program. The possibilities are endless, since societies can be viewed as intersecting sets of minorities and majorities, defined by an infinite number of criteria, all of different relevance at different times.

The organization of society on the basis of rights or claims that derive from group membership is sharply opposed to the concept of a society based on citizenship, which has been such an important aspect in the development of modern societies. The individual makes claims as a citizen, a status common to all members. T.H. Marshall has traced[49] the development of citizenship rights and the manner in which they have served the process of class abatement, and Parsons has recently drawn on Marshall's ideas about citizenship as central to the development of the system of modern societies. They are essential also to the development of modern egalitarianism. First civil rights provided equality before the law, then political rights allowed participation in government, eventually social rights brought about education, health, and decent living standards and some measure of equality of condition. As Parsons has said: "The emergence of 'full' modernity thus weakened the ascriptive framework of monarchy, aristocracy, established churches and an economy circumscribed by kinship and localism to the point at which it no longer exercised decisive influence."[50]

Citizenship rights are essentially universalistic whereas group rights are essentially particularistic. One of the reasons why many developing societies cannot be compared with modern societies is that they have not yet embodied some, or indeed any, of these citizenship rights in either their value systems or their social organization. They remain essentially premodern, emphasizing tribalism and localism and resolving their ethnic conflicts, sometimes even to the point of genocide, with the particularistic focus. In modern western nations that have established democratic procedures and, albeit inadequately, but nonetheless perceptively, have developed the social rights of citizenship, ethnic conflict is about equality of condition and full participation in a modernizing opportunity structure as well as the political community. To resort to the group basis of settling claims, if necessary, is regrettable.

I now return to the matter to which I referred earlier, that ethnic groups, because they are biological descent groups, are a regressive means of safeguarding and transmitting culture, a responsibility which many would assign to them. No doubt cultural survival can be most efficiently achieved through the biological descent group because when coupled with another principle firmly embedded in our values—that parents have the inalienable right through cultural transmission to make their children the vehicles of their values—recruits are always available. The use of the family for ethnocultural transmission requires that groups impress upon their members the value of marrying within their own group. If they do not they will lose the primordial link with tribe or nation and the exclusive ethnic claims on culture will be eroded. Endogamy is a process of exclusion. There was a time when lowering rates of endogamy could be taken as an index of lessening prejudice in a more liberal and open society. In the current return to ethnicity it seems a different judgment, that such lowering rates can be interpreted as a loss of ethnic communal strength, is being made. The metal of endogamy is more attractive because it is unmeltable.

When descent groups are the principal carriers of culture there are dangers of new forms of racism. If "races" have been evaluated as inferior and superior, so can cultures be. Racism and "culturism" stem from the fact that both are linked to the maintenance of descent-group solidarity and endogamy. After all, if ethnicity is so important, if cultures are so different, then it is easy to extend the argument that those of different ethnic groups and cultures must also be different with respect to qualities which are thought important in different parts of the work world and for entrance to elite status. It may not take very long before that view becomes extended even further, to include the notion that qualitative cultural differences are inborn. When that point is reached we have come full circle and we begin to realize that those theories of race and ethnic differences which we thought destroyed or at least highly discredited by the Second World War have reappeared in a new guise with culture replacing race.

Along with the arguments supportive of the revival of ethnicity can be found also the view that cultures have a right to live and individuals and societies have an obligation to see that they survive, although surely history is as much the graveyard of cultures as it is of aristocracies. The desirability and responsibility of preserving culture through historical, archeological, and anthropological study, because we want to know how people lived at different times and places, is beyond question. Often, in discussions of the survival of culture, one gets the impression that the reference is to cultural artifacts such as dance, folklore, cuisine, music, crafts, and the like. Cultural artifacts always will survive, because people enjoy them, and that is good because they add variety. However, they do not require descent-group identification to survive. Artifacts are unlike values, some of which when embedded in particular cultures are particularly inappropriate for modernity—for example, the low evaluation of education for girls.

If there are dangers of biological descent groups preserving cultures through living them, there are available associational ways of conserving culture. Some people find the culture of ancient Egypt fascinating and rewarding to study. But if the culture of ancient Egypt is of value the various groups that preserve it—archaeologists who get money to investigate it and amateur Egyptologists who make it a hobby—must recruit new members to carry on their interests. One way would be to require as a condition of membership that members marry within the Egyptology group, and, given the traditional role of the family as the unit of cultural transmission, ensure the survival of the culture of ancient Egypt through the generations. Alternatively, they can do as they always have done and that is to recruit members by persuading others that studying and keeping alive this particular culture is a good thing.

The obligation to conserve culture is different from the obligation to live it. In Canada, for example, it is at times suggested that the Eskimos should be left alone to live their traditional hunting and nomadic culture rather than be encouraged to modernism even though, for the individuals involved, life is more often than not nasty and brutish and seldom long, at least until modern government health services are delivered to even the most remote areas. Yet few would argue that medical attempts to control tuberculosis should be abandoned in favor of the more primitive harshness.

Not all cultures have equal claims on our moral support. Some cultures treat human beings in profoundly inhumane ways. As Conor Cruise O'Brien has said in a recent discussion of the rights of minorities in developing countries:

> The culture of a group may include systematic violations of basic human rights. When we are told to respect the cultures of groups we are being told to respect things which may include for example the Hindu caste system, the treatment of women in Islam and a number of other cultures, female circumcision in certain cultures, ostracism of twins, for example in others, and so on.[51]

So strongly are cultural rights advocated that people in modern nations, particularly those that make claims to being democracies, are reluctant to persuade developing countries to be either democratic or modern. Perhaps considering their histories of imperialism and aggression they do not speak with much moral authority. But our claim to the judgment of cultures is not put forward because we have created a perfect society, but because in the course of social evolution some principles of social life have emerged which are more morally supportable than others.

So far my emphasis has been on the costs of ethnic saliency in modern societies. Are there no benefits? One strong argument for ethnic pluralism, widely accepted to support the idea of multiculturalism in Canada, is that it creates diversity. A society with a number of different ethnic cultures in which the members of relatively exclusive groups behave alike, it is said, will be heterogeneous rather than uniform. Yet it could be that such diversity is more enjoyed by the beholder—whatever Olympus he might be viewing it from—than any of the actors within their enclaves. Moreover, modern societies are the most differentiated of all. Diversity is almost a defining attribute for them, but their diversity is one of choice rather than of descent. Indeed, the call to ethnic loyalty stems largely from the fear of the descent group that members will desert it for the diversity of an associational rather than a communal type.

A strong case can be made for the role of ethnic group affiliation in solving problems of personal identity in the modern world of bureaucracy and technology. There is no doubt that ethnic groupings can play this role, but, as I have argued, at the possible cost of perpetuating ethnic stratification. Identities and psychic shelters can be found in other forms of association and interest groups which are not based on descent, for it is this aspect of the ethnic group which is the source of irrational invidious comparison.

The psychic shelter function of ethnic affiliation has been and continues to be important in Canada and no doubt in other modern societies as well, in two special contexts. One is that of recently arrived immigrants, of which Canada continues to have large numbers in its population. The other is the positive function which ethnic affiliation has for the raising of the self-concept of members of low status groups.

For the immigrant the transition to a new social environment can be fraught with psychic hazards, particularly if he comes from the Azores or the Abruzzi to metropolitan Toronto. The question from the point of view of general social goals is whether the useful staging-camp role of the ethnic community becomes permanent, or whether some dispersion into the wider society of the various groups increases his chances of achievement and mobility in the receiving society.

Commitment to the receiving society on the part of immigrants may not be as strong now as it was sixty or seventy years ago. Immigrants come in modern jet aircraft, settle into enclaves in the receiving metropolis, and charter aircraft to take them home for visits. What the jet aircraft does between Milano and Toronto, fast special trains do from Torino to Amsterdam. So the link with the society of origin is not as completely broken as it was in the time of the long steerage passage across the Atlantic, and with this shrinking of distance the social status of migrating labor will be ever more ambiguous in the societies to which it moves to work. The social status of permanent stranger is something new for modern societies. But where the status of citizenship can be acquired, as in the United States and Canada, social mobility and achievement almost imply a commitment to the values of modernism and a movement away from the ethnic community with each succeeding generation.

There remains the positive function that ethnic identification can play in raising the self-concept of members of low status groups. The enhancement of self-concept can serve contrary ends. One is to compensate for low status without doing anything about it, very much as evangelical religions do for lower classes in ethnically homogeneous societies or low status ethnic groups in ethnically heterogeneous societies. The other is to provide a firm base from which to achieve, although many cultures do not emphasize individual achievement, nor do they provide the appropriate skills for it. From the point of view of the Indians, does promoting their own culture help them toward equality in the postindustrial society?

If strong ethnic identification is to enhance the self-concept of an individual and thus provide a firm base from which to achieve, it is important to emphasize language rather than culture. Identification with and the use of their own language, particularly in school, may be important in providing opportunity for very low status groups. For example, the use of an immigrant language, say, Italian or Portuguese and certainly the language of native peoples in Canada, may help a child in overcoming learning impediments that arise from using one language at school and another at home. He acquires some self-confidence when his language is not despised. But such use of language is quite different from the goal of having ethnic communities become a permanent compensation for low status, or as psychic shelters in the urban-industrial world. We would hope for a society in which the compensatory role of the ethnic community is not necessary.

I have tried to argue what, particularly in my own country, is an unpopular view, and that is that the saliency of ethnic differences is a retreat from the liberal notions of the unity of mankind. But I would be naive indeed—an inappropriate state for a professional sociologist—if I were not aware of the political realities in those modern societies where deprived minorities seek to redistribute social resources to redress grievances. Political realities are not principles although they are often confused with them, and hence, the question is whether interethnic conflicts can be solved in ways which are both ethically acceptable and sociologically possible.

It is my view that in Canada, in the emerging postindustrial phase, with its one culture of science and technology and its extensive transnational network, bilingualism can survive. But that phase can scarcely be bicultural, much less multicultural. If bilingualism is to be a part of Canada's future, we will require more exogamous marriages to offset the falling fertility rates in Quebec. We will also require vastly improved language learning programs. Under such circumstances, there would be no need to rely only on group exclusiveness and endogamy for Canada's two languages to survive.

What of cultures? Cultures are traditionbound. Anthropologists view cultures as established ways of doing things, or of viewing the world, or as designs for living and survival passed from generation to generation, and, while for societies more simply organized than those of today, the role that cultures played and for many continue to play was important, they are less and less relevant for the postindustrial society because they emphasize yesterday rather than tomorrow. Can cultures of the past serve societies facing the coming of postindustrialism? The one recurring theme in many of the analyses of the next twenty-five years is the rapidity of change, of the shock of the future. One can almost speak of the end of culture, as some have written of the end of ideology. Many of the historic cultures are irrelevant to our futures. Opportunity will go to those individuals who are future-oriented in an increasingly universalistic culture. Those oriented to the past are likely to lose out.

One would like to think, too, that in the United States the morally desirable and sociologically possible would take the direction of solving problems of non-white deprivation and all inequalities through the liberal emphasis on individual rather than group rights. In the short run in both Canada and the United States it may not be possible, but we should be aware of the danger of institutionalizing short-run policies: if we do we may well be turning back on the principles which have been evolving in our histories and which the revival of ethnicity contradicts.

Notes

1. The title of a widely read book by Pierre Vallières, Éditions Parti Pris, Montréal, 1968. Reprinted as *White Niggers of America* (Toronto, McClelland and Stewart, 1971).

2. Les éditions du boréal express. Montreal, 1972. The original is *French Canada in Transition* (Chicago, University of Chicago Press, 1943).

3. See for example, Sheilagh Hodgins Milner and Henry Milner, *The Decolonization of Quebec* (Toronto, McClelland and Stewart, 1973).

4. The idea of French Canadians as an ethnic class was first discussed by Jacques Dofny and Marcel Rioux in a 1962 paper reprinted in Marcel Rioux and Yves Martin, *French-Canadian Society* (Toronto, McClelland and Stewart, 1964), as "Social Class in French Canada." There has been criticism, particularly from Marxist writers, of the "dubious metaphor" of an ethnic class. See Stanley B. Ryerson, "Quebec: Concepts of Class and Nation," in Gary Teeple, ed., *Capitalism and the National Question in Canada* (Toronto, University of Toronto Press, 1972). In the same volume see also Gilles Bourque and Nicole Laurin-Frenette, "Social Class and National Ideologies in Quebec."

5. *A Preliminary Report of the Royal Commission on Bilingualism and Biculturalism* (Ottawa, Queen's Printer, 1965), p. 13.

6. *Report of the Royal Commission on Bilingualism and Biculturalism*, Book I, *The Official Languages* (Ottawa, Queen's Printer, 1967), p. xvii.

7. The main instrument was the Official Languages Act of 1969, *Statutes of Canada*, 17–18 Elizabeth II, Chapter II.

8. One of the provisions of the Official Languages Act of 1969 was the appointment of a Commissioner of Official Languages whose task was to ensure compliance with the spirit and intent of the Act. On the whole his annual reports (Information Canada, Ottawa) have tended to be critical of the rate of progress toward the objectives of the Act.

9. *La Presse*, Montréal, October 30, 1973.

10. "Diplomatic" and "executive" federalism are terms to describe the ways in which provincial and federal cabinet ministers and committees of federal and provincial bureaucrats bargain on a wide range of issues, like urban problems and higher education, and work out the responsibilities of the two levels of government. The federal Parliament and provincial legislatures become almost ratifiers, an unusual role for them in the traditional parliamentary system. See R. Simeon, *Federal-Provincial Diplomacy* (Toronto, University of Toronto Press, 1972), and Donald V. Smiley, *Canada in Question* (Toronto, McGraw-Hill, 1972).

11. Proportions based on mother tongue. There are bilinguals in both French-speaking and English-speaking groups. The 19 per cent includes immigrants in Quebec whose mother tongue would be neither English nor French. *Census of Canada, 1971*, vol. I, pt. 3, Ottawa, Statistics Canada, 1973. If "ethnic origin," the definition of which is dealt with later in this chapter, is used the proportions are non-French in Quebec, 21 per cent; French in Ontario, 9.5 per cent; and French in New Brunswick, 39 per cent. *Census of Canada, 1971*, Advance Bulletin, *Population by Ethnic Group* (Ottawa, Statistics Canada, 1973).

12. *Report of the Royal Commission on Bilingualism and Biculturalism*, Book III, *The Work World* (Ottawa, Queen's Printer, 1969), p. 559.

13. *Report of the Commission of Inquiry on the Position of the French Language and on Language Rights in Quebec* (Montreal, l'Éditeur officiel du Québec, 1972).

14. For a series of interesting papers on contemporary Quebec see Dale C. Thomson, ed., *Quebec Society and Politics* (Toronto, McClelland and Stewart, 1973).

15. Norman Webster, "French Language Education: For Anglophone Bigots the Going Is Tough," *The Globe and Mail*, Toronto, December 1, 1973.

16. *Vital Statistics* (Ottawa, Statistics Canada, 1973).

17. *Report of the Royal Commission on Bilingualism and Biculturalism*, Book IV, *The Cultural Contribution of the Other Ethnic Groups* (Ottawa, Queen's Printer, 1970), p. 32.

18. *Census of Canada, 1961*, Bull. 7.1–6. There is a brief history of the ethnic origin question in Warren E. Kalbach, *The Impact of Immigration on Canada's Population* (Ottawa, Statistics Canada, 1970), pp. 3–9.

19. *The 1971 Census of Population and Housing: Development of Subject Matter Content* (Ottawa, Statistics Canada, 1969), p. 13.

20. Instructions accompanying 1971 census self-enumeration forms (Ottawa, Statistics Canada, 1971).

21. Kalbach, *The Impact of Immigration*, p. v.

22. N.B. Ryder, "The Interpretation of Origin Statistics," *The Canadian Journal of Economics and Political Science*, 21.4 (1955), 466–479.

23. *Census of Canada, 1971, Population by Language Most Often Spoken in the Home and by Official Language* (Ottawa, Statistics Canada, 1973).

24. Some comparison between the two censuses has been made by Joel Smith, "Melting Pot—Mosaic: Consideration for a Prognosis," in *Minorities North and South*, Proceedings of the Third Inter-Collegiate Conference on Canadian-American Relations, Michigan State University, 1968.

25. *Canadian Slavonic Papers*, 7 (Toronto, University of Toronto Press, 1965).

26. *The Globe and Mail*, Toronto, December 16, 1968.

27. *Report of the Royal Commission on Bilingualism and Biculturalism*, Book IV, *The Cultural Contribution of the Other Ethnic Groups* (Ottawa, Queen's Printer, 1969).

28. *Report*, Book I, *The Official Languages*, pp. 155–169.

29. "Statement by the Prime Minister, House of Commons, October 8, 1971," Office of the Prime Minister, Ottawa.

30. Guy Rocher, "Les Ambiguités d'un Canada bilingue et multiculturel," paper presented to the 1972 Annual Meeting of the Canadian Association of Sociology and Anthropology, mimeo, Département de Sociologie, Université de Montréal.

31. See editorial in *Journal of Canadian Studies* (November 1971).

32. *A Preliminary Report of the Royal Commission on Bilingualism and Biculturalism* (Ottawa, Queen's Printer, 1965), p. 128.

33. "Notes for Remarks by the Prime Minister to the Ukrainian-Canadian Congress, Winnipeg, Manitoba, October 9, 1971," Office of the Prime Minister, Ottawa.

34. *The Globe and Mail*, Toronto, May 1, 1972.

35. Press release of minister's address, Office of the Provincial Secretary, Toronto, March 20, 1972.

36. *The Globe and Mail*, Toronto, October 15, 1973.

37. Citizenship Branch, Department of the Secretary of State, Ottawa (undated).

38. *The Globe and Mail*, Toronto, October 17, 1973.

39. Donald L. Noel, "A Theory of Ethnic Stratification," *Social Problems* 16 (Fall 1968), 157–172.

40. See, for example, Tamotou Shibutani and Kian M. Kwan, *Ethnic Stratification: A Comparative Approach* (New York, Macmillan, 1965); Stanley Lieberson, "A Societal Theory of Race and Ethnic Relations," *American Sociological Review*, 36 (December 26, 1971), 902–910; Burton Benedict, "Stratification in Plural Societies," *American Anthropologist* 64 (1962), 1235–1246; John Rex, *Race Relations in Sociological Theory* (New York, Schocken Books, 1970); R.A. Schermerhorn, *Comparative Ethnic Relations; A Framework for Theory and Research* (New York, Random House, 1970); M.G. Smith, *Stratification in Granada* (Berkeley, University of California Press, 1965). For two earlier statements see J.S. Furnival, *Colonial Policy and Practice* (Cambridge, Cambridge University Press, 1948), and Everett C. Hughes, "Queries Concerning Industry and Society Growing Out of Study of Ethnic Relations in Industry," *American Sociological Review*, 14.2 (April 1949), 211–220.

41. See, for example, Madison Grant, *The Passing of the Great Race* (New York, Scribners, 1921).

42. Hans van Houte and Willy Melgert, *Foreigners in Our Community* (London, Research Services Ltd., 1972). See also "Immigrant Laborers in Western Europe," *New York Times*, September 21, 1973, and "Europe's Hired Poor," *New York Times Magazine*, December 9, 1973.

43. John Porter, *The Vertical Mosaic* (Toronto, University of Toronto Press, 1965), chap. 3; and Bernard R. Blishen, "Class and Opportunity in Canada," *Canadian Review of Sociology and Anthropology*, 7 (May 1970), 110–127.

44. See the typologies in R.A. Schermerhorn, *Comparative Ethnic Relations*, and Stanley Lieberson, "A Societal Theory of Race and Ethnic Relations."

45. Talcott Parsons, *The System of Modern Societies* (Englewood Cliffs, N.J., Prentice-Hall, 1971), chap. 5.

46. Frank G. Vallee and Norman Shulman, "The Viability of French Groupings Outside Quebec," in Mason Wade, ed., *Regionalism in the Canadian Community* (Toronto, University of Toronto Press, 1969), p. 95.

47. See Andrew Greeley, "The Rediscovery of Diversity," *The Antioch Review* 31 (Fall 1971), 349; and "The New Ethnicity and Blue Collars," *Dissent* (Winter 1972).

48. *Report of the Royal Commission on the Status of Women in Canada* (Information Canada, 1970).

49. T.H. Marshall, *Class, Citizenship and Social Development* (Garden City, N.Y., Anchor, 1965).

50. Talcott Parsons, *The System of Modern Societies* (Englewood Cliffs, N.J., Prentice-Hall, 1971), pp. 81, 86.

51. In *The Times*, London reprinted as "In Secession a Case for the Individual," in *The Globe and Mail*, Toronto, January 27, 1973.

6

Melting Pot or Mosaic:
Revolution or Reversion?

Differences between Canada and the United States have fascinated historians for a long time and more recently other social scientists also. Interpretations of these differences are often produced by tracing them back in American history to the revolution which created the United States, and in Canada through the evolution or even counter-revolution which is said to have been central to Canada's development. Historical interpretations are not, in the main, propositions testable in the scientific manner, but they can be subject to critical scrutiny and re-examination in the light of evidence continuously accumulating through the scholarly enterprise.

It was with such an objective in mind that Professor Richard Preston of Duke University, an historian in charge of that university's Canadian Studies Program, planned as part of the Bicentenary celebrations at Duke a conference on Canada-U.S. differences to which he gave the title "Revolution or Evolution." The contributors included both Americans and Canadians and covered a wide range of subjects in which it might be expected that revolutionary and evolutionary motifs might be relevant.

I was asked to address the matter of whether or not the ways in which the two countries went about absorbing great quantities of immigrants had anything to do with their evolutionary or revolutionary beginnings. "Melting Pot" and "Mosaic" were the two labels most widely used to describe what were thought to be the two contradictory modalities. I had a lingering suspicion that both were false labels. Ethnic revivalism, discussed in the previous paper, was strong in the United States, and I was always puzzled about how the notion of the Canadian mosaic got started. How firmly rooted were these respective ideas in the histories of the two countries? With unscholarly temerity and no little risk, given the limitations of a single paper, the sociologist ventured into history. It was a fascinating summer's undertaking for 1976, and the pursuit of an answer to the question was intriguing and rewarding. The reprinted paper comes from the volume

139

of the conference edited by Richard Preston, Revolution versus Evolution.*

What is revolutionary about the idea of the melting pot? It is, perhaps, that beyond its crude and metallurgic metaphor it calls for a rejection of the past. It suggests that human beings can be culturally transformed and set on a path which leads to the creation of a new nation with a new national type, a new modal character. Such of course are the objectives of our latter-day revolutions which seek to obliterate bourgeois or other traditional cultures and collective personalities and to replace them with those conforming to some preferred "socialist" ideal. The leaders of the revolutions of our epoch, in Cambodia for example, seem really to believe that if they are thorough in the eradication of the former, the latter can be cultivated. What distinguished the American experience was that the process of cultural transformation, if such it was, was to come through free institutions and not through the force and oppression which contemporary revolutionaries, perhaps more realistically, employ.

However, it is doubtful that the leaders of the American Revolution, or their successors, ever held doctrines about the transformation of human beings of different cultures into a new cultural type. George Washington, who may not have been typical of the leaders, wrote in a letter to Gouverneur Morris in 1776, "I do most devoutly wish we had not a single foreigner among us except the Marquis de Lafayette who acts upon very different principles from those which govern the rest."[1] This feeling about outsiders, to be echoed long after by the American nativistic movement, was scarcely an anticipation at the time of the laying down of the American charter of the seemingly boundless immigration that was to come in the following century.

Cultural transformation—using the term culture in the broad, anthropological sense—of "huddled masses yearning to be free" through some sociological crucible was a vision of the late nineteenth century. It implied a universalism and a rejection of all ancestral past. Where one came from, one's descent group, one's color or paternal language should not be the basis for the distribution of social rights. All are welcomed by the "mighty woman with a torch," although the inscription on the Statue of Liberty does not suggest that cultural parricide was a condition of entry or a likely prospect. The welcome was primarily to those who were

---

* *Duke University Press, Durham, North Carolina, 1979.*

seeking freedom from autocratic social structures.

The rejection of the European father, a collective oedipal syndrome analogous to the rejection of the authoritarian father on the part of the individual in Freudian psychology, was, according to Geoffrey Gorer, the British anthropologist, an essential element in the development of the American national character. Gorer quotes an order of the day issued by General Patton to American troops at the time of the invasion of Sicily in 1943, a statement which might be construed as the ultimate outcome of the American transformation of Europeans. The flamboyant general said:

> When we land, we will meet German and Italian soldiers whom it is our honor and privilege to attack and destroy. Many of you have in your veins German and Italian blood, but remember that these ancestors of yours so loved freedom that they gave up home and country to cross the ocean in search of liberty. The ancestors of the people we shall kill lacked the courage to make such a sacrifice and continued as slaves.[2]

In cultural terms all this rejection of historical bonds is radical enough, but with the melting pot theory, in one of its versions at least, there is the even more radical notion that the host society of old American descendants should combine itself with the elements it was transforming. There has been much confusion of terminology in both the popular mind and in serious writing of how immigrants should be incorporated into the receiving society. For some the melting pot is just another expression for assimilation to the values of the host society, for others it means that host and newcomers all melt together into a new people. It is in the more radical sense that I am using the term melting pot. Of course the melting pot vision did not appear until the new immigration, and Zangwill's play,[3] which is considered to be the origin of the term, was not written until 1909.

The old immigration of English and Irish laborers, of Germans and Scandinavians, although it may have generated some romantic speculation about "racial" mixture, had brought people who had some cultural affinities with native-born Americans. They differed from native Americans in religious observances and they bore the marks of poverty, but they were, except those from the Celtic fringe of Britain, Protestant and redeemable within the framework of American cultural patterns.

In the postrevolutionary period the founders of America continued to be Anglo-Saxon in culture and outlook, shaping their new society from a heritage they had brought with them. Northern Europeans were similar to Anglo-Saxons, and it was easy for all to be absorbed by the expanding frontier. The Revolution was political, in a minor way social, and probably not at all cultural in the sense of taking in the foreigners, whom Washington so strongly disliked, to create a new people. As revolutionary as it was, the most we could say is that the melting pot idea when it appeared was consistent with some of the themes of universalism and equality and citizenship that were part of the Revolution. When the idea of "racial" intermixture did appear with the new immigration it was met with such a degree of hostility on the part of large numbers of the host society that it is difficult to imagine that the radical melting pot, which would have included themselves, was a part of their values. It was too revolutionary for that.

If the melting pot is revolutionary in its rejection of the ancestral past, the mosaic is, beyond its subtle and picturesque metaphor, a reversion to ancestral patterns because it implies, particularly as it is found in its recent expression in Canada, that ethnic origin and descent group identification should be salient features of social structure. It emphasizes the particular rather than the universal and requires individuals to seek out some segment of historical humanity with which to associate and identify. It detracts from the unity of mankind and the fundamental equality of humans because of its concern for differences.

The justification for labelling the mosaic a reversion is that its ultimate logic requires the endogamous descent group to be the carrier of culture. If that logic is pursued there is the danger of arriving at the point where cultural differences, which it is the duty of the descent group to embody, are attributed to genetic qualities and so we return to a social biology of race and ethnic differences. It was this social biology of the early part of the present century which supported nativistic movements in both the United States and Canada, and which had its impact on the exclusiveness of immigration policy.

With the current development of "mosaics" around the world, from the tribalisms of new nations emerging from colonialism, to the separatism, language rights and regionalism in the most advanced nations of Europe, ethnic claims are among the major themes of contemporary politics. These movements emphasize claims of descent groups rather than individuals and hence diverge from the principle of universalism and the unity of mankind.

If it is difficult to find the melting pot doctrine in the intellectual history of the United States until almost the present century it is equally difficult to find the mosaic image in the history of Canadian thought and institutions although that image with its emphasis on cultural traditions would seem to be more consistent with the conservative counter-revolutionary foundations in Canada.

Despite the apparent compatibility of the images of melting pot and mosaic with the dominant values of the two societies, both are rather romantic views of the development of the social life of the two countries and the incorporation of immigrants within them. Neither is a statement of the realities of immigration to the New World. There are probably more similarities than divergencies between the two countries in their reception of new-comers. Both came close to demanding assimilation to the culture of the host society despite the contrary images evoked by the colorful metaphors with which we are familiar. Moreover, technological change was to make assimilation almost inevitable, if not to American or Canadian values, perhaps not as different as we would like to believe, then to the more general values of modernism.

It is important to remember that the two countries shared in the massive population movements and in the process exchanged with each other large numbers of their native-born, creating the extensive ties of kinship which are an unusual feature of two neighboring states. In the 130 years between 1820 and 1950 an estimated 3.2 million Canadians (including Newfoundlanders) went to the United States with the peak year of the movement, to emphasize its recency, being 1924.[4] In fact, if Canadians were ever allowed to consider themselves as an ethnic group they would perhaps have now displaced the Russians as the sixth largest national group to have gone to the United States. A good number of these were French from Quebec moving in the last century to the New England textile and forest industries.

Reciprocally, there was the movement of Americans into the Canadian West when the expansion there in the early part of the present century coincided with the end of it in the American West. Then, ". . .the Canadian West received a basic stock of experienced, resourceful, English-speaking North American farmers."[5] Over a million Americans came to Canada between 1897 and 1914, almost as many as from Great Britain, and more than from other sources.[6] It is interesting to note that in the 1970s once again the United States has become a major source of immigrants to Canada. Now they are the highly skilled counterpart of the flow of American capital. Despite the clamor that is made about multiculturalism, neither Canadian officialdom nor the statistics it produces recognize a United States or an American ethnicity— a neighborly rejection of the melting pot process either through a blindness to the existence of a real American type or through a sharp perception that the melting has not taken place after all, and that non-North American ethnicities have survived.

As well as the exchange of their own native-born populations Canada and the United States shared up until 1914 in the large-scale "new" immigration from Europe. Some of these were leap-froggers whose thoughts about where they wanted to go in the New World were less fixed than their determination to leave the old one. Although there can be no strict accounting of this movement there is little doubt that the United States was the net beneficiary. However familiar one might become with the Canadian estimates one is always struck with the observation that between 1850 and 1950 something like 7.1 million people came into Canada, but 6.6 million left leaving net migration to contribute little to population growth.[7] With this great outflow, mostly no doubt to the United States, Canada lost large numbers of both native-born and foreign-born.

Given this confluence of population movements from abroad and between the two countries it might well be expected that in the settlement and the incorporation of immigrants there would be as many parallels as divergencies, and some convergence in the face of tradition-destroying modernization towards a modest cultural pluralism, an escape from the extremes of melting pot and mosaic. If I earlier presented melting pot and mosaic in extreme terms, as polar models of how people of different cultural groups can relate, the revolutionary and the regressive, it is for the purpose of demonstrating that in reality in North America neither approximates the truth, in practice neither has been practicable and neither has been particularly valued by the respective societies despite the rhetoric in prose and poetry that has been devoted to it. The reality, in both countries, lies somewhere between the two poles.

It is doubtful that the melting pot was ever descriptive of the history of intergroup relations in the United States. Even with the old immigration from northern Europe of similar cultural elements there were areas of group settlement where some of the important elements of culture, particularly religion and language, were retained. It is true that common exposure to frontier conditions may have led to similar patterns of response to the physical environment, creating something of a homogeneous technological or material culture and giving the impression of a frontier melting pot, but non-material aspects of culture survived and still do. Moreover, the old immigration, excluding of course the Irish, made up the human element of the expanding frontier, and so its successive flows passed over the old colonial cultures or released native Americans to move further west,[8] thereby lessening the physical contacts under which intergroup conflict might arise, or the first stirrings of the melting pot might have taken place. While many of the old immigration over the generations became assimilated—which is not the same as the melting pot—some retained some degree of ethnic identity through to the present, the Irish perhaps being the most obvious, but Germans and Scandinavians also in some regions of the country.[9]

It is with the new immigration, from Eastern and Southern Europe, very much a rural to urban movement as well as a transoceanic one, that the idea of a melting pot may have been appropriate. However, intergroup hostility and rivalry and even hatred became marked to the extent that it is unlikely that the host society was willing to merge with the newcomers to create a new American type. Racial as well as religious fuel, added by the Irish, helped to heat up the feelings of hostility which many native Americans felt towards the incoming groups. George Washington's feelings about "foreigners among us" were shared strongly on the part of some Americans a century later. There is something of a contradiction in the outbursts of American nativism against those who were the fearful embodiment of alien cultures, or as it was more crudely put in the biological theories of the time, inferior racial stock, but on the other hand were an essential component to the expanding economy. In our day we find an analogous situation in the ambivalence felt in many European countries towards imported labor or guest workers who are essential, but less than welcome. It is a remarkable reflection of American ideals that the newcomers to America, despite the hostility expressed towards them, could acquire citizenship, a status most unwillingly granted by European nations of our epoch.

In the long run American nativism won out with the immigration quotas specifically designed to maintain an Anglo-Saxon dominance. The new immigration laws of the 1920s, which put an end to the laissez-passer system, were the outcome, too, of theories of racial superiority articulated in Europe by Gobineau and Chamberlain, trumpeted by Richard Wagner and echoed in the United States by such writers as Madison Grant. If a melting pot process was taking place, if the "Great Alchemist. . .was fusing. . .with his purging flame," as Zangwill so graphically put it,[10] old Anglo-Saxon Americans were holding back and resisting being drawn into the crucible, to use yet another metaphor employed by romantics to describe what was happening to host and newcomers. Moreover, the block settlement of the frontier was being reproduced in the ghetto settlement of the cities leading to, not the melting pot, but two peculiar patterns of American intergroup relations: ecological invasion and succession so extensively studied by Park and his associates in Chicago; and the entrenchment of ethnic realities in American city politics. The hostility shown to the foreigners of the new immigration, and their languages, which is reflected today in the low level of foreign language training in the United States, scarcely indicated a willingness to forge with them a new culture.

Two forces were working against the melting pot: the superiority felt by the old Americans and the strong communal identities felt by "the unmeltable ethnics," to use Michael Novak's term. It has been pointed out[11] that much of the new immigration was from national ethnic groups whose cultures and primordial identities were suppressed by the great multinational empires of the times, the Russian and the Austro-Hungarian, and that for many of the immigrants their hopes were to save or revive their cultures in the New World. They may have chosen American freedom, seen not so much as the freedom of individual rights, but as collective rights for groups to be able to live their own cultural life away from oppression. Even the settlement houses in American cities created by Americans to assist in immigrant adjustment became shelters for European folkways.[12] In American social structure the myth of the melting pot is too revolutionary to be a statement of reality, however much it might express a universalistic millennium.

If not the melting pot, what does characterize the course of ethnic relations in the United States? The answer as far as it is provided by American sociologists who have studied the matter are two somewhat contrary processes. One is assimilation to the social life of the dominant old Americans, the process which Milton Gordon has called "Anglo-conformity,"[13] and the second is a modest form of cultural pluralism which attests to the strength of ethnic identities across the generations. Initially strong ethnic communal ties developed because of the need for collective self-help in American urban squalor in the heyday of social Darwinism and laissez-faire capitalism. Immigration was linked to labor force needs developing an association between ethnic groups and particular kinds of jobs. As a result the ethnic group became the one which helped to provide protection against exploitation, poverty, and threats to occupational rights. While some of these associations have been retained to the present time, others have disappeared because the members of some groups have been occupationally mobile or because they have taken the assimilation option. In an analysis of the March 1971 Current Population Survey in which respondents were asked what their origin or descent was and were provided a list to choose from such as British, Polish, Italian, and so on, over 30 per cent of men between 18 and 65 classified themselves as "Other" or "Don't know."[14] Most of these, the author of a report on the survey suggests, were mixtures of specified groups or "must have no ethnic identity at all and have forgotten their ancestry." On the other hand, one can find other examples of how ethnic and occupational communities survive sufficiently to belie the melting pot thesis.

The cultural pluralism that has developed in the United States is a very muted one, falling far short of language rights, political representation on an ethnic basis, and separately controlled educational systems. At least that was the case until recently when American non-white ethnic groups, who were never seriously considered as elements in the melting pot, began to demand recognition and redress as members of groups, creating something of a group rights movement in the United States quite different from the principles of individual rights upon which it had been founded and which were central to its revolutionary principles. The demand for community control over schools, for affirmative action in the work world and language rights in the case of Chicanos, Puerto Ricans and other Spanish Americans were expressed by ethnic movements.[15] There was also to burst out the repressed hostility of the descendants of the survivors of the aboriginal peoples of America. If their story is left out of this account it is not because it is any less significant in human terms, but rather because a comparison of Indian policies of the two countries deserves a paper in its own right.

The relative deprivation of non-white ethnic groups in the United States is the main reason for the renewed emphasis on the descent group as one of primal identity and as a protective device, as had been earlier ethnic communal ties among immigrants. Their demands for recognition and redress—quite justified by any ethical standards lest these remarks are misunderstood—has set a new value on ethnicity and means a reversion in the sense of moving back from universalistic principles. If the demands of non-whites were in ethnic terms so were the responses to them. Sometimes ethnic occupational interests were threatened—Jewish school teachers in New York, for example—bringing a response in the same key. If black was beautiful so was Irish and Italian or other parentage. Both melting pot and assimilation were far from complete.

For many who cannot or will not respond to ethnic questions on surveys the ancestral past has been obscured and assimilation to Anglo-conformity has been complete. The "brutal bargain" has been a part of "making it,"[16] of upward occupational mobility, and this occupational assimilation has been achieved at the price of cultural assimilation. Rather than the melting pot it is these assimilative processes involving the loss of ethnic identity on the one hand, and the muted form of ethnic pluralism inherent in the present ethnic revival on the other, which are descriptive of the incorporation of immigrant nationalities in a predominatly "Anglo" America.

If the melting pot is descriptive of neither the attitudes towards nor the reality of immigrant absorption in the United States, the mosaic is equally faulty as an account of the same processes in Canada. One thing is clear: in Canada the phenomenon of mass migration has not attracted the attention of historians as it has in the United States. We have no Marcus Lee Hansen, Oscar Handlin or John Higham concerned to analyse these vast population movements within the framework of charter values and myths. One reason might be that we have few myths, revolutionary or evolutionary, against which to examine the unfolding of our story. Indeed, it is difficult to find any extensive discussion of immigrant adjustment in Canadian historical writing let alone its analysis in terms of some desirable mosaic. If the task of historians is to produce myths and counter-myths they have been particularly silent on the Canadian mosaic. At the most they give a few pages in their general histories. It is remarkable that in a volume of essays entitled *Historical Essays on the Prairie Provinces*[17] the only ones devoted to immigrants or the national origins of the people were on the Mennonites and Hutterites, yet the story of the new immigration to Canada was as dramatic as it was in the United States. One must go back to contemporary accounts such as that of Winnipeg in the first decade of the century by J.S. Woodsworth in *Strangers Within Our Gates*[18] or to ethnic histories themselves such as Senator Paul Yuzyk's *The Ukrainian Peasants in Manitoba.*[19] Not only has the great migration of Europeans to Canada failed to inspire Canadian historians, but they have failed also to create or develop the mosaic concept as the trend in Canadian social development.

The expression "mosaic," as far as one can tell, was coined by an American about ten years after Zangwill created his melting pot image about the many groups that were living together in the growing American cities. Victoria Hayward referred to the varieties of church architecture that grew with the block settlement of prairies as a "mosaic of vast dimensions and great breadth." The book was called *Romantic Canada*[20] and I believe it has not been among the spate of reprinted material that has come with the current wave of Canadian nationalism, perhaps because she was American or because her book has no other merit than its metaphor.

The term was given further currency by John Murray Gibbon in his book published in 1938 entitled *Canadian Mosaic*,[21] with the subtitle, "The Making of a Northern Nation." Originally conceived as a radio program for the Canadian Broadcasting Corporation, the book is a catalogue of the various national groups (they were not called ethnic then) who had come to Canada and of the contributions they had made and could make to Canadian society. Like others which were to appear during the war a couple of years later, the book was aimed at racial (the word then in use) understanding. There is no consistency in the discussion about the incorporation of immigrants since the assimilative implications of the Canadianization program of the Imperial Order Daughters of the Empire are reported without comment, and the I.O.D.E. is identified as one of the organizations cementing the mosaic—to which the book is dedicated. The confusion about the integrative processes taking place is illustrated by the following quotation:

> The Canadian race of the future is being superimposed on the original native Indian races and is being made up of over thirty European racial groups, each of which has its own history, customs and traditions. Some politicians want to see these merged as quickly as possible into one standard type, just as our neighbors in the United States are hurrying to make every citizen a 100 per cent American. Others believe in trying to preserve for the future Canadian race the most worthwhile qualities and traditions that each racial group has brought with it.[22]

Here we have something of an anticipation of the federal government's multicultural program of the 1970s, and since the Gibbon book is largely a recording of folk arts and high culture, and quite neglects culture in the wider anthropological sense, there is a further resemblance. Gibbon made no attempt to discover if the mosaic had any roots in Canadian history or whether there were ideas about incorporating immigrants that might distinguish Canada from the United States. It is unlikely he would have found much since the theme seems to have had little interest for Canadian historians. Neither commanding the attention of the historian nor taking the fancy of the general public, his book was not reprinted.

And so the image of the mosaic is not at all prominent in social comment or historical writing in Canada. Ideas of the melting pot or some version of it in the variety of metaphors, many of them biological, which the subject seems to have prompted, can be more easily found. Writing a piece of war propaganda prepared for radio, and like Gibbon's book concerned with interethnic understanding at a time when some groups might be viewed with suspicion in 1941, Watson Kirkconnell spoke of ". . .the varied human ingredients that history has poured into the huge mixing bowl of Canada's national life," and of the "richness of the national amalgam."[23] A decade later J.M.S. Careless suggested that between 1901 and 1911 "Canada for the first time became what the United States long had been, a melting pot of peoples,"[24] although the group settlement of foreign-born in the West proved the most difficult to absorb.

A.R.M. Lower, who was not reluctant to express what he considered to be the evils of immigration, added to the imagery: "Ukrainians, Hungarians, Poles and Germans all had to be ground through the mill of the public school, taught English and painfully and roughly trained in that English tradition of law and government which was not understood too well by the natives themselves. . . by mid century a new people had been begun in the West, neither 'British' nor 'foreign,' simply Canadian."[25]

While the observation could be construed as suggesting either the melting pot or assimilation to Anglo-conformity, there is certainly nothing of the mosaic in it. It would seem that in Canada, as in the United States, public education was to be the main road to assimilation. "It was taken for granted," wrote W.L. Morton of European newcomers to Manitoba in the early part of the present century, "that they would be and should be assimilated, and it was to this end that the flag legislation of 1906 had been directed and that the agitation for compulsory school attendance was now being raised."[26]

In his more recently published account of immigration and colonization in Canada to 1903,[27] Norman Macdonald has managed to confuse the two images in a chapter entitled, "The Melting Pot Era: Group Settlement," suggesting at least that neither of them was particularly salient during the long period of immigration which he surveys.

If, as in the United States with the image of the melting pot, in Canada the image of the mosaic is difficult to locate in charter mythology or historical writing, one might look to immigration policy as it was formulated by governments and discussed by public commentators. If one wanted to locate the origin of the mosaic it might be tempting to start with the reserve system of block land grants to national and religious groups in the early phase of prairie settlement in the 1870s. There was a kind of official desperation about the Canadian government's attempt to make Canada more attractive than the U.S., which was getting the bulk of European immigration. To do this they were prepared to reserve blocks of land for particular national groups whose members might settle together and maintain their old national ways even, as in the case of the Mennonites in Manitoba, overlooking the provisions of the

Dominion land policy to provide for common rather than individual ownership.[28] Blocks of land were set aside for Mennonites, Germans, Icelanders, Hungarians, and Doukhobors, some of it through group negotiation rather than by a flow of individuals. The Canadian Pacific Railway and the Canadian government, who at that time may have been considered identical, shared a desire to populate the newly opened spaces, hence the tendency to recognize collective rights over individual rights in matters like landholding and the schooling of children, questions which over time were to become greatly disputed. The U.S. government legislated against this practice, but the difference between the two governments was not so much because of differing views about whether they were creating melting pots or mosaics, but rather because of Canada's desire to get people to the West.

Although the block settlement in Canada, both negotiated and free, as a response to the need for settlers, may have been initiated in a different fashion than in the United States, the outcomes were probably not that different. In the westward expansion national groups would congregate together. Perhaps the main difference was the far greater hardships suffered by the settlers in Canada than in the United States, where in large measure already opened land was purchased from native Americans.[29] However, there is no reason to suppose that the community life based on national origins would be more intense in Canada than in the United States. By this time in the United States the hardship was in the cities, and in the role of overcoming it national communities probably were no less important there than in rural Canada. It is difficult then really to differentiate the melting pot and mosaic in the processes of settlement in the two countries.

Another important parallel between the two countries can be found in the discussions about how much immigration and from where. In Canada, there was certainly little of the generosity displayed towards other nations and other cultures which would be necessary for the building of a cultural mosaic. The Canadian counterpart of American nativism, expressed by the group whom Carl Berger has called the Canadian imperialists, was aimed, as in the United States, against the new immigration from eastern and southern Europe. Canada, thought G.R. Parkin, was to belong to ". . .the sturdy races of the North-Saxon and Celt, Scandinavian, Dane and Northern German."[30] Parkin and others thought Canada had a purifying ally in its climate and for that reason felt that the disastrous effects of the new immigration in the United States could be avoided.[31] While it could have been a matter of dispute whether natural selection would work better in the pure air of a harsh prairie winter or the overcrowded slums of American cities,

Parkin thought the United States was welcome to Hungarians, Poles, and Italians and what Canada needed was "more of the hardy German and Norwegian races."[32]

In the early part of the present century Sir Clifford Sifton's[33] search for his stalwart peasants for prairie development gave rise to concern not only in Winnipeg, but also in Toronto and Montreal. No one was to be more persistently against non-British immigration throughout his life than Stephen Leacock. He thought a small number of eastern Europeans might, "like a minute dose of poison in a medicine,"[34] be helpful. In an address to the Canadian Club of Ottawa in the first decade of this century, he said, "Poles, Hungarians, Bukowinians and any others. . . will come in to share the heritage which our fathers have won. Out of all these we are to make a kind of mixed race in which is to be the political wisdom of the British, the chivalry of the French, the gall of the Galician, the hungriness of the Hungarian and the dirtiness of the Doukobor."[35]

Many English-Canadian writers were caught up in the strident tones of the racial phobias of the time. One denounced the melting pot in saying ". . .that instead of the pure race from which we have come, we shall have a mongrel race, and this mongrel race is making itself known in Canada as a result of the immigration we have had."[36] That was in 1920. There was more of the so-called undesirable immigration to come before it stopped almost entirely at the time of the Great Depression.

It is impossible to know whether these influential writers and men of affairs were reflecting or moulding public opinion, but there is little in the sentiments they expressed to conclude that Canada was building a plural society. Although it might have been preferable in their view to keep the foreigners out, once they were in the country the ideal method of their absorption was Anglo-conformity, or Anglo-Canadianization and there was a general faith that Canadian-British education and institutions would do their work and all these people and their descendants could be accommodated to the benefit of empire. Education was certainly to play a role. In *The Education of the New Canadian*, J.T. Anderson, a one-time premier of Saskatchewan, wrote in 1918, "No better material can be found among our newcomers from which to mould a strong type of Canadian citizen than is found among these Ruthenians."[37]

There is little then in Canadian history that suggests an image of the Canadian future as one of ethnic pluralism. The United States and Canada have been remarkably alike in attitudes towards immigration and desirable types of immigrants. Both, in time, became exclusive in immigration policy, the United States with its blunt instrument of quotas and Canada with its more subtle understandings of preferability. It may seem strange that the two countries with their different histories and their different archetypes and preferred fantasies—revolution and evolution if they are the correct labels—should have run parallel with respect to immigrants and how they should be absorbed into the developing social structure. These parallels seem surprising since there are several reasons to expect that the two countries might have taken different courses.

One is that Canada remained a British colony until 1867, and after that British influences remained strong not only in those areas where the British government retained some constitutional prerogatives. As we hear so often there was no revolutionary rejection of the past aimed at creating free institutions. Rather what were sought were new arrangements that might lead to better exploitation of a vast hinterland. Sir John A. Macdonald's desire to die a British subject was never seriously threatened, and the great heroes of Canadian railway building bought their way into or were rewarded with seats in the British House of Lords. Indeed until the 1930s Canadians of distinction, dubious or merited, might legitimately aspire to ennoblement by the British monarch without losing their Canadian citizenship. Even that recent penalty does not undermine the high status which Canadian-born press peers enjoy in their country of origin. One had to wait until the present Governor General to have a head of state whose plain and austere tailoring is without monarchical trappings. These strong British links might have resulted in less tolerance towards non-British immigrants than in the United States, but Americans seemed no more tolerant than Canadians toward those nationalities which American nativism saw as responsible for "the passing of the great race," that is, the Anglo-Saxon.

Canada's links with Britain survived that country's ever-falling proportion of the population, 43 per cent in 1971. That proportion still makes it an important minority and accounts for the continuing strong cultural linkages. Moreover, throughout its history Canada has always seen Britain as the major and preferred source of immigrants. Although they no longer make up a majority of newcomers, the British are still the largest of the incoming groups which have become greatly varied in recent years. Up to the present day the British have retained their special place in the elite structure of Canadian society.

A second reason why it might have been expected that Canada and the United States would develop differently in the way in which immigrants would be incorporated in the society is the fact that Canada was a binational state from the beginning. The uneasy tolerance which French and English were to show towards each other was not extended to foreigners who resisted assimilation or were believed to be unassimilable. The French were no more welcoming to outsiders than were the British and their hostility to a pluralism beyond the historic dualism is as strong as ever in the present day.

Among English Canadians at times even the binationalism of Canada was in question. Religion and racial conflict, exemplified by the battle over bilingual schools in Ontario, Manitoba, and the North-West, Orangeism, and the British Empire orientations of the Toronto "imperialists" created ambivalence about the future of the French within Canadian society. There were even thoughts that ultimately the French would assimilate to Anglo-conformity so taken would they be by British institutions, and indeed French-Canadian collaborating elites seemed to accept ennoblement by the British monarch as readily as their English-Canadian counterparts. The less ethnocentric of the articulating British in the early part of the century romanticised about the survival of French-Canadian culture, but saw it as no threat because of what they hoped would be boundless British immigration. It is a remarkable fact of Canadian demographic history that unlike the ever diminishing proportion of British, the French have managed to retain their proportion of the population at around 30 per cent through the present century with scarcely more than a trickle of immigrants.

The French always seem to have been conscious of the threat which immigration posed to them in terms of both cultural survival and economic development. Consequently, towards the end of the last century when the great waves of immigration were passing over them, the Quebec officials looked for immigrants in France, Belgium, and Switzerland, and more importantly, for they were seen as the most likely to respond, to the French Canadians in New England. Thus repatriation of their own rather than a search of the world for others was Quebec's response at the height of the human movement across the Atlantic. Neither the European Francophone nor the expatriate French Canadians responded with enthusiasm.[38]

Rather than foster a tolerance towards pluralism Canada's fundamental duality might well have worked against it. In Manitoba one of the reasons given for withdrawing the right of the French to French-speaking schools at the turn of the century was that all national groups that were being swept in by immigration would demand their own language rights and thereby hinder the process of assimilation. Those rights were taken away in 1915.[39]

Although the French up to the period after the Second World

War continued to express hostility to immigration and its predominantly British character there is very little they were able to do about it because English-Canadian politicians were skilful in countering Quebec's objections. The development of immigration policy rested primarily with the federal government that implemented it through the activities and location of its immigration offices abroad. The French were to become bitter critics of federal policy and of what they perceived as its discriminatory character until finally they set up their own immigration department in 1968.[40]

The French saw their own falling birth rates and the continuing Anglo-assimilation of non-English ethnic groups in Montreal as major threats to the survival of their culture. The act which set up the immigration department in Quebec in 1968 made some slight acknowledgment of pluralism by including among its responsibilities, in addition to all the usual tasks of an immigration department, the preservation of ethnic customs, but this was in the late 1960s when the revival of ethnicity had well begun, and so is a reflection of contemporary events rather than historical values. Moreover, Quebec was faced with the same conflict of interest as any other host society wanting to attract newcomers: on the one hand the need to integrate them in Quebec society and to teach them French, and on the other hand to make the assimilative process more attractive by allowing the preservation of ethnic customs. It was a particular conflict for the French, who so intimately link language and culture. Their dilemma was nowhere more acute than in the Quebec reaction to the federal government's multicultural program in 1971. "You will have gathered," wrote Premier Bourassa to Prime Minister Trudeau shortly after, "that Quebec does not accept your government's approach to the principle of multiculturalism."[41] The position of the Quebec government and of Quebec intellectuals seemed to be that multiculturalism would detract from the essential Canada that was bilingual and bicultural, conditions which should prevail if Canada was to survive. "Je veux souligner que pour la communauté canadienne-française, cette nouvelle politique multiculturelle représente un immense pas en arrière dont, je crois, les Canadiens français n'ont pas encore pris conscience."[42]

There is, however, one curious way in which Canada's duality might be a reason for the saliency of ethnicity which now exists and which has helped to keep national origin groups alive, and that is the effect the duality has had on the Canadian census. Before Confederation in 1867 the censuses which were taken classified the population as "French origin," "not of French origin," and "Indian." Out of that simple and logical classification has grown, to account for the large and varied immigration, the complex one we know today.

Although there was some inconsistency in the censuses after Confederation, generally "origin" was defined as the birthplace of the individual or that of his paternal ancestor before coming to North America. Over time, as immigrants came increasingly from Europe and as international boundaries changed, the problem of an origin classification became more complicated. The matter was not helped by the fact that census administrators were never quite sure what they were about.

There is a good illustration in the discussion of the origin question in the 1931 census. (Here one is following a lead suggested some time ago by Joel Smith that an examination of how the two countries have treated ethnicity in their respective censuses would be an indication of orientation to melting pot or mosaic.)[43]

> It is a well known fact that there are "Austrian," "Swiss," and "Prussian" types of Germans, and if these regard themselves as belonging to separate races, it is a question whether this distinction should not be carried out in Census enumeration. If a distinction is made between Norwegian and Dane, it seems reasonable to distinguish between Austrian and Prussian. . . .

> The question may arise as to whether a grouping of ten races, some of them differing widely, is of value, even though the grouping is done solely to effect an adequate comparison between censuses. The answer mainly depends upon the particular purpose for which the information is required. Such a grouping has little or no value for ethnical study, but it is doubtful that this has ever been the purpose of taking a census of races. When the races have fused and their differentiation is no longer important from a *social* point of view, a census of races will be unnecessary but, up to the present time, the races in Canada show several important points of differentiation which are of great social significance.[44]

One is left wondering what racial fusion might have meant in the minds of these officials, but the fact that they thought it might come is some further evidence that the mosaic is not firmly rooted in the Canadian past.

In the preparation for the 1961 census the Canadian government under John Diefenbaker, who felt very keenly that hyphenated Canadianism was undesirable, attempted to get rid of the ethnic question. Strong resistance came from the French who might have been satisfied with a language question—say language first learned in childhood—except that there would then be no way of measuring French descendants who had lost their language, and thus assimilated. It is only by measuring this phenomenon that the threat to French survival in Canada could be monitored. By the time of the preparation of the 1971 census the ethnic revival was well begun, the Royal Commission on Bilingualism and Biculturalism had exploited what it could of the ethnic data of the 1961 census, and so it became increasingly difficult to abandon it.

One of the working documents in the preparation of the 1971 census dealt with the ethnic question. "This question," it said, "has given rise in the past to emotional feelings on the part of respondents but while its inclusion is sometimes criticized, there is a heavier demand for data on ethnicity than on most other items."[45] The listing of pros and cons for including the ethnic question indicated the difficulties surrounding it. For example:

> Great use is made of census data on ethnicity by national and cultural organizations who are anxious to retain their identity.

> A cross-classification of ethnic groups with mother tongue or language now spoken provides a good measure of the degree of assimilation of different groups.

> Collection of data on ethnic groups is viewed in some quarters as tending to perpetuate distinctions along ethnic lines to the detriment of Canadian society as a whole.

> This question irritates some respondents who think of themselves as Canadian but are expected to report themselves as English, Irish, Norwegian or some other nationality with which they no longer associate themselves.[46]

If these officials were alert to public feelings on the issue, and they probably were since representations would have been made to them, it was clear that even at this late date there appeared to be no clear commitment to mosaic or melting pot for Canadian society.

With all its sociological absurdities the question was included in 1971. It has long been known that the question has provided a very unreliable picture of ethnic structure. Even in 1971 the census planners were saying, "There is a relatively high degree of reporting error since respondents may not know their ethnic background."[47] The absurdity of the question lies in requiring the citizen to answer, "To what ethnic or cultural group did you or your ancestor (on the male side) belong on coming to this continent." The exclusive patrilineal descent ignores the important socializing and cultural role of the mother, particularly in language learning. Moreover, it does not allow for a Canadian or American ethnicity, except for native Indian and Eskimo. Census administrators, somewhat exasperated, have dealt with the few who insisted on reporting Canadian or American by classifying them under "Other."

Thus the picture we have of the ethnic structure of Canada is an artifact of the census. It requires all Canadians to have an ethnicity whether they feel it or not. The American census, which has had only a birthplace question and not an ethnic origin one, has been clear throughout as Joel Smith pointed out with this quotation from the American census of 1880:

> . . .the census statistics will often appear inadequate to the facts of population. Thus a visitor in Cincinnati is likely to be told that in that section of the city which is called "Over the Rhine" there are 90,000 Germans. In one sense of the word German this may be true. It is not incorrect to speak of a child of German parents, perhaps himself speaking the German language and living in a community almost exclusively of that nationality, as a German. But this is not the point of view of the census law. For the purpose of the tables immediately following, those only are Germans or Irish, or French, who were born in Germany, Ireland or France. Their children born on the soil of the United States are known and ranked as Americans.[48]

So a new nationality or ethnicity takes root—by law! The outcomes of the law are not, however, clear. Does the fact that in a survey in 1971 at least 30 per cent of men could not give their ethnicity indicate a measure of success in creating a new nation, in the assimilation and melting of immigrants, or does the continued vitality of ethnic groups in American society suggest that the primordial links are more secure than supposed? There are some interesting parallel Canadian data on this matter of wanting to identify not with the past but with the present. In a 1972 national survey involving a very large sample for the purpose of analysing occupational mobility, respondents were asked the census question on ethnic origin in order to determine the effects of ethnicity on mobility. But they were also asked another question immediately following, "To which ethnic or cultural group do you feel that you now belong?" As responses, "American" and "Canadian" were allowed as well as those which appeared in the census responses.

The results show strikingly that most Canadians identify more strongly with Canada than with their "origin" groups. Eighty-six per cent chose Canadian as the cultural group to which they now felt they belonged. When the foreign-born are taken out about nine-tenths of male respondents saw themselves as Canadian. Thus while in the United States the objective of the census law to obliterate descent group identification after the first generation has not been an unqualified success, neither has the Canadian census been wholly successful in providing a picture of Canadian ethnic structure which would correspond to a set of identities. It might be surmised that in the long and difficult history of migration to the New World the migrants in leaving their place of origin sought to identify, because of their aspirations if nothing else, with their new country. However, the difficulties that they faced, two world wars and the recognition of old and new nationalities that followed the wars, and the resurgence of nationalism and demands for self-determination have had for the descendants of these immigrants a countereffect. In both the United States and Canada neither the metaphors of mosaic nor of melting pot are apt descriptions of what has taken place.

We have to look not to their histories or to their charter values of revolution and evolution—if these are not themselves questionable labels—but to the recent past and the worldwide revival of ethnicity to understand why, in both countries, ethnicity has found new strengths expressed in Canada by multiculturalism and in the United States by the return to the old idea of a nation of nations. Ethnicity became salient in both countries in response to similar internal and world conditions.

The revival of ethnicity after the Second World War brought into question the dominant trend to Anglo-conformity in both Canada and the United States, and can be traced to several sources. There was first of all decolonization when European powers were forced to retreat from their former empires in the face of nationalist movements of liberation, which, after initial success, were in turn to revive traditional tribal hostilities finding expression in the gamut from separatism from the new nation to outright genocide. Often the European retreat was not accomplished without bitter struggles greatly heightening the sense of peoplehood on the part of those who had been colonized. The war in Vietnam was another factor because it appeared that the United States was assuming the role of white domination in the affairs of the world. There were also the émigrés from eastern Europe who feared that the socialist revolutions were obliterating national cultures and that these had to be preserved by émigré communities. In Canada, postwar émigrés played an important part in strengthening the ethnic identities of earlier arrivals and second and third generations. There was also reaction against the large centralized and powerful states where tensions between centre and periphery, metropolis and hinterland were ethnic tensions. Devolution as it developed in contemporary Britain could be viewed as an accommodation to ethnic demands by the Celtic fringe. In France, too, peripheral regions contained ethnic and linguistic groups who sought to free themselves.

Within North America perhaps the most important forces in the revival of ethnicity were the existence in both Canada and the United States of large deprived minorities whose positions, although very different in the two countries, called for redress. The civil rights movement in the United States, the civil rights legislation and the equal opportunity legislation had their counterparts in Canada with the extended proceedings of the Royal Commission on Bilingualism and Biculturalism and the subsequent legislation on language rights, bilingual districts, and French representation in the federal public service.

These developments, often because they had repercussions in the occupational structures, raised the consciousness of other minorities, and eventually women. So we find ourselves in the decade of the organized minorities demanding rights as members of groups rather than as individuals, and making ethnic affiliation or descent group identification an essential part of a person's selfhood. The revival, as shown by the extensive review in the book edited by Glazer and Moynihan,[49] is worldwide. Many view it with approval because they feel that these primordial havens provide a new stability in the merging mass societies and "global villages." Thus Canada's mosaic, scarcely adumbrated in its historical development, took on its firm design in the postwar years and at the same time the fires were dampened under America's melting pot.

It is difficult to say what future course the modest cultural pluralism which has followed from these developments might take. Stronger ethnic group identification, a more sharply delineated mosaic, could be viewed as a reversion to the saliency of endogamous descent groups as a principle of social organization with all the dangers of invidious rankings and comparisons where such types of social organization have existed. A melting pot course towards the development of a universalistic modern character and culture emphasizing common human qualities and the unity of mankind and shedding the particularisms of history continues as the revolutionary option. In the revolution, human history and human cultures need not be forgotten or abandoned; they might simply be released from the custody of the descent group to the responsibility of all.[50] One might hazard a judgment that despite the current revival of ethnicity the United States veers more towards the revolution than does Canada.

Notes

1. Quoted in Samuel S. Busey, *Immigration: Its Evils and Consequences*, New York, 1856, reprinted by Arno Press, New York, 1969.

2. Geoffrey Gorer, *The Americans*, London, 1948, 13.

3. Israel Zangwill, *The Melting Pot*, New York, 1909.

4. Oscar Handlin, *Immigration as a Factor in American History*, New York, 1959, 16.

5. J.B. Brebner, *North Atlantic Triangle*, Toronto, 1945, 227.

6. *Ibid.*

7. The original estimates are those of Nathan Keyfitz. See the discussion in John Porter, *The Vertical Mosaic*, Toronto, 1965, 29–30.

8. Marcus Lee Hansen, *The Immigrant in American History* reprinted in Oscar Handlin, *op. cit.*, 43 ff.

9. See the discussion in Nathan Glazer, "Ethnic Groups in America," in Morroe Berger, *et al., Freedom and Control in Modern Society*, New York, 1954, 156.

10. In *The Melting Pot*, quoted in Oscar Handlin, *op. cit.*, 150.

11. See e.g. Nathan Glazer, *op. cit.*, 167 ff.

12. John Higham, *Strangers in the Land*, New York, 1969, 121.

13. Milton M. Gordon, *Assimilation in American Life*, New York, 1964.

14. Geoffrey Carliner, "Has The Melting Pot Worked?" Institute for Research in Poverty, University of Wisconsin, Madison, 1975, mimeo.

15. In their foreword to the revised edition of *Beyond The Melting Pot*, Cambridge, 1970, Nathan Glazer and Daniel P. Moynihan use the terms "ethnic group status" and "separatism" to describe the alternative possible developments of ethnic group relations in 1970, p. xxiii. They seem convinced of a movement away from assimilation in the direction of a less muted pluralism than now exists.

16. For an insightful account see Norman A. Podhoretz, *Making It*, London, 1968.

17. Donald Swainson, Toronto, 1970.

18. Missionary Society of the Methodist Church, 1909.

19. Toronto, 1953.

20. New York, 1922.

21. Toronto, 1938. The term had also been used in a Y.W.C.A. publication in 1926 by Kate Foster.

22. John Murray Gibbon, *Canadian Mosaic*, Toronto, 1938, vii.

23. Watson Kirkconnell, *Canadians All*, Directorate of Public Information, Ottawa, 1941, 7.

24. J.M.S. Careless, *Canada: A Story of Challenge*, Toronto, 1953, 304.

25. A.R.M. Lower, *Colony to Nation*, Toronto, 1957, 429–430.

26. W.L. Morton, *Manitoba: A History*, Toronto, 1957, 297.

27. Norman Macdonald, *Canada: Immigration and Colonization*, Toronto, 1966.

28. *Ibid.*, 201.

29. Marcus Lee Hansen, quoted in Oscar Handlin, *Immigration as a Factor in American History*, 45.

30. Quoted in Carl Berger, *The Sense of Power*, Toronto, 1970, 131.

31. *Ibid.*

32. *Ibid.*, 147.

33. The minister in the Laurier government responsible for immigration.

34. *Economic Prosperity in the British Empire*, Toronto, 1930, 195.

35. Quoted in Berger, *op. cit.*, 151.

36. *Ibid.*

37. Quoted in Gibbon, *op. cit.*, 301.

38. Macdonald, *op. cit.*, 99–100.

39. W.J. Morton, "Manitoba Schools and Canadian Nationality, 1890–1923," in *Minorities, Schools, and Politics*, University of Toronto Press Historical Readings, No. 7.

40. Freda Hawkins, *Canada and Immigration*, Montreal, 1972, 227.

41. Howard Palmer, ed., *Immigration and the Rise of Multiculturalism*, Toronto, 1975, 151.

42. Guy Rocher, "Les Ambiguités d'un Canada bilingue et multiculturel," *Le Québec en Mutation*, Montreal, 1973.

43. Joel Smith, "Melting Pot-Mosaic, Consideration for a Prognosis," in *Minorities North and South*, Proceedings of the Third Inter-Collegiate Conference on Canadian-American Relations, Michigan State University, 1968.

44. *Seventh Census of Canada*, 1931, Vol. 1, 235.

45. Census Division, Dominion Bureau of Statistics, "The 1971 Census of Population and Housing, Development of Subject Matter Content," mimeo, Ottawa, 1969, 13.

46. *Ibid.*

47. *Ibid.*

48. Quoted in Joel Smith, *op. cit.*

49. Nathan Glazer and Daniel P. Moynihan, *Ethnicity: Theory and Experience*, Harvard University Press, Cambridge, 1975.

50. I have dealt with this notion in greater length in "Ethnic Pluralism in Canadian Perspective," in Glazer and Moynihan, *op. cit.* That paper is reprinted in the present volume.

7

Mr. Trudeau and Canadian Federalism

Social institutions are based on habit. It is, therefore, a good first principle of social analysis to assume that, short of a revolution, things are more likely to remain as they are than to change. Even at dramatic historical events when we are poised eagerly or fearfully for change, a built-in stabilizing mechanism—custom and habit—comes into play to re-establish equilibrium at some point not too far off where change began. In Canada the most recent dramatic event which seemed to herald headlong change was the election of the Parti Quebecois in 1976. But it was not long before equilibrating forces came into operation and the Lévesque government's posture rapidly adapted to the habitual haggling that had previously marked Quebec-Ottawa relations, and the concept of separatism came increasingly to look like that of the old special status.

Perhaps it is this inertia of social habit that makes it possible for a paper on Canadian federalism written in 1968 (at the beginning of the Trudeau era from which so much change was expected) to be still relevant. Mr. Trudeau's views about how the Canadian polity should develop took no special clairvoyancy to predict because he had written it all out before and published it in English at the time of his projection onto the national political stage. Curiously, many commentators, and even some who were to become members of his cabinet, never read Federalism and the French Canadians *and were surprised at some of the ways Trudeau sought to change federal-provincial relations and to make constitutional reforms.*

Since I had some familiarity with Trudeau's writings I thought, when I was invited to give a paper at the Department of Political Science at Duke University in the spring of 1968, I would try to forecast, should Mr. Trudeau win his first election as prime minister, how the structure of Canadian federalism might take shape under his leadership. I do not wish to make any great claims to have been prescient, but much of what I suggested would happen did happen, and the pattern of provincial-federal relations with its unending squabbling has been a continuing and constant feature of Canadian politics, all the more so as provincial governments have become stronger, in terms of the disposition of tax dollars, than formerly.

Although this paper is about federalism and Canadian political structure, it is not out of place, in my view, in a set of papers concerned primarily with problems of equality in Canada. In Trudeau's view, equalization grants to the provinces are an important federal responsibility and a means through which the poorer provinces might achieve equality with the others in areas like education and health care. It is difficult to know how, other than in the statistical sense, provinces can be "poor." People are poor, and some of their poverty could be caused by protected privilege and regressive policies within provinces which in no way change through equalization transfers. To equalize provincial averages in some resource need not affect within-province distributions. Yet constitutional dogma remains that (beyond the transfer payments for childhood and old age) the federal government should not tax to give grants directly to Canadians but should "equalize" through provincial governments.

Thus, with all its legal and political sophistry, federalism can stand as a formidable barrier to equality. Mr. Trudeau does not agree, of course. As he puts it, "Federalism must be welcomed as a valuable tool which permits dynamic parties to plant socialist governments in certain provinces, from which the seed of radicalism can slowly spread."

The paper, "Mr. Trudeau and Canadian Federalism," contains also some public opinion data on attitudes to federal and provincial governments from a survey undertaken in 1965. If the governors think this is a difficult country to govern, the governed are very confused about their governors. Whether Trudeau has improved matters for either governed or governors, as he so clearly wished to do, there is no way of knowing for certain. I suspect at the most any change is glacial.

TRUDEAU'S FEDERALISM

The last year has been an unusual and exciting one in Canadian politics. The great binge of centennial celebrations and Expo 67 distorted our views of reality, and helped to inflate our economy. Two leadership conventions have brought new persons and personalities to head our major national parties. The government suffered the unusual humiliation, even for a minority government, of being defeated in the House of Commons on a money bill, thus precipitating a parliamentary crisis. There was a spectacular conference of federal and provincial political leaders. Now we are in the middle of a general election. From a scarcely noticeable point on the horizon, to become the dominating landmark on the Canadian political landscape, has loomed the presence of Pierre Elliott Trudeau.

It is not surprising, therefore, that many observers are talking about the "new politics." But as with old products which are rewrapped every year and put on the supermarket shelves as "NEW," the newness of politics is often no more than package-deep, as least as far as policies are concerned. The new prime minister has been called many things, but the most ominous label I have heard attached to him is "Mackenzie King in a Mercedes." If that is so, and there may well be truth in that considering Trudeau's own assertion of his pragmatic approach to problems and his coldly smooth takeover of power, then political packaging is wondrous indeed!

One development which contributes to the appearance of newness is the way in which Canadian politics is being put in new containers by a greatly expanded corps of political journalists. One gets the impression in Ottawa, from the increased facilities for the press, that there are more journalists on Parliament Hill than there are politicians. Television has brought to Canadian politics a new dimension, the consequences of which are not at the moment possible to assess. In the recent fiasco over the government's defeat on its tax measures, when the opposition tried to argue that the government was no longer in power, the foyer of Parliament became a television studio which most of the party leaders were happy to use since they had pretty much rendered the Commons itself speechless. The two leadership conventions have been closely planned and organized around television in a way which is new. Also the federal-provincial conference of prime ministers and premiers (and a federal minister of justice) performed their act entirely before television cameras. One can surmise that at the expressive and symbolic level of politics—which no doubt is important—this phenomenon is something new for Canada. One is reminded, however, of Lord Keynes' observation that political decisions are not made in monkey houses, and brought back to the reality that there is a politics taking place off-camera and it is deeply rooted in the continuing rigidities of social structure. (The state of Canadian political science being what it is, I doubt if any Canadian department has a project analysing the effects of this new element in Canadian politics.)

The ephemeral and superficial qualities of our "new look" in politics has been the product of the political journalist turned gossip columnist. Political journalists produce their daily drivel (a term once used by Mr. Pearson to describe the efforts of one well-known columnist), search out the sensational, the inside dope, and show more interest in the prime minister's birth certificate and whom he kisses than in his views on Canadian society. These views can be found in his collection of papers, *Federalism and the French Canadians*,[1] which contains more answers to what he stands for than are to be solicited through the inane questioning of the press conference and the television interview. One gets the impression that the prime minister has been brought to his present position by the mass media, and in the process he himself has found his new milieu of the television lights and the autograph seekers congenial—in fact he has said so. One can see in the trade-offs between political leaders and political journalists that symbiosis which binds together those who live for politics and those who live off politics.

One is struck by how abysmally ignorant some of these journalists are. We lack the sophisticated political journalism that one finds in Washington or in Paris. Whatever their merits the mass media are playing a new role in Canadian politics and this new element needs very much to be studied. The academic investigator has to set aside all the current fanfare and try to go below the superficialities to discover whether or not there are any changes and if so what the trends are. The task is sobering and unspectacular and I say that more in envy than in self-righteousness, because the answers do not come to me as readily as they appear to come to so many.

There is a difference between new styles, if that is what we have, and new policies. In political systems, as in other social spheres, practices are based on habit and so have a built-in conservative quality of inflexibility, of obstinancy. The Canadian political system has been unable to provide leadership, to give coherence, to define, and to mobilize resources to achieve goals for Canada as a total society. Trudeau has very clear views about how the Canadian polity should work. If he *really* becomes prime minister on June 25th he will face an enormous challenge. If he succeeds we can, I think, look forward to a very significant shift in federal-provincial relations which could have far-reaching consequences for Canada at the threshold of the postindustrial, postmodern, or "active" society. I want to do two things. First of all to look at Trudeau's theory of Canadian federalism in the light of current social requirements, and secondly, to present some attitudinal data on the public evaluation of the federal system of government.

We now have a prime minister who not only reads books, but writes them. (It is tempting to recall that an earlier prime minister wrote about industry and humanity before entering politics and later concluded, in the exigencies of performing the art of the possible, that it was more important to prevent than to accomplish.) Thus Trudeau's views put forward in *Federalism and the French Canadians* may be softened in the face of the intractability of Canadian life, but it is important to know what his views are.

Mr. Trudeau is a constitutional conservative, as he says, "Essentially a constitution is designed to last a long time."[2] He believes that the British North America Act was, and continues to be, in the main, a satisfactory instrument by which to govern Canada even with the complex changes which have come about in the one hundred years since it was enacted. The division of powers between the federal and provincial governments needs very little change because it enables each level of government to satisfactorily discharge its obligations: ". . .our Canadian constitution gives provinces the widest possible jurisdiction in matters of social security."[3] The main trouble with Canadian federalism has been that the federal government has encroached on provincial responsibilities particularly after the Second World War, while the provincial governments have willingly or unwittingly allowed federal encroachment. As far as the constitution is concerned the provincial governments have all the powers they need if they are given back their taxing rights by the centralizing federal government.

Perhaps Mr. Trudeau reflects his legal training, because he does not support Canadian federalism with the usual arguments about cultural pluralism and cultural particularism, although he does not ignore these. He must relegate them to a less important role because he rejects the embodiment of French-Canadian nationalism in the Quebec state, and he rejects ethnocentricity as the basis of political units. Rather the main purpose of federalism is to prevent monolithic power concentrated in one centre. Federal systems ". . .divide the exercise of sovereignty between the various levels of government, and give none of them full powers over the citizen."[4] Federalism serves the theory of checks and balances. It creates counterweights, competition, and creative tensions between provinces and between the federal government and the provinces. "Since regionalisms do exist in Canada, such feelings should be exploited to further the cause of democracy: each community might enter into a state of healthy competition with the others in order to have better 'self-government'; thus the whole Canadian system of government would be improved by creative tensions between the central, the provincial, and even the municipal administrations."[5] In the early 1960s he was advising his socialist friends that contrary to all their theorizing about the need for strong central government to implement socialist policies, provincial autonomy could be the vehicle through which socialism could be realized. "Federalism must be welcomed as a valuable tool which permits dynamic parties to plant socialist governments in certain provinces, from which the seed of radicalism can slowly spread."[6]

Federalism, moreover, can better ensure democracy by bringing some important governmental operations close to the people. Thus the fathers of Confederation were wise to put such things as education, welfare, property, and so forth within provincial jurisdiction and to leave such far away things as external affairs and defence in federal hands. Mr. Trudeau accepts the fact that the federal government has an important role in economic stabilization and in the equalization of living standards among the provinces to be achieved by fiscal transfers, but he warns us very firmly about the growth of centralized, paternalistic federal power. It is only when the two levels of government stick closely to their own constitutional responsibilities that the electorate knows which to hold accountable for what; otherwise, as he puts it, ". . .the democratic control of power becomes impossible."[7]

It is incorrect to consider Mr. Trudeau's liberalism firmly rooted in the nineteenth century, as some have said. He is quite positive in his assertions about the role of government in improving the quality of social and cultural life, the need for welfare services, and so forth. But he is equally positive that the federal government has no role in these through shared programs if there is no constitutional basis for such sharing in well-defined concurrent powers—and that rules out any constitutional sophistry about the "power of the purse" or the "spending power." The federal government has no constitutional grounds for taxing citizens to perform provincial functions, and on no subject is he more adamant than federal aid to universities—not just education but to universities. Nowhere is he more eloquent in his denunciation of constitutional impropriety than in his paper, "Federal Government Grants to Universities," written in 1957.

> If, for example, a province began to tax its electorate for the purpose of financing the Canadian Army, giving as its excuse that Ottawa was too poor to protect us from the threat of Russian invasion; or if Ottawa regularly subsidized the construction of schools in all provinces on the pretext that the provinces did not pay sufficient attention to education, these governments would be attacking the very foundation of the federal system, which as I have pointed out, does not give any government the right to meddle in the affairs of others.[8]

On federal government aid to education he makes an interesting (and no doubt vital from his point of view) distinction between equalization and centralization. Equalization grants redistribute money from the wealthier provinces to the poorer ones. How these are used is for provincial governments to decide. Federal grants to universities were offered to all provinces regardless of their respective wealth and according to a single schedule of payment. As Trudeau writes, ". . .the federal government collects funds from all ten provinces and redistributes them to all ten provinces, to finance a service that is not within its jurisdiction. This may be called centralization, but certainly not equalization."[9]

If provincial governments are dilatory, inefficient, backward, reactionary, and do not provide the quality of services that their citizens wish, then they will throw the government out at the next election, and this will be more easily done when the responsibilities are clear, but cannot be if they are blurred. For the citizens who desire medicare or higher education for their children, do they fire the federal Liberals for refusing to provide these or do they fire their provincial governments? The present confusion of powers, of shared programs, of opting-out formulas, leaves the electorate completely confused. There should be no question of regional poverty preventing the provision of services, because equalization payments will have taken care of such disparities. Thus, in the wide range of services, by which in the modern industrialized world governments are judged, provincial governments alone are responsible for quality, for performance, and for priorities. For all this no constitutional changes are required, only constitutional observance.

There are ways in which Mr. Trudeau would change the constitution, but these changes would not involve the division of powers. He proposes an entrenched Bill of Rights which would be binding on federal and provincial governments alike. In the past it has been provincial rather than federal governments which have abused individual rights, because they are responsible for the administration of justice. Also, through commission in the case of restrictive labor legislation, or omission in the case of fair employment practices legislation, they have been responsible for violating the rights of collective bargaining and labor practices which are a part of the modern world. Thus his argument that democracy is better served by provincial autonomy is in danger of being refuted on the grounds of past and present provincial practices. For this reason a Bill of Rights is an essential element in Mr. Trudeau's system. An entrenched Bill of Rights, and the jurisprudence that would develop out of it, could, in time, have an important normative effect on Canadian political culture.

Another way in which Mr. Trudeau considers the present

constitution to be unsatisfactory is the absence of French language guarantees across the whole country. Almost all the recommendations to be found in the Report of the Royal Commission on Bilingualism and Biculturalism (another of this year's important happenings) can be found in Trudeau's various papers. It is necessary to make Ottawa a bilingual capital; to make the federal civil service truly bilingual (and even cabinet meetings!); to make the armed services bilingual; to give educational rights to French Canadians in other provinces in communities where they make up over 15 per cent of the population for two successive censuses; to give French language rights in the courts; and in cultural services such as broadcasting. French Canadians would then feel at home in all of Canada. Mr. Trudeau rejects totally the notion that Quebec represents the French-Canadian nation; that Quebec or any other province for that matter should be based on the concept of ethnicity or nationhood. Quebec is just like any other province, that is, a unit of government geographically closer to the people and more aware of their needs in the provision of important services. He recommends also changes in the Senate, and in the Supreme Court where the latter deals with constitutional questions.

I do not think I have ever read a more coherent, consistent, and articulate blueprint for contemporary Canada than in this collection of papers. One is astounded at the clarity and the logic of it all. But one is also left with the feeling of his being legalistic and mechanical and unaware of, or perhaps ignoring, social forces at work in modern political systems. One cannot suggest that a person who has done so much to liberate Quebec from the darkness of its Duplessis days, and who has played such an important role in the organization of labor in Quebec, is naive about irrationality in human affairs. Yet Trudeau appeals like a nineteenth-century rationalist to the rationality which he projects into all humans. If he is not naive, he is certainly optimistic.

On these constitutional and legal matters, we can anticipate endless discussion and argument which will be referred to euphemistically as "dialogue," but which will make politics even more of a lawyers' game than in the past. We stand in danger of neglecting correspondingly those policies necessary to make the quality of Canadian life worthwhile in the future, and to prepare the country to take a place as a strongly independent force in the postmodern world.

Mr. Trudeau is in the unusual position—I would hesitate to say fortunate—of having articulated a scheme of government, and is now prime minister, with the opportunity to implement his ideas. He is undoubtedly rowing against the tide of strong political opinion in Quebec, and also in respect of a Bill of Rights. It is unlikely, given the present climate, that the provinces will stand out against the provision of language and educational rights to French Canadians, but they will stand out against a Bill of Rights, for they enjoy their power too much to restrict it voluntarily. All the political parties in Quebec are for some degree of "special status" as is the federal N.D.P., but the position of the federal Conservative party is not clear.

For some observers the analysis of Mr. Trudeau's position which I have presented would be considered irrelevant to present-day politics because, they argue, now that he is on the federal scene he will become a centralist, if not because he thinks it a good idea, then because the system is so unchangeable that even he will be forced to conform to the dominant pattern of federal-provincial relations which have been established for the last quarter century. These observers misinterpret, I think, some of his more recent statements to the effect that when Ottawa was too strong he was for provincial autonomy, and now that the provinces have, in his view, become too strong he has entered federal politics to help redress the balance. Also his doctrine of creating "counterweights" is taken as an indication that he has become a centralist. However, I think it would be safe to say that since he is a convinced federalist he wants to redress the balance between the two levels. He would preserve present constitutional arrangements such as the federal government's total responsibility for external affairs and its role in equalization payments which would require it to keep its share of taxation. Even where he proposes reforms, such as with the Senate and the Supreme Court, they are changes in the federalist direction rather than towards a unitary state. It would be very surprising if he now repudiated the views he has held for so long, to argue for an aggrandizement of federal power at the expense of the provinces. If he repudiates his intellectual past so firmly he is a Mackenzie King indeed.

For all the arguments which are made in favor of a strong federalism for Canada, equally strong and logical ones can be made to the contrary. Where one stands in the debate depends on personal preferences, one's view of history, one's view of the best means of maximizing the country's welfare and its contribution to the international community. One has only to look at the important role of the federal power in the United States in the development of civil liberties and the role of the Supreme Court in articulating principles of human rights to realize that strong central institutions can be democratic instruments against unjust state legislation, and that, as a general principle, federalism is no more democratic per se than unitary forms of government, as far as safeguarding civil liberties is concerned. Mr. Trudeau recognizes this in his desire for a Bill of Rights. In the long run these rights depend on a society's traditions and political culture. In response to calm or crisis, the view of what is appropriate for liberty will oscillate between permissiveness and control.

In the specific way that Canadian federalism has developed, democracy has not been well served by strong provincial governments. These governments usually stay in office for a long time. Their premiers are the most experienced of our political leaders and they exercise a strong influence over their cabinets and legislatures. At the present time the veritable jungle of federal-provincial joint responsibilities makes government policies a matter for negotiation between cabinet ministers and bureaucrats from both levels, while the legislatures become rather passive and perplexed observers, thus removing the political process from the participatory democracy that federal systems are supposed to serve. Mr. Trudeau of course recognizes that centralizing tendencies are inherent in any modern industrialized society and that frequent and extensive provincial and federal consultation and agreements might be necessary for such problems as minimum standards of social security, labor legislation, and economic stabilization. No one could disagree, but Mr. Trudeau does not seem to accept the fact that the federal electorate will probably never have the occasion of voting for two *functionally independent* governments.

In sociological terms I think there are serious weaknesses in the doctrine of a strong federalism. It assumes that the provinces constitute real communities representing real cultural differences which must find expression through their own governments. With the exception of Quebec—although Mr. Trudeau opposes the idea—it is pretty difficult to establish that the provinces represent so much cultural homogeneity. They may have in the past. But in the world into which we are moving and in which governments will play entirely new roles, the dogma of cultural particularism will be increasingly meaningless. I have previously observed that it is rarely made clear, even in the present, what the cultural differences are, or why they are more important than the similarities. Interprovincial migration, modern means of travel and communication, economic integration through the growth of the national corporation, all suggest that any theory of sectionalism or cultural particularism needs to be re-examined. Most provinces, New Brunswick and Manitoba are striking examples, have a greater variety of ethnic cultures within them than most provinces have between each other. It is difficult to see how these intraprovincial cultures are protected by a federal system. Another argument in favor of federalism is that regions and provinces have specialized economic activities and that these require strong provincial governments to safeguard and develop them. But equally strong counterarguments could be made that regional economies could better develop and be better planned and stabilized through integrative policies at the national level. National corporations undertake such integrative policies. Decisions about closing down Nova Scotia coal mines are taken in Montreal, when they are not taken in London or New York. In the case of Dosco, it was assumed the federal government would participate in ameliorating the effect of closing down the Sydney steel plant.

It could be questioned that Canada can move into the postmodern world based on science and technology with the constitutional balance in favor of provincialism, particularly when education appears to be unalterably a provincial power. It seems absurd, for example, to search for a national science policy and to see research as a national enterprise, while the training of scientists and researchers, and the curricula by which they are taught, are not matters of national concern. But then, Canadian politicians are past masters of constitutional sophistry.

Strong provincialism and entrenched provincial power can inhibit the emergence of a strong sense of political community in Canada. A sense of responsibility and shared goals among the Canadian people ought to be fostered, not simply for sending a brigade of troops to NATO or a delegation to the United Nations, but in cultural and social concerns that touch very much on the quality of life. It is not only the French Canadians who want to feel at home in the whole of Canada. Many other Canadians, new and old, do as well.

In the absence of any concrete information about public feelings one way or the other, it would be as wrong to take an antifederalist stand as it is to take a federalist one on this matter of the communal needs served by provincial autonomy. Where Mr. Trudeau's analysis of Canadian particularisms tends to be misleading is that it is based almost exclusively on Quebec experience. Of course, Quebec *is* a special case of cultural particularism. By aspiring for strong federalist systems for all provinces, Mr. Trudeau appears to reject the view that Quebec is different, but what he is really saying is that all the other provinces are like Quebec and should make a great effort to retain their rights against the encroachments of the federal power.

PUBLIC OPINION AND FEDERALISM

Most discussions about how federalism in Canada serves social or cultural needs go on without much information about how Canadians actually feel about their society. Obviously there is the conventional wisdom produced by historians, historically-oriented political scientists, journalists, and others. There is also the rhetoric of the convention hall and the election platform. We are never sure whether this conventional wisdom is little more than what Mosca would have called a "political formula" helping to create a sense of legitimacy for the way in which power is exercised. If federalism has some social basis, threats to change could create reactions, which in turn could be reflected in currents of opinion in the society at large. On the other hand, if strong provincialism is felt to weaken national purposes or goals then such views should be ascertainable. We need, then, some attitudinal data on the operation of the Canadian political system, but, as I have said, the kind of political science that might elicit such data is very poorly developed.

From time to time the Canadian Institute of Public Opinion has asked questions on federal-provincial responsibilities. Setting aside the problem of the quality of the questions, some of which are rather leading, it would appear that between 1943 and 1960 at least half the respondents in national samples disapproved of any increase in federal powers, and the proportions approving increases were rarely more than one-third. For example, in 1944, in response to the question of whether or not the Dominion government should give back powers which belonged to the provinces, 50 per cent indicated that they should be given back, while 33 per cent said the Dominion government should keep them. In 1946, 50 per cent of the respondents—we are dealing with national samples here—thought that Canada would be worse off if all provincial governments were abolished and the whole country governed from Ottawa, while 25 per cent thought that this drastic step would make Canada better off. In response to the same question in 1960, 62 per cent said "worse off," and 17 per cent said "better off." Of course, the question is extreme because it deals with the abolition of the federal system rather than a modification towards a unitary state. Thus, even when the country was mobilized in a major war effort, the national focus did not override provincialism. But then a large segment of the population was against participation in the war in any case. On the questions relating to much less drastic change involving only a shift of powers, at least for those questions presented by Dr. Schwartz in her *Public Opinion and Canadian Identity*,[10] views in favor of the federal system seem less strong, but always there seems to be more opinion against change than for it. As Dr. Schwartz states, "In this image of Canada, the legitimacy of federalism and biculturalism is increasingly recognized."[11]

In a study primarily concerned with the public evaluation of occupations in which I am engaged with Professor Peter Pineo, we asked a national sample a variety of questions on contemporary Canada (1965). Three of the questions were related to federalism and designed, we hoped, to improve upon those which had previously been asked. The first question was "Canada is a country with two levels of government, the provincial and the federal. Which of these two levels do you think is more important for the future development of the country?" The three responses were Provincial Government, Federal Government, and Don't Know. The second question was "Which of these do you think has more effect on your welfare and future as an individual?" The third was "Do you think the provincial government should have more power than it now has, or do you think the federal government should have more power?"

In response to the first question, 64 per cent indicated that they thought the federal government more important for the future development of the country, while 20 per cent thought the provincial government was (3 per cent volunteered that both were important). There was very little difference between English and French in this view, 65 and 60 per cent respectively, thinking the federal government more important. (French here is the language of the interview.) In the city of Montreal, which we oversampled, the patterns were similar although the English and French differences were more marked than in the national sample, with 70 per cent and 60 per cent respectively, considering the federal government more important. The numbers of the Montreal English are very few. In terms of political party supporters a higher percentage of Liberal and N.D.P. supporters in federal elections thought the federal government more important (70 and 74 per cent respectively) compared to 64 per cent of Conservative supporters. For party supporters in provincial elections 74 per cent of the N.D.P. supporters thought the federal government more important while Liberal supporters dropped to 66 per cent, the same as the Conservative supporters in provincial elections. Although the numbers are small, 56 per cent of the Union Nationale supporters in Quebec thought the federal government more important (see Table I).

There is remarkably little difference in the responses by province or region. In terms of the degree of urbanization, those in larger cities and farm and rural dwellers saw the federal government as more important (67, 65, and 64 per cent respectively) to a greater degree than those in small-sized cities. White-collar workers, more than blue-collar workers, with the exception of the pro-

TABLE I

LEVEL OF GOVERNMENT THOUGHT TO BE MORE IMPORTANT FOR FUTURE OF COUNTRY

(per cent)

	Language		Region					Education			Support In Provincial Elections					Ethnic Origin					TOTAL
	English	French	Atlantic	Quebec	Ontario	Prairies	B.C.	Elementary	Secondary	Postsec.	P.C.	Liberal	N.D.P.	S.C.	U.N.	Canada	U.K.	France	N. Europe	S.&E. Europe	
Provincial	19	22	22	20	19	16	27	24	18	14	22	20	19	21	30	18	20	23	19	17	20
Federal	65	60	62	62	66	63	66	54	68	75	66	66	74	68	56	64	68	59	61	67	64
Both	3	2	—	2	4	3	4	3	2	5	2	3	1	3	—	4	3	2	3	2	3
Don't Know	12	16	15	15	11	16	3	18	11	6	10	12	6	8	15	14	10	15	16	14	13
No Answer	1	1	—	1	1	3	—	1	1	—	—	—	—	—	—	1	—	—	—	—	1
TOTAL	100	101	100	100	101	101	100	100	100	100	100	101	100	100	101	101	101	99	99	100	101
Ns	607	186	79	213	273	154	74	281	380	127	180	229	69	71	27	111	310	133	88	97	793

fessionals, were of the same view. There is little difference by age, but substantial difference by educational level with 75 per cent of those with some form of postsecondary education thinking the federal government more important compared to 68 per cent with secondary school and only 54 per cent with elementary school. Moreover, the more education the smaller proportion of "Don't Know" responses, the proportions dropping from 18 per cent to 6 per cent from elementary to postsecondary levels. Thus in terms of the future development of the country, the federal government is viewed as being more important fairly consistently by most segments of the population.

As we all know, the way questions are asked can have considerble effect on the response. In our present problem, it would seem that the context about which judgments on federalism are made is crucial, as can be seen from the responses to our second question. "Canada is a country with two levels of government, the provincial and the federal. Which do you think has more effect on your welfare and future as an individual?" For this question the responses were reversed. Forty-seven per cent said the provincial government was more important and 38 per cent the federal (see Table II). Unlike the first, with this question there were important differences between English and French (language of interview). The English divided their opinion equally (43 per cent) between the two levels of government, while 61 per cent of the French thought the provincial government more important, and only 21 per cent thought the federal government more important. For the Montreal French, however, the distinction was much less (46 per cent and 33 per cent), suggesting that the French in this highly urban culture share more in the national opinion trends. If the low numbers of Montreal English mean anything, 59 per cent thought the federal government more important for the future of their welfare and only 28 per cent thought the provincial government was. At least we could hypothesize for future testing that the English in Montreal are more federal government oriented than any group in the country. If it should prove to be correct it would no doubt be because they feel threatened.

Greater variability is shown in responses to the second question than to the first. For example, 57 per cent of Conservative supporters in federal elections thought the provincial government more important while only 31 per cent thought the federal government was. Conservative supporters in provincial elections were a little less provincially oriented. Federal election Liberal supporters broke about evenly on the importance of either the provincial and federal governments (46 and 44 per cent), but Liberal supporters in provincial elections veered somewhat more to the pro-

TABLE II

LEVEL OF GOVERNMENT THOUGHT TO HAVE MORE EFFECT ON WELFARE AND FUTURE OF INDIVIDUAL
(per cent)

	Language		Region					Education			Support In Provincial Elections					Ethnic Origin					
	English	French	Atlantic	Quebec	Ontario	Prairies	B.C.	Elementary	Secondary	Postsec.	P.C.	Liberal	N.D.P.	S.C.	U.N.	Canada	U.K.	France	N. Europe	S.&E. Europe	TOTAL
Provincial	44	61	52	53	42	36	57	48	48	46	54	48	45	54	59	42	48	65	44	34	47
Federal	43	21	42	30	43	45	39	32	41	47	34	41	46	38	26	41	42	20	40	45	38
Both	1	—	—	1	1	1	1	—	1	2	—	1	3	—	—	—	1	1	1	2	1
Don't Know	12	17	6	16	14	16	4	20	10	5	12	11	6	8	15	15	9	14	15	19	13
No Answer	1	1	—	—	—	2	—	1	—	—	—	—	—	—	—	1	—	—	—	—	1
TOTAL	101	100	100	100	100	100	101	101	100	100	100	101	100	100	100	99	100	100	100	100	100
Ns	607	186	79	213	273	154	74	281	380	127	180	229	69	71	27	111	310	133	88	97	793

vincial government than the federal (48 and 41 per cent). Union Nationale supporters were heavily provincial government supporters.

For this question there were also important regional differences. Atlantic provinces and Quebec respondents saw the provincial government as more important than the federal (52 and 53 per cent respectively) as did British Columbia (57 per cent) while Ontario residents were about evenly divided. A greater proportion of Prairie respondents, even for this question, saw the federal government as more important. They seem generally to have a low estimate of the importance of provincial governments.

In large cities (over 30 000), opinion was equally divided between provincial and federal government importance, but in smaller cities and in farm and rural areas particularly, provincial governments were seen as more important. For occupational levels, manual and farm workers and farmers were more likely to see the provincial governments as more important for them to a greater extent than did white-collar workers. The educational level of the respondents provides some differences in the response. For those with postsecondary education there is an even division between those who feel the provincial government more important than the federal government for their welfare, whereas for those with elementary education only a much larger proportion (48 per cent) feel the provincial government more important than the federal (30 per cent). As with the first question, the higher the education, the greater certainty. Those with completed secondary education fall somewhere in between. For age levels there is no difference.

Our third question was "Do you think the provincial government should have more power than it now has, or do you think the federal government should have more power?" The most striking thing about the response here was that almost one-third said "Don't Know." Perhaps the previous questions had left them bewildered. This applied to both English and French respondents. Overall, a greater proportion thought the provincial government should have more power; that is, 36 per cent, with only 29 per cent believing the federal government should (see Table III). However, the provincial government was chosen to have more power by 54 per cent of the French with only 12 per cent of them thinking the federal government should have more. More Quebec respondents than those in any other region (49 per cent) thought the provincial government should have more power. In Ontario the proportion so thinking was only 27 per cent. Conversely, Quebec had the lowest proportion (18 per cent) selecting the federal government for greater power, but 35 per cent in Ontario did, which, it will be not-

TABLE III

LEVEL OF GOVERNMENT WHICH SHOULD HAVE MORE POWER
(per cent)

	Language		Region					Education			Support In Provincial Elections					Ethnic Origin					
	English	French	Atlantic	Quebec	Ontario	Prairies	B.C.	Elementary	Secondary	Postsec.	P.C.	Liberal	N.D.P.	S.C.	U.N.	Canada	U.K.	France	N. Europe	S.&E. Europe	TOTAL
Provincial	30	54	39	49	27	33	31	40	34	32	34	32	33	51	63	40	33	54	34	29	36
Federal	35	12	28	18	35	31	38	20	32	41	31	35	48	13	11	23	35	16	24	39	29
Both	1	—	—	—	2	—	—	1	1	2	2	2	—	—	—	1	—	—	—	—	1
Don't Know	32	30	33	29	34	33	27	35	31	24	32	29	19	35	22	32	29	28	40	31	32
No Answer	2	4	—	3	2	3	3	4	1	1	1	2	—	1	4	4	1	1	1	1	2
TOTAL	100	100	100	99	100	100	100	100	99	100	100	100	100	100	100	100	99	100	100	101	100
Ns	607	186	79	213	273	154	74	281	380	127	180	229	69	71	27	111	310	133	88	97	793

ed, is a greater proportion than favored the provinces. In the Atlantic provinces, 39 per cent said more power to the provinces compared to 29 per cent for the federal.

Liberal and N.D.P. supporters in federal elections favored greater federal powers than did Conservative supporters, and they are a little more certain about it. A greater proportion of the N.D.P. would give more power to the federal government while, for the Liberals, the proportions giving more power to either are about equal. These differences narrow very much for party supporters in provincial elections. Here both the Social Credit in Alberta and British Columbia, and the Union Nationale in Quebec favor the provincial governments having more power more than do any other groups. It is likely that these same voters support the Conservative party in federal elections and their doing so accounts for the differences between the two sets of Conservative supporters.

On the rural-urban continuum those in large cities were about evenly divided between federal and provincial governments having more power, whereas in all other categories, except rural non-farm, the provinces were favored by considerably greater numbers. As with the other two questions, there seemed to be little difference between older and younger age groups. For occupational levels, white-collar workers in greater proportions favored greater powers for the federal government, while the reverse held for manual workers. Again we find the more highly educated are more in favor of federal power than are the less educated. Forty-one per cent of those with postsecondary education favored the federal government compared to 20 per cent for those with only elementary school education.

Ethnicity is the one background characteristic which I have left to deal with separately. In Canada cultural differences are often thought of as ethnic differences, and it is this pluralistic aspect of the society which often gets confounded with provincialism and the ideology of federalism. I am coming increasingly to feel that ethnicity may well be an artifact of the census rather than the social reality it is claimed to be, and this is because of the way in which the census question asks for the original or the first North-American ancestor on the father's side. This excludes both the U.S. and Canada as ethnicities. We asked a number of questions relating to ethnicity, but the one tabulated for the problem we are dealing with here was "What country would you say most of your ancestors on your father's side are from?" Since we permitted Canada as a response, differences between French Canadian and English Canadian might not be as clear as if we had excluded Canada. (It is language of interview we have been using for French-English differences previously.) Although in response to the first question about the future development of the country, all ethnic origins favored the federal as opposed to the provincial government, for British origins it was 68 per cent, but for French it was 59 per cent. British-French differences were much greater on the subsequent questions. Sixty-five per cent of the French thought the provinces more important in respect of the individual's welfare while only 20 per cent favored the federal. For the British, 48 per cent thought the provinces and 42 per cent the federal. For "Canada" as an origin the division of opinion between the two levels of government was about even. On the question concerning more power for either government, 54 per cent of the French said more power for the provincial government and 16 per cent for the federal, but the British were about evenly divided between the two, 33 per cent for the provincial and 35 per cent for the federal. For those who gave "Canada" 40 per cent were for more provincial power and 23 per cent for more federal power.

One final set of findings. If we cross-tabulate the first two questions, it is possible to take those who gave the provincial government or the federal government for both questions, and to designate them as "provincialists" and "centralists" respectively. Only 14 per cent could be classed as provincialists but 32 per cent could be centralists. While 37 and 38 per cent, respectively, of the British and Canadian origins were centralists, only 13 per cent of the French were. Of the regions, Ontario was the most centralist with 36 per cent, the Prairies and the Atlantic region had 33 per cent each, and Quebec 26 per cent. Thirty-nine per cent of those with postsecondary education were centralists compared to 25 per cent of those with elementary schooling only, while 18 per cent of those with elementary schooling were provincialists compared to 10 per cent of those with postsecondary. On the basis of the language of interview 36 per cent of English were centralists compared to 17 per cent of the French.

It is possible, I think, to draw some conclusions from these admittedly meagre findings. The first is that there is no overwhelming desire for change in any direction. Obviously opinion is anything but fixed on the question of the relative importance of provincial and federal governments and their powers, although the context about which judgments are made will bring different responses. No doubt, the present division in the public mind is reflected in the party system in the sense that since 1962 no party can claim to be a national party able to devise policies appealing to all segments of the country. Party supporters, moreover, will vary depending on whether or not they are party supporters in provincial or federal elections. Liberal supporters in federal elections are modestly more centralist than Conservative supporters although I suspect in this election it will be the Conservatives who are centralist and the Liberals provincialist.

Another conclusion which emerges clearly is that the French in Canada are much more provincialist than the other parts of the population which we have analysed. Whether the French are determined by language of interview, ethnic origin, Quebec residence, or support of the Union Nationale party they consistently see the federal government as less important and as not having claims to more power. In this sense, they are different and it would seem that the political demands for special status have some foundation in social attitudes. This provincialist orientation is not shared by Ontario residents, a greater proportion of whom would give the federal government more power, while the Prairies are about equally divided on the subject, although their people, as we have noted, felt the federal government to be more important on both scores. The Atlantic provinces are less centralist oriented than the Prairies and that might arise because of the isolation of the former. British Columbia, also isolated from the rest of Canada, is split in terms of provincialist or centralist orientations, and this is reflected to some extent in their voting behavior. The two-party system flourishes in British Columbia. The N.D.P. has for a long time been a strong opposition party, and their supporters as we have seen are decidedly more centralist than other party supporters.

Since on the whole public opinion is in a very mixed up state, political leadership has an important role in resolving the dilemma and giving direction. Earlier in this paper I tried to show the direction I would expect Mr. Trudeau to take. There are obviously grounds for the alternative option of a new federalism which would give a special status to Quebec and at the same time seek to draw the rest of Canada together in a stronger centralist frame.

Moreover, as one regards this opinion data against the processes of social change, those components of the population which are emerging and will become increasingly important in the future, that is, the large-city dweller, the white-collar workers, the better educated, indicate that there is more future for centralism than for provincialism.

Canada is in a transition period in very many ways. As one watches the election which is now underway with the increasing use of the mass media and jet travelling of party leaders, one can see Canada becoming a McLuhanite village—at least an anglophone village—in which national identification will increasingly lead to more coherent and strengthened national policies and goals articulated and realized through national political institutions. If that is the case, I suspect that Mr. Trudeau is keeping to his usual practice of rowing against the current.

Notes

1. Toronto, Macmillan of Canada, 1968.
2. *Ibid.*, 42.
3. *Ibid.*, 26.
4. *Ibid.*, xxii.
5. *Ibid.*, 147.
6. *Ibid.*, 127.
7. *Ibid.*, 80.
8. *Ibid.*, 81.
9. *Ibid.*, 82.
10. Mildred A. Schwartz, *Public Opinion and Canadian Identity* Berkeley, University of California Press, 1967.
11. *Ibid.*, 95.

8

Postindustrialism, Postnationalism, and Postsecondary Education

However generous or niggardly governments or publics might be towards their universities, these institutions play an important part in nation building and nation sustaining. They "produce" highly qualified members of the work force; they transmit the higher culture that has shown itself worth preserving and transmitting; they undertake pure and applied research as the foundation of an industrial economy; they provide a safe harbor for critical intellectuals; they contribute through humanistic and social studies to the sense of national identity and purpose.

Until the 1960s (when there was that frantic period of catching up) Canadians neglected their universities, which were open to only a small fraction of the more privileged young people in the population. Federal government money helped from modest beginnings in 1951, after grants for veterans' education were running out, through Mr. St. Laurent's announcement of the formation of the Canada Council in 1956, and over the next twenty years. Mr. St. Laurent found no difficulty in articulating a clear national and federal interest in universities.

Because universities engage in "higher" education, there is the view that they are the exclusive concern of the provincial governments. That is a view firmly held by Mr. Trudeau, a point which I have made in the paper "Mr. Trudeau and Canadian Federalism." Apart from Quebec, which under Mr. Duplessis for some time refused the federal grants, provincial governments did not object strenuously to this federal assistance to university growth. After 1967, however, when under the Fiscal Arrangements Act of that year the federal government agreed to pay fifty per cent of provincial postsecondary budgets, all of

185

which were to escalate dramatically over the next few years, new doubts were being expressed about the constitutional propriety of these federal transfers because they were so large and open-ended and forced priorities on provincial governments they might not otherwise have chosen. Over a period of years there were commissions, discussions, conferences, and federal-provincial trucking over the Fiscal Arrangements Act. In 1977 the federal government pulled out altogether and transferred tax points to the provinces to do what they wished with the money previously earmarked for postsecondary education. After that, the only federal money going to universities was through federal departments and agencies making research grants and contracts.

By the late 1970s, then, the position was that there was no national interest in the universities such that the federal government had an obligation to support through the formation of a distinctively national universities policy. The preceding twenty-five years of federal grants seem to have been a political aberration, because for all the money that was transferred no policies were ever developed.

It has always seemed to me to be an absurd position that there is not a national interest in the higher learning that needs to be served by the federal government. But the view one holds depends very much on whether one thinks of Canada as a nation or as a loose connection of subnations. As I have suggested in other commentaries to the papers in this volume, the present ideology—one would not grace the matter with the word theory—and practice of Canadian federalism is in the direction of fragmentation. The greater strengthening of provincial political power can only be at the expense of a growing national coherence. For those who hold a principalities theory of Canadian society, the question of a national interest in universities does not arise. I never have. That is why I argued in the present paper the need in the emerging transnational, postindustrial world for a national system of higher education. It was prepared for one of those many conferences on financing postsecondary education. This one was organized by the Institute of Public Administration of Canada and held at Queen's University in June 1970. Events have taken us yet farther away from national objectives.

Canada's needs in postsecondary education must be considered in the light of social changes now taking place and likely to accelerate over the next decade or so. Because the lead time in establishing educational resources and producing educated people to the level of the high qualifications required is long, we must look forward to our needs for some time into the future. Also because, as everybody knows, the costs of postsecondary education are astronomical and will, if not checked, take off on their own, the need for planning and co-ordination of postsecondary development is mandatory. It will be the argument of this paper that we need to plan a national system of postsecondary education, and that there is, because of the nation-wide importance of the higher learning, a vital role for, and obligation of, the federal government to take new initiatives in planning. The continuation of the present educational non-policy of fiscal transfers is to neglect Canada's interests as a national society.

We need to assess the nature of the ongoing social change and consider what we might anticipate about the future of our society in a world that increasingly moves towards McLuhan's global village, and a world of interpenetrating societies and institutions. We are familiar with the multinational corporation as such an interpenetrating institution, but there are others also, intellectual and cultural, which tend to weaken national identities and to obscure national interests. But however continentalist or internationalist Canada might become, presumably enough Canadians will desire to preserve a Canadian identity and to make a unique Canadian contribution. On this last point, Canada's continentalism and internationalism of the past has been largely passive, and it may be that in the future our identity will emerge more clearly when we assume an active rather than a reactive stance. Our capacity to be active in the world of the future will depend on how we develop our human resources.

The Postindustrial Society

The social change which we should now be monitoring more carefully, not only for our postsecondary needs but also for many others, is the transition from the industrial to the postindustrial society. The postindustrial society is one based on the culture of science and technology. It has various other names: the cybernetic society, the service society, and so forth. Its coming is viewed by many with apprehension because of what is believed to be its inevitable dehumanizing qualities, but it has, if its capacities are properly used, a great potential to improve human life. Unfortunately we cannot deal with these issues here.

The beginnings of the postindustrial society are already with us. According to Daniel Bell, who has written much about it, there are five main characteristics.[1] The first is the creation of a service economy with the majority of the labor force producing services rather than goods. This condition is simply a continuation of the expansion of the tertiary-level occupations which we have been experiencing. Kahn suggests that a quaternary level of occupations is developing. He describes this level as rendering services ". . . to tertiary occupations or to each other."[2] Bell's second criterion is what he calls the pre-eminence of the professional and technical class. There are the rapidly expanding occupations, and the workers in them are the symbols of postindustrialism as the semiskilled worker was the symbol of the industrial period. His third characteristic is the centrality of theoretical knowledge. It has long been said that knowledge is power, but for postindustrialism it is theoretical and abstract knowledge which is the basis of innovative power. Thus the postindustrial society is organized around knowledge. Fourthly, this society has a commitment to growth and innovation which gives rise to the need for planning and forecasting and controlling the advance of technological change. Finally, there is the creation of the new intellectual technology of linear programming, systems analysis, information theory, all of which are important in the macro-analysis of masses of data. Decision making must increasingly have such a technological base.

Because knowledge is central to the postindustrial society the dominant figures who are emerging are the scientists, the engineers, the mathematicians, the economists, all at home with the new computer technology. These stand in contrast to the dominant men of the industrial period, the entrepreneur, the businessman and the industrial executive. Consequently, Bell says, ". . . the dominant institutions of the new society will rest, not with businessmen or corporations as we know them . . . but with the research corporation, the industrial laboratories, the experimental stations and the universities."[3] He continues: ". . . if the business firm was the key institution of the past one hundred years, because of its role in organizing production for the mass creation of products, the university will become the central institution of the next one hundred years because of its role as the new source of innovation and knowledge."[4]

A further feature of the postindustrial society, which it is important to note, is the greatly increased role of government in exploiting the potential of postindustrialism and the establishing of national goals. Most of the great planning problems left by the industrial period—urbanization, pollution, common standards of social rights which are expected—will be solved in the postindustrial period through the political system. Consequently, there will be a great reduction of the importance of the concept of profit. Already the rapidly expanding industrial sectors of the economy are the not-for-profit ones and this is likely to continue as governments at all levels assume greater responsibility in the planning and direction of social change.

A more familiar and a less optimistic view of the emerging society is provided by Galbraith in *The New Industrial State*. However, like Bell, he emphasizes the importance of trained intelligence and gives a central role to educational and research institutions. "They stand," he says, "in relation to the industrial system, much as did the banking and financial community to the earlier stages of industrial development."[5]

Bertram Gross, another writer concerned with social change, points out another feature of the postindustrial world as the societies that comprise it penetrate and intervene in each other's activities, and that is the need for transnational legitimation for such activities and the provision for co-operative transnational actions.[6]

National Identity in the Postindustrial World

If there is any validity in the views of Bell, Kahn, Gross, Galbraith and others about emerging postindustrialism, how can their images of the future help us make some assessment of Canada's need for higher education? To some extent our answer will depend on what image we ourselves have of the future of Canada as a continuing independent polity with some degree of separate identity. How important is such a survival of identity in any case? Why not simply accept the inevitable interpenetration of other postindustrial societies and go along for the ride? Can we forget about the fact that knowledge is the new power and that universities with their highly educated people constitute the new locus of power? Perhaps we do not need power in this innovative sense since all the benefits can come from elsewhere. In a recent convocation address Harry Johnson indicated some of the benefits of this interpenetrating system.

> Apart from expanded higher-level education, the main requirement for participation in the modern world is willingness to accept and welcome the application of new technology.
>
> Unfortunately in many ways, the application of new technology is largely implemented through the agency of the large corporation which has been extending its activities from the national to the international sphere. I say unfortunately because the fact that it is a corporation with a national domicile obscures the fact that it is an agency for the diffusion of new technology, and hence an agency for the destruction of local industrial monopolies and the world-wide transmission of the benefits of technical progress.[7]

If postindustrialism requires a great expansion of universities and research institutes why not continue, as in earlier periods of our history, to neglect educational development and "import" or accept the invasion of postindustrialism from elsewhere, as we did with industrialization? We seem to have become industrialized despite ourselves. In 1951 we were magnificently unprepared for industrial expansion, with over half our male labor force with eight years of schooling or less. Canada's transformation into mature industrialization after the Second World War was achieved in considerable measure by the importation of foreign capital and highly trained people. In case anyone doubts the latter, let me present briefly some evidence. The proportions of those in professional occupations who were postwar immigrants at the time of the 1961 census have been indicated in a number of studies.[8] On this subject, the 1961 occupational census data have been analysed in an interesting way by Bernard Blishen.[9] By devising an occupational scale based on income, education, and prestige, the three main components of occupational rank, he was able to assign scale values to 320 occupations. He then arranged them into six classes by rank. For the top two of these classes, that is, the occupations having the highest scale values, the proportion of the native-born labor force compared to the postwar immigrant labor force in them is strikingly different. In Ontario the proportion of the native-born labor force in these two classes was 9.9 per cent, but that of postwar U.K. immigrants was 13.8 per cent, and of postwar U.S. immigrants 28.2 per cent. In the western provinces the proportions were 8.7 per cent of the native-born labor force, 14.4 per cent of the U.K. and 31.8 per cent of the U.S. In Quebec the Canadian-born proportion was 7.35, the U.K.-29.6 and the U.S.-born 35.3. These proportions indicate how much richer in trained capacity than the native-born labor force were the postwar immigrants who came from the United Kingdom and the United States. Some further evidence is to be found in a 1965 labor force survey which found that 23.6 per cent of the native-born male labor force had completed high school and attended university compared to 34.1 per cent of the postwar immigrants. For those with university degrees the percentages were 5.3 and 8.9 respectively.[10]

The reliance on external resources to bring us into the industrial stage of development can be seen in almost all industrial and institutional sectors. We have heard a good deal of irrational discussion of it in the university context. In his study published late last year on the performance of foreign-owned firms in Canada Professor Safarian presents some evidence on Canadian representation at the top level of foreign-owned firms and he raises questions about the failure of Canada to provide the range of trained managerial talent our industrial system requires. "It is not evident," he says, "that the quality of Canadian managerial personnel is so high that Canadian interests could be served by reduced resort to imported persons."[11] He also quotes the Economic Council to the effect, ". . . the average educational attainment of the owner and management group in Canada shows a greater shortfall below the educational attainment of the corresponding group in the United States, than is the case with almost any other major category of the labor force."[12] These observations about the educational level of Canadian management are, I think, important because we often fail to include managers in the international flows of highly qualified manpower, and hence tend to underestimate our needs. Our needs are indeed great if "Canadianization," as one government member has said, depends more on management rather than ownership.[13]

The overall differences in the educational attainment of the Canadian labor force and that of the U.S. are also well-known. In 1966, of the male population 25–34 years of age, 30.5 per cent in the United States had some university education or a university degree compared to 14.6 per cent in Canada. Of that age group in the U.S. 17.7 per cent had university degrees, but in Canada only 8.2 per cent had them.[14] Thus whether we compare Canada with the United States or whether we look at the high level of external recruitment (we still are recruiting professional occupations heavily abroad) it is clear that Canadian institutions of higher learning fell far short of meeting the needs of Canada's development into the industrial stage.

Should we proceed to the next stage of development by a similar route, by undertaking a minimum of educational planning, by continuing to hold the position that the provinces have the exclusive right to plan higher education? Should we keep on relying on the international market for the highly qualified manpower we will need or on the multinational corporations as they rationalize their Canadian operations? Is Canada damaged seriously in any way, or are Canadian interests neglected when recruitment from abroad is relied upon to fill so many of the higher occupational needs? A somewhat related question which has an important bearing on our higher educational needs is that of research and development in Canadian industry. Why be concerned about R and D programs in Canadian industry when we can import the benefits of R and D from elsewhere through foreign corporations? Is a Canadian mousetrap so much better than an American or a Belgian one? If it is not, then what are our future demands for research and development scientists in industry, a question surely to which educational planners should have an answer? What might we expect of future government policy with respect to meeting some of the critical points of the recent OECD review of science policy in general, and industrial research and development in particular?[15]

At this point it might be appropriate to stand up and waffle about closing the forty-ninth parallel. In some areas we do attempt to close it off with our insistence on Canadian content in the broadcast media and football teams, our concern about the ownership of the printed media, or the chartered banks. Some would have the universities protected. We have become concerned about the ownership of uranium mines in a very curious reversal of our normal response to foreign takeovers. Somewhere, somebody seems to think there are areas of Canadian life where we cannot safely afford to let in outsiders. If that is so, and if such areas should become more numerous, our higher educational needs are very much related to those areas. We should produce more highly qualified bankers, or greatly extend football scholarships. If Canadian content of the mass media is all that important we should have many more faculties of fine arts, drama schools, academies of music, but these are only slowly developing in Canada, because they have in the past been considered as a kind of frosting on the educational cake.

In posing all these questions I have tried to indicate how the answers to some rather fundamental problems facing Canadian society must be found before we can realistically talk about Canadian needs in higher education in a world increasingly integrated through postindustrialism. I think those are right who say that the barrier-erecting nationalism is to cut this or any other country off from many of the advances of science and technology.

There are, however, at least two alternatives to the isolation that would result from an overconcern for Canadianization. One is for Canada to make sure that every opportunity is given Canadians through the educational systems we have, to maximize their potential and to exploit the possibilities for upward social mobility that postindustrialism willl bring. There is also geographical mobility, and perhaps if the modern international corporation is the principal transmitter of the benefits of scientific and technological development we should be less concerned about where Canadian graduates end up. What I am suggesting is that Canadian young people are entitled to all the educational opportunity they can use and perhaps more than they are properly motivated to use in some segments of our society. Thus the trends which enrolment figures have established of increasing proportions of the age group taking postsecondary education must continue to a much greater degree of democratization. I will say something more about democratization a little later.

For those who are worried about Canada's future, continued vigorous expansion of educational opportunity is a far more positive approach than intellectual protectionism. In fact I am sure a case could be made that Canada's survival in a world whose development I have tried to describe depends on its being prepared for the culture of science and technology and on its contributing in its own way to that culture. If that is so, our educational needs become very considerable.

The second alternative which I have in mind is for Canada to decide what it can do in the postindustrial world and that decision is very much bound up with our future science policy. In this respect Canada can take a very positive stance rather than the reactive one which I mentioned at the beginning. A good example of a positive role for Canada in the world is the recently established development agency.

Universities or Multiversities

So far I have put a great deal of emphasis on national manpower requirements to keep Canada salient in the postindustrial world. Today many people would argue that it is not universities' business to be concerned with training manpower or to be engaged in scientific research. Research and training can be done in research institutes and technical institutes. Professional training can be done in professional institutes. Universities, it is argued by many, should really be intellectual communities which, as Robert Hutchins has recently said, are made up of ". . . people at various stages of development, physical and intellectual, who are trying to understand major issues that confront or are likely to confront mankind."[16] Many of us working in the universities feel that the criticisms of the multiversity are well founded and that before very long the universities will have to change in the direction of the intellectual communities they should be. It is not possible here to present a model of what the universities should be or might become. Once again it is important in attempting to determine Canada's future needs for some planning to be considered before decisions are to be made. We often hear of proposals to shift more of the cost of university education on to the student because presumably he is more the direct beneficiary of his education than society at large. But the costs can be shifted in another way, directly onto industry whose profits benefit from the use of personnel trained at public expense. The same could be said for government departments whose goals are directly served by trained people they secure from the universities. Both industrial and governmental research, as well as training, could be excluded from educational costs as such.

Canadians ought to think much more about this possible line of development as being more suited to the existing federal structure. Federal government sponsored mission-oriented research, with or without the collaboration of industry, could be the responsibility of newly established research institutes. It should be remembered that mission-oriented research might not coincide with the mission of the university. The provinces could then foster their intellectual communities without the enormous costs involved with the present orientation of universities to prestigious graduate programs. We should recognize the fact that if we do not want to import all our science and technology we must encourage our own research and training of scientists. However, we might well raise questions about where that function should be undertaken, and according to our answers our university needs will vary a great deal.

Democratization of Higher Education

There is another criticism of the manpower approach to postsecondary development and that is that education is a social right and the amount of it available should be determined by the demand—not of employers' job requirements—but of young people's desires to consume education as a good which is essential to the development of personality, and to acquire a capacity to participate intelligently as a citizen in the community. Earlier it was thought that the demand was determined by student's ambition to be upwardly mobile through the occupational structure, but this element of the demand, although still important, appears to be decreasing as students look for new experiences in education.

Whatever the source of the demand, public policy in many countries has sought to meet it and to let student enrolment be the regulator of growth. This position is illustrated by the policy that "university places will be provided for all qualified applicants." In the present situation where many more qualified applicants than estimated are produced at the secondary levels, governments would like to see the universities take in more students with a less than corresponding increase in costs or plant. The universities would view this as a dilution of that elusive thing called academic quality which apparently depends so much on low staff-student ratios. Thus the universities' defence of standards can well force governments into taking political decisions which might restrict enrolments. Governments, on the other hand, seem sure that there are economies to be achieved through innovation, particularly in such a labor intensive industry, that will help to lower costs per student without diluting quality. There seems much logic in the governmental position. The universities should be obliged to innovate both in teaching and in the development of new structures, although these innovations will be experimental until tried out over time and subsequently evaluated. One wonders how much of this is actually going on in our universities at present. I think it is inescapable that the full democratization of higher education requires innovation.

There is still much of the old conservative and elitist quality about universities and some considerable suspicion within them of the democratizing process. The elitist view holds that higher education can be assimilated by relatively few. This high standard ideology and the fear of dilution of quality leads to the argument to restrain enrolments. With the elitist position universities can be either expensive to the student or cost nothing if the brightest children can be sorted out at an early age, given special treatment and supported financially. With the elitist system, whatever the financing, the universities are open mainly to the middle and upper classes because of the advantages of early upbringing, home environment and educational experience. Thus some groups deprived by regional, ethnic, and class subcultures have greatly reduced chances of higher education. At the present time, and certainly in the postindustrial world, elitism is dead in education except perhaps in a very special way which I will develop a little later.

It is the egalitarian or democratic principle which is alive. A democratized system means more than that implied by "places for qualified applicants," because that is still tinged with high quality elitism. A democratized system is one in which substantial efforts are made to remove the complex economic, social and psychological barriers to becoming qualified. What does "qualified" mean in any case? Does it mean rigid and arbitrary entrance requirements based on some preconceived scale of performance, or does it mean entrance based more on the person's potential? The only barrier which we have made any attempt to break down—much more in some provinces than in others—is the financial one, by keeping down the proportion of operating costs represented by fees and by student award programs. On this last point a student award program based on performance or scholarship is elitist rather than democratic, since it gives much better chances to middle- and upper-income groups. These minimal efforts to reduce financial barriers are scarcely enough to lead us to believe that we have democratized the system although we have no doubt improved it in the latter half of the 1960s.[17] The direction of change, then, is towards greater democratization, which has become an important political goal of the twentieth century. This process has been helped by new manpower requirements and talent searches, but also, for Canada, by the demonstration effect from the United States where universities and colleges will continue to expand, where they will be opened up increasingly to deprived groups in a variety of ways including the financial involvement of the federal government along the lines suggested in the recent reports of the Carnegie Commission on Higher Education.[18]

Thus it would seem, with the changes now taking place, that for the question of numbers, of how many should continue to the postsecondary level, there are no clear answers. Even the old notion that a given range of the intelligence spectrum, say the top 25 per cent, should be the guide, is scarcely acceptable. For one thing such a guide is very much culture-bound to time, place, educational experience, nutritional levels and so forth, but it is also an elitist guide because it could be argued that those lower in the range could also improve their potential through further education. Perhaps our best guide is the United States. It is somewhat more along the road to postindustrialism than we are, and whilst there are many valid criticisms of the quality of American civilization it must be remembered that the centres of these criticisms are in the universities and within groups of educated young people. So a case could be made that our policy objectives ought to be the gradual closing of the gap between Canada and the United States in the proportion of the relevant age group in postsecondary education. That is something of a calculable national goal, but we need institutional changes as well.

Towards a National System of Higher Education

I want to elaborate on what I think are Canada's major needs at the postsecondary level, needs which are very much determined by the emergence of postindustrialism, the difficulty of retaining national identity and the desire for democratization. In general terms the need is for a national system of postsecondary education. We are slowly emerging as a national society, but we still lack goals or guides to wherever it is we are going. The Science Council of Canada has sought to outline goals in its document *Towards a National Science Policy for Canada*.[19] These are very important: national prosperity, health, education, freedom and unity, leisure, personal development, world peace. Economic growth was always thought to be a goal although that now seems to be subject to some questioning. On this point the Chairman of the Economic Council, Arthur Smith, has made an important observation that economic growth by itself is not enough unless it is ordered and controlled. "But in addition to good growth performance, we will need highly effective regulatory and control measures, with vigorous monitoring and enforcement procedures . . . it is essential that economic growth does not take place in an uncontrollable and irresponsible fashion."[20] (If nothing else Smith is pointing out the expanding need for highly qualified manpower in the social sector, but his notion of a government role in the establishment of economic growth as a national goal is consistent with our outline of the postindustrial society.)

National goals will increasingly require national standards, something recognized in Canada's long held doctrine of equalization. National goals should have their origins in the intellectual centres of the nations, be widely discussed, and implemented through the political system, since ultimately national goals are achieved through political leadership. If Canada is to develop as a national society distinguishable in some way from the United States, then its parts must become increasingly interdependent so that what happens in one part has its effects in other parts. As I have tried to argue, what distinguishes us from the United States will be very much at the cultural level and in terms of our own positive contribution to the postindustrial world. Crucial to our achievement of such national goals is a national system of higher education, and in this the federal government has an important planning role.

I want to present a few ideas about this national system and how it might develop, largely for purposes of discussion, but if it is too radical for Canada's conservative tastes to be worth the dialogue I will as well make an argument for federal involvement in planning even within the more narrow and restrictive limits of the present constitutional outlook. On this matter, the old notion that the federal government has no role in university development is as out of date as the carriages that existed in 1867. In the light of the broad historical changes which are taking place, so is the argument so eloquently advanced by the present prime minister at the time of the first federal grants to universities.[21] It is as wrong, he argued, for federal governments to build universities because the provinces had failed to as it would be for the provincial governments to establish armies because they felt the federal government had neglected defence. The fact is that today, in the face of the more silent conquest by foreign takeover, knowledge is our defence. A highly-educated population is far more important to our survival than are our armed forces.

In outlining a possible national system of higher education I must once more acknowledge a debt to Daniel Bell, who has been writing on this subject a good deal in the United States.[22] The functions which are performed by a system of higher education are varied, but they are often summarized under the envelope expression as the preservation, semination, and extension of knowledge. The last of these, that is research, is specialized, and as I argued earlier may not be viewed as educational in the most strict sense of the term. The other kind of specialization also concerned primarily with training is in the professional schools. Higher education also involves the lower level technological training which is beyond high school but is vocationally oriented and less demanding than university education of the traditional scholarly kind where, in an intellectual community, people deal with the problems confronting mankind.

It is clear that a higher educational system must be differentiated or pluralistic to allow not only for different functions, but as well for different choices, inclinations, and ability levels. In the past we have tended to place a high value on one model of a university and that is the model of the mainline university, Columbia, Oxford, Harvard, the Sorbonne, and the like. All of our universities have wanted to become outstanding and to achieve world stature. They set up elaborate programs, hire a few star professors, start a journal or some other activity to emulate their models. As Daniel Bell has said, "The difficulty hitherto has been that every institution of higher learning has sought to be with a few exceptions, like every other. What we need is a greater variety, serving different aims in a differentiated division of labor. There is no reason why some institutions cannot be primarily in the service of scholarship and learning, with little need to take on added responsibilities. Some institutions can be oriented primarily to research, and others to training."[23] I am not competent to say to what extent the costs of postsecondary education have been pushed up because of this emulation of the mainline model, but perhaps some planning in the direction of a more pluralistic system might help to check costs, but even if it does not, a more differentiated system is more functional for the emerging society.

At the top of this differentiated system there might be, to follow Bell's suggestion for the United States, a national system of autonomous elite universities carrying on the traditional role of scholarship and enjoying the traditional immunities that universities have always enjoyed. In Canada these national universities could be located strategically and regionally. They could be developed out of existing universities or created anew. They would be appropriately anglophone or francophone. They would govern themselves independently, but they would draw their funds from federal sources and their students would receive federal grants. Their research interests would be pure rather than applied. They would be truly national resources and the centres of excellence that we hear so much about in discussions of science policy. The provinces would continue to have their universities of course, but they would put greater emphasis on local needs and on professional and technical training. The provinces would also continue to run their college level postsecondary institutions. Essential to this national system of higher education would be a research and service system, as was suggested previously, to undertake client- and mission-oriented research associated with or separated from the national universities. These research institutes, for the social sciences as well as natural sciences, could be entirely federally supported or could be jointly supported by federal and provincial governments. More likely provincial governments would buy services from them. In such a national system the federal government would assume the planning and support of the highest level scholarship and research in the light of national goals while the provinces would continue to provide postsecondary education of a less costly and a more local kind.

There is no doubt that such a national system contains an important elitist element, but the fact is that it is unlikely that Canada warrants more than a few outstanding universities. The elitist character would have to be countered by making the provincial universities attractive and no less expensive to the student so that the poorer students do not go to them because of differential fees. This is what is happening in the Ontario system where the Colleges of Applied Arts and Technology draw their students in the main from lower social class levels than do the universities. The fact is, however, that the provincial universities and their colleges would remain attactive because of their more direct manpower function.

In order to develop such a system it would be necessary to establish a federal government agency responsible for planning higher education and not just for supporting provincial demands. The planning should be done, of course, in association with the provinces, but the point to be made is that the federal government has a responsibility to look after the nation's needs, which are in so many respects over and above the needs of the individual provinces. There has been little planning, even within provinces, although one may have a distorted view from the Ontario experience. The most we have done is to respond to pressures, some of them having very little to do with educational needs. A good amount of the planning, particularly that related to research institutes, would have to be linked in with Canadian science policy, whatever that might become.

I realize of course that a proposal such as the one which I have just made may be thought to be a way-out pipe dream, particularly among those who under the pressure of day-to-day exigencies have to keep the system going rather than plan for its future. For such people there may be a more acceptable approach, although planning is pretty much inescapable if costs are to be controlled. In keeping with my general theme that the task of a system of higher education is to serve national needs as well as provincial ones, and that this requires national planning rather than simply fiscal transfers which the provinces use in the way they see fit, there are two points which I want to make. One is that there are important federal responsibilities that the universities in particular serve (it is interesting that the manpower retraining scheme—education at its lowest and most parochial level—has a heavy federal commitment and constitutes almost all of federal manpower planning) and for that reason the federal government should plan its inputs. The prototype is the Royal Military College which presumably has its constitutional legality in the federal government's responsibility for defence. There are also federal government agricultural research stations on university campuses. Why not extend this principle with institutes of international affairs, programs of area studies (the Pacific Rim, for example), modern language schools, institutes of public administration, institutes of penology and so on through the whole range of federal responsibilities. Here again a federal government agency could co-ordinate the federal needs and deal directly with universities. Since many of these specialized areas concern research and graduate studies their support would be a sizable financial contribution.

No doubt the federal government response to such suggestions would be that it is because of these federal responsibilities that it supports postsecondary education through the present fiscal arrangements, and that somehow national needs are met by the ten provinces acting by themselves without any co-ordination. Therefore, no national planning is required. Surely national planning is required. It is not likely that any agency is at present engaged in extensive planning. In the meantime we may find that some provinces are making contributions to national goals which place an unfair burden on them.

Over and Beyond the Provinces

As I have tried to argue, there are national needs for postsecondary education that constitute something more than the simple addition of all provincial needs which are exclusive to the provinces themselves. One interesting way to measure these extraprovincial contributions is to look at the "demography" of university enrolments. Components of this extraprovincial contribution would be the proportions of students from each province who are studying in other provinces, the proportions of students who come from abroad, and the interprovincial migration of those with university education.

With respect to the first of these, the Atlantic Provinces lead all the others in the proportion of their young people who are attending university outside their own province. In 1967–68 the proportions were 28.4 per cent for P.E.I., 18.5 per cent for New Brunswick, 14 per cent for Nova Scotia, and 13 per cent for Newfoundland. Other provincial proportions ranged downward to Ontario's 4.9 per cent.[24] It could be expected that a higher proportion of the interprovincial enrolments would be those from neighboring provinces or perhaps from the regional groupings with which we are used to viewing Canada, particularly the Atlantic Provinces, and the Prairie Provinces. Thus one would anticipate in the Atlantic Provinces, for example, that most of the out-of-province students would come from the region, a fact which would call for the provinces developing regional university systems. However, the proportion of students from regional neighborhoods is not nearly as great as the proportion from outside the region combined with that from outside the country. The pattern can be illustrated by Nova Scotia where 8 per cent of the students come from outside Canada, 10 per cent from outside the region, and 13 per cent from other regional provinces. New Brunswick has a similar pattern. In Manitoba 7 per cent of students come from outside the country, about 4.5 per cent from outside the Prairie region, and 4.5 per cent from regional neighbors. The Ontario-Quebec exchanges are much less between each other than between, for each of them, those outside the country and those from other provinces. With each other in 1967–68 these two provinces exchanged 4800 students, but between them took in 10 124 students from outside the country and 3279 from other provinces besides themselves. The proportions of students are not large, however, since 13 per cent of Ontario's students come from either outside the country or from outside the province, while 7.2 per cent of Quebec's do. These proportions of students from outside the province and outside the country can, of course, be interpreted in different ways. They can be regarded as some sizable cross-provincial educational contributions or as relative provincial self-sufficiency. It is important to interpret them in the light of federal policy aims. If one policy aim is through fiscal transfers to make each province self-sufficient in the provision of student places in and for itself, then low or decreasing proportions of interprovincial student migration would be considered a good thing. Other policies, however, might not be so regressive or so parochial. It could be argued that increasing rates of such cross-provincial student migration are an important factor in promoting national unity, and that such migration should be encouraged. If the protection of interprovincial student migrants who are graduate students is greater than those who are undergraduates then a higher proportion of university costs are involved than implied by enrolment figures. There are good grounds for believing that this is the case, and so policy aims more likely become those of national highly qualified manpower needs.

With respect to the second component of the demography of university enrolments, students from outside the country raise different policy questions, but scarcely those which concern provinces. What are Canada's obligations to the international exchange of educational facilities? There is not only the recognized obligation to the developing world, but the obligation to balance the foreign educational resources used by Canadians. Moreover, cross-national migration of students is an important factor in international understanding. As with internal student migrants, there is little doubt that the proportion of foreign graduate students greatly exceeds the proportion of undergraduates, making the proportions of university budgets involved higher than simple enrolment figures would suggest. In Ontario, for example, where enrolments make up about a third of all Canadian enrolments and about one-half of all graduate enrolments in Canada, the percentage of students from outside Canada was in 1967–68 6.5 per cent, but of graduate students it was closer to 40 per cent.[25] Thus the question arises: is it Ontario as a province or Canada as a nation which should determine policy with respect to foreign students?

With respect to the third component, some evidence on the mobility of university-trained people can be found in a 1966 Labour Force Survey.[26] In the age range 25–44 of those with university education 17 per cent did their university work in a different province and 20 per cent in a different country. In the 45–64 age group it was the reverse, 20 per cent in a different province and 17 per cent in a different country. Thus in both age groups only about 60 per cent of university-trained people received their education in the province in which they resided. The proportions are considerably less for those with less than university education. Generally it can be stated that the higher the educational level attained the greater is the mobility and the greater, therefore, is the university contribution to national manpower needs. To quote the Macdonald Report, "The fraction of graduate students employed in the province of their graduation is small; only Ontario retains more than half of its Ph.D. recipients."[27]

Overproduction or Overspecialization?

For some time there has been a fear of overproducing highly qualified manpower and a consequent unemployment of professional workers and waste of educational resources. Until very recently these fears were unwarranted. During the last year, however, it appears that many Ph.D. students both in Canada and the United States are facing difficulties in getting jobs which they consider suitable for their qualifications. In part their difficulties arise from present economic restraints which have led to cutbacks in appropriations for research activity. The present tight job market for Ph.D.s trained to do research might, therefore, be temporary and does nothing to lessen the argument that the trend of postindustrialism is the absorption of more and more highly qualified workers. For societies experiencing rapid technological change there never will be a tidy fit or a realization of a theoretical maximizing of the use of trained manpower. If the observation that ". . . the disequilibrium between the supply of and the demand for human resources cannot be overcome in the short run,"[28] is correct, then we must expect such discrepancies, as upsetting as that may be for some.

To take another view, perhaps there should be some overproduction to establish standards of quality. University degrees are not a uniform commodity, and it might be useful in a difficult job market to sort people a little more on the basis of quality than is possible when there are substantial shortages of people rather than jobs.

We also assume that there is a low level of substitutability of highly qualified manpower. Perhaps this assumption is not correct. Perhaps highly qualified people can adapt their training to a variety of jobs. At least the possibilities have not been fully explored as to whether with a minimum of retraining the stock of highly qualified workers can be made more adjustable to changing occupational needs. It is almost impossible to forecast occupation by occupation, labor force requirements with any degree of accuracy, but we do know there is a persistent growth in the category of professional occupations. For this reason we might consider that we have a problem of overspecialization rather than overproduction. In that case, our educational planning is at fault because we place too great an emphasis on specific discipline content rather than on content common to all disciplines. This condition exists at both undergraduate and graduate levels, although it is slowly being corrected at the undergraduate level where the output of highly trained honors students is no longer the primary objective. At the graduate level, however, there is still a high degree of specialization and professionalization. It is difficult for Canadian universities to innovate and reduce this element of specialization in their graduate programs because many of them are young and their faculties take as their models the more prestigious departments in the mainline universities in the United States. Such orientation is thought to be necessary to be recognized. Perhaps, as is so often the case, the initiative will have to come from outside. The postindustrial society is one of accelerated rates of change. Therefore, those who leave our universities should have skills which are flexible and adaptable in a rapidly changing world.

We should consider also that our lack of planning is now having some undesirable consequences. Perhaps we are producing too many chemists and not enough city planners or whatever it is that we need. It is doubtful whether we have really overproduced to any extent in the scientific and engineering fields, but if we have done so, then these mistakes, if such they are in the long run, should not lead us to conclude that we have overinvested in the educational field in the light of our overall needs or that we can slacken our efforts to build across Canada a system of higher education that will be appropriate to our needs over the next ten years or so.

Postscript

After writing about the need for a national system and rereading Mr. Trudeau's 1957 paper "Federal Grants to Universities," it occurred to me that perhaps I have overstated his opposition to federal participation, or that time and circumstances might have changed his views. At one point he says,

> I am not saying, *a priori*, that education (at least university education) should never fall under concurrent federal jurisdiction: it might well be in the general interest for the central state to undertake immediately an enlargement of our cultural horizons, or to cooperate in the large-scale production of technicians to come to grips

with our own underdeveloped state, our economic rivals, and our ideological enemies. But this needs to be proved. Above all, as a citizen I would require that such a revolutionary interpretation of our constitution be made the object of a conscious choice. I would demand that political parties take a clear stand on the matter and make their reasons public, thus allowing the electorate to decide with full knowledge of the issues involved.[29]

In this paper I have tried to present a line of argument and offer some evidence (falling short of proof no doubt) of what might be ". . . in the general interest for the central state . . . ."

Notes

1. Daniel Bell, "The Measurement of Knowledge and Technology," in E.B. Sheldon and W.E. Moore, *Indicators of Social Change*, New York, Russell Sage, 1968, pp. 145 ff.

2. Herman Kahn and Anthony J. Wiener, *The Year 2000*, New York, Macmillan, 1967, p. 63.

3. Daniel Bell, "Notes on the Post-Industrial Society," *The Public Interest*, Winter 1967, p. 30.

4. *Ibid.*

5. J.K. Galbraith, *The New Industrial State*, Boston, Houghton Mifflin, 1967, p. 282.

6. Bertram Gross, *The State of the Nation*, London, Tavistock Publications, 1966, p. 80.

7. As reprinted in *Ottawa Journal*, May 25, 1970.

8. E.g., Economic Council of Canada, *First Annual Report*, p. 167.

9. Bernard R. Blishen, "Social Class and Opportunity in Canada," *Canadian Review of Sociology and Anthropology*, vol. 7, no. 2, 1970, pp. 110–127.

10. Michael D. Lagacé, *Educational Attainment in Canada: Some Regional and Social Aspects*, Ottawa, DBS, 1968 (Special Labour Force Study No. 7).

11. A.E. Safarian, *The Performance of Foreign-Owned Firms in Canada*, Montreal, The Private Planning Association, 1969, chap. 2.

12. *Ibid.*

13. C.M. Drury, as reported in OECD, *Reviews of National Science Policy: Canada*, Paris, OECD, 1969, p. 434.

14. Lagacé, *Educational Attainment in Canada*, corrected Table C3.

15. OECD, *Reviews of National Science Policy: Canada.*

16. "U.S. Universities Don't Know What They're Doing or Why, Robert M. Hutchins Says," *The Chronicle of Higher Education*, March 9, 1970.

17. I have tried to analyse some of the student award data: see John Porter, "Canadian Universities: Democratization and The Need For a National System," *Minerva*, Summer 1970.

18. Howard R. Bowden, *The Finance of Higher Education*, New York, Carnegie Commission on Higher Education.

19. *Report No. 4*, Ottawa, Queen's Printer, pp. 13ff.

20. Reported in *Ottawa Journal*.

21. P.E. Trudeau, *Federalism and the French Canadians*, Toronto, Macmillan of Canada, 1968, p. 81.

22. Daniel Bell, "Quo Warranto ?—notes on the governance of universities in the 1970s," *Public Interest*, Spring 1970, pp. 53–68.

23. *Ibid.*, p. 64.

24. Z.E. Zsigmond and C.J. Wenaas, *Enrolment in Educational Institutions By Province 1951–52 to 1980–81*, Ottawa, Economic Council of Canada, 1970, Appendix D.

25. *Survey of Citizenship of Graduate Students Enrolled in Master's and Doctoral Degree Programs at Ontario Universities in 1969–70 (With Comparative Statistics for 1968–69)*, Research Division of the Committee of Presidents of Universities of Ontario, April 1970.

26. Lagacé, *Educational Attainment in Canada*, p. 11.

27. John B. Macdonald *et al.*, *The Role of the Federal Government in Support of Research in Canadian Universities*, Ottawa, Queen's Printer, 1969, p. 202.

28. Gottfried Bombach, "Manpower Forecasting and Educational Policy," *Sociology of Education*, vol. 38, no. 5, 1965, p. 344.

29. Trudeau, *Federalism and the French Canadians*, p. 83.

9

Power and Freedom in Canadian Democracy

Egalitarian values find their outward expression in socialist movements. Socialism, like Christian denominationalism, comes in many forms in both ideology and practice. In its name have been imposed cruel and dictatorial regimes as well as moderate reforms within a framework of democratic institutions and civil liberties. It is the latter "weak socialism" of reform which has become the objective of the social democratic movements of Europe and the New Democratic party in Canada.

The strength of socialist ideology, whether it is of the strong variety represented by Marxism or the weak variety of democratic socialism, lies in its powerful critique of the inequality that has emerged with modern capitalism. Much less convincing have been socialist programs for change. The world has now seen two generations of socialist development in the Soviet Union and one generation in several eastern European countries under the hegemony of the Soviet Union. To the western egalitarian there is not much that is attractive about these developments. They have not been terribly productive and whatever gains they might have accomplished in an egalitarian direction have been at great cost in civil liberties and human freedom.

Democratic socialist programs have had only modest success in changing the fundamentally unequal structures of modern capitalist society. They have been scarcely successful at all in North America, including Canada, which had by the late 1970s advanced somewhat more into the "welfare state" than had the United States. The extent to which welfare programs are redistributive and therefore serve egalitarian ends has been limited because they are based on regressive tax structures, and because groups in the middle level of resource distribution are able to ultilize them disproportionately. As long as western economies remained buoyant and continued to grow, it was possible to enjoy improved standards of living and some welfare programs based more on an insurance principle than on that of redistribution. Unlimited growth and the sense of perpetual affluence was to end by the

207

middle 1970s, and, in a resurgence of conservative sentiment, welfare systems came very much into question. Thus, both the strong and weak varieties of socialism have done little to reduce the structure of inequality in modern societies, and so in large measure socialist literature remains critical rather than programmatic.

In a paper written in 1960, I attempted to make a contribution, which was critical and prescriptive, if not programmatic, to social democratic theory. The occasion was the desire on the part of a group of Canadian social scientists with a "left-of-centre viewpoint" to produce a collection of critical papers on the Canadian economy and society reminiscent of Social Planning for Canada *which had served as a framework in the 1930s for C.C.F. policy making. The later book,* Social Purpose for Canada, *coincided with the founding of the New Democratic party in 1961. The edtior of this volume, Michael Oliver, became the first national president of the New Democratic party, which replaced the C.C.F. as the "inside left" of Canadian politics.*

The paper, which is reproduced here with some outdated statistics on economic concentration removed, deals not so much with the usual left critiques of capitalist enterprise, but with two of the major problems of complex modern societies which seemed to me to be independent of the ownership of the means of production. One was the inescapable social need to concentrate power in such broad realms of social organization as the economic, political, military, and so forth, regardless of whether a system was socialist or capitalist. The second problem was the capacity that large-scale bureaucracy, the major instrument of power, has to destroy human creative potential. I wrote of freedom as a condition necessary to be creative, and of power as the capacity of some to monopolize creativity. Power expands at the expense of freedom in the authority and work structures of contemporary society.

Some of the observations which this paper contains anticipated criticisms that became popular by the late 1970s in books like Harry Braverman's Labor and Monopoly Capital. *Work was becoming degraded, as Braverman put it, by the continuously extending division of labor in both the blue- and white-collar occupations. How this seemingly inexorable process of bureaucratization and alienation might be halted and at the same time high levels of productivity maintained is a fundamental question for the next stage in social development which some call postindustrial. The renouncing of capitalist modes of production may be necessary but can by no means be sufficient.*

Reading "Power and Freedom in Canadian Democracy" almost twenty years later, I think I would have to give less credit to the welfare state for what it then appeared to have already accomplished. It was still a period of hope for equality through reform, and only recently has the failure of the welfare state become apparent in part because of our improved methodologies for measuring inequality, but also because there has now been enough time to show how minimal in many countries the degree of redistribution has been. I would probably want also to modify my views about how the changing occupational structure which has come with industrialism really provides upward mobility. In fact, other essays in this book on education and equality indicate how my views are changing. Time has also shown me to be overly generous about the productive potential of socialist economies, or at least about their capacity to provide some of the basic human needs, such as for privacy in living space.

The paper, I think, remains a strong critique of the effects of bureaucratic forms of organization, and its call for worker participation in management and democratic planning processes is still very contemporary although advances in that direction, particularly in Canada, must be measured in millimetres rather than miles. Similarly, the idea is still very much alive that democratically planned societies, even when they are based on large-scale industry, must solve the dilemma of power by building in mechanisms of achieving political and social consensus which are responsive to human needs as these are expressed by mobilized publics. Some of the other essays pick up these themes and make a due acknowledgment to Amitai Etzioni's The Active Society.

Power is the right that some people have to direct the affairs of others. It is a product of human society, and therefore appears wherever human beings associate. Most discussions of power are concerned with the power of the state because, at the national level, holders of power have effective means of enforcing their wills. It is wrong, however, to exclude from consideration the power which exists in all our institutions and associations, in small social groups as well as in large ones. Also, if we wish to understand the nature of power, we must look both geographically and historically beyond our own society. Even at the lowest levels of social development, where society is little more than a collection of related families, the power of some over others can be found. This ubiquity of power has its roots in human psychology, and power grows within social relationships. Even the commonly experienced social relationship of love has this quality of power. Tyrannical demands can be made in the name of love, and love can also lead to abject submissiveness.

Freedom is the very antithesis of power because in simplest terms it means the ability to direct one's own affairs. Throughout human society there is a struggle between freedom and power. Like power, this desire for freedom can also be traced to human psychology. It stems from needs which must be met if the human organism is to survive. The satisfaction of organic needs provides an elementary freedom; but it is of paramount concern only in societies near the borderlines of subsistence. At higher levels of social development a new order of needs appears which might be called cultural needs. An example is the need to acquire complex skills in order to realize one's potentialities. If these cultural needs are not fulfilled the individual's life is so restricted that he feels he is not free. As social development proceeds these cultural needs become much more varied and therefore the struggle for freedom is never won.

Thus, freedom is relative, depending on the level of social and cultural development. No discussion of freedom can be confined to its primitive aspects of satisfying material needs and removing despotic political restrictions. Rather, we must keep in mind that at higher levels of social development freedom must be assessed in terms of the quality of social life, and particularly in terms of the manner in which these derived cultural needs are satisfied.

Human beings are such complex organisms that it is not surprising that they have such contradictory psychological elements. Throughout history an explanation of these contradictions has been sought in the analysis of human nature. In the modern period explanations have been sought in the nature of human society. Even psychology, which has taken over from theology the task of understanding the individual soul, recognizes that social institutions mould human behavior. An enormous range of consequences follows from the fact that human beings are social animals, and that their very existence and survival depend on relations with other human beings. Here we are concerned with only a narrow range of the consequences of man's need for society—the co-existence of power and freedom.

However simple the social structure, ordered relationships are essential. Among these ordered relations are those which grant the right to a few to make decisions on behalf of the group. At the primitive level the kinds of decisions which have to be made may seem to us elementary, but for the primitive group they may be crucial. Someone has to decide when the hunt should begin and the direction it should take, when planting should begin, whether or not the distribution of the catch or the harvest conforms to the customs of the community, whether or not a neighboring tribe is to be attacked, and so forth. These decision-making rights, essential at any level of social development, inhere in the leadership roles of particular social institutions—head of the kin group, tribal elder, magician, shaman, managing director, prime minister, arch-bishop, and so on.

It follows also from the nature of social organization that there can be no power or authority without obedience. There would be no point in assigning decision-making rights to individuals who hold particular institutional positions unless there was a high probability that their orders would be carried out. Men control or suppress their desire for freedom or, more likely, they are trained at an early age to accept particular systems of authority as good. In return they get some security and a stable set of expectations about the behavior of their fellows. Power and authority often bring personal gain as individuals appropriate rights beyond those granted for their institutional roles. A privileged ruling class based on a hereditary principle emerges when a number of power-holders transmit these appropriated rights to their children.

An individual's personal freedom can depend on the power that he has over other men. In the pre-industrial stage of social development the power that some men had to extract tribute from other men ensured their elementary freedom, and at the same time left them free to pursue other interests. Conversely the man who labored so that he could deliver his tribute had a very restricted area of freedom. It is not possible here to trace the long historical struggle between these contradictory qualities in social life nor the developments, particularly the personal appropriation of rights, that have strengthened personal and class power, hereditary ruling classes, and the development of ideologies such as the divine right of kings.

It is important, however, to remember that social organization cannot exist without power. Power cannot be shuffled out of the world by utopian philosophies; nor can the dangers associated with giving power rights to individuals—capitalists or planners—be completely removed. With a great deal of imaginative experimentation we could no doubt create an institutional order in which the risks were minimized. Such a goal requires a psychological transformation in our industrial masses, whose apathy perhaps constitutes the greatest impediment to the growth of a free society in which human creative potential can be released. There is, as Erich Fromm and others have pointed out, a widespread fear of freedom, because of the sense of isolation and impotence which individuals feel in the modern mass society. There is, moreover, a readiness to accept the standards of consumption provided through the supermarket, the credit card, and the finance company, as the indexes of freedom. If a society is to be built in which human beings are free to develop and to experience the satisfaction of the higher order of needs which we have called cultural, it can only be done by the use of power. I shall return later to the problem of power in relation to democratic planning. First we must look at some of the reasons why capitalism with its dominant theme of private appropriation is so widely accepted as the basis of the industrial order.

The Plutocratic Ethos

In western industrial economies, the principle of power over other men through property rights became perpetuated, even though the legal binding of serf to master which had existed in the previous stage of development had been abandoned in favor of a common status of free citizens who could make their own contracts. Individual property rights meant that those who owned the instruments of production controlled their use and access to them. In many respects the new urban proletariat of the industrial revolution was less free than the feudal serf who had at least some legally defined claims against his master.

The statistics of misery, squalor, and filth that describe the human cost of the nineteeth century's transition to industrialization are a part of every history student's notes. They were the evidence for the socialist condemnation of private ownership of productive instruments. Private ownership of property gave power to the privileged few over the many. There were various views about the condition of the new industrial masses, but the one which played such an important part in socialist thought was the Marxian doctrine of increasing misery, which held that at some point the intolerable conditions would explode into a class war in which private property, the source of all evil, would be abolished. While not all socialists agreed with the Marxian method of getting rid of private ownership, most of them agreed that private ownership of productive resources was an instrument of class oppression. Political institutions were thought, not without justification, to be mere agents of privately owned economic institutions. It followed that if the instruments of government were used to protect capitalist society, they could also become the means of destroying capitalism and thus enter into the service of the socialist principle of economic equality. Thus, to capture the state, either by bomb or ballot, became the goal of proletarian movements.

History never did follow the course predicted for it by nineteenth-century socialists. In the long run, rather than increasing misery, there has been a constant improvement in material standards, as measured by personal consumption, in societies where capitalism reached its highest development. Proletarian revolutions have taken place where capitalism has been retarded, or where there has been colonial rule. Moreover, in some capitalist countries with universal manhood suffrage, working-class socialist parties have never come to power and in others they have been in power for only very short periods. It was not until 1945 in England that a working-class party won a decisive victory at the polls. In Canada, although the socialist movement has had considerable strength in urban areas, it is in an agrarian province that it has acquired power. It is little wonder that socialist theorists, in the face of this widespread acceptance of the capitalist order, have begun to re-examine some of their fundamental ideas about social organization.

It is worth considering briefly some of the changes that have come about and confounded socialist doctrine. In the first place, within the economic system powerful trade unions have developed which, to some extent, have been able to counter the power of private ownership of productive instruments with the power of collective refusal to work them. Furthermore, the occupational structure of modern industry does not break the work world into two classes, one working in dirt and drudgery, and the other with more refined tasks and the power of command. Instead we find occupational gradations, involving increasing degrees of skill and supervising rights. The increasing complexity of industrial techniques has had its counterpart in the wide range of values we assign to the various occupations. Prestige attaches to the different kinds of skills that the industrial system requires. The recruiting ground for these skill groups has been the formerly unskilled laboring classes. While the Horatio Alger myth can be refuted by the facts of occupational inheritance at the very top levels of the industrial world, what cannot be refuted is the widespread movement upwards that is possible within the boundaries of the lower and middle levels. Along with an improved material standard of living has gone an increasing opportunity to improve one's status or to have one's children achieve higher status, however slight, than oneself.

Industrial societies have been upwardly mobile societies, at least sufficiently so to reduce resentment and frustration throughout the working classes. Along with this actual mobility has gone a very intense belief, particularly in North America, in unlimited opportunity to get ahead. While there is a great discrepancy between the image of a mobile society and the reality of the social impediments to getting ahead, the image is widely enough held to counteract most charges about the inequality of opportunity. Recent studies[1] would suggest that there is more mobility in some European societies than there is in North America, even though the latter continent is thought to provide greater opportunity. The image of opportunity in North America is to some extent a retention from an earlier period, when immigrants were escaping from political oppression or the misery of economic change. The fact is that some opportunity is inherent in the industrial growth which has been experienced in both capitalist Europe and America.

Another change in the twentieth century is the cumulative welfare measures which have created the "welfare state." While the associations of the corporate and some professional worlds still view these developments with horror, some basic welfare measures are a part of our social life. Most of these changes have been in response to popular demands expressed in the platforms of working-class movements. Nowadays no political party of the right would think of removing them. In fact they have reached the status of electoral bribes. The development of social welfare can be seen as a series of concessions within the capitalist order, but these concessions are very important and have gone a long way towards destroying the doctrine of increasing misery. Along with welfare measures there has been some redistribution of income through the transfer payments and the taxation of corporate wealth to bear the cost of heavy government expenditure on defence and other services. Capitalism in other words has undergone sufficient transformation that it is difficult to relate present reality to the model built up in socialist theory.

While we have been talking about capitalist industrial society in general, what we have said applies also to Canadian experience. A strong labor movement, even though it is threatened from time to time, acts as an important check against economic exploitation. With the transition in Canada from agriculture to industry the occupational structure has become more complex, making for differentiation of occupational status and some mobility into skill classes. Although our welfare measures are not as extensive as in other countries, and anything but uniform from province to province, there is an improvement over earlier conditions. The doctrine of increasing misery is no more applicable to Canada than it is to other societies based on capitalism. These historical developments have meant that the power of economic exploitation of individuals through capitalist institutions has been curbed. Socialism's *raison d'être* therefore has to be reformulated. Particularly in need of examination is the idea that the solutions to the problems of power lie exclusively within the economic realm.

We must accept the fact that industrial capitalism has raised individual consumption standards, and provided in the process of its growth a new level of occupational opportunity. The words individual consumption standards have been used purposely to avoid the popular illusion that capitalism has brought the highest standard of living ever known. Such a notion implies the use of a measuring device or index which is rarely made more explicit than the per capita ownership of automobiles and refrigerators. International and historical comparisons using such indexes are frequently pointless. In some countries with a different population distribution automobiles are not so important, and in others climate does not make refrigerators so essential for the preservation of food. A more important question is why are particular indexes chosen rather than others? The answer in part is that in the capitalist ethos standards are erected in terms of individual ownership of things, but there are many other indexes which could be used with equal or perhaps greater claims to validity. Canada, for example, ranks eighth in the world for its infantile mortality rate.[2] It has nothing to be proud of in its educational systems. No one would argue that our cities are places where human beings can live a good life in an atmosphere free from pollution and traffic hazard. The condition of Lake Ontario prevents the inhabitants of the large urban mass in the vicinity of Toronto from swimming in it. None of our cities are likely to be held up as models of town planning. Of the billions of dollars spent in housing construction in the last decade it is safe to say that no more than a small fraction has been spent on projects that would conform to accepted standards of community planning. Statistics of owner-occupied dwellings are also used to demonstrate a high standard of living, but these figures ignore the fact that a large number of lower-income families who do manage to find a down payment on a house can keep up their payments only by renting out a part of the house they have bought. Owners do not always have the exclusive use of their homes.

Within any measure of a standard of living there would have to be included that income which can only be derived from social investment: education, health and hospitalization, planned cities, roads, parks, and so forth. In an index that did include these items capitalist Canada would probably do less favorably than some European countries in which capitalism has been modified by the presence, and in some cases a period in office, of powerful socialist parties.

Even if one accepted the argument that, measured by any index, capitalism has created the highest material standard of living ever known, it does not logically follow that it will continue to do so. We are only now beginning to see something of the enormous productive potential of the Soviet Union. It would simply be an extension of the error which I have pointed out if we tried to compare indexes of production and consumption of capitalist North America and the Soviet Union. At higher levels of development social life cannot be compared in material terms, but if capitalism chooses to be compared on the criterion of material things it may well take fright at the challenge now presented to it by other systems.

The reformulation of socialist theory must start with the fact that, despite the material levels it has created, capitalism has not lost its exploitative character. There is no longer the exploitation by entrepreneurs of a disorganized proletariat, but what has emerged with the new bureaucratic and corporate forms of capitalism is the monopolization of a society's creative potential. The new scale of corporate organization is such that our institutions become moulded to corporate needs. What we might become as a society, judging by the manner in which we welcome outside capital of corporations, is measured in terms of our exploitability by corporations.

Social goals are now established by a much smaller number than in the days of entrepreneurial capitalism. Because of the traditional rights of private property, enshrined in the myth that corporations are individuals, the corporate elite hold the creative privileges available. Only a few men have the creative privilege of building a new industry or destroying an old one, of establishing a new university, planning a new hospital, or developing a new resource. Often it is the same men who do all these things. From large industrial complexes to organized philanthropy, creative rights continue to be monopolized by the corporate elite. So accustomed are we to seeing progress solely in terms of increased material wealth, the gross national product, or real wages, that we ignore the fact that the vast majority in our mass democracies do not participate in any kind of creative behavior.

Freedom, as we have suggested, is relative to the level of social development. We recognize this relativity in material things when we include in the cost of living index items which half a century ago would have been considered luxuries, but we rarely think of creative experience either in the individual sense or in the sense of group and social achievement as an item in the index of the good life. Such behavior continues to be a class privilege because those who engage in it are educated, or have inherited a way of life which is essential to its realization, or they occupy commanding positions in our institutional systems—economic, religious, educational, and so forth. Since our institutional elites are predominantly recruited from the higher segments of our class structure, our social and cultural values tend to be defined in class terms. In religious behavior, for example, the enriched ritualism of the Anglican Church is thought to be more refined and appropriate to high status than evangelical forms of worship, and it is not unlikely that as a person improves his status he will change his religion, if he is Protestant, and start to read T.S. Eliot. Another cultural value which seems to be built into our institutional structure is that an individual's status is related to the number of men he controls in his work—which implies that power itself is a value.

The pervasiveness of class values can be seen to some extent in the modified goals of proletarian movements. Often their aims are no more than to capture the items of bourgeois conventionality, or to achieve a style of living as advertised in *Life*, a style that takes its cue in turn from the bourgeois values of the *New Yorker* and *Harper's Bazaar*. Recent studies in the United Kingdom would suggest that the reduced popularity of the Labour party can be accounted for by the improvement in the material standard of living among some of the working class.[3] The name "Labour" party, it would seem, is regarded as not quite respectable. Why it is that the material items, often cheap and gaudy, of the bourgeois way of life should have such an appeal must ultimately be explained in terms of social psychology. Perhaps it is the result of the continuous assault on the mind by the advertisers. Instead of producing what it needs, a plutocratically controlled society must sell what it produces. Eventually we are convinced that the color of a soap affects its cleansing qualities or that a triangularly shaped soda cracker is "dainty."

A further consequence of the creation of artificial demand through advertising is the standardization of taste and the obliteration of regional and ethnic cultures. Of all our ethnic groups the French Canadians are most aware of the possible loss of regional and ethnic identity. Frequently these fears can be exploited in the most Machiavellian fashion by our elites, but the French desire for cultural separation can be justified both psychologically and socially. A massive homogeneous national culture can only intensify that sense of isolation and powerlessness of which we have spoken. Democratic social planning must preserve and foster group differences, because it is through identification with small rather than massive social aggregates that the individual can avoid the feeling of isolation. The national mass is much more susceptible to the manipulative techniques of modern power and modern demagogues. A well-drilled uniformity ensures an uncritical predisposition to obedience.

If bourgeois values are to be transferred to the working classes why should capitalism not carry on, prodded from time to time by working-class movements? The answer surely lies in the desirability of social participation in defining and achieving goals, in the release of the potential for a creative life shared with others, governed not through competitiveness and authoritarianism but through co-operation.

The use of words like creativity and spontaneity can be criticized on the grounds of their vagueness, and the difficulty of attaching them as labels to particular kinds of behavior or to particular subjective states. In simplest terms what is meant by these words is the expression of the self. When a child is given the opportunity to paint or draw with his own choice of colors whatever he likes, what results is a creative act. Similarly, a group of children dancing will rarely be watching each other. Their movements are free and express feelings which are exclusively individual. Adults too experience this creative expression when they become amateur artists or join classes in writing or learn to play the flute. It is no doubt such a need for expression which is behind the do-it-yourself movement and the great zeal of suburban gardening. Whatever may be said of the architectural uniformity of suburban developments there is always some self-expression with house color and landscaping or interior decorating. (One of the failures, incidentally, of public housing schemes is that tenants are frequently denied this freedom of expression.)

Bodily movements also permit the expression of the self. The heightened feelings which come from the skilful use of the limbs are akin to the satisfactions of creative activity. We recognize too that to be creative limbs must have freedom from clothing and therefore we make "appropriate" varying degrees of undress which in other situations would be considered immodest. Often the creativity of bodily movements is achieved in partnership with physical surroundings. The exhilaration of the skier comes as much from the sensory delight of sun and snow as it does from the control which he has over his movements. Creativity is not always self-expression. At the appropriate times we can be creative with others. Social organization requires us to work with others. What we must seek are the conditions under which working with others towards common goals produces the kinds of satisfaction and feelings which we associate with individual creativity.

The close and intimate atmosphere of the family affords the best conditions for individuals to work together to create bonds of affection and mutual support. It is in the primary social grouping that individuals can learn love and respect for others. The acquisition of these primary sentiments leads in turn to the establishment of social bonds outside the family, particularly within the community. It is doubtful that, except in unconscious perversions of them, such sentiments can be extended beyond community and region to encompass such large aggregates as modern nations, and for that reason, as I shall argue later, decentralization is essential in the democratically planned society. It is important to realize that creative expression cannot develop without policies to foster it. We place a great value on the family as a social institution and yet we require families to live in dismal surroundings which are scarcely conducive to the building of creative relationships. The vast conurbations which are beginning to sprawl out from our metropolitan areas are more likely to brutalize the senses than to spark that sensual element in creative behavior. What a struggle it is to preserve parkland in our large cities from the subdividers and the developers!

Many will argue that continued socialist piety in an age of so-called affluence is a form of obsessive neurosis, but we can point to many indexes of socially derived disorder—delinquency, mental illness, drug addiction, alcoholism, suicide and the like—which would suggest that we are not producing human happiness. It must be remembered too that these pathological conditions are not confined to a single class, although each class has its peculiar kind of deviant behavior. The fate of a drunk or a mentally disturbed person will depend on his class position, so that statistics of any particular form of deviance will not reflect its true class incidence.

It was the great achievement of Emile Durkheim, the French sociologist, to show that the indexes of deviant behavior are as likely to be high in periods of prosperity as in periods of poverty. In periods of prosperity, when individual gain is the prevailing value there is an absence of an encompassing moral order which binds people together for common social ends. Even the rich comforts of *Crestwood Heights*, as the authors of that book have shown, do not make its members immune from anxieties and psychic strains.

In Canada we have seen recently many cases of corruption in public life and of the exploitation of responsible social roles for personal gain. Many of these instances lie in the financial and commercial worlds, whose institutions lend themselves so readily to this kind of behavior. Businessmen do not really see restrictive trade practices as criminal behavior, nor does their prestige fall when their firms appear in court. The stock manipulations of certain former Ontario cabinet ministers did not preclude them from running again for public office. Nor did they prevent their associates from continuing in office. This lack of conscience can only be explained in terms of habituation to the capitalist ethos and the complex of attitudes which legitimates predatory behavior. Our elites do not endanger the public interest because the public so readily accepts their definition of its interest.

We tend to draw examples of the exploitative character of power roles from the economic realm, but they can be found in other institutions as well. The mass media, with their close ownership links with our local and national plutocracies, help to define the moral basis of capitalist institutions through their constant repetition of the stereotyped benevolence of these institutions. Among these images is the one that plutocratic power has the right to exploit the new medium of television for economic gain. Recent hearings before the Board of Broadcast Governors show how elites of Montreal, Toronto, Winnipeg, and Vancouver seek to extend their power over the mass media by capturing a new set of rights. The unhappy problem is that public ownership of mass media is no guarantee of freedom of ideas, as long as so many other institutions are dominated by private interests. The controllers of the CBC frequently take on the role of guardian of our moral sensibilities when they prevent our contamination by an intellectual virtuoso like Simone de Beauvoir. No doubt they are responding to some extent to the elites of the church hierarchies, but the fact that they feel obliged to do so simply points out the ubiquitous quality of power. The organized pressure of religious groups in their complaints about the portrayal of the life of a woman who became a saint and the withdrawal by a large corporation of its sponsorship of a television drama show how the authoritative principle inevitably pervades the creative arts. The grotesque morality which underlies the brutality so typical of the mass media receives singularly little critical analysis. It is interesting also that in a 1959 television series in which members of the corporate elite were interviewed about big business not a single critical idea emerged.

The exploitive, predatory, and restrictive character of capitalist institutions rests on a morality defined by those at the apex of our institutional hierarchies. This is not to suggest that they consciously propagate a morality which enhances their own worthiness—although the emergence of the modern advertising myth-makers would suggest that even this element of control is within their grasp—but rather that their view of the world is a product of institutional behavior. Habitual behavior within an institutional order provides its own justification by the psychological transformations, subtle and frequently beyond our grasp, which tell us that what we have done and continue to do is right and good simply because of the fact of doing it.

In turn this process of habituation permits class control of total social morality. By its control of philanthropic institutions, an elite with its own dubious morality watches over the morality of the underprivileged and the deviants of the lower class. It is no accident that professional social welfare has replaced social reform as the principal method of dealing with social problems. Reform suggests too much institutional change with a consequent erosion of privilege, but welfare permits the patching up of the casualties of a predatory economic system. As I have said, capitalism has been forced to accept a welfare state within its own institutions, but this it has done without giving up the creative privileges of its leaders.

The Reins of Power

Socialist policy then must be directed towards releasing the spontaneous and creative forces within human society. Such a change can only be brought about through democratic planning and co-ordination. Planning, of course, means for some a restriction of freedom, but it is illusory to suppose that with our present institutions we live free of restriction. I have tried to argue that freedom is restricted by the monopolization of the creative role, but it is also restricted because we do not plan. We exercise little control over disordered social forces which because of their effects imprison us within an environment of accident. With almost primitive mentality we attribute these accidents to impersonal forces such as "the market," "public opinion," "temporary adjustment," and so forth. Social science has done something to reduce this animistic world of the social environment, and to provide us with some tools for the implementation of social policy, but at the most these tools are used as negative controls rather than as positive techniques for social planning.

It is wrong of course to argue that we are without planning, because as I shall try to show, modern industrial society could not get along without it. The planning is done through the machinery of corporate bureaucracy countered from time to time by the bureaucracies of organized labor and government. The aims of corporate organization determine the shape of social development. This is the creative role. The countervailing role of government and organized labor is negative. As the Trans-Canada pipeline case indicates, at times the government gives positive aid to corporate power.

What is alarming on the contemporary scene are the erstwhile socialists who argue that all that is necessary is the extension of negative controls to keep the corporate world in order. As our society proceeds along the course of industrialization a greater degree of co-ordination and planning will be necessary if we are not to have a proliferation of the kind of dislocation that results from such things as the decision on the Avro Arrow, Nova Scotia coal mining, the uranium industry, and so forth. The deficiencies in our educational systems and the crisis in our universities are no less examples of the absence of co-ordinated planning. As long as our institutes of higher learning must live by the corporate hand-outs and unplanned government grants the crisis in which they find themselves will continue, thus reducing the contribution they might make to social development. Similarly, our defence needs, agricultural policy, the rapid growth of our cities, immigration policy, and aid to underdeveloped countries require planned co-ordination rather than unplanned plutocratically directed growth restricted only by negative government controls.

However, planning will fail to be democratic unless we devise new administrative techniques. Socialists have never given enough attention to how social participation in the definition and achievement of goals can be brought about. With the present bureaucratic machinery which governs most of our institutions the ends of the creative life can scarcely be served. The simple notion that a new age of socialist glory will be ushered in by changing the ownership of productive instruments overlooks the depressing quality of bureaucratic organization. Since bureaucracy can be a device equally of the corporate world or of a socialist world, for the masses there is little difference. Bureaucracy belongs to the industrial order, and while changes in the institutions of property and ownership may be necessary to solve the problems of power inherent in the bureaucratic structure of industry, it would be wrong to think that these problems are automatically solved by public ownership. Moreover, there seems little point in preparing for the first stage without some clear ideas about how the bureaucratic problem is to be solved.

In contemporary societies based on industry, most essential social activities are carried out through large-scale bureaucracies. If we want to understand modern forms of power we must first understand this organizational machine. The word bureaucracy has both a technical and pejorative meaning. In simplest terms it means rule by officials, but in the popular mind it is associated with cumbersome and irritating administrative machinery. Everyone at some time in his life has been enmeshed in the nets of private and public officialdom. The wrong order has come from the department store; the railway company has given the same berth to two people; the government department has lost the papers submitted to it. Quick to condemn the bumbling clerk and the pompous official, we ignore the fact that without large-scale organization our social life would be chaotic. If they are to run smoothly, someone must organize and control the intricate schemes of social relations with their multifarious points of human contact.

Modern bureaucracy in its organizing of production and distribution has created an enormous range of middle-level occupations between the factory bench and higher management, between the rank and file and the general staff. This white-collar "salariat" keeps the accounts and records for corporations, governments, churches, trade unions, and many other organizations. Modern production of material goods, television programs, engineers, missionaries, and politicians requires knowledge—knowledge of consumers and incomes, congregations and collections, taxpayers and taxes, members and their dues, servicemen and their dependants. Someone, and in most cases more than one, records our birth, inoculations, school attendance, marriage, offspring, mortgage payments, hospitalization, car licences, monthly instalments, our sins if we transgress, and eventually our demise. We have all become facts in the filing cases of numerous offices, carefully accounted for, documented, and punched on to cards, ready to be sorted, resorted, cross-indexed, and catalogued in an infinite variety of ways. Somewhere in the organizational hierarchy we are the guardians of our statistical selves.

It is easy to condemn this unenchanting world of record and routine, but it is essential to the institutional planning without which our high standard of living would be impossible. There is, of course, a substantial tradition of criticism of the growth of bureaucracy, a process which has been called among other things "the new despotism," "the road to serfdom," "the managerial revolution," and "Parkinson's Law." Most of these critiques are directed at government bureaucracy, and ignore completely the massive bureaucracies of private industry, trade unions, churches, and universities. Consider, for example, the huge army of officials required to operate bodies such as the Canadian Pacific Railway, A.V. Roe, Eaton's, Canadian Breweries, Metropolitan Life, Bell Telephone, the University of Toronto, the Anglican Church, and the United Steel Workers of America.

It is frequently argued that these private bureaucracies are benevolent rather than despotic, because they have to contend with competitors and satisfy consumers. Nor are they, it is claimed, as pervasive as government bureaucracy. This view comes from a very distorted perspective of their behavior, and the behavior of the men who dominate them. Many of these organizations impinge on our lives in myriads of ways. It may be a uniform kind of beer from the breweries, a standard rate of interest from the banks, the transferable academic credit, the industry-wide contract, or the Christian view of divorce. Corporate "despotism" can be much more far-reaching, as, for example, when it holds the future of a community in its hands by deciding to move its operations from one city to another. Within the white-collar mass, work procedures, personnel policies, and career lines are not dissimilar, whether the bureaucracy is private or public.

It is not here that I want to argue the relative despotic quality of public and private bureaucracy. I want simply to point out the principal feature of modern social structure based on industry. These battalions of officials must provide the productive system with a constant flow of information. They can do so only if they are organized into an orderly division of tasks, and governed by rules and regulations to cover all imaginable contingencies. The end of organizational activity and efficiency is served by the new social sciences. No longer, as in the nineteenth century, is the role of social science to criticize, but rather its new function is to improve the techniques of bureaucratic control. Personnel psychology, industrial relations, rational accounting, and linear programming are all bureaucratic tools. Even the university, which should be the last resting place of the independent soul, has become absorbed, through the research contract, in the world of large organizations, to which by tradition and nature it has been opposed. The graduates of business and public administration are the direct descendants of the human engineers and the stop-watch holders.

Despite occasional blunders bureaucracy is efficient. Without its techniques masses of people could not be mobilized into the gigantic productive units that we have today. It is inconceivable that we could ever revert to more haphazard administrative devices and still support large populations at high standards of living.

The success of bureaucracy—its efficiency—is also its danger, because it becomes a power instrument par excellence. Hierarchically organized bureaucracies are systems of command and co-ordination. Those who work in them—and they are gradually absorbing us all—acquire habits of obedience. Orders are followed and if orders cease to come the systems come to a halt. Whoever controls administrative machinery controls increasingly large segments of our institutions. There are psychological by-products of bureaucracy which deaden the critical faculties of men and, by narrowing their spheres of activity to the appropriate "office" or "position," leave them experiencing only a fragment of life. There is little opportunity for the worker, whether in overalls or white-collar to relate his own activity to the productive aims of his society.

Bureaucracy provides socialist theory with a built-in contradiction. Socialism, which seeks to release men from productive drudgery, envisages larger productive units, more intricate co-ordination between these units, and more extensive planning of the total social effort, none of which can be achieved without a very great increase in administrative machinery. With the nationalization that took place in the United Kingdom during the first Labour government, large productive units, such as railways and coal mines, were brought under the centralized control of national boards. Neither workers nor consumers became conscious of increased freedom or dignity. The increase in the scale of operations can result in a greater alienation of the worker and consumer from the productive goals of the society.

Moreover, such large centralized units are easily transferable between public and private ownership. These changes in ownership and control resemble palace revolutions, in which elites change without a noticeable effect on the lives of the workers. In a system of political democracy, socialist gains under one government may be demolished under a subsequent government. The less that is done to change the quality of industrial bureaucracy, the easier it is to return to capitalist forms of organization.

Early socialist writers cannot be blamed for failing to see the bureaucratic explosion which has attended modern industrialization. They dreamt of a smaller world, based more on the community, where the harmonious relations between workers followed from common goals mutually understood and arrived at. Even in the early part of the twentieth century, the guild socialists visualized a society in which democratically organized functional groups would become associated in a co-operative productive system. It was easy to denounce private ownership, human greed, and profit making as the barrier to this Eldorado of co-operation. Indeed it was a barrier at the time, and may still be today, but the world of large-scale organization makes a far more formidable barrier to socialist ideals. Socialists have not given enough thought to how this barrier might be removed.

It has been suggested that the last electoral defeat of the Labour party in the United Kingdom was because the public, consumers and workers, had had enough of nationalization, and therefore public ownership, the core of socialist policy, should be removed from the party's platform. The fact that nothing was done, other than to replace private managers with public ones, probably more than anything else left the public susceptible to the massive corporate propaganda against nationalization.

If some of the time and talent spent on sharpening managerial tools could be spent on devising methods of democratic control of industry or eliciting consumer opinion, we would be much closer to the kind of industrial order which socialists desire. What, for example, should be the role of trade unions in that part of the economy which passes to public ownership and in which some form of worker participation in management is introduced? Trade unions themselves have used the organizational weapon of bureaucracy in their struggle against the capitalist order. In productive units where there is some semblance of industrial democracy, the role of unions must obviously be different.

Workers' representatives on boards of nationalized industries or crown corporations may simply be trade union leaders who have enhanced their own position. How many of them would be prepared to establish democratic work processes at the expense of the systems of power which they have built up in their struggle against capitalism? Some of the fruits of this struggle can be seen today with the appointment of workers' representatives to all kinds of boards, commissions and regulatory agencies. Because they are appointed by organized labor, these people are not so much workers' representatives as they are organizational watchdogs. Trade union leaders and corporate officials share places on these boards because both groups command organizational machinery. Trade unions can suffer the same kind of bureaucratic ossification as any other organization if their only postures are those of consolidating gains or of winning more tournaments before labor relations boards. Unless they pass to their next creative stage and map out new territory of social development, they will find themselves economic fossils.

Account then must be taken of bureaucratic control in any analysis of power and freedom in modern society. The picture which nineteenth-century theorists drew of society was of human beings living as a large collection of independent units. The problem of freedom was simply one of creating the physical conditions under which human atoms could attain their self-determination. The picture which twentieth-century theorists are drawing is of bureaucracy and counter-bureaucracy. The control of materials and men lies within these large administrative systems. The lines of control, like the reins of a thousand horses, come together in a relatively small number of hands. The drivers are few. It is they, the elites at the top of our bureaucratic pyramids, to whom are given the creative privileges, and to whom we entrust the job of directing us into our brave new worlds. If we can identify the main social institutions which have taken on this shape, we can in turn identify the groups who are in effective control at the top. In a short essay it is impossible to analyse all the institutional hierarchies within which power coalesces. Economic institutions are selected because of their advanced stage of bureaucratization and the tendency for other institutions to be patterned after them.

Concentration of economic power and the separation of ownership from control are two of the most profound changes in twentieth-century capitalism. Capitalism is no longer a system of independent entrepreneurs making their profit according to the logic of classical economic theory. It is one of the greatest achievements of the contemporary myth-makers that the image of the business world is still that of the nineteenth century. Despite the enormous range of evidence which tells us otherwise we still see the economic system as being made up of men and their businesses. As long as this picture of the economic world is maintained all ambitious men can cherish the hope that they too can achieve the status of ultimate worth—that of the independent businessman. The public vocabulary of the corporate world as it finds its way into the Chamber of Commerce brief and institutional advertising is a collection of words from a dead language. "Free enterprise," "private enterprise," "competition," "the freedom of consumers," and the like are as outdated labels as "fief" and "benefice." It is significant that in their perennial attack on trade unions the corporate world draws a picture of giant trade unions crushing out the businessman whose only concern is the public interest. In actual fact, the giant unions which we have are a direct response to the centralized control of the productive system.

The concentration of economic power means simply that a large proportion of the economic activity of the nation is in the hands of a very few large firms, and furthermore these very large firms become linked together and to the main financial institutions, the banks and insurance companies, through interlocking directorships. One only has to take the directors of the four largest banks in Canada—Bank of Montreal, Royal Bank of Canada, Canadian Bank of Commerce, Bank of Nova Scotia—to see the far-ranging economic power that lies in the hands of a few men. Professor Ashley has shown[4] that thirty directors of the Bank of Montreal held, at the time of his study, between them "220 or more" directorships in other companies. Similarly the twenty-five directors of the Royal Bank of Canada held 240 other directorships; the twenty-two directors of the Canadian Bank of Commerce held 225 directorships in other companies; the twenty directors of the Bank of Nova Scotia held 220 directorships. Altogether these ninety-seven men held between them 930 directorships in corporations operating in every sector of the economy.

There are in Canada some very powerful holding companies which have within their portfolios the control of an enormous range of corporations. Outstanding among these is Argus Corporation. Twelve directors of Argus Corporation hold 150 directorships in banks, insurance companies, trust companies, and in operating companies.

Elsewhere I have tried to outline the concentration of economic power in Canada that follows from the dominating position that a relatively few large firms have in the economic system.[5] Each of these large corporations is bureaucratically organized into a careful division of tasks, hierarchy of offices, graduated careers, systems of promotion, and so forth. At the apex of each pyramid, in effective command is a small group of senior officers and directors. The bureaucratic machines which they control produce for profit. They function too as channels of communication and supervision. In this sense is power (the directing of the affairs of other people) downwards throughout the system. One salaried official carries out the directives from another salaried official above him and directs those below him.

The attitude of obedience is essential if the objectives of those at the top are to be reached, but it is also necessary for getting on in the bureaucratic system. The criteria of worthiness for promotion become related to the individual's efficiency in carrying out directives and showing good judgment, a bit of corporate sophistry meaning that his opinions are more or less the same as those of his seniors, or that time and luck proves his judgment to be good. He is a good "family" man, the family being the corporation to whose well-being he has committed himself. Historians have written of the devotion and servility of the domestic servant class of earlier periods. The modern counterpart of this group is the "organization man," devoted and servile to a bureaucratic order. I do not think I have been overdrawing this mentality of obedience. Even if the individual does not want to get on, he wants at least security, and since he has no property rights in his job, docility becomes the wise policy. Compensation for the loss of position is a right only at the very top where a chief executive who is ousted when his corporation has passed to the control of a new group is able to demand some kind of settlement. It is true that at the lower levels, workers' associations have been able to counter the arbitrariness of corporate officials with seniority clauses and the like. In the future, as the occupational structure shifts with accompanying undertones of white-collar respectability and bourgeois identifications, more and more workers will become fully bureaucratized without the benefit of worker organizations.

The significance of all this for the problems of power is surely in the fact that a few control men and resources and therefore inevitably control the many who are prevented from full participation in the creative life. The more the culture of bureaucracy develops—and economic concentration is an indication of how it has developed—the more the appropriate mental habits become those of servility. The case for public ownership to produce more material things may be weak, but the case for it as a means of allowing social participation and the humanizing of bureaucracy may be overwhelming.

The drift to centralized control of the economic processes is now well advanced. Centralized control means absentee control through a complex bureaucratic apparatus. More and more local industries become absorbed in these economic empires. When the dominant plant or mill in a small and remote community is brought into the network of a Toronto holding company and the former owners are replaced by corporate personnel, community responsibility and obligations change. This is not to suggest that privately owned local plants were operated with great beneficence or that absentee owners ignore community feelings. With absentee control economic forces become much more impersonal, and the responsibility for the social effects of economic change much more difficult to place.

As increasingly salaried officials implement remote decisions, the channels of control become more narrow. We have already spoken of the small group of men at the apex of industrial complexes like Argus and A.V. Roe, and there has been much talk in recent years of the yet remoter control which results from foreign investment. The small fraction of men who control the economic processes can be seen from the extensive interlocking directorships among large corporations. In a group of 170 large corporations in 1952 some 200 men held half of all the directorships in these companies as well as directorships in banks, insurance companies, and trust companies.[6]

The corporate elite do not limit their activities to the direction of their economic empires. Their roles have the magnetic effect of drawing to them numerous other creative privileges, in the form of governorships of hospitals, universities, artistic associations, and philanthropic organizations. There is scarcely a large city or large university whose board is not graced by representatives of the corporate world. There are obvious reasons for their being there. They can raise money.

In her fascinating study of the control of philanthropy in a large Canadian city, Professor Ross has shown how the business world views fund raising as a means of legitimating its governing of the economic system. "Philanthropy rests squarely on the shoulders of big business," said one corporate executive; "we use that as a weapon to try to force business to give. We tell them if they want the system of free enterprise to continue they must continue to give."[7] The success too of any charitable campaign depends on the right people heading it up. Businessmen engage in reciprocal exchange of donations. Thus throughout the country, welfare agencies depend on the economic elite sponsoring them.

Other papers in this volume outline techniques to reduce the power that comes from economic concentration, but if these solutions involve little more than capitalism with controls, we will not be much farther ahead. Governmental control or all-out public ownership by itself will do little if anything to expand creativity, widen responsibility, or increase participation in the productive processes or solve the problems of bureaucracy.

Values and Attitudes for a New Society

Democratic planning for freedom requires us to make advances on two levels: the psychological and the institutional. The creation of a democratic environment depends on rational inquiry guided by humanitarian values. The good society can never be achieved as long as we carry around in our minds our fictional accounts of social reality. Nor is it fostered in the current climate of anxiety: anxieties about economic stability, technological change, international relations, and personal status. Humanitarianism cannot come about without a shift in emphasis from the current social value of self-interest to the neglected value of common social interests.

We never cease to hear that in order to get essential social tasks performed we must reward men, particularly businessmen, with high incomes and opportunities to acquire great wealth, and to pass fortunes on to their families. The sense of social duty and the public good does not depend on such a grotesquely selfish account of human motives. The point is that we do so very little to develop the opposite motives. The opposite motives are demonstrated in those men who assume important social roles without high monetary rewards, and men who in their work are guided primarily by the desire for public service. Able and responsible men work in the federal public service, for example, for a fraction of what their talents could bring them in the corporate world. Teachers, clergymen, welfare workers, scientific researchers, and some doctors and lawyers do not see themselves primarily as serving selfish ends. Their reward comes often in the form of prestige, but prestige does not lead to the accumulation of fortune and excessive power. This type of person contradicts the theory that material rewards alone are the appropriate incentives to get social functions performed. It is, of course, necessary to pay people sufficient to induce them to undertake prolonged and rigorous training, but such differential rewards do not mean the huge incomes and capital accumulation that is alleged to be necessary to get businessmen to do their jobs properly.

We recognize the fact that public institutions are likely to contain some men whose prime motive is power per se. The very fact that decision-making roles are essential to social organization means that there is always a risk of personal appropriation. In a rational and humanitarian environment we would recognize the person motivated by power per se as deviant to our desired model. No one would suggest that there is a higher concentration of that type in our present public institutions than in our private ones. What is important here is that public institutions are much more open to inquiry than are private ones. It is the nation's business to know what is happening in the CBC, for example, but how often do we think it the nation's business to know what is happening in Argus Corporation? The public official accepts inquiry into his work and operations. If he resents it, his resentment is mainly because he is confronted every day with the kind of inquiry that seems to have as its aim political exploitation rather than genuine concern for the proper functioning of the public service. But his resentment is nothing compared to that of the businessman's resentment of inquiries about restrictive trade practices.

This shift in emphasis on motives can only be achieved through educational systems and through some control of our ideological systems, particularly the mass media. We must plan to educate people to be democratic and humanitarian, a process which does not stop at the school- or college-leaving age. Perhaps, too, we should give some thought to social control of the mass media, particularly newspapers which increasingly become controlled by fewer and fewer people. We accept the idea of public trusteeship for some of our educational institutions, provincial universities for example, and we never suggest that they are not free. Freedom of the press from capitalist control would mean a liberation, and some of the greatest newspapers in the world, such as the London *Observer*, and in Montreal, *Le Devoir*, have just this freedom to perform their proper social function. There is no reason why some of our large metropolitan dailies when they come up for sale could not be bought through public funds and operated under trusteeship. Such a publicly endowed paper may drop in circulation, but its educative value would be immense.

What we need in positions of power in a democratically planned society is a changed quality of leadership. Many writers have pointed out that men who desire power exhibit irrational elements in their behavior, and that competitive institutions put a premium on pathological traits. It is the ruthless and the ambitious who get to the top. Actually such men are perceived with ambivalence. They conform to the model of determined competitiveness which capitalist institutions reward, yet their behavior our humanitarian feelings deplore. Psychoanalytic writers have thrown much light on the importance of love and hate in all our social relationships, and how hate feelings enter into the power-seeking motives. To desire a social structure in which feelings of mutuality, co-opera-tiveness, and love prevail is to desire an almost revolutionary transformation in our psychology of social relationships.

Such a change, however, must be the goal firmly in our minds as we move towards a new social order. In a democratically plan-ned society the aims of leadership—that is the decision-making process which accounts for the ubiquity of power—must be the social good rather than personal gain. No doubt some differentia-tion of monetary rewards will always remain, but, as I have said, we do not need great fortunes and concentrated power. Men with a passion for such great rewards can only be satisfied at a cost to their fellows.

The role of leadership in a freely planned democracy is two-fold: to aid in the searching out and articulation of social needs, and, secondly, to direct social operations to implement socially expressed choices. In our age of complex industrialization we must depend very heavily on men with expert skills and particu-larly on the social scientists, since it is the social order we seek to change. We cannot do without men of leadership quality, but in our training for leadership our emphasis must be on social obliga-tion rather than personal ambition. In the economic realm, for example, contemporary leadership attitudes would be expressed as: "How can I persuade people to buy what I am producing, and how can I control the fellow who comes into the market I create?" The attitudes of democratic leadership should be: "How can I find out what is socially useful and desired, and enlist the support of others in producing it?" We have plenty of evidence too that power can lead to feelings of indispensability in the men to whom it has been given. This "Bonapartiste" psychology can only be inimical to the democratic way, and to combat it we must devise the necessary institutional checks.

Changes in the psychology of the masses are no less impor-tant than changes in the psychology of leadership. In both cases it must be remembered there is no such thing as a rigid psychologi-cal structure called human nature. There are rather social natures in the sense that the prevailing psychological dispositions are socially created. It is possible to create a society in which the prevailing personality is marked by humanitarianism and rationality, and while such a goal may be far distant, it is the goal we must keep in mind. In all likelihood we need to discover the appropriate child-rearing techniques in the home and pedagogical methods in the schools. Where we do not know the appropriate methods we must look for them. If we spent less on such things as motivational research to discover how our unconscious feelings can be exploited in the interest of merchandising and allocated more to the discovery of the kind of training necessary for democratic living, we would be better off. Unfortunately much of the research in social psychology underwrites the value of conformity rather than the value of individual differences. The conformist belongs to the totalitarian industrial system, not to a democratic one, and it matters little from the point of view of individual freedom whether the conformity stems from political indoctrination or commercial beguilement. There are many ways to wash brains. The stereotyped minds of our modern mass societies may feel free, but their potentiality for growth becomes reduced by the standardizing effects of our current systems of education and communication.

Although educational methods are important instruments in the development of personalities more congenial to the democratic milieu, the fact remains that educational systems reflect the values of the dominant institutions within the society, and their influence in bringing about the desired psychological changes is thereby reduced. To achieve some measure of social change it may be necessary to find ways of changing the institutional structure before changing modes of thought. One obvious step which a government devoted to social planning could take through its investment policies is to reverse the influence which now flows from dominant economic institutions to other areas of social life. In the present phase of corporate capitalism such things as education, research in all fields, the social services, the arts and entertainment, and the content of the mass media depend very largely on corporate support, and as a consequence of this dependence take on the shape and values and attact, in many instances, the same kind of leadership as the corporate world.

In education, from the businessmen who sit on local school boards to the corporate elite who sit on boards of universities, the incumbents derive prestige and status, but the inevitable feedback is the dominance of business and corporate mentality. How often is a great educator invited to the board of a large corporation? Why should such a practice be any less common than a corporate leader being on the board of a university?

In the many fields of research there is a similar waiting upon corporate initiative. Within industry the aims of research are overwhelmingly of the "building a better mouse trap" variety or the application of science to the creation of marketable commodities. In a recent television advertisement we were told that after years of research the company concerned had now produced a spray shoe polish. Such a breakthrough in the field of personal grooming may serve us well, but it is the dominance of capitalist modes of thought that makes us value that kind of "scientific" advance rather than research in the fields of medicine, health and welfare, or basic work in physics.

These latter will at times be given a fillip as a by-product of our present economic institutions, but more often they proceed with what support governments have been prepared to give them. The elite of the corporate world will donate funds, set up a research institute, endow a chair at a university, or establish a foundation, but there is always the waiting upon corporate profits or the successful accumulation of personal fortunes. The Canadian elite are far behind those of other countries in the supporting of this kind of activity. In fact it is to American foundations and sometimes those of other countries that people in Canada interested in fostering research so often have to turn for funds. The economic elite in Canada complain that their accumulation took place after income tax had become a standard form of government revenue. While income tax has probably imposed some limit on personal accumulation, it is significant that the tax proceeds of the estates of two men were sufficient to establish the Canada Council.

The arts and what might be called without snobbish connotations the higher forms of entertainment have been in an even worse condition than research and education, no doubt because their value is almost entirely aesthetic and there is little probability of long-term profitability. Metropolitan and community centres for the performing arts could be developed through social investment. It is typical of a capitalist society that in Toronto such a centre should have to wait upon corporate benefaction. The O'Keefe Centre came from Argus Corporation through its subsidiary Canadian Breweries Limited. As was revealed in the recent trial of the latter firm, the directors were convinced of the great advertising advantages that would follow from building it.

Living as we do in a milieu dominated by the corporate philosophy we have come to look upon various kinds of social investment as something which can be afforded only if it does not interfere with the stability of the corporate economy. This stability is threatened when avenues of profit are encroached upon by government, or when government has to tax in order to invest in what it considers desirable. We are frequently told the country cannot afford old age pensions, or other welfare measures because of their costs. Obviously there are costs to such measures, but principally the cost is a sacrifice of the prevailing economic order. The direction of the flow of institutional influence becomes clear when the corporate philosophy assumes the status of social doctrine for the entire community.

If this reciprocal relation between institutional behavior and modes of thought is to be broken, the creation of new kinds of institutions through investment might be more effective than joining battle directly with present economic power, particularly if long-run goals are kept in mind. With the development of new institutions come new career systems creating in turn possibilities for new types of leadership which would not be modelled on that of the modern corporation. If this argument appears strange it should be remembered that within the last twenty years there has developed an entirely new type of career system within the federal public service. Although there is some interchange between corporate and public service careers, there are many men in public service who would not find the big business firm congenial to their personalities. New institutional development can be planned and in time be the source of new values and attitudes. Consider some of the possible lines of development beyond the generally accepted forms of social investment such as schools and hospitals. Why not establish a national university devoted to advanced study in all fields of intellectual inquiry, or a national medical research centre, or a national science foundation on a larger scale than the present National Research Council, or a national foundation for the arts which could greatly expand the work now being done by the Canada Council? We also need a well-endowed national organization to develop physical fitness and to take athletics out of its present commercial imprisonment.

In a democratically planned society there must be a desire for participation in the establishment of social goals. There is now a great deal of literature which seeks to explain the widespread apathy in our western industrial societies, and the common theme which these studies have is that the apathy results from the sense of powerlessness and inability to have any effect on the great social issues of the day. It is not only the great social issues which seem beyond the grasp of men in the mass society. Nowhere is apathy more marked than at the level of urban local government, the level at which there is direct impingement on individuals and their families. Yet we know there have been instances when large segments of a community can be brought together to undertake particular community projects. The drama in Canada will be permanently indebted to the public-spirited individuals in Stratford who worked so hard for the Festival. It was a project furthermore which required the kind of leadership we have been mentioning. It is often said that the modern metropolitan mass cannot participate in governmental and social process of this kind. Why do we not search for the techniques of local government more appropriate for democracy in metropolitan communities?

There is as much in our western traditions which supports the principle of democratic social planning as there is that speaks out against it. It is not a revolutionary doctrine. The values which are implied in the democratic personality are as much a part of our inheritance as are those values implied in the aggressive and personally ambitious model of our contemporary folk heroes. We need to ensure that our next epoch brings forward the desired type.

Equally important as these psychological changes are the changes which must come at the institutional level. In particular we must search out new techniques to deal with the problems of bureaucratic organization. In part we must move towards some system of industrial democracy, and since large productive units do not lend themselves well to worker participation, planning must result in decentralization. There is no reason to suppose that the breaking up of large industrial agglomerations into relatively autonomous units is incompatible with the idea of centralized planning. Decentralization furthermore helps to strengthen regional, cultural, and sometimes ethnic differences.

Within these decentralized economic units the machinery must be found which permits and encourages worker association with management. Although at the moment we have only vague ideas of how this goal can be achieved there are some possible lines of approach. Needless to say an adequate system of worker participation can only be discovered by constant study and some experimentation. Creative social development must be experimental in its search for new techniques. The aim of worker identification with management decisions might be achieved through the election of direct representatives to the boards of the various regional levels of publicly owned industry. It is anomalous in Canada that the management of a publicly owned railway system behaves no differently in respect to its workers than a privately owned one. Rather the two managements behave as one. Another possible line of development is the creation of consultative bodies in industry corresponding to the various levels of the administrative hierarchy. Whatever the method the goal must be the replacing of the authoritarian character of bureaucratic structure by feelings of co-operation and common purpose.

In the future the pace of social development will depend to a great extent on the willingness and the ability of a society to experiment with its social machinery. We have lived now for a long time in a scientific age. This acquaintance with science and its achievements has given us the attitude that we can eventually master our physical environment, but as yet we are still bound by a built-in conservatism when it comes to mastering the social environment. Within the field of industrial relations there is tremendous scope for social experiment, but the capitalist corporation is limited in the extent to which it can experiment. One reason for this limitation is that experimentation would interfere with the structure of bureaucratic control and authority. This is why the so-called democratic work processes which have been tried in some corporations have as their aim the acceptance of management decisions rather than any democratic participation in policy making. Workers are allowed to talk their way into accepting decisions from above. A further reason is, of course, that a corporation in competition with other corporations cannot afford to embark on experimentation in human relations except within narrow boundaries. Since efficiency is measured solely by profit, experiments concerned with the welfare of workers are always judged against the profitability of increased output or reduced absenteeism rather than against the criterion of welfare itself.

The possibility of experiment in industrial organizations free from the hazards of corporate enterprise is a strong argument for public ownership in some sectors of the economy. Social experiments, like any other kind, cost money and are subject to failure. There must therefore be flexibility in experimental policies. The belief that publicly owned economic enterprises should behave just as privately owned ones has been an important factor in the criticism of nationalization programs. There seems to be an unwillingness to search for other criteria to judge the social as well as the strictly economic effects of public ownership.

Many people would view with alarm the setting aside of the economic criteria of technical efficiency and output. Their importance of course cannot be denied, but we must be prepared to accept some losses in the search for new social techniques. We do not hesitate to put a large proportion of our resources into experimenting on armaments that become obsolete within such a short time. Industrial nations blow up millions of dollars every year in rocket research and we accept these losses as a part of our scientific way of life. Could we not say of social experiments also that there may be temporary losses but in the long run we are going to find a better way for human beings to work in industrial organization?

Such government-undertaken social experiments could be viewed as an extension of other kinds of research and experimentation which the government already conducts through a variety of agencies such as the National Research Council, the Defence Research Board, Forest Products Laboratories, and the system of experimental farms. The agencies are necessary because the work they do would be neglected if we applied economic criteria to their operations. Why do we not go a step further into experimenting in the social field?

A central part of the argument in this essay has been that in its present form bureaucracy is inimical to the growth of the co-operative spirit. Yet an important fact to be remembered from the point of view of socialist theory is that people have become accustomed to working as salaried officials without personal property rights. At the level of management some form of teamwork in the planning and implementation of policy is now the accepted practice within industrial organization. It should not be impossible to create in industry the attitudes conducive to socialist goals rather than the maximizing of corporate profit.

As social planning proceeds there must be some change in the functioning of our political institutions. The fear is widespread that all social planning must be totalitarian and despotic. Often these fears can be exploited as an ideological weapon against social change. The fact remains, however, that social planning can lead to individual appropriation of power. We can, of course, devise institutional checks against such appropriation, but in the long run the safeguard depends on the democratic spirit which I have described as rational inquiry guided by humanitarian values. The psychological changes, which I have suggested are necessary for a democratically planned order, cannot take place overnight. They can probably only emerge from the processes which they are intended to support in the same way that the current adaptation to a capitalist order is the result of a long period of habituation. What gives the present crisis its sense of urgency is that we stand at the point of choosing in the present epoch between planning by concentrated private interests with continuing public indifference and acquiescence or democratic planning towards socially expressed goals.

Notes

1. See the review of these studies in S.M. Lipset and Reinhard Bendix, *Social Mobility in Industrial Society* (Berkeley, 1959).

2. *Canada Year Book*, 1959 (Ottawa), 229.

3. See the account of R.T. McKenzie, "Labour's Need for Surgery," *Observer*, London, Oct. 25, 1959.

4. C.A. Ashley, "Concentration of Economic Power," *Canadian Journal of Economics and Political Science*, vol. XXIII, no. 1, Feb., 1957.

5. John Porter, "The Concentration of Economic Power and the Economic Elite in Canada," *Canadian Journal of Economics and Political Science*, vol. XXII, no. 2, May, 1956.

6. *Ibid.*

7. Aileen D. Ross, "Organized Philanthropy in an Urban Comunity," *Canadian Journal of Economics and Political Science*, vol. XVIII, no. 4, Nov., 1952.

10

Education, Equality, and the Just Society

I was invited by York University to inaugurate a new annual lecture series established in memory of the distinguished Canadian historian, Edgar McInnis. I could choose any topic I wished. The following two papers are the lectures delivered in 1977.

I have always argued that education was the main bridge between the deprived environments of the least privileged classes in any society and the opportunity represented by economic growth such as the industrial expansion in Canada during the post-Second World War period. Some of my early research in the 1950s showed how retarded in educational development Canada was and how closely linked was the amount and kind of schooling a Canadian received and his social class background. Higher education was in an abysmal state for a society about to become an industrial and commercial power. We made our great development in large part through the importing of highly qualified workers much as we imported the capital.

Gradually, of course, our educational systems improved with the education industry becoming a major object of investment. School retention rates increased, postsecondary education was opened up although access to university remained heavily biassed in favor of the more privileged. The link between education and equality, it was believed, was that investment in individuals through education would improve their skills which they could in turn convert into income in the labor market. Greater investment in human capital, it was thought, would lead to higher productivity of the economy, and if the educational system were open, the benefits of social investment in education could be spread around. Thus, equality of educational opportunity was seen as a crucial step in educational reform. I wrote a good deal about this and argued for and participated in the planning of the tertiary level in Ontario.

I have never doubted that equality of access to all educational institutions was and should continue to be an important objective of social reform. As the western capitalist economies had been stum-

bling through their crises of the late 1970s and there appeared to be surpluses of educated manpower, the role of education in economic growth came seriously into question. Similarly, its contribution to expanding equality was being critically assessed. Equality of educational opportunity alone was not enough to bring about some measure of redistribution of wealth through economic opportunity and the increased marginal productivity of workers. I am not sure that I ever thought it was sufficient, but I was certainly seen by my critics as representing something of a tired liberal school who thought that all that was necessary was to open up the schools and universities, through which young people would proceed to an Eldorado that lay beyond.

While all reassessment of education was going on, John Rawls published his very influential treatise on equality, A Theory of Justice. *I sought in these two McInnis lectures to link education in the mid-1970s to the controversies about social equality as these were being conducted by contemporary scholars and other intellectuals. It was in part to reassess my own position that I undertook this task. In the process I clarified much for myself. I hope I might have done this for others as well.*

I

EDUCATION AND EQUALITY: THE FAILURE OF A MISSION

If the question were asked which of the major social innovations of the twentieth century had most failed in its mission a likely answer would be public education. None of our society-wide collective enterprises is subject to greater critical scrutiny at the present time than education. The disparagement can be heard and read in all industrial societies of the West. Perhaps criticism would be current also in the socialist East if dissent from major social policies were more tolerated than it is.

Public education's false promise was that it would be one of the chief instruments to achieve social equality. We distinguish public education here from private education which has always been available to the dominant classes of the advanced societies and which has always been important in those classes maintaining their positions of dominance. Public education was to challenge inherited privilege by providing opportunity for the children of the less well-off sectors of society. In providing conditions for "la carrière ouverte aux talents" it was to strike at the exclusiveness of aristocracy or plutocracy.

There were other more practical and less lofty objectives, not the least of which was to meet the more highly skilled labor force needs of the developing industrial nations. Both liberal reformers and laissez-faire capitalists found they could support the extension of public education. The former because it was to provide opportunity, and the latter because the hitherto untrained masses could be taught the virtues of hard work along with some modicum of marketable skills. There were also what might broadly be termed citizenship objectives, illustrated by the expressed need with the extension of the franchise to "educate our masters," or to set out on the more diffuse "pursuit of happiness."

While the demands of a swelling industrial economy for trained manpower—for human capital as it was to become appropriately labelled in the capitalist economy—may seem to have been the most pronounced purpose, the equality and citizenship justifications were also emphasized. Certainly the basic reforms in English education in 1944 were achieved because of the wartime coalition in which the Labour party members were most insistent that among the victories that were to come must be that of greater equality of opportunity for the British working class.

Perhaps at times and in places the equality theme in the expansion of public education was a spiritual sugar-coating or an ideological wrapping to conceal the hard materialism of economic reasoning. Equality appeared as an exalted goal more acceptable than the profane accumulation of wealth. Most of the commissions which in many countries including Canada examined the state of education and made recommendations about its future, and much of the political rationalization at the point of introducing legislation for changes, were as likely to emphasize equality as they were the economy.[1]

While we have devised techniques—many of them of dubious quality—to measure the contribution of education to economic growth, very few tools are available to measure the contribution of education to equality or the broad citizenship effects which education is supposed to have produced, and so it is not surprising that an assessment of these dimensions has been neglected. Recently, however, there have been new attempts to develop ways of looking at education and its effects on equality. In these lectures I want to look at some of them and in the light of them to reassess the extent to which the principle of equality has been served by the growth of public education. Such a review cannot avoid taking into consideration some of the other declared objectives of education such as manpower creation and economic growth. Ironically, just as the contribution of education to social equality has been called into question, so too has its contribution to the production of trained manpower. We have to weigh evidence of great training robberies and of over-educated Canadians and Americans, or British or French for that matter. My plan for these two lectures is to examine the equality issue in the first and the manpower questions in the second, but to discuss both in the context of the just society.

The equality issue is of relevance to our contemporary societies for a number of reasons. One is that equality has been an emerging value in the course of the western tradition and is becoming increasingly a test of the good society. The OECD, for example, has recently published a comparative study of inequality of income distribution in member countries, among which, of course, is Canada.[2] Deprived groups have been mobilizing to demand redress (our native peoples, for example) over a range of economic and social rights denied to them. Perhaps most important of all is the fact that our capitalist economies are in a critical period of low or no growth and are no longer able to meet demands for higher standards of living through increased output. When growth falls off the increased increment dwindles or disappears entirely, and the demands for equality become more vocal. As Heilbroner has said, in a growthless economic system the control over incomes becomes a conflict over rights.[3] Finally, the advanced societies can no longer ignore the gross inequalities in the world system. What has been called the OPEC syndrome of the less developed resource-producing countries is likely to take new forms—as indeed it has with the abortive North-South conference of 1976—among countries with yet fewer resources and no leverage other than appeal to moral principles. All these are sufficient reasons, however they might affront our conservative values, to examine closely the case for equality and to assess the contribution that education has made to serve better that principle.

At the outset it might be useful to recall the familiar distinction between equality of condition and equality of opportunity. The former implies that whatever is valued as good in the society—material resources, health, personal development, leisure—should be distributed among all the members of society in relatively the same amounts regardless of the social position which one occupies. Equality of opportunity, on the other hand, implies a society in which resources are distributed unequally—as indeed has been the historical experience—but in which access to the structured inequality should be open to all without regard to the individuals' social class origins, their parental resources, their religious affiliations and, in more contemporary discussions, their membership in minority groups or their sex. For many, the principle of equality in a liberal society is satisfied by providing equal opportunity to seek out and compete for unequal rewards.

However, while it is possible to make the distinction between the two types of equality in an analytical sense, in the real world the distinction is a questionable one because inequality of condition can nullify the effects of whatever might be introduced to implement equality of opportunity. Educational and occupational opportunity as it now exists can be regarded as a series of prizes to be awarded through competition, but with greatly disproportionate odds to win in favor of those who come from better-off origins. For example, for many industrial countries including Canada, it is now possible to calculate the probabilities of a person ending up with a university degree or a professional occupation if he comes from particular types of social background.[4] Those coming from better-off origins always have the higher probabilities of success despite whatever social policies the welfare state might have provided in the hope of equalizing the odds.

It is not surprising therefore, that increasing attention is being given at present to inequality of condition and that at both the philosophical and political levels the case is being made for a more radical egalitarianism. The discussions of inequality and equality are of course as old as philosophy itself, but the subject is never talked out, or written out, because the context of relevance changes with changed social circumstances. Thus, whatever Aristotle, Rousseau, Louis Blanc, or Marx may have said about the subject, the ideas have to be looked at afresh in different times and places. Do new capacities for affluence of the advanced societies strengthen or weaken the arguments for equality of condition? How much liberty and efficiency need be or should be traded off against it? How much can any form of progress towards equality continue to be made in the rich nations while the poor ones continue in their deprivation? All these questions have to be debated anew in our own time.

The simple assertion of extreme egalitarianism, "all humans are equal," is not very helpful since it is both absurd and useless.[5] It is absurd because, over a wide range of characteristics, human beings are obviously not equal; and the statement is useless for analytical purposes if it simply states a circular identity that all human beings are the same as other human beings. It fails to describe any reality, for clearly humans are not equal with respect to strength, naturally endowed intellect, experience from age, physical disabilities, to mention some natural inequalities noted by Rousseau. Thus "all humans are equal" fails as a descriptive statement.

As a prescriptive statement that all humans ought to be equal, it encounters many problems of conflicting principles. What are the relevant respects in which they ought to be equal? Are working and non-working adults to receive equal income? Are pensioners to be treated like students? Are large families to be treated like small ones? One does not have to go very far with these questions to see the absurdity of extreme egalitarianism, and so the objective becomes one not so much of equality itself as of a choice between different principles of inequality or of distributive justice such as that individuals should be rewarded according to need, according to merit, or according to their contribution to society.

These principles can conflict when we might reward top job holders so well because of what we believe they are doing for society (a principle firmly upheld by our own pay and tax structures) that we could neglect the more menial contributors to the social good to the point of denying them the basic minimum for culturally acceptable living standards. Conversely, we might place such an emphasis on need or extreme equality that we neglect to provide incentives to get the onerous tasks of direction and responsibility undertaken, although no capitalist democracy, least of all our own, has come near that. Thus, our search is not so much for equality as for fairness or a balance of the various distributive principles that might be applied.

We may find that balance through a game in which the participants consider chances they might have to acquire wealth or to experience poverty, to enjoy comfort or to suffer discomfort. The game, which has been invented and modified by philosophers for a long time, we can call contract. In its most recent version it has been designed by John Rawls in his book *A Theory of Justice*.[6] Rawls' work, a philosophical undertaking of great importance for contemporary discussions of social life, has been widely disseminated through all the social sciences. A voluminous critical and interpretative literature, including at least two books,[7] has developed around the work.

In order to derive principles of social justice Rawls imagines an original position in which equally free, rational men, through discussion, would arrive at a set of social arrangements for providing social order and for distributing the economic and social benefits of working together. They engage in this rational discussion behind a "veil of ignorance" in that, when the game is over, they do not know what their intellectual capacities will be, nor their social-class position, nor strength, nor health, nor to which generation they belong. Thus practical questions in which the discussants might have vested interest such as whether or not the more intelligent should receive more than the less intelligent, those in authority more than those in inferior roles, are settled without the participants knowing where they themselves will end up. If a person does not know whether he will be bright or stupid, a boss or a worker, born wealthy or poor, he cannot argue from the point of view of his vested interests, and since Rawls claims they will all have a high aversion to risk, since there are no rational grounds for calculating risks, they will not take a position on the chance of being wealthy, bright, and powerful when they might well be poor, stupid, and weak.

Two principles of justice would be agreed upon. The first holds that everyone is equally entitled to a set of basic liberties which is compatible with a similar set of liberties for everyone else. The second is that whatever economic and social inequalities there are must be so arranged that they are of the greatest benefit to the least advantaged. In addition, all positions must be open to all under conditions of fair equality of opportunity. Since these principles might be in conflict it is necessary to decide priorities. The first goes to liberty, which can only be restricted for the sake of liberty, and "a less than equal liberty must be acceptable to those with the lesser liberty."[8]

The kernel of this elaborate theory is the notion that inequalities must be to the benefit of the least advantaged—what Rawls calls the difference principle—and this principle of justice takes priority over efficiency even though a more efficient arrangement might maximize the sum of advantages. However, fair equality of opportunity—open access to all positions—is more important than the difference principle. Rawls' general conception of justice is then stated: "All social primary goods—liberty and opportunity, income and wealth, and the basis of self-respect—are to be distributed equally unless an unequal distribution of any or all of these goods is to the advantage of the least favoured."[9]

The principle that inequalities can only be justified if they benefit the least advantaged is considerably more constraining than the principle that inequalities can be justified if they lead to greater advantage for all, an idea which provides support for the extreme differential reward structures of contemporary societies. Great differences in income are thought to be necessary to get essential tasks performed so that productivity and output will be increased, thus providing a larger pie to be cut into grossly unequal pieces. This was the dominant ideology, for example, expressed during the history of the Carter Commission on taxation and the debates on tax reform in Canada. Inequality of income is justified on more than grounds of efficiency in the liberal capitalist doctrine. People are said to deserve higher incomes because they work harder or they devote more to the social good. Great differentials in income and life chances to the point of amassing fortunes have been justified with doctrines of this kind, and this acceptance of inequality is raised to the ruling faith of our everyday life.

Rawls' main institutional arrangement to bring about the just society is the social minimum by which redistribution to the least advantaged takes place. In his discussion of the social minimum[10] and efficiency he seems something of a liberal rather than the socialist some think him to be, but since justice is prior to efficiency and efficiency is judged in terms of making the least advantaged rather than everyone better off, he does seem to be arguing for a rather fundamental egalitarianism.

Not everyone, perhaps not a majority, sees the just society in terms of equality in the distribution of social and economic benefits. Many in Canada would agree that the just society involves no more than equality before the law, but beyond that how far the concept of rights should extend, say to education, health, housing and the like, is not a particularly lively debate in this country. That is not so elsewhere, and there are many examples of anti-egalitarian writers, perhaps the most articulate being those who have been dubbed the "new conservatives" of *The Public Interest* and *Encounter*. One of these, Robert Nisbet, who might be called the Milton Friedman of sociology, has just published a strong denunciation of the wider egalitarianism. Equality, he says,

> is by now tantamount to a religious article of faith carrying with it, at least in the minds of many intellectuals, leaders of special interest groups, and a rising number of politicians and bureaucrats, much the same kind of moral fervor and zeal, much the same sense of crusade against evil, and much the same measure of promise of redemption which have historically gone with religious movements.[11]

To him "Envy is the secret canker of equality—that is equality of result or condition."

Nisbet is also concerned about the effect that Rawls' doctrines would have on liberty, and he has little hope that by giving liberty priority it could survive the powerful bureaucratic apparatus that Rawls sees as necessary to oversee and manage the just society he outlines. The concept of equal liberties seems absurd and dangerous to Nisbet. Liberty cannot be shared. To take some from some people to give it to others is to restrict it for all and such ideas can only lead down the road to servitude. Echoing von Hayek of a generation earlier, he asks: Are we to be equal free men or equal serfs?

Perhaps the most immediate counter-proposal to that of Rawls comes from his Harvard colleague, Robert Nozick, who in his recently published *Anarchy, State and Utopia*,[12] advances what he calls the entitlement theory, or justice in holdings. If holdings are justly acquired or justly transferred (and those qualifications raise a lot of issues), then the person is entitled to them. Thus, a person is entitled to goods acquired through bequests providing the initial acquisitions were just. He is also entitled to goods received through luck, say a fair lottery, or if, as in the case of a popular entertainer, people are prepared to pay to be entertained, the entertainer is entitled, so to speak, to take the money and run, presumably after he has delivered the goods. Since lotteries have been elevated in this country to a new status in social policy, we might guess that lottery winners would be the least egalitarian and would be against sharing their winnings with the least advantaged. That is, of course, why Rawls puts those in the original position behind his veil of ignorance, because if they do not know whether or not they are going to win they might have different views about equal sharing. Rawls specifically rejects luck as a basis of reward.

Nozick would deal with unjust acquisition through a principle of rectification of injustice in acquisition which is fair enough in the here and now, but the historical case is more difficult, particularly in view of the long intergenerational transfer within families of capital, and of the fact that our gross inequalities arise from inheritance. Since the descendants are not responsible, Nozick finds it difficult to determine how far back it is necessary to go in "wiping clean the historical slate of injustice," to provide what we might call laundered justice. Nozick claims his entitlement theory is historical, that is, the justice of any distribution depends on how it came about, whereas most welfare theories such as Rawls' are structural or time-slice in principle, which attempt to optimize trade-offs in a hypothetical end-state distribution.[13]

How do we choose between the various and opposing views about equality? There is always the elegance and the reasonableness of the argument, and in the work I have just reviewed I have no more than sketched lightly the intricately latticed thought structures their authors have created. Or we might feel strongly that history or comparative anthropology reveals an emerging normative structure in rationality, mutuality, and democracy. Or distributive justice can be considered as an extension of citizenship rights which began in the civic and political realms.[14] Or we might consider the evidence provided from psychology such as Piaget's children creating rules and administering them with a sense of justice because without that there could be no games.[15] That might suggest to us an inherent drive for equality which we can also see among siblings who are our first reference groups in making judgments about how we are being treated and how we might treat others. Finally, our judgments may be visceral and based on feeling. Perhaps Rawls' people in their original position would sense how humans would feel about justice and liberty and that understanding may be the ultimate appeal of egalitarianism. It has been for me, at least.

I hope that this most summary review of equality and justice might serve as a framework for these two lectures. I will now return to the theme of this one: how public education has failed in its mission as an instrument of equality.

Education has been central to any discussion of equality of opportunity since it was to be the means of intervention between the existing structure of inequality into which children were born and the existing structure of unequal rewards to which they might aspire. For liberal reformers, education was to be the equalizer at the beginning, but not throughout or at the end of life in the work world. They did not think that the structure of inequality would be eliminated through education, but rather that there would be some movement of individuals up and down the class structure as education fostered talent from below and removed advantage from above. Moreover, if the system worked freely everyone would end up pretty much where their talents, energies and motivations would take them. The reward structure, though unequal, reflected talent and merit. People would deserve their rewards and society would benefit maximally because of the production of talent.

The contribution that education was thought to make to equality of condition is more obscure. I had always believed that there was no causal link from education to equality of condition, although I had long been an advocate of the view that if we must live with inequality of condition, education has an essential role in equality of opportunity. Equality of condition was to be achieved by other instruments, abolition of unjustified levels of inheritance, progressive taxation, reduction of differential wage structures, and the elimination of occupational monopolies. Recently in the United States, largely as the result of the work of Christopher Jencks and his colleagues (which I will discuss later), education has been condemned because it has failed to achieve equality of condition.

The notion that it might seems to come from a theory of human capital which holds that given a system of wage competition a worker is paid whatever his marginal productivity might be. Those who invest more capital in themselves, or have it invested on their behalf through more education, will increase their skills and create for themselves higher marginal rates of productivity and hence higher earnings. When workers generally increase their educational and skill levels, the productivity of the labor force as a whole goes up, and indeed a good proportion of the economic growth of industrial societies has been attributed to increases in educational levels. The equalizing force of education, it was thought, would come into play because although skilled workers had higher earnings, an increase in the pool of skilled workers would tend to reduce their earnings, a belief the strength of which is demonstrated in the history of guilds and craft unions. And since the pool of unskilled workers would be smaller their wages would go up.

Something of this kind is suggested in the following quotation from Clark Kerr and his associates in their book *Industrialism and Industrial Man*. They say:

> Education is intended to reduce the scarcity of skilled persons and this after a time reduces the wage and salary differentials they receive: it also pulls people out of the least skilled and most disagreeable occupations and raises wage levels there. It conduces to a new equality which has nothing to do with ideology.[16]

Thus wage competition in a free labor market would promote overall income equality by reducing the scarcity value of skill. Of course, this is a highly abstract model and could be clung to faithfully only with eyes tightly shut to what goes on in the real world, notably all those practices which interfere with free competition in the labor market, including those by which the better educated are able to protect their superior income-creating advantages. Even with the increased supply of better-educated people, some association between income and education remains rather than diminishes, and so young people are still well advised to keep educating themselves if they wish to have higher incomes.

The process has been well described by Thurow.[17] As the number of university-educated workers expands they begin to move downwards into jobs and income ranges previously held by the best high school-educated workers. Workers with high school education are forced lower in the income range and since that group, too, will have expanded, they will take jobs formerly held by the best workers with only elementary school education. Thus, the middle group would have higher incomes relative to the least educated group, but lower incomes relative to the university-educated. What develops is an educationally segmented labor market where educational credentials become a screening device. While there may be some equalization of incomes within educational levels there will be continuing inequalities between them. After presenting the empirical evidence Thurow concludes that if present trends continue in the U.S., income would be almost totally segregated by education. Thus, while it seems logical to think that when an advantage becomes as widespread as education has, it ceases to be an advantage and becomes valueless through debasement, that equalizing consequence does not seem to have happened.

The belief that by making educational opportunity more equal there would follow a greater equality of condition, was the central proposition which Christopher Jencks and his colleagues sought to test in what has become one of the most controversial books of contemporary social science, *Inequality: A Reassessment of the Effect of Family and Schooling in America.*[18] The book brings together a vast array of research findings on the inheritability of intelligence, the way in which family characteristics affect IQ tests, school grades, tests of cognitive skills, the amount of education received, the jobs people get, and finally how all these combine to affect the amount of income they receive. Jencks submits all these factors to a statistical analysis of great virtuosity and comes to the conclusion that education does not make for equality of result whatever the human capital theorists might think. Even when the number of years of schooling is combined with genetic endowment, the social background of the family, academic achievement in school and the job a person gets, altogether they account for about one-quarter of the differences of white male incomes in the United States. That does not leave much for education to explain by itself. This finding that variations in education do little to explain variations in income may seem odd when we see, as in our discussion of Thurow, there is still an association between income and educational level. Of course we cannot infer from this association that education causes income; it may simply be a way through which other causes work indirectly. But in Jencks' study, even when all these elements which have always been objects to be manipulated by or compensated for through educational policy are combined, there are still about three-quarters of the differences in income unaccounted for. What does affect income then? It is important to know if we are interested in achieving equality through policy intervention.

Jencks' answer, *faute de mieux*, is a bundle of things which he wraps up under the label of luck. In part, luck is pure chance for the individual such as being in the right place when particular jobs become available or entering the labor market at a propitious time, but also important are competences acquired on the job informally through experience and personality traits, such as an accommodative mentality appreciated by employers.

If the inequality of income that existed were a matter of luck, as Jencks concludes, the extra that the better off enjoy would be undeserved according to Rawls. Jencks, who is also an egalitarian, would employ some kind of income insurance to neutralize the effect of luck, which is probably not a commercially attractive concept of insurance. However, as some of Jencks' critics have pointed out, there is much besides luck that creates inequality of income: the rigidities of the occupational structure, the capacity of workers, manual as well as professional, to control entrance and acquire differential bargaining power and to seal off exclusive jurisdictions for themselves.[19] No amount of educational reform can overcome these entrenched privileges.

Jencks does not limit himself to the relationship between schooling and income inequality. He spends a great deal of time demonstrating that education has also failed to equalize cognitive skills, that is, what people learn quite apart from what they earn. People, of course, do learn things in educational institutions, and whatever they do learn they take into the labor market. It is simply that when they are in the labor market more education tends not to be automatically converted into more income. The failure to equalize what people learn means that education has failed at the first stage of a process which might be described in this way: equalize cognitive skill—equalize chances on the job market—equalize earnings and so arrive at equality of condition.

Jencks' findings on the incapacity of public education to reduce inequality appeared when professional educators were still recovering from and debating the consequences of the path-breaking study of James Coleman, whose work was commissioned by the United States Congress to establish the extent of educational inequality between whites and non-white minorities.[20] Coleman approached this problem of educational equality from an entirely different angle. Up to then it was believed by most educational planners and politicians who put up the tax money that equality was simply a matter of seeing that schools got equal resources. If that happened, the average level of skills among schools would become equal, that is, variations between schools would disappear. The more resources the higher the quality of schooling that could be expected. Such things as smaller classes, better-educated teachers, better school libraries and equipment, better school physical plant and so on were all thought to be central to producing better-educated children. In fact, the great expansion of the education industry was based on just such notions.

If all these things make a difference, Coleman argued, that difference should show up by comparing what those children learn who go to schools with superior resources with what other children learn who go to schools with inferior resources. His sensa-

tional findings were that differences in resources between schools
do not matter very much as far as effective education of children
is concerned. Substantial inequalities in cognitive skills between
groups persist that cannot be blamed on differences in school
resources: children do as well if they go to poor schools as they do
if they go to better-off ones. A summary conclusion of all this
research would be that despite the deficiencies which all such
studies have, schools do not now have a great effect on
achievement.[21]

That of course is a tremendous indictment and needs to be
examined more fully, but it is not surprising that such findings
should be seized upon by economy-minded tax guardians at all
levels of government as arguments for curtailing expenditures on
education. They have been used, too, by liberal reformers as reasons for pursuing egalitarian objectives in other directions, by putting available funds into such things as housing, health, and pensions. Not surprisingly the education industry, which combines
vast administrative bureaucracies with well organized, disciplined,
professional organizations has counter-attacked against this
threat. Since a large proportion of the costs of education are the
salaries of these bureaucracies and teachers, and since there is no
evidence that the schemes they dream up or the extra qualifications they acquire make any difference, the threat is serious from
their point of view.

An important difference in the treatment of equality between
Jencks and Coleman is that the former deals with large aggregates
of data to demonstrate inequality between individuals, whereas
the latter deals with inequality between groups and is concerned
to equalize group averages. For example, we might in this country
be concerned with equality among all Canadians or we might be
concerned with equality among English, French, and others. Thus
if all three groups had equal average income, equal average years
of schooling and so forth, the Coleman model of equality would
be met even though within each group inequalities existed. In the
Jencks model of equality, which is fairly extreme, individuals are
not classified into groups, but are all considered together, and they
must all be near the average. The difference between the two
approaches to measuring inequality is not simply methodological. The Coleman model says equality is met if there is no discrimination because of group membership. For example, women and
men are equal in the labor force when their average rates of pay
are the same. Jencks would say they must all be considered
together to calculate the average and must all be near it.

If not public education, what does make the difference in
what children learn? The only answer is the one which has been

provided for a long time, and that is differences in family background and cultural milieu which are favorable to learning, the resources which children bring to school. These cultural differences are a reflection of the already existing inequalities of our social class structures.[22] If these socially derived inequalities are added to differences in natural endowment they make up the private resources that the individual brings into the educational system. Such resources are enormously unequal and the weight of the evidence from Coleman and Jencks is that public education, despite the huge expenditures that are put into it in general or for special programs in particular, has failed to reduce the continued inequality that flows from the inequality of social backgrounds. Thus, the evidence against schooling as it presently exists mounts. It does little to equalize cognitive skills; variations in the amounts of monetary and policy resources employed have little effect on educational outcomes; and public education has little consequence for the reduction of income inequality.

Rather than offset the inequalities of class, public education has served to perpetuate them. This class reproduction is the central thesis of two Marxist writers, Bowles and Gintis, in their *Schooling in Capitalist America*,[23] a study which can be considered the latest assault on public education and which no doubt will be widely read because it comes at a time of economic crisis, underutilization of educated young people, and increasing disillusionment with corporate capitalism as it has developed. These two writers see the educational processes as a mirror image of the capitalist system of production, all legitimated by what they call the technocratic-meritocratic ideology which holds that the task of education is to sort people out on the basis of their inherent ability and to give them a training commensurate with those abilities. They enter the work world at an appropriate level and progress upward according to the competences they demonstrate. Rewards are based on technical qualifications and merit and since these are unequal, so is pay. Unequal rewards exist because these inducements are believed necessary to prompt people to put up with education and take on responsibility. The technocratic-meritocratic ideology is easily recognized. It underlies much of our educational practice and the inequalities of pay in our work situations. As can be readily seen it is an extension of the liberal ideology supporting equality of opportunity referred to earlier. It is also the rational model of capitalist economic organization—or we might go beyond that and say it is the model of production of the industrial society in the bureaucracies of both private and public sectors.

Educational reformers generally have accepted the ideology because of its apparent support of equality of opportunity. However, sociologists in many countries have shown that meritocratic systems do not benefit the majority of working-class children, which is to say the majority of children in our societies, because of the emphasis on early selection based on tests of intelligence and cognitive skills weighted in favor of middle- and upper-class children. In part, the tests measure the kinds of things that middle-class children have an advantage in learning. The meritocracy is based on attitudes and motivations, the dispositions to learning and other cultural elements that middle-class parents transmit to their children. Being selected and sponsored by educational institutions means special treatment in superior academic streams, entrance to the higher learning and finally into positions of responsibility and control in the work world.

Social class selection for preferred educational treatment seems inescapable when both secondary and postsecondary levels are divided into the more routinized vocational training on the one hand and the more creative and more demanding academic learning on the other. Vocational streams are often referred to as providing "no-nonsense programs" while, as we know so well, there is lots of nonsense in the more leisurely, intellectually luxurious academic programs. These divisions within learning correspond to those of the work world: "no-nonsense" disciplined work in the lower levels and increasing possibilities for creative and independent work as the occupational structure is ascended, although the degree of creativity allowed for within the constraints of existing bureaucracies must not be overestimated. The different levels of schooling, even if they are not internally stratified by streams and tracks, permit different degrees of creativity and independence. Thus, those who leave at lower levels and who do not make it through to university but instead go to work—and that is always the sizable majority in Canada—are more disciplined, have had less opportunity to be creative or to find personal development than those who continue, and are therefore more accommodative to the discipline expected of them at the lower levels of work. Schools and work places are similar in their ambience, and so students are taught the appropriate patterns of personal behavior which fit them into their job situations. Drill, obedience, routine standardization, and rewards for the right work characterize both, with the teacher as foreman and the principal as manager.

This training for servitude at work, a lifetime without spontaneity or creativity or individuality—and that continues to be the condition of work for most—helps to produce the necessary false consciousness to legitimate alienated labor, where work is marked by a fragmented division of labor and over which the workers themselves have no control. Schooling provides what Ivan Illich calls pre-alienation.[24] Thus by a process of selective streaming, varying rates of retention and differential subjection to discipline, the educational system serves to reproduce from generation to generation the existing structure of inequality. Even when we consider that some proportion make it through from the lower levels to the higher (the layers of inequality have some permeability) it would not be an unfair judgment to say that egalitarian objectives have not been achieved.

Authoritarianism and rigidity in schooling have long been criticized by commentators and investigators of varying ideological persuasions. Their criticism of schooling is that it has been a form of aggression against the primordial spontaneity and creativity of childhood and adolescence, a "destructive denaturing."[25] Schools have been seen as prisons isolated from the crowded flux of everyday life in society, prisons from which eager and exuberant spirits are forever seeking to escape, but are prevented by their teacher guardians, laws, truant officers, and in some places even the police. Some would go so far as to suggest that compulsory schooling has become a form of bondage or legal encumbrance limiting the civil rights of the young.[26] Many of these criticisms have been aimed at teaching methods, educational bureaucrats, curricula, classroom and school structures. Although there has been a strong radical element in this body of criticism, conservative teachers and academics acknowledge that both compulsion and social pressure force them to deal with students whom they see as having no interest in learning, or at least learning in a fashion which from a position of authority teachers are able to impose.

We are familiar enough with these criticisms since they have been around for a long time in the writings of Paul Goodman, Edgar Friedenberg and Ivan Illich, and in an earlier epoch John Dewey.[27] The fact that all these people are still widely read suggests that despite their influence on educational commissions of inquiry and some reforms aimed at making schools less authoritarian, less lock-stepped, less graded and freer in choice, these criticisms must still have some validity. My concern with this type of criticism, and some of the changes to which it has given rise is not in the effects they have on personality but rather how these changes relate to inequality of class structure. The relationship is not altogether clear. Some writers, like Paul Goodman for example, describe the helplessness of the working-class or minority-group child as he confronts the discipline and the middle-class orientation of the school. They are not disposed to learn in this conventional way and since there is no other, they become docile or rebellious. The school fails to transmit the middle-class tools and virtues which are essential to climbing the success ladder. Success-oriented schooling has been criticized abroad also for its destruction of working-class cultures or ethnic cultures in more recent years. Certainly there are aspects of working-class life, job insecurity, poverty, limited leisure, poor living environments and the like which are not worth preserving, and it seems desirable to provide through education a mechanism for people to pull themselves out. But we know that not all can move out because opportunity is limited, and consequently the preparation is not for opportunity so much as for competition. Thus, rather than using education as an escape route for the few, there should be ways of reforming it to alleviate some of the lower-class hazards for the many; to develop their survival skills, their capacity to participate, and to encourage their cultural activities. As for the other radical critique—education as preparation for alienated labor—it should be possible to devise educational changes having other objectives such as sensitizing working-class children to the conditions which the system creates for them and preparing them to have more control over their work activities. Equality can be as well served through education to change deprived environments as through education to compete for limited opportunity.

However, the anti-authoritarian critics of schooling are not confined to middle-class radicals speaking on behalf of their working-class clientele. The middle classes have been vocal, too, and the middle class are more articulate, have more clout as taxpayers and voters and participate more in voluntary organizations related to schools. I would interpret much of the freeing up of the schools which we have seen—according to some with deplorable results—as a response to the demands of the middle class whose children were also unhappy with the restrictive characteristics of the school. After all, their children are disciplined at home through manipulative child-rearing practices, they have the motivation to do as well as or better than their parents. Moreover, they are well supplied with learning devices and situations outside of the school. For them school was not so much a prison as a bore. So the demands for freer schools and the search for alternatives were middle-class activities.

I once interpreted these activities as working against equality and opportunity because it seemed to be a matter of the middle class reorganizing the schools for their benefit. The changes were coming at a time when school retention rates—in Canada particularly—were reaching new levels, which meant that a larger proportion of working-class young people than formerly were continuing into the higher levels of schooling. The absence of objective evidence of achievement (what university admissions people are now looking for) would not much harm the middle-class student since he had social and cultural advantages in getting on despite whatever schooling he had rather than because of it. On the other hand the certificate of achievement for the working-class young people, minorities, and women gave them claims to consideration for work or further education on an equal basis with others better off than they. I do not hold this view so strongly now and have come to the conclusion that achievement credentials create new forms of inequality and injustice—a problem with which I want to deal in the next lecture.

Perhaps the most widely debated aspect of the relationship between education and equality is the question of how it is paid for, particularly at the higher levels. We have seen extraordinary ingenuity in the attempts to measure and partition the costs and benefits between individuals and society. The debates have led to a variety of patchwork student aid programs, their promoters suggesting equality is being served. I do not propose to review this debate here because I have, with others, discussed it extensively elsewhere.[28] But the conclusion which is extremely important in the present context is that the less well-off contribute substantially in relation to their resources for educational services which they do not use or do not see as useful to them. When we asked Ontario high school students a few years ago how much further they planned to go in education after leaving high school their responses ranged from taking training in vocational and trade schools, for which in most cases they would have to pay, to carrying on through university to postgraduate work. Those going to the fee-paying trade schools were predominantly of lower-class origin while the higher classes were overrepresented among those who were going to the tax-endowed highest educational level. That gives us a brief glimpse of the failure of the welfare state: not that its generosity to the least advantaged has brought us to the shoals of disaster, but the way in which the best advantaged become the more skilful consumers of publicly supplied services. That the present form of financing higher education contains substantial subsidies to the better-off in society seems an inescapable conclusion. Thus the obstacles to equality, among them the ways of financing education, have proved formidable.

All of these criticisms of public education add up to a rather severe indictment. The evidence against schooling as it presently exists should not be accepted without critical scrutiny, and there has been plenty of that—witness the storm of controversy that has surrounded the work of Jencks and Coleman. There is always the technical quibbling of course, but more important is the response that school effectiveness or school outputs are judged very narrowly by verbal and other tests which measure cognitive skills alone. Of course schools are supposed to produce cognitive skills, but there are broader educational objectives such as cultured, mature, and civic-minded individuals and it is not easy to devise measures of how well schools are doing in these affective domains. However, even with respect to the more measurable cognitive skills it is important to keep the findings in perspective. It is not to say that children have failed to learn in schools so much as variations in school resources do not account for the variations in what children learn. If schools had no resources at all, clearly there would be no learning. Nor are these critics saying that schools have failed to educate. Clearly some young people do very well in the educational system, but if they do they are more likely to come from the more advantaged groups in the community or bring some private resources to school with them. It is in this way that education helps to reproduce the structure of inequality. The crucial point is that education has failed to equalize.

Perhaps it was naive to think that it might have or that educational reform alone was sufficient to deal with the basic structure of inequality, which in its consequence is much more pervasive and deep-rooted than we think. Coleman has made the point in a wide-sweeping criticism of Rawls that egalitarianism is impossible without the destruction of the family and that would be a costly measure because families invest far more resources in a psychological and cultural sense in children which do far more for their learning than any educational system could.[29] Thus, families are an important social resource that equality should not destroy, and if family resources are unequal that is a fact of social life.

Those who hold that the just society involves some considerable degree of equality—if not extreme egalitarianism—need not concede on this point of the family. It does, however, involve a shift in strategy from educational institutions to other social domains, and it would involve plans for equality of condition to reduce the undeserved advantages that are transmitted through the family. What those social policies might be are beyond the scope of these lectures.

However, we have by no means exhausted the questions that can be raised on the relationship between education, equality, and opportunity. Do our economies continue to be the Eldorados of boundless opportunity we once thought they were or have they run out of opportunity? Have we overemphasized economic consumption as the realm in which to strive for equality of condition? Are there no other conditions? If we were misled about the capacity of our systems for opportunity, or overly preoccupied with equality of condition as equality of consumption, what role might education play in the light of answers to these questions? These are the subjects of the next lecture.

Notes

1. In Canada the equality theme was muted until after the Second World War. It is difficult to find any clear articulation of it in the history of Canadian education before then. In the nineteenth century in Upper Canada (Canada West) it was thought that the social problems of crime and pauperism among juveniles might be reduced through education, a view strongly held by Egerton Ryerson. See Egerton Ryerson, *Report on a System of Public Elementary Instruction for Upper Canada* in J. George Hodgins, *Historical and Other Papers and Documents of the Ontario Educational System*, vol. III (Toronto, 1912). For contemporary scholarship and interpretations of Ryerson's social philosophy about education see Parts I and II of Paul H. Mattingly and Michael B. Katz (eds.), *Education and Social Change: Themes from Ontario's Past*, New York University Press (New York, 1975).

2. Malcolm Sawyer, "Income Distribution in OECD countries," *OECD Economic Outlook* (Paris), July 1976.

3. Robert Heilbroner, *Business Civilization in Decline*, Norton (New York, 1976), 109.

4. Following the work of Boudon in France. See Raymond Boudon, *Education, Opportunity, and Social Inequality*, John Wiley (New York, 1974).

5. I am indebted to my Carleton University colleague Z.A. Jordan for many enlightening discussions of the concepts of equality and social justice.

6. Harvard University Press (Cambridge, 1971).

7. Brian Barry, *The Liberal Theory of Justice: A Critical Examination of the Principal Doctrines in a Theory of Justice by John Rawls*, Clarendon Press (Oxford, 1973); Norman Daniels, *Reading Rawls*, Basic Books (New York, 1974).

8. John Rawls, *A Theory of Justice*, Harvard University Press (Cambridge, 1971).

9. *Ibid.*, 303.

10. *Ibid.*, 276 ff.

11. Robert Nisbet, "The Fatal Ambivalence of an Idea," *Encounter*, December 1976. See also his review of Rawls, "The Pursuit of Equality", in *The Public Interest*, Spring 1974.

12. Basic Books (New York, 1974).

13. See "Distributive Justice", in Robert Nozick, *Anarchy, State and Utopia*.

14. See T.H. Marshall, *Citizenship and Social Class and Other Essays*, Cambridge University Press, 1950.

15. Jean Piaget, *The Moral Judgment of the Child*, Free Press (Glencoe, 1948).

16. Quoted in John H. Goldthorpe, "Social Stratification in Industrial Society," *The Sociological Review Monograph No. 8*, Keele, 1964.

17. Lester C. Thurow, "Education and Economic Equality," in Donald M. Levine and Mary Jo Bane, *The "Inequality" Controversy: Schooling and Distributive Justice*, Basic Books (New York, 1975).

18. Basic Books (New York, 1972).

19. See Levine and Bane, *op. cit.*, and *Perspectives on Inequality*, Harvard Educational Review Reprint Series No. 8.

20. J.S. Coleman, *et al., Equality of Educational Opportunity*, Washington, D.C. U.S. Department of Health, Education and Welfare, U.S. Government Printing Office, 1966. For discussions of the Coleman Report see Frederick Mosteller and Daniel P. Moynihan, eds. *On Equality of Educational Opportunity*, Random House (New York, 1972) and *Harvard Educational Review*, Winter 1968.

21. The effects of education are dubious in more than one context. For example, a committee of the Ontario legislature examining highway safety sought ways of improving the driving habits of young people. They suggested driving improvement courses to be taken after the third offence in the first five years of driving. "Although a driving improvement course is recommended, the committee was told by the research staff last week that driver education courses don't improve safety records", *The Globe and Mail* (Toronto), 26 January, 1977.

22. For some evidence from Ontario see, Marion R. Porter, John Porter, and Bernard R. Blishen, *Does Money Matter? Prospects for Higher Education*, Macmillan of Canada (Toronto, 1979).

23. Basic Books (New York, 1976).

24. Ivan Illich, *Deschooling Society*, Harper and Row (New York, 1972), 66-67.

25. The expression comes from Edgar Z. Friedenberg, *Coming of Age in America*, Random House (New York, 1963).

26. *Ibid.*, 249. See also Paul Goodman, *Public Mis-education and the Community of Scholars*, Random House (New York, 1962), and Charles E. Silberman, *Crisis in the Classroom*, Random House (New York, 1970).

27. For Canadian variations on similar themes see Loren Jay Lind, *The Learning Machine*, House of Anasi (Toronto, 1974) and Joel O. Loken, *Student Alienation and Dissent*, Prentice-Hall of Canada (Scarborough, 1973).

28. Porter, Porter, and Blishen, *op. cit.*

29. James S. Coleman, "Equality of Opportunity and Equality of Results," *Harvard Educational Review*, vol. 43, February 1973, and "Inequality, Sociology and Moral Philosophy," *American Journal of Sociology*, vol. 80, no. 3, November 1974.

II

EDUCATION AND THE JUST SOCIETY

In the preceding lecture I made a case for equality as one of the goals of the just society, drawing a great deal on the contemporary philosopher John Rawls. I considered a body of rather persuasive evidence that the great expansion of public education in the present century had failed in its promise of promoting either equality of opportunity or equality of condition. The concern has been, however, primarily with equality of opportunity to learn and develop skills that could be taken into the labor market and converted into a career, income, and other social and economic advantages. Now I would like to move beyond educational institutions to consider the work world and the structure of occupations to see whether they can be properly designated as a structure of opportunity, so better to assess the linkage between education and work. The expansion of education was justified not only because it was thought to serve equality, but because of its economic benefits. At present I am only tangentially interested in the economics of education and I am happy to leave that to the incisive analytical tools of the economists. What concerns me is whether we can properly say whether the great expansion of industrialization was also—and continues to be—an expansion of opportunity such that we must consider access to it through education, or any other means, as essential to the just society.

It would be helpful, first of all, to sketch out the regnant model which social scientists use to account for occupational or job opportunity and the relation of education to it.

The model goes something like this. The advances of industrialization and technology have brought with them a greatly increased number of jobs requiring higher levels of skill than formerly. This upgrading of the labor force has been achieved through the increased education which has accompanied industrial growth. Jobs themselves have increased educational content and jobs requiring higher levels of education have become a greater proportion of the total. The model extrapolates these trends into postindustrialism with more and more education-loaded, white-collar, service, brain work and less and less education-limited, blue-collar, goods-producing work. In this upgrading model the education-occupation link is integral.

Nation-wide studies of intergenerational occupational mobility in Canada and elsewhere (in which the changing structure of opportunity implied by the model just outlined is captured by comparing jobs which men have with those their fathers held) all conclude that education is a most important facilitator for those who move up. In part, this conclusion results because some important factors like level of ambition or attitudes to work or sheer luck get left out of large national surveys. However, from the limited set of factors examined, it has been demonstrated that education can overcome disabilities that might attach to low social origins, and hence some empirical support is given to the doctrine of education serving to equalize opportunity. Recently, however, there have appeared trenchant criticisms of the model of upgrading and opportunity and those who pursue this kind of research (among whom I include myself) cannot ignore them.

The model is under attack because it is held to be a misrepresentation of the processes at work. Instead of upgrading there has taken place and will continue to take place what Harry Braverman has called the degradation of work in the twentieth century.[1] That might sound like an odd subtitle for a Marxist to give to a book in view of the degraded conditions of work in nineteenth-century capitalist England from which Marx drew his prophetic inspiration. Braverman's work has to be taken seriously because what he is saying is that the upgrading trend that science and technology were supposed to bring to improve the conditions of work through more skilled, creative, and independent work by better-educated workers, has in fact not taken place. Rather the trend has been toward the opposite—a degradation. And so the picture of upward occupational mobility that is implied in the kind of occupational movements we measure is called into question.

Braverman gives many examples of degraded work for they are not difficult to find. Here is one describing how what might have been a "crusty, wholesome loaf of bread becomes a 'product' with the 'resiliency of a rubber sponge.' "[2]

> . . .the production process for the manufacture of this bread is a triumph of the factory arts. Continuous mixing, reduction of brew fermentation time, dough which is metered, extruded, divided, and panned to the accuracy of a gram in the pound, conveyorized baking and automatic depanning, cooling, slicing, wrapping and labelling have effectively rid the bakery of the troublesome and unprofitable arts of the baker, and have replaced the baker himself with engineers on the one hand and factory operatives on the other. The speed with which the operation is conducted is a marvel of efficiency, and, apart from its effects on the workers, if only it were not necessary for the people to consume the product the whole thing could be considered a resounding success.

In the destruction of the industrial arts of the skilled worker, technology has created a great range of semi (which is really to say minimally) skilled and unskilled operatives. Service industries and clerical occupations of the tertiary sector, the expansion of which is claimed to represent an important element of upgrading, are also being degraded by technology. The routinization of clerical work by automated office machinery and the increasing fragmentation of office work have removed an element of independent judgment on the part of clerks whose jobs earlier embodied a range of skills. The promotional ladders that clerical workers could once look up have had rungs knocked out of them, making upward mobility difficult. Office occupations which were once thought to be more desirable for pay and prestige have been reduced through streamlined administration to resemble factory work.

Occupations surrounding the computer, which is the symbol of automated office work, are thought also to represent upgrading because of the need for technical qualifications. The fact is, however, computer functioning depends on a large base of unskilled key-punch operators, a job which according to one report

> can be learned in a matter of a week or two, and satisfactory production skills can be attained within some six months. Despite most employers stated preference a high school diploma is not essential for satisfactory performance. . . .a ninth-grade reading level and equivalent proficiency in arithmetic provide a good starting base.[3]

We are all familiar with examples of stripped-down, simplified skills in automated office work. Bank tellers no longer need to add, but simply push bank books into computer terminals; library clerks run optical scanners over electronically sensitized labels attached to the books and thereby activate the entire recording of the circulation process. One wonders now what requires a graduate degree in library science or how much formal training is now necessary for library technologists, a new job to emerge from our educational machinery. They both have demarcated jurisdictions within the library, but we might well ask in the light of the automated work how much of their formal educational requirements are really necessary. And so we might proceed through a wide area of the clerical and white-collar work world to find jobs which require fewer skills nowadays than formerly. Cooks in restaurants become thawer-outers and secretary typists become automated word processors.

It has been argued that while a great deal of labor may have been degraded, because for many jobs in both blue- and white-collar production lines the worker has been moulded into the exigencies of technology, at the same time there has been built up behind the ranks of automated factory workers or the banks of white-collar card punch operators an army of highly qualified and creative engineers and maintenance workers. But the maintenance worker has become the not-so-skilled component replacer, and the battalion of creative scientists seems but a corporal's guard.

Why, Braverman asks, has the upgrading thesis been so firmly entrenched as the conventional wisdom of both labor economics and sociology? The answer he provides is a difficult one to refute. Much of the upgrading is a statistical artifact of census occupational categories rather than changes in the real work world.[4] Many occupations which over time continue to be classified as skilled are just not as skilled as they used to be: the baker, for example. "Semiskilled" was a census statistical category created to classify, somewhere in the occupational hierarchy, newly emerging factory operatives working on machines in production lines when these became a feature of modern factory work. It seemed proper that they should be higher than occupations classified as laboring, but lower than those classified as skilled. But when one looks at what semiskilled workers and laborers do, there is often very little difference in terms of skill or educational qualifications required. One study of the New York State Department of Labor reported that "two-thirds of all the jobs in existence in the state involved such simple skills that they can and are learned in a few days, weeks, or at the most months of on the job training."[5] I can report from our own experience of attempting to build an occupational classification from the new Canadian occupational titles used in the 1971 census that large segments of the semiskilled labor force, both blue- and white-collar, require minimal training.[6]

Those of us who have used the upgrading model as the basis of mobility studies have always been puzzled about how to deal with urban workers whose fathers were farmers and farm laborers. Given the relative recency of the rural-urban transition the Canadian labor force includes a large number of people of farm origin. The pattern of off-farm migration which has been noted for many countries is that the sons of farmers become in large proportions unskilled and semiskilled urban workers, and in any study of occupational mobility this is recorded as movement upward because of the assumption that these two classifications require more skill than farming and hence are higher in the class structure. A good amount of recorded upward mobility or upgrading is just that process. But the farming father, whether hired hand or proprietor, commanded a range of knowledge and skills involving plants, animals, and machines which could be placed well above that required by an urban factory worker.[7] Yet most censuses say the reverse. I myself suggested many years ago, in trying to assess the effects on the Canadian class structure of the great rural-urban transition of the present century, that the great fall in the number of farms and farmers represents the loss of a class of independent owners to a class of low-level wage earners and might well be considered downward movement rather than upward.[8]

Another of Braverman's interesting examples is the occupation of teamster and its transition from the age of horses to that of cars and trucks. In both stages they have been and are a large occupational group. When teamsters drove horses they were considered unskilled because harnessing and driving a horse was an activity with which large numbers were familiar, particularly if they came from farm backgrounds. But when motor cars appeared, representing the advance to machinery with which fewer people were acquainted, teamsters became classified as semi-skilled. Nowadays when cars are driven from an early age the job seems scarcely a skilled one, but the skills of harnessing horses are somewhat rare.

To argue as Braverman has that much of the upgrading of the labor force is a statistical artifact is not to deny that there have appeared a large number of highly qualified occupations based on the natural and social sciences, the law, and so forth. However, the numbers are small relative to the rest of the labor force. But because typically they rest on the higher learning they send up the average educational requirement of the labor force. Moreover, the labor forces of industrial and postindustrial societies are increasingly assuming a bimodal distribution with respect to skill requirements, the highly qualified at one end and the mass of less qualified at the other, creating a polarization which as it increases will have great implications for equality, not only of incomes but of authority and power, thus providing a further dimension to the segmentation of the labor force.

Along with the degrading of work noted by Braverman, has gone a very considerable increase in the levels of education of people at work, making for a substantial lack of fit between the skill requirements of jobs and the level of education brought into the work world, the condition which Ivar Berg has called "the great training robbery."[9] It is a fact that over time new jobs have appeared requiring high levels of training. However, it has been estimated for the United States that only about 15 per cent of the increased level of education of the labor force between 1940 and 1960 came about in this way. The rest, 85 per cent, came about by workers doing the same jobs having more education.[10] No doubt in some cases the same jobs do require somewhat greater skills with technological change than formerly. However, when the truth in Braverman's degrading thesis is considered along with the increased educational levels of workers in the jobs which have been degraded, we must pay attention to the critics of our over-educated labor forces.

As Berg and others have pointed out, what we may have seen is not a response of educational institutions to the occupational demands of a highly industrialized labor force but a response from employers throughout the economy to the supply which has been produced by educational institutions. That is, education has become a screening device, and credentialism a new form of property holding involving the right to work. The uncredentialled become a new minority (and in some respects they may be a majority) and subjects of discrimination. In many places the uncredentialled overlap as a group with other groups subject to discrimination who become shunted by economic forces into segmented labor markets of high risk and little opportunity: ". . .instead of equalizing chances," Illich notes, "the school system has monopolized their distribution."[11]

Credentialism, the holding of various types of diplomas and certificates bestowed by the educational system, is not altogether the fault of employers. Many really believe that better-educated workers are a better bargain despite the fact that it has never been demonstrated that the characteristics of the good worker, future trainability, productivity, adaptability, and so forth are related to level of education. Some of the evidence reviewed by Berg, although not conclusive, suggests the opposite. So employers might well be advised to be much more sceptical than they have been about educational qualifications.

Sometimes the new property rights provided by credentialism have legal enforcement as in the case of doctors, teachers, and a wide range of professions. But the use of credentials as dubious screening devices by employers of almost everyone from keypunch operators to professors means that credentialism is an essential entitlement to work. The relationship between unemployment and low level of education is some evidence of this phenomenon. The link between educational qualifications and job opportunity, which has been the central theme in educational public relations, has added to credentialism. I think in all fairness, or perhaps in self-defence for my own pronouncements, the link between skill level and in-school training seemed plausible, and we were all too prepared to ignore alternative ways of becoming skilled.

Ivan Illich bases a good deal of his exhortation to deschool society on the evils of credentialism. While we might have some doubts about taking seriously anyone who states as he does that "escalation of the schools is as destructive as the escalation of weapons but less visibly so,"[12] his criticism of conventional forms of learning is not without persuasiveness and his sketching out of what might take place of schools, what he calls learning webs, is not without attraction.

Credentialism provides a clue to the relationship that is found between education and occupational success. It helps with the first jobs people get, with the early stages of a career and with selection for early training and promotion, although as we have noted, Berg makes the case in his review of the evidence, that workers with better educational qualifications are not any better than workers with lesser qualifications. Overeducation through credentialism provides the illusion of preferability for future job performance.

It would seem that educational institutions as suppliers of labor and employing institutions as creating the demand formed an umbilical link, a feedback loop through which they nourished each other rather than examining closely just what the skill content of jobs might be in the light of the labor force changes taking place.

Thus we find with credentialism yet another example of how the expansion of public education has had the unanticipated consequence of bringing a new form of inequality rather than reducing the existing structure of inequality. That consequence is all the more serious from the point of view of the just society because the lack of credentials can often be traced to factors of social inequality as I tried to argue in my first lecture. The role of credentials in the service of inequality is aptly stated in the following quotation:

> The development of the diploma from universities, and business and engineering colleges, and the universal clamor for the creation of educational certificates in all fields make for the formation of a privileged stratum. . . .When we hear from all sides the demand for the introduction of regular curricula and special examinations, the reason behind it is of course, not a suddenly awakened "thirst for education," but the desire for restricting the supply for these positions and their monopolization by the owners of educational certificates.

The quotation does not come from any of our radical critics of education but from Max Weber's celebrated analysis of bureaucracy which dates from early in the present century.[13] The case against credentialism is a fairly strong one in that it can effectively cut people off from opportunity as it operates to exclude the supposedly unqualified whether at the highest or the lowest levels. It is also seen as supporting monopoly pricing of services and a differential wage structure.

There is, however, another side of the credential story in the consideration of equality. From the point of view of the deprived or least advantaged—the lower class, minorities, and women—to obtain a certificate through public education was to obtain a passport to upward occupational mobility and an escape from low social origins or discrimination. It was also a way of selecting out the talented from the disadvantaged and opening opportunity to them often through special programs of redress. The survival of programs in the light of the evidence that they seem to have little pay-off in equalizing achievement in school or incomes at work comes into doubt. They may, however, promote equality by dispensing credentials to those who formerly were not able to acquire them and so improve their access to the job market.

Thus as long as credentialism is firmly entrenched the defenders of redress programs have a strong case when minority group members or women go into an employment office or a dean's office with a welding certificate or a Ph.D. degree; they cannot be told they are unqualified and shown the door, although alternative subtle devices might be found to exclude them in the course of their subsequent careers. At least the job barrier can be breached by making credentials a qualification for entry. Because it has made this contribution to equality of opportunity credentialism should not be abandoned lightly and so reopen the way to discrimination in employment.

However, we must try to strike a balance; the retention of credentialism maintains a discrimination against those who are without the new form of property and imposes something of an artifactual demand on educational institutions. Of course, educational institutions are themselves the great offenders with their graded hierarchies where movement from one to the other is almost impossible without diplomas from below. Some chinks are beginning to appear in this academic bastion as well with open admissions policies, with alternative forms of credit such as units of work experience, and the acceptance of discontinuous learning patterns. Recommendations along these lines can be found in almost all recent provincial commissions on postsecondary education. Some university senates have moved slowly in that direction, but almost as a secondary activity with part-time students in the light of the falling clientele in their primary market. Others remain fixed and protect the dispensing of academic credits as do banks the dispensing of other forms of credit.

A good argument can be made, then, from the standpoint of equality and the just society that credentialism should be abandoned, and—an even more radical notion—forbidden under fair employment practices legislation, so that the lack of formal educational qualifications cannot be the reason for exclusion from hiring any more than ethnic origin or sex. Evidence of competence acquired in other ways than certificates must be considered. Nor should employers be able to raise competence requirements higher than are necessary for the jobs they seek to fill. Nor should occupational groups be given the right to set their own educational qualifications for entry—whether plumbers or professors—for that is the most effective device for exclusion and high incomes. In what is considered as a mildly radical document, the Hall-Dennis Report on schooling in Ontario, one reads, ". . .plans should be made to transfer the licensing of teachers to the teaching profession."[14] One of the main arguments seems to have been that that is the mark of a self-governing profession, and that with the growing acquisition of formal certificates teachers have achieved that high status. One must not single out teachers particularly when the privilege of occupational closure is endemic to the labor force. To extend the privilege rather than remove it is scarcely a movement in the direction of equality.

The abolition of credentialism in employment was recommended by as conservative a group as can be found, those who produced the Report of the Special Program Review for the Government of Ontario. They said, "Full support should be given to the recommendations of the Commission. . . to discourage the use of academic achievement or paper credentials as a job-screening mechanism."[15]

The Commission referred to is the Commission on Postsecondary Education in Ontario. Weber, it will be recalled from the earlier quotation, was concerned with the way in which diplomas became property and hence linked to class reproduction. But he also feared the inequality that was emerging with the growing power of bureaucracy. In the contemporary world the terminology changes somewhat—Galbraith's power of the technostructure, Daniel Bell's ascendancy of the professional and technical class—but the picture is much the same, the steady march of the expert and the official towards the capitals of power, armed with certificates from the ever expanding educational institutions.

If certificates stand in the way of the tendency towards equality why not get rid of them altogether by forbidding educational institutions to bestow them? To live without certificates seems a horrible thought—like living in a Canadian winter without heat—horror because of the twin supports they provide, the conferring of status and occupational rights, and secondly, signifying competence to employers. We have dealt with the former, but what about the latter? There is no reason why employers who want to match people to their skill requirements cannot test recruits themselves providing they do not impose artificially high standards.

This would not be a great burden on employers since so much can be learned quickly on the job. The point is that no certificates should be awarded that can serve as future property in the labor market. There is of course the public interest to be maintained for some highly skilled and professional tasks, but the licensing could be provided by public agencies and anybody who wants to could apply to be licensed. The point would be to remove certification from educational institutions—the whole gamut of them—because of the way in which credentialism has grown and contributed to inequality.[16]

Any steps taken to abolish or reduce the effects of credentialism would of course bring about enormous changes in educational institutions as we now know them. If they were no longer linked to vocational or occupational futures the reasons for coming to them would be quite different although they might still prepare people to meet the demands of advanced knowledge. In any case they could give themselves over to learning for those who were interested in learning, and providing they were accessible to all and sufficiently varied and flexible in approaches and method, they would do less to contribute to inequality.

If education has done little to serve the principle of equality or distributive justice, and if we have overestimated the opportunity we attached to the new industrial labor force, and if we were to reduce if not eliminate credentialism what is to be the future of our present day educational institutions? The question is timely because governments everywhere are reducing the priority they once gave to education as competing demands are heard for funds. The liberal capitalist state seems to have exhausted its capacity to pursue the just society through welfare measures. If that is so education has weaker claims than it formerly had for such a pride of place. One has only to compare the needs of the young and healthy with the old and disabled to see the challenges to the education case. Jencks, for example, says, after his striking revelation that education does not have much of a pay-off in later life, that it should nonetheless be preserved because it can provide pleasant activity and surroundings for the young and they should all be equally entitled to it.[17] But the needs of the young as against the old—or any other category—are not immediately self-evident, and once the economic productivity argument is seriously weakened, education as a kindergarten (baby and "teen" sitting many critics call it) has to make a stronger claim than formerly.

The point from which I would embark on the search for how education might be transformed to serve better equality and social justice would be those criticisms stemming from Marxists like

Bowles and Gintis and other writers like Illich, Friedenberg, and Silberman, some of whom I reviewed earlier. We might put their views all together under the heading of the "psychologistic critique," including such notions as education as prealienation and education for docility. Their concern is more with personality effects of schooling than with cognitive effects: the failure to develop the self rather than the failure to learn. They provide variations on the same theme of how education suppresses human potential. To link these psychologistic critiques with some philosophic views of C.B. Macpherson will help locate our point of departure.

In a paper called "The Maximization of Democracy," Macpherson speaks of the distinction made in western liberal thought between humans as consumers of utilities, with unbounded desires to satisfy wants, and humans as possessors of capacities.[18] The free market society which we still retain as a millenial myth is considered morally desirable because it serves this acquisitive nature of humans by facilitating their pursuit of unlimited personal accumulation and consumption. We are filled with desires not even dreamt of until the ingenuity of capitalist enterprise unlocks them in an endless sequence. (It might be added parenthetically that unhappily for large populations, socialist economies unlock few desires.) As I suggested earlier, for those who are not well served by free market economies, and who become casualties to its imperfections, their amelioration—our concept of welfare—is to supply culturally minimal standards which ascend along with the increasing consumption of an acquisitive society. Macpherson has made the point that liberal theories of distributive justice, among which he would include that of Rawls, are often cast in terms of this first aspect of humans as consumers of utilities: justice, that is, in terms of some equal or fair distribution. Thus we may say that justice is served when there is some redistribution to the less advantaged in terms of the consumption of things, which, if a person does not have much, is important enough, but it serves only one aspect, and overemphasizes that one aspect of the dual nature of humans. We think of a society with high levels of consumption shared in fair measure by well-paid workers and others with guaranteed annual incomes as coming close at least to the desirable society. But how good is a society of alienated and routinized labor even if it does produce the big bash on Saturday night and takes care of the effects on Sunday morning?

Then there is that other aspect of humans distinguished in western thought as possessors of capacities. The market economy has also failed to serve humans, as Macpherson says, "in their potential for using and developing their uniquely human capacities." To quote him further:

> The claim is based on a view of man's essence not as a consumer of utilities but as a doer, a creator, an enjoyer of his human attributes. These attributes may be variously listed and assessed: they may be taken to include the capacity for rational understanding, for moral judgement and action, for aesthetic creation or contemplation, for the emotional activities of friendship and love, and, sometimes, for religious experience. . . .Man is not a bundle of appetites seeking satisfaction but a bundle of conscious energies seeking to be exerted.[19]

It is, therefore, the task of the liberal democratic society to "maximize each man's ability to use and develop his essentially human attributes or capacities,"[20] and we must increasingly think of the good society in terms of the "egalitarian maximization of powers." There is a certain affinity between this type of analysis and the concept of alienated labor, at least in that context of man as a worker, whose instinct of workmanship, to borrow Thorstein Veblen's term, is suppressed because his powers are exploited by others.

It is not my task here to provide an account of alienated labor in capitalist or socialist societies. There is an impressive literature available on these subjects. Nor, since my subject is education, can I here provide a blueprint to make work places or factories more participative and more democratic, more equal or more just. There are many indications of how we might proceed, most of which are ignored or resisted by the entrenched interests of both capital and labor. My point rather is that inasmuch as education serves alienation, and inasmuch as it fails to equalize chances for maximizing human potential, it fails also to serve the just society, in much the same way as it fails to serve the just society through encouraging undeserved inequalities in acquisition and consumption.

Many will sense a certain similarity between the quotations from Macpherson, the terminology of the "psychologistic" critiques and the rhetoric of many of the commissions on education which we have had in Canada. Perhaps as a result of these commissions we have gone some way towards changing the authoritarian structure of schools, but I doubt that we have done much to undermine the objective of producing quiescent labor force participants, and indeed, as we ascend to the higher levels of the educational system the entire apparatus is increasingly oriented to and judged in terms of labor force considerations. Even students seem to be overwhelmingly concerned with this labor force participation, but largely, I would surmise, because it improves their capacity to acquire and to consume. In fairness perhaps, it would be less so if we had not in a misguided concern for their futures persuaded them that it was good to get into debt. Whatever the reason, credentialism is as rampant in the universities as anywhere, and with the vast majority being in arts faculties, that seems to be a mockery of the traditional view of education as development of personality or self-actualization.

Of course it must be recognized that as far as changing the condition of work is concerned education has a limited role. It can do something, as I have suggested, about changing the outlook and expectations of future workers, but can do nothing to the corporate and bureaucratic structures within which they will work. Such change must come from political and social movements in the society at large. This fact leads me to another consideration; how education might serve the just society by developing citizens to take a more active role in their communities against the structure of power, and all the inequalities that flow from it.

As one looks at the major social trends emerging in our epoch, it is possible to see the threat of increasing concentrations of power and decision making. Science and technology, which have done much to provide our high levels of productivity, have at the same time given extraordinary power to the experts and those who control them. A related trend is the enormously expanded body of information which is available to decision makers. They dispose of and have often exclusive access to the highly sophisticated machinery, physical and intellectual, to make that information serve their needs. Paul Goodman wrote of the incredible power of capital to pre-empt talent,[21] but public sector bureaucracies are acquiring similar powers and would like to make themselves as impenetrable as private bureaucracies. Power and decision making are shifting into a transnational context, as the interdependencies of both the advanced and developing world become more complex. The range and complexity of these issues are increasingly beyond the understanding of most of us for whom the media of mass culture—symbolized by the hours of television viewing per week—act as a functional diversion.

It is interesting to note that none of the critics of education about whom I have spoken rejects technology in itself. They object rather to the enslaving effect it has had on humans, denying them their essentially human qualities, particularly in the productive processes, and they object to the way in which education has prepared them for such enslavement. But these critics also express the belief in technology's potential for good, and call neither for its abandonment nor for a return to more primitive ways of life.

From the trends which I mentioned there is the danger of a continuing polarization between the controllers and the controlled, and that is congruent with the polarization of the labor force that I have referred to earlier. The highly qualified component essential to the scientific and technological base of our culture becomes widely separated from the less qualified and more routinized workers. What happens in the world of work happens also in broader social contexts, or there is the great danger that it can.

In this emerging condition it seems to me that education has a new task not related to economic efficiency, nor to humans as acquisitive consumers, but rather to their having some measure of control over their destinies in the broader sense. We now have societies with enormous powers for direction at the social or global level, but with populations with increasing powerlessness and apathy at the individual level.

Such a society can never be an authentic democracy however legitimate power holders might appear to be within existing legal frameworks and as a result of electoral processes which become more and more plebiscitary. Controlling centres—that is, institutional elites and decision makers, public and private governments—have prodigious powers of management and guidance, which can only become authentic, as contrasted with being merely legal or legitimate, by increasing and widening participation in the formation of consensus. In part, this depends on sharing in the knowledge and the capacity to understand it, and reducing the pre-emptive power controlling centres have over talent. I am trying here in a most fragmentary fashion to outline what Etzioni calls the "active society."[22] An active society is one in which mobilized publics are alert to and prepared to speak and act against the unauthentic behavior of controlling centres. To the extent that our education so far has produced docile workers and inactive citizens, authentic democracy is not well served.

Where do these thoughts leave us with respect to our present-day educational systems? We try to get rid of credentialism, we try to create more active, knowledgeable people, we try to counter the continuing aggrandizement of power on the part of elites and their experts. At the same time we are required to supply a labor force with a relatively small proportion of highly qualified and a majority of routinized workers. Important as these labor force needs are, our model of the just society states that the efficiency of the economy does not necessarily have prior claims over other desirable ends. However, the just society in both its distributive and participative senses, with its extensive freedoms and liberties, which, we are told, we are in danger of losing if we listen too closely to the siren calls of equality, is in fact a luxury that belongs to highly productive societies. Thus we would not want to destroy those benefits which science and the higher learning have contributed. That would be throwing the baby out with the bath water.

It would seem to me that both distributive justice and equal opportunity to maximize one's potential are more likely to be achieved by accessibility and openness in education than by elitism and meritocracy. As Rawls has pointed out in his discussion of fair equality of opportunity, it is unjustified to devote extra resources in the hope of making the brightest yet brighter if their brightness is because of genes, an area in which God still throws dice although man may be coming closer to calling the shots. Some proportion of brightness is not the capriciousness of genes, but the contingencies of social arrangements. Extra educational benefits to the bright ones arising from social contingencies are also undeserved. "No one deserves," says Rawls, "his greater natural capacity, nor merits a more favorable starting place in society."[23] Rather than give so much to the intellectually superior there might be policies of redress to give a disproportionate amount to the less able and the socially disadvantaged, particularly in the early years of schooling.

If accessibility and openness are more just, that means educational resources should be equally available to those in need of them and who can make use of them and wish to have access to them at any time in their lives. The lack of formal certification from any previous level should not be an obstacle to making use of educational resources at higher levels if people can show their ability to cope with the work or handle the machinery. Where resources are limited—and books and other learners are never that limited—it is not particularly just that they should be distributed on the basis of ability to pay or superior ability in that narrow sense in which we measure it.

These suggestions no longer sound outrageous because they are not unlike many that have been made, as I have said earlier, by commissions reporting on the future of education in several Canadian provinces.[24] Steps taken in the direction of openness have been faltering and often reversed as reaction sets in to what is seen as reduced capacity to perform conventional academic chores. Some educators in Ontario look back nostalgically to the old province-wide Grade 13 examinations and declare in despair that students are not what they used to be. But how relatively few students we had then, and in what few numbers we drew them from the lower levels of our class inequality! What sort of evidence is there to confirm an hypothesis of falling standards? I know of no trend data that could establish an association between the democratizing of education and these so-called lower standards. But we must also remember that we are meeting different students, with different standards, different concerns, and changed values compared to those in whatever golden age lightens our nostalgia.

Where does that leave us as far as excellence is concerned? Excellence is the irresistible mystique by which we academics are impelled to reproduce ourselves. As I look back on my own experience of the endless debates about ideal educational programs, about how indispensable some practitioners think their subjects to be I feel that the good students get on despite our carefully laid plans for their good, rather than because of them. And I have long ago given up the notion that we should treat those with superior ability as a special gift from God to be endowed with privilege in learning and forever thereafter. Not because I do not think ability is an important social asset. On the contrary it obviously is, and we must certainly facilitate its flowering.

Rawls in his Theory of Justice points out that superior ability can be an essential asset in a highly productive economy and recognizes there is an efficiency problem in its use, which may require at the higher levels the allocation of unequal educational resources to the brightest because the least favored could benefit in the long run. He suggests that individual talents should be considered as social resources to be developed for the benefit of all, particularly the least favored.[25] In the past we have too readily accepted the view that the accidents of genetic endowment and the effects, whatever they may be, of social investment in education at the higher levels should become personal capital for unlimited acquisition. Such a view scarcely has a place within a framework of social justice.

Able students need more freedom and less guidance. I have had some very able students, and I am old enough for this judgment subsequently to have been verified, but it is my recollection that if I helped them at all it was by opening doors, removing barriers, sharing my own experiences including my errors with them, being available when the going got tough and helping them avoid the pathology of bureaucratic rules which we foster, but above all letting them teach themselves with the tools at hand. Less able students need other kinds of help, but I am here talking about that special social asset of higher ability that some feel will disappear if we open up our educational structures. I see all that as a minor problem compared to the ability that we have left deserted in environments inimical to intellectual development, and to whom in many cases our learning machines have failed to build a bridge.

In these lectures I have tried to argue that so far educational reforms of the twentieth century have failed in their task of promoting equality of either condition or opportunity, and that public education has been overly concerned with labor force objectives, with the questionable faith that the labor force in its changes with increasing industrialization represented constantly unfolding opportunity for all. For the future orientation of education, if it is to help in the creation of a fair and just society, there must be a new concern for developing more participant workers and more active citizens than we have had in the history of our liberal market systems. The task is of increasing urgency not only in matters of distributive justice, but in the creation of authentic democracy.

Notes

1. Harry Braverman, *Labor and Monopoly Capital*, Monthly Review Press (New York, 1974).

2. *Ibid.*, 209. The description appears to be that of Siegfried Giedion in *Mechanization Takes Command* (New York, 1948).

3. Braverman, *op. cit.*, 332.

4. *Ibid.*, Chapter 20.

5. Charles Silberman, *The Myths of Automation* (New York, 1966), 52. Quoted in Braverman, 433.

6. P.C. Pineo, John Porter, and Hugh A. McRoberts, "The 1971 Census and the Socio-Economic Classification of Occupations", *Canadian Review of Sociology and Anthropology*, 14(1), 1977, 91–102.

7. Braverman, *op. cit.*, 434.

8. John Porter, *The Vertical Mosaic*, University of Toronto Press (Toronto, 1965), 141.

9. Ivar Berg, *The Great Training Robbery*, Praeger (New York, 1970). See also Richard B. Freeman, *The Over-Educated American*, Academic Press (New York, 1976).

10. Berg, *op. cit.*

11. Ivan Illich, *Deschooling Society*, Harper and Row (New York, 1972), 17.

12. *Ibid.*, 14.

13. H.H. Gerth and C.W. Mills, eds., *From Max Weber*, Kegan Paul (London, 1947).

14. Ontario, Department of Education, *Living and Learning: The Report of the Provincial Committee on Aims and Objectives of Education in the Schools of Ontario*, Toronto, 1968, 133.

15. Ontario, *The Report of the Special Program Review*, Toronto, 1975, 128.

16. The certification by educational institutions is in many cases indirect because for many professions governments have delegated the licensing role to boards and agencies which the professions control. Broader lay representation on these boards might better safeguard the public interest.

17. Christopher Jencks, *et al., Inequality: A Reassessment of the Effect of Family and Schooling in America*, Basic Books (New York, 1972), 29.

18. C.B. Macpherson, *Democratic Theory: Essays in Retrieval*, Clarendon Press (Oxford, 1973).

19. *Ibid.*, 4.

20. *Ibid.*, 10.

21. Paul Goodman, *Growing Up Absurd*, Random House (New York, 1960), ix.

22. Amitai Etzioni, *The Active Society*, Free Press (New York, 1968).

23. John Rawls, *A Theory of Justice*, Harvard University Press (Cambridge, 1971), 102.

24. E.g., Ontario, Commission on Postsecondary Education in Ontario, *The Learning Society*, Toronto, 1972; Manitoba, Task Force on Postsecondary Education in Manitoba, *Report*, Winnipeg, 1974; Alberta, Commission on Educational Planning, *A Future of Choices: A Choice of Futures*, Edmonton, 1972.

25. Rawls, *op. cit.*, 101.

Appendix

THE WRITINGS OF JOHN PORTER

Appendix

THE WRITINGS OF JOHN PORTER
Compiled by Wallace Clement and Richard Helmes-Hayes

The essays noted with an asterisk (*) are included in this volume.

BOOKS

1961   *Canadian Society: Sociological Perspectives*, edited with Bernard R. Blishen, Frank E. Jones, and Kaspar D. Naegele. Toronto: Macmillan. Second edition (revised) 1964; third edition (further revised) 1968; abridged edition 1971.

1965   *The Vertical Mosaic: An Analysis of Social Class and Power in Canada*. Toronto: University of Toronto Press.

1967   *Canadian Social Structure: A Statistical Profile* (compiled and with an introduction and commentary). Toronto: McClelland and Stewart, Carleton Library No. 32.

1970   *Macrosociology: Research and Theory*, with James S. Coleman and Amitai Etzioni. Boston: Allyn and Bacon. Includes "Research Biography of a Macrosociological Study: *The Vertical Mosaic*", pp. 149-181.*

1971   *Towards 2000: the Future of Post-Secondary Education in Ontario*, with Bernard R. Blishen, John R. Evans, et al. Toronto: McClelland and Stewart.

1973   *Does Money Matter? Prospects for Higher Education*, with Marion R. Porter and Bernard R. Blishen. Toronto: York University Institute for Behavioural Research. (Revised and enlarged edition, retitled *Does Money Matter? Prospects for Higher Education in Ontario*, Toronto: Macmillan, Carleton Library No. 110).

1979   *The Measure of Canadian Society: Education, Equality, and Opportunity*. Agincourt: Gage Publishing.

1982   *Stations and Callings: Making It Through the School System*, with Marion R. Porter, Bernard R. Blishen, et al. Toronto: Methuen.

1985   *Ascription and Achievement: Studies in Mobility and Status Attainment in Canada*, with Monica Boyd, John Goyder, Frank E. Jones, Hugh McRoberts and Peter C. Pineo. Ottawa: Carleton University Press.

PUBLISHED PAPERS

1954 "Two Cheers for Mental Health" in *The Canadian Forum* 34 (October):145, 152-3.

1955 "Karl Mannheim" in *The Canadian Forum* 34 (January):222-3.

"Elite Groups: A Scheme for the Study of Power in Canada" in *Canadian Journal of Economics and Political Science* 21:4 (November):498-512.

1956 "Concentration of Economic Power and the Economic Elite in Canada" in *Canadian Journal of Economics and Political Science* 22:2 (May):199-220.

1957 "The Economic Elite and the Social Structure in Canada" in *Canadian Journal of Economics and Political Science* 23:3 (August):376-394.

1958 "Conserving the Bureaucracy" in *The Canadian Forum* 38 (May):27-28.

"Political Parties and the Political Career" in *The Canadian Forum* 38 (May):54-55.

"Higher Public Servants and the Bureaucratic Elite in Canada" in *Canadian Journal of Economics and Political Science* 24:4 (November):483-501.

1959 "The Bureaucratic Elite: A Reply to Professor Rowat" in *Canadian Journal of Economics and Political Science* 25:2 (May):207-209.

1961 "Power and Freedom in Canadian Democracy" in *Social Purpose for Canada*, edited by M. Oliver. Toronto: University of Toronto Press, pp. 27-56.*

"Social Class and Education" in *Social Purpose for Canada*, edited by M. Oliver. Toronto: University of Toronto Press, pp. 103-129.

1963 "The Power Structure in Canadian Society" in *Canadian Public Administration*, 2 (June):140-147.

"Canada" in *McGill Journal of Education*, 1(2) (Fall):125- 130.

1967   "Occupational Prestige in Canada" with Peter C. Pineo in *Canadian Review of Sociology and Anthropology* 4:1 (February):24-40.

"Canadian Character in the Twentieth Century" in *Annals* of the American Academy of Political and Social Science 370 (March):49-56.*

"Some Observations on Comparative Studies" in International Institute for Labour Studies, *Bulletin* 3 (November):82-104.

"The Human Community" in *The Canadians: 1867-1967*, edited by J.M.S. Careless and R. Craig Brown. Toronto: Macmillan, pp. 385-410.*

1968   "The Future of Upward Mobility" in *American Sociological Review* 33:1 (February):5-19.*

"Why the Shortage of Highly Qualified Manpower?" *Labour Gazette* 68(5) (April):195-239.

"The Class Bias of Canadian Education" in University of British Columbia Alumni *Chronicle* 22:2 (Summer):10-15.

"Inequalities in Education" in *Canadian Counsellor* 2:3 (July):136-147.

1969   "La mobilité sociale: facteur de croissance économique" in *Synopsis* (mars-avril).

"Canadian National Character" in *Cultural Affairs* 6.

"Una problema sociale: l'alta qualifazione de lavoro umano" in *Mercurio* 12:1.

1970   "The Democratisation of the Canadian Universities and the Need for a National System" in *Minerva* 8:3 (July):325-356.

1971   "Post-Industrialism, Post-Nationalism and Post-Secondary Education" in *Canadian Public Administration* 14:1 (Spring):32-50.*

1972   "Dilemmas and Contradictions of a Multi-Ethnic Society" in Royal Society of Canada *Transactions* 4:10 (October):193- 205.

"Reply" [D.W. Livingstone, 'Inventing the Future: Anti- Historicist

Reflections on *Towards 2000*'] *Interchange* 3(4):120-121 [see Livingstone's "Rejoinder" (pp. 122-123) in the same issue].

1974   "Educational and Occupational Opportunity in the Canadian Mosaic" in *Canadian Counsellor* 8:2 (April):90-105.

"Equality and Education" a keynote address for the Annual Conference of the Canadian Society for the Study of Education. Toronto (June). Published in two parts in *Integrateducation* 13:4, 5 (July-August, September-October, 1975).

1975   "Ethnic Pluralism in Canadian Perspective" in *Ethnicity: Theory and Experience*, edited by N. Glazer and D.P. Moynihan. Cambridge: Harvard University Press, pp. 267- 304.*

1976   "Melting Pot or Mosaic: Revolution or Reversion?" presented to Bicentennial Conference "Revolution and Evolution," Canadian Studies Center, Duke University (October).* Published in *Revolution versus Evolution*, edited by R.A. Preston. Durham, N.C.: Duke University Press, 1979.

"Différences dans la mobilité professionnelle des francophones et des anglophones" with Hugh A. McRoberts, Monica Boyd, et al. in *Sociologie et Societes* 7:2 (October):61-79.

1979   "The Future of the University" in Carleton University (Ottawa) *Arts Faculty Forum* (March):14-20.

"The Canadian National Mobility Study", with Monica Boyd, John Goyder, Hugh A. McRoberts, Frank E. Jones, and Peter C. Pineo, *Canadian Population Studies*.

1981   "Status attainment in Canada: findings of the Canadian mobility study", with Monica Boyd, John Goyder, Frank E. Jones, Hugh A. McRoberts and Peter C. Pineo, *The Canadian Review of Sociology and Anthropology* 18:5 (December):657- 673.

REVIEW ARTICLES

1969   "Bilingualism and the Myths of Culture" in *Canadian Review of Sociology and Anthropology* 6:2 (May):111-118. A review of Books I and II of *The Report of The Royal Commission on Bilingualism and Biculturalism*.

"Do Canadians Get the Best Jobs?" in *Canadian Business* (November):44-51. A review of *The Performance of Foreign- Owned Firms in Canada*, A.E. Safarian.

1972   "Structured Inequality Down Under" in *Social Forces* 50 (June):531-533. A review of *Equality and Authority: A Study of Class, Status and Power in Australia*, S. Encel.

1973   "The Limits of Sociology" in *Contemporary Sociology* 2:5 (September):463-467. A review of *Inequality: A Reassessment of the Effect of Family on Schooling in America*, Christopher Jencks, et al.

REVIEWS

1948   *Italy* (by Elizabeth Wiskeman) in *Clare Market Review* 48:2 (Lent):39-40.

1954   *The Origins of Psycho-Analysis: Sigmund Freud's Letters to Wilhelm Fliess, Drafts and Notes: 1887-1902* (edited by Marie Bonaparte, Anna Freud, Ernst Kris: authorised translation by Eric Mosbacher and James Strachey: Introduction by Ernst Kris) in *The Canadian Forum* 34 (October):163-164.

1958   *Problems of Power in American Democracy* (by A. Kornhauser) in *Canadian Journal of Economics and Political Science* 24:4 (November):589-591.

1959   *Political Power and Social Theory: Six Studies* (by Barrington Moore) in *Canadian Journal of Economics and Political Science* 25:1 (February):522-523.

Social Stratification: A Comparative Analysis of Structure and Process (by Bernard Barber) in *Canadian Journal of Economics and Political Science* 25:1 (February):86-87.

"Statistical Review of Canadian Education", *Census*, 1951 by Dominion Bureau of Statistics, Education Division, Reference Paper 84) in *Canadian Journal of Economics and Political Science* 25:1 (February):73-77.

Philadelphia Gentlemen: The Making of a National Upper Class (by E. Digby Baltzell) in *Canadian Journal of Economics and Political Science* 25:2 (May):230-232.

1968   *Pouvoir dans la société Canadienne-française* (edited by Fernand Dumont and Jean-Paul Montminy) in *Social Forces* 46:1 (September):134.

        The Power Structure (by Arnold M. Rose) in *American Sociological Review* 33:2 (April):301-302.

1970   *Class and Conformity: A Study of Values* (by Melvin L. Kohn) in *Science* 170:1183-1185.

1972   *Minetown, Milltown, Railtown* (by Rex. A. Lucas) in *Canadian Historical Review* 53:4 (December):455-457.

1975   "Where the juice runs" in *Books in Canada* 4:12 (December):3-5. A review of *The Canadian Establishment*, Peter C. Newman. (Originally entitled by Porter as "The Vertical Power Trip: Peter Newman and the Canadian Establishment.")

        Elite Accommodation in Canadian Politics (by Richard Presthus) in *Contemporary Sociology* 4:2 (March):120-121.

        Social Stratification and Career Mobility (edited by W. Müller and Karl Ulrich Mayer) in *Contemporary Sociology* 4:2 (March):166-167.

1978   "Kvetcher in the rye" in *Books in Canada* 7:10 (December):8-9. A review of *Bronfman Dynasty: The Rothschilds of the New World*, Peter C. Newman.

UNPUBLISHED PAPERS AND REPORTS

1966   "French-English Differences in the Evaluation of Occupations, Industries, Ethnicities, and Religions in the Montreal Metropolitan Area" with Peter C. Pineo. Report to the Royal Commission on Bilingualism and Biculturalism. Ottawa: Carleton University (October).

        "Politics and Minorities: Canada and the United States" a paper delivered to the Third Annual Intercollegiate Conference on Canadian-American Relations, Michigan State University (February).

        "Mr. Trudeau and Canadian Federalism," a paper delivered to the Political Science Department, Duke University (May).*

"Mobility, Stratification, and Highly Qualified Manpower," a paper delivered to the Cornell Conference on Human Mobility, Cornell University (October).

"Native and Foreign-born Differences in the Evaluation of Occupations, Industries, Ethnicities, and Religions and in Mobility Patterns" with Peter C. Pineo. Ottawa: Department of Manpower and Immigration.

"The Future of Excellence," a paper presented at Hart House, University of Toronto, Toronto.

"Education Values and Social Change", a paper presented as part of the Althouse College of Education Lecture Series 1967-68 (March).

1969   Comments on "The Humble and the Proud: The Comparative Study of Occupations," an address by E.C. Hughes at the American Sociological Association annual meeting. San Francisco (September).

"The State versus the Individual," a paper presented at a Conference on Canada: Two Nations or Two Cultures, Vanier College, York University, Toronto (November).

1971   *Report on the Situation in the PSA Department, Simon Fraser University*. Mimeo, American Sociological Association. Washington, D.C.

1972   "Some Questions About Ethnic Pluralism Asked from a Canadian Perspective," a paper presented at a Conference on Ethnic Problems in the Contemporary World sponsored by the American Academy of Arts and Science, Boston (October).

1974   "The 1973 Canadian national mobility study in a comparative context," a paper presented at the Mathematical Social Science Board Seminar, Toronto (August).

"The Pluralistic Society in a Modern State," a paper presented at a Colloquium on "Cooperation and Conflict: The Tension Between Nationalism and Internationalism in the Americas and Western Europe" of the Liberal International, Ottawa (April-May).

"Some Observations on Perspective Canada [Statistics Canada, Ottawa, 1974]," a paper presented at a seminar convened by Statistics Canada, Ottawa (November).

"Macrosociology: Some Problems with the Nation State as the Unit of Analysis" a draft prepared for use in Sociology 602, Carleton University (Spring).

1975   "Towards a Macrosociology: Further Notes", a draft prepared for use in Sociology 602, Carleton University (April).

"Notes as a Commentator for the Macrosociological Issues" in Canadian Sociology session at the Canadian Sociology and Anthropology Association annual meeting. Edmonton (May).

1976   "Thoughts About Unionization of Faculty", Ottawa (February).

"The Social Sciences and the Future of the National Statistical System: Some Comments on a Paper by Philip Hauser," a paper presented at a Conference on Statistics, Social Science Research Council of Canada and Statistics Canada, Ottawa.

"The Canadian National Mobility Study: Some Preliminary Findings" with Monica Boyd and Hugh A. McRoberts, presented at the International Seminar on Research in Social Stratification and Mobility, Hebrew University, Jerusalem (April). "The Canadian National Mobility Study: Some Preliminary Findings" was also presented to the Institute of Philosophy and Sociology of the Polish Academy of Sciences, June, 1976.

1977   "Immigration and Ethnic Effects on Occupational Status in Canada" with Monica Boyd, presented at the International Sociological Association Research Conference on Social Stratification, Trinity College, Dublin (April).

"Education and Equality: The Failure of a Mission" and "Education and the Just Society" presented at the Edgar McInnis Memorial Lectures, York University, Downsview.* Reprinted here as "Education, Equality, and the Just Society."

"Address by John Porter" in Options for Canada, a Report on the First Options for Canada Colloquium, St. Patrick's College, Carleton University, Ottawa (September).

Survival of a Grade 8 Cohort: A Study of Early School Leaving in Ontario, with Bernard R. Blishen and Maria Barrados. Toronto: Ministry of Education.

"Guest Lecture at Nipissing University College", North Bay (October).

1978   *Part-Time Studies and University Accessibility* with Elizabeth Humphreys. Toronto: Ministry of Colleges and Universities.

"Education for Its Own Sake," for a seminar on higher education, International Association of Universities, Halle, German Democratic Republic (May).

"Who Are Minorities? What Do They Want and Why?" and "Some Limits to Self-Determination," presented at a conference on minority rights, McGill University, Montreal (November).

1979   "Ethnic Origin and Occupational Attainment", co-authored with Peter C. Pineo and "Canada: The Societal Context of Occupational Allocation" as contributions to the planned publication of the project Occupational and Educational Change in a Generation: Canada, with Monica Boyd, John Goyder, Hugh A. McRoberts, Frank E. Jones, and Peter C. Pineo.

"Regionalism as Rhetoric", Ottawa (April).

n.d.   "Evaluation and Status: Some Theoretical Perspectives." Department of Sociology and Anthropology, Carleton University, Ottawa.

MISCELLANEOUS

1968   "Maclean's Interviews John Porter [by Douglas Marshall]" in *Maclean's* 81:6 (June):9, 51-54.

1972   "Conceptual and Theoretical Problems in *The Vertical Mosaic*: A Rejoinder" in *Canadian Review of Sociology and Anthropology* 9:2 (May):188-189.

1975   "Foreword" to *The Canadian Corporate Elite: An Analysis of Economic Power*, Wallace Clement. Toronto: McClelland and Stewart, Carleton Library No. 89, 1975, pp. ix-xv.

1977   "The 1971 Census and the Socio-economic Classification of Occupations" with Peter C. Pineo and Hugh A. McRoberts in *Canadian Review of Sociology and Anthropology* 14:1 (February):91-102. A research note.

1977   "John C. MacDonald, 1925-1977: A Tribute" in *Canadian Review of Sociology and Anthropology* 14:3 (August):365.

1978   "Comments by John Porter" in a symposium on Braverman, *Alternate Routes: A Critical Review* 2:23-25.

"The Vertical Mosaic: Some Further Thoughts on Ethnicity and Education".

"Labour and Management in the Changing World of Work".

"Beyond the Bursary: Some Non-Financial Aspects of Social Class and Education".

"Statement to Commission on University Government: University of Toronto", Toronto.

"Canada's Class Structure: Implications for Education" (March).

"Fair Employment and the Fair Career". A paper prepared for "Canada at Work" (a radio series).

Untitled manuscript re Social Change: Comments on Conference Papers.

"Educational Needs in a Changing Society".

"Christopher Beattie: A Memorial Note".

As far as we have been able to determine, this is a complete listing of John Porter's writings. It is considerably more extensive than the Bibliographic Appendix that was published in the original edition of *The Measure of Canadian Society* (1979). Reprints, however, have been omitted from this listing. Many of the new entries are unpublished works which came to light in the process of reading through the John Porter Papers in the Public Archives of Canada, material which was not available at the time of the publication of the first edition of *The Measure of Canadian Society*. In addition to the material listed here, there are a number of other kinds of material to be found in the John Porter Papers in the Public Archives of Canada. Specifically, there are several poems written by Professor Porter during the Second World War, some short (incomplete) fictional prose manuscripts, and a long manuscript describing events in London during the Battle of Britain. In addition, there is amongst his course lecture notes, a number of manuscripts dealing with topics in political science and sociology. We wish to thank Bernard Blishen, Dennis Forcese, Dennis Olsen, Peter Pineo, and Marion Porter for their assistance. They are not responsible, of course, for any errors or omissions.

WRITINGS ABOUT JOHN PORTER AND HIS WORK:

AN ANNOTATED BIBLIOGRAPHY*

Richard C. Helmes-Hayes

INTRODUCTION

John Porter is, without question, the dominant figure in the history of Canadian sociology. Not only did he do more than any other person to reinforce, if not establish, the scholarly credibility of sociology within the Canadian academic community at large[1], he also simultaneously did much to set the agenda and standards of debate within the discipline itself[2]. The most important means by which he achieved these goals, of course, was *The Vertical Mosaic* (1965); the most significant piece of scholarship in the history of Canadian sociology. *The Vertical Mosaic* had a tremendous, immediate impact on the discipline during the 1960s and early 1970s, but it had an important long-term influence on the discipline as well. For more than two decades now it has acted as a kind of Original Source; a point of inspiration and reference for literally scores of research projects in a wide variety of subfields within the discipline.

However, while it is important to acknowledge the significance to Porter and to Canadian sociology of *The Vertical Mosaic*, it is also important to appreciate the fact that Porter's reputation does not rest entirely on the merits of this one book. During his career, Porter was involved in one important project after another; studies of major scope and impact such as the National Study of Occupational Prestige (1967), *Towards 2000* (1971), the Ontario High School Students' Aspirations study (1973, 1979, 1982), and the National Mobility Study (1986)[3]. Clearly, none of these studies were as ambitious in scope as *The Vertical Mosaic*, and none had the same kind of overwhelming impact. Nonetheless, each of them did play a key role in the academic and public debates that surrounded these issues. The number of entries in the bibliography that deals with Porter's research other than *The Vertical Mosaic* reflects the importance to the discipline of these studies.

The fact that Porter's work has long stood at the centre of the Canadian sociological enterprise has made the task of assembling this bibliography difficult, for there are literally hundreds of references to his work in the *Social Sciences Citation Index*. Obviously, it would be inappropriate to include all of these references in the bibliography and so what follows is a selective list. The list contains two kinds of material: (i) book reviews and (ii) critical essays. I have included all of the book reviews that I could find on the grounds that they constitute an index of the immediate scholarly response to Porter's work. However, making the selections from amongst the large number of critical essays that refer to Porter's writings was more difficult. In making these selections I was guided by the following considerations. First, entries were limited to those which appeared in the academic press[4]. Second, they had to be 'first-generation' critiques which took one or more of Porter's writings as the explicit focus of an extended analysis. By 'first-generation' critiques I mean works which were the 'first'[5] to respond to his writings or ideas on a particular subject rather than works which picked up these first-generation critiques and extended them. Thus, Clement's research on the economic and media elites is included[6], while later, related research by those attempting to assess, for example, the validity of the 'merchants against industry' thesis is not[7]. While space limitations were an important practical consideration, there are scholarly reasons for making this decision as well.

There is no doubt that in making the decision to limit the bibliography to 'first-generation' critiques something is lost in terms of its completeness. However, as Wallace Clement noted in reviewing this manuscript, a complete bibliography would be impossible, for in some ways almost all of Canadian sociology since 1965 could be considered as a footnote to *The Vertical Mosaic*. Furthermore, since people are still using it as a take-off point for research, new entries are being created all the time. Those interested in more contemporary, what might be termed 'derivative' assessments of Porter and his work — assessments which call into question many of the important conclusions of *The Vertical Mosaic* — are referred to excellent recent overviews of Canadian sociology written by Robert Brym and Patricia Marchak[8].

The bibliography is structured as follows. Section I lists book reviews or review essays that deal with one of Porter's works in particular. Not surprisingly, most of them are book reviews of *The Vertical Mosaic*.[9] I have listed Porter's works chronologically with the reviews listed under the appropriate book title. Section II lists critical essays. These essays are broader in scope; they tend to be based on a number of his writings and/or discuss a number of the important overall themes in his work. Two especially rich sources of information of this type are the December, 1981 "Special Issue" of the *The Canadian Review of Sociology and Anthropology* "In Memory of John Porter, 1921-79", and James Heap's, *Everybody's Canada* (1974).[10] The former contains a number of essays written by Porter's colleagues in which they assess his views on a wide range of important sociological themes, i.e., class, power and elites, prestige and mobility, education, and ethnicity. The latter contains reprints of a number of book reviews of *The Vertical Mosaic* and a long critical essay by Heap. Remarkably, given the recent surge of interest in the historical development of Canadian sociology, there is no in-depth study of Porter's life's work to compare with the studies of S.D. Clark by Harry Hiller and Deborah Harrison or the book on Carl Dawson by Marlene Shore.[11] Only the series of essays by Wallace Clement (combined and condensed here in the Introduction to this volume) and the essay by Dennis Forcese in the "Special Issue" of the *Canadian Review of Sociology and Anthropology* (1981) mentioned above attempt to provide an overall assessment of Porter's work. Section III lists a number of sources of biographical information.

* Readers should note that I have abbreviated *The Vertical Mosaic* to *TVM* in the summaries in the bibliography. I would like to thank the Social Sciences and Humanities Research Council of Canada for their financial support during the preparation of this manuscript (Post-doctoral Fellowship No. 456-86-0020). I would especially like to thank Wallace Clement both for his comments on a draft of this bibliography and for undertaking to supervise the larger research project — an intellectual biography of Professor Porter — of which this bibliography is a part.

Notes:

1. It is not my intention, in emphasizing Porter's influence, to deny the important role played by Carl Dawson and S.D. Clark in helping to establish the discipline. Nonetheless, it is true that despite their best efforts there were — even as late as the early 1960s — very few sociologists in Canada and sociology had achieved autonomous departmental status at only two Canadian universities, i.e., McGill (1922) and Toronto (1963). At least part of the explanation for this situation rests with the low status of sociology, particularly in its 'American' guise, within the Canadian intellectual community. In this regard, the publication of *The Vertical Mosaic* could not have occurred at a better time. It coincided precisely with the boom in post-secondary education in the mid-1960s and allowed sociology to take its place amongst the social science disciplines then benefitting from this growth (see H. Hiller, *Society and Change: S.D. Clark and the Development of Canadian Sociology*, Toronto: University of Toronto Press, 1982; R. Helmes-Hayes, "Images of Inequality in Early Canadian Sociology, 1922-1965", unpublished Ph.D. dissertation, University of Toronto, 1985).

2. This point is made by Robert Brym ["Anglo-Canadian Sociology" *Current Sociology* 34(1) (Spring, 1986):74] as follows:

> John Porter's *The Vertical Mosaic* (1965) has been called 'the most important book in Canadian sociology'. . . . If intellectual significance can be gauged by the degree to which a work sets the terms of a debate —

by the degree to which it is paradigmatic — then the evaluation seems entirely appropriate.

3. The complete references for these studies are as follows: "Occupational Prestige in Canada" with P. Pineo in *Canadian Review of Sociology and Anthropology* 4:1 (February):24-40; *Towards 2000: The Future of Post Secondary Education in Ontario* with B. Blishen, J.R. Evans, et al. Toronto: McClelland and Stewart, 1971; *Does Money Matter? Prospects For Higher Education* with M. Porter and B. Blishen, Toronto: York University Institute for Behavioural Research, 1973 [revised and enlarged edition, retitled *Does Money Matter? Prospects For Higher Education in Ontario*, Toronto: Macmillan, Carleton Library No. 110, 1979; and a final expanded version entitled *Stations and Callings: Making it Through the School System* with M. Porter, B. Blishen et al., Toronto: Methuen, 1982]; *Ascription and Achievement: Studies in Mobility and Status Attainment in Canada* with M. Boyd, J. Goyder et al., Ottawa: Carleton University Press, 1986.

4. Some of Porter's writings, particularly *The Vertical Mosaic* and *Towards 2000* were reviewed in newspapers and popular magazines.

5. Some of these are quite recent, obviously, since *Stations and Callings* (1982) and *Ascription and Achievement* (1986) have been published only recently. The bulk of such 'first-generation' critiques, however, dates from the late 1960s and early 1970s.

6. See Wallace Clement, *The Canadian Corporate Elite: An Analysis of Economic Power*. Toronto: McClelland and Stewart, 1975, and *Continental Corporate Power: Economic Linkages Between Canada and the United States*. Toronto: McClelland and Stewart, 1977.

7. See R. Brym (1986) [cited Note 2 above] for a critical review of recent literature on this and related issues.

8. See P. Marchak, "Canadian Political Economy", *Canadian Review of Sociology and Anthropology* 22(5):673-709; and Brym (1986)[cited above].

9. I have not included reviews of M. Oliver (ed.), *Social Purpose for Canada* (Toronto: University of Toronto Press, 1961) because there were very few explicit references to Porter's work in these reviews. I have not included reviews of B. Blishen, F.E. Jones, K. Naegele and J. Porter (eds.), *Canadian Society: Sociological Perspectives* (Toronto: Macmillan,1961, 1964, 1968, 1971) for the same reason.

10. See the *The Canadian Review of Sociology and Anthropology* 18(5) (December 1981) and J. Heap (ed.), *Everybody's Canada: The Vertical Mosaic Reviewed and Re-examined*. Toronto: Burns and MacEachern, 1974.

11. For the Hiller reference, see Note 1 (above). See also D. Harrison, *The Limits of Liberalism: The Making of Canadian Sociology*. Montreal: Black Rose, 1981; and M. Shore, *The Science of Social Redemption: McGill, the Chicago School and the Origins of Social Research in Canada*. Toronto: University of Toronto Press, 1987.

Critiques of Porter's Work

I. ABOUT SPECIFIC WORKS:

BOOK REVIEWS AND REVIEW ESSAYS

1959 Rowat, D.C., "On John Porter's 'Bureaucratic Elite in Canada'" in *Canadian Journal of Economics and Political Science* 25(2) (May):204-7.

Rowat suggests that Porter is unwise to use Weber's ideal type of bureaucracy as a point of reference and "normative ideal" (204) in his analysis of Canada's upper-echelon civil servants for, in his view, 'representativeness' rather than 'technical efficiency' is the key to an effective, democratically-responsive bureaucracy.[See Porter's response, "The Bureaucratic Elite: A Reply to Professor Rowat" (pp.207-9) in the same issue.]

The Vertical Mosaic (1965)

1965 Fortin, G., "Compte Rendu" in *Recherches sociographiques* 6(2) (Mai-Aout):200-2.

Fortin briefly outlines Porter's findings noting that while it is an important book, it has a number of serious deficiencies. On the subject of class, Fortin notes that it is unfortunate that there are no data on the subjective element of class with which Porter might have supplemented his analysis of objective classes. He contends, though, that Porter's use of the term 'class' is problematic because statistical classes are not social classes. Similarly, he objects to Porter's use of a positional form of power analysis, arguing that it is wrong to assume that only those who hold positions of formal power actually exercise power. He concludes by noting that Porter's analysis indicates that Canadian society is not democratic and is unlikely to become so.

Maclennan, H., "Two Books on Canada" in *The Tamarack Review* 37 (Autumn):90-7.

TVM is reviewed along with George Grant's *Lament for a Nation*. Maclennan summarizes each of the books and says that they corroborate each other in painting a very pessimistic picture of Canada's future. The major theme of the book, in his view, is that "though Canadians are worshippers of progress, their business and technological elites are so lacking in initiative and advanced training that not even within their own country can they compete successfully with foreigners"(94).

Marshall, T.H., "Class and Power in Canada" in *Canadian Review of Sociology and Anthropology* 2(4) (November):215-222.

While acknowledging the importance of *TVM*, Marshall argues that Porter's analyses of both class and power alike are flawed by conceptual and methodological problems. Porter defines classes according to "objective dimensions" only. This reduces them to "statistical categories". As subjective consciousness is an element of class, however, Porter is not then dealing with classes. His untested assumption of in-group consciousness amongst elites based on similarity of position and background is no more than a suggestive hypothesis.

Smiley, D., "Book Review" in *Western Political Quarterly* 18(4) (December):943-5.

Smiley deals only with Porter's discussion of elites and power. He expresses dissatisfaction with Porter's definitions of both terms and with Porter's choice of the positional method to analyse power. He concludes, however, with the remark that *TVM* is a "monumental work [which] makes our understanding of Canadian society immeasurably richer"(945).

Horowitz, G., "Creative Politics, Mosaics and Identity" in *Canadian Dimension* 3 (November-December):14-15,28; and 4 (January-February, 1966):17-19.

Horowitz discusses Porter's claim that Canada is prevented from being a more democratic nation because it has no national identity to override its many ethnic and regional ones. He contends that only a strong left-wing political party could create the class-based, dynamic "creative politics" that Porter desires.

Chapman,R., "Book Review" in *Political Studies* 15:132-4.

In the context of a review of five books on Canadian politics, Chapman provides a brief and positive description of *TVM*. He notes that it links social theory with "a mass of data" and should become "required reading for anyone who who wishes to know about Canadian society" (134).

1966   "Editorial Comments" in *Marxism Today* 10(3) (March):68.

The editor makes very brief mention of some of the main findings of *TVM* and suggests that the evidence Porter marshalls to "polemicize" against Marxism actually provides "material in its support".

Robin, M., "*The Vertical Mosaic*: Reviewed" in *The American Political Science Review* 60 (March):153-4.

Robin provides a basic summary of *TVM* and commends Porter's analysis of class and power for being both empirically and theoretically sound; falling prey to neither the "cabalist mentality" of the Marxists nor the liberal view of Canada as a "pluralist utopia" (153).

Blishen, B., "Social Structure in Canada" in *Queen's Quarterly* 73(1) (Spring):130-5.
This is a thorough and well-written summary of the main points of Porter's findings. It is positive throughout offering no criticism of his method or findings.

Geisel, P., "Book Review" in *Canadian Welfare* 42(2) (March-April):103-4.
This is a brief, basically positive description of Porter's findings which underlines the impressiveness of the undertaking, especially given that it was a one-person effort.

Prang, M., "Book Review" in *Canadian Historical Review* 47(2) (June):156-8.
This is a generally favourable review which, rather than critically assessing the strengths and weaknesses of *TVM*, uses some of its main findings and arguments to frame a series of questions designed to provoke Canadian historians into doing research in areas where Porter's work shows that lacunae exist.

Lower, A.R.M., "Book Review" in *Canadian Historical Review* 47(2) (June): 158-61.
Lower is scathing in his criticism of *TVM*. He condemns Porter (and sociologists more generally) for using jargon, for reducing reality to statistical categories, and for belabouring the obvious. He argues that Canadians do not subscribe to the myth of classlessness that Porter suggests they do and he criticizes Porter for — among other things — his use of a statistical definition of class, his failure to consider the impact of "metropolitanism" ("American financial imperialism")(159) on Canada, for his failure to take an historical approach, and for his attempt to develop an overly materialist explanation of Canadian society (i.e., for failing to acknowledge sufficiently the impact of ideas and ideals on social development).

Harris, R., "Education" in *University of Toronto Quarterly*, Letters in Canada:1965 35(4) (July):487-91.
Harris provides a good overall description of the major findings reported in *TVM*, but he focusses his comments on Porter's view of the role of education. He criticizes Porter for not addressing the issue of exactly how it is that the processes of selection and exclusion work

within the schools to make them class-biased. He also questions the criteria by which Porter selected some of his elites.

Hughes, E.C., "Book Review" in The *Annals* of the American Academy of Political and Social Science 366 (July):196.
Hughes' review offers a brief and glowing description of *TVM*.

Seeley, J.R. "Review" in *American Journal of Sociology* 72:3 (November)321-2.
Seeley highlights the main points of Porter's argument in a very complimentary way.

Ross, A.D., ["Book Review"] in *McGill Journal of Education* 1(2) (Fall):131-3.
Ross contends that the value of *TVM* is that for the first time it allows students of Canadian society to draw on Canadian rather than American data to illustrate sociological theories. She outlines the basic findings of *TVM* with relation to class and power and discusses Porter's assessment of education's role vis-a-vis social mobility. She concludes by praising Porter for adopting an explicit value position in *TVM*.

Bottomore, T.B. "Review" in *Canadian Journal of Economics and Political Science* 32(4) (November):527-8.
Bottomore begins his review by stressing the sociological advantage of starting one's analysis from a consideration of a society's class structure. He praises Porter's work in *TVM*, arguing that as "a documentary account of differences between classes" it is an "outstanding achievement" (527). He notes, however, that *TVM* is flawed by Porter's failure to recognize and examine factors such as the rise of the NDP, for such developments challenge his argument that Canadians generally adhere to a view of their society as classless.

Horowitz, I.L., "*The Vertical Mosaic*: A Review" in *American Sociological Review* 31 (December):862-3.
Horowitz suggests that the purpose of *TVM* is to explain why, given the existence of such a large number of divisive forces, there has been no open conflict in Canadian society. He provides a summary of the book, and praises Porter's use of social theory. While generally congratulatory, he does note Porter's failure to discuss American domination.

Mandel, E., "Book Review" in *Dialogue* 4(4) (December):546-8.
This review, written by a philosopher for an audience of philosophers, makes a few interesting but cryptic observations about Porter's

alleged adoption of a form of sociological and economic 'determinism'. Mandel also examines Porter's view of the academic establishment, his statistical conception of class, and his Hobbesian theory of power and the social contract.

1967   McEachern, G.A., "Book Review" in *Canadian Journal of Agricultural Economics* 15(1):145-6.
McEachern offers a brief description of Porter's findings.

Ellis, R., "Book Review" in *Social Forces* 45(3) (March):449-50.
Ellis' review is descriptive and generally complimentary. The exception is his comment that Porter is strongly influenced by an ideological commitment which causes him to paint "an overdrawn portrait of social inequality in Canada that often departs from the facts presented"(450).

Young,W., "Canadian Elites" in *Canadian Literature* 32 (Spring):74-5.

This brief review of *TVM* is basically descriptive and favourable. It is noteworthy in that it is the only one to make extensive reference to the labour elite. Young's basic point is that Porter's data confirm what social critics and those in the trade union movement have known for a long time; i.e., that they are peripheral to the real power structure of Canadian society.

Bottomore, T.B., "Book Review" in *Journal of Commonwealth Political Studies* 5(3) (November):245-6.
Bottomore notes that *TVM* is "one of the very few successful attempts to depict the class structure of a whole society"(246). He takes Porter to task, however, for not paying attention to recent social and political trends; particularly with regard to how they might indicate the development of a degree of class consciousness. He also argues that Porter could have more fully examined the apparent contradictoriness of the co-existence in Canadian society of both a class structure and a myth of classlessness. Bottomore criticizes Porter for not examining either the changing class structure of Quebec or the emergence there of nationalism and class consciousness. He also takes Porter to task for failing to note the American influence on Canadian society and for failing to compare developments in class structure and political movements in the two countries.

Dofny, J., "Book Review" in *Political Science Quarterly* 82(4) (December):654-6.
While commending Porter's effort, Dofny criticizes him on a

number of counts; eg., his use of a statistical conception of class and his consequent failure to discuss factors (such as social movements) which seem to suggest the existence of class consciousness, his theoretically-impoverished description of French-English relations, and his premature dismissal of Marx.

Longstaff, S., "John Porter's [The] *Vertical Mosaic*: A Critique with Some Reflections on the Canadian Scene" in *Berkeley Journal of Sociology* 12 :82-90.

Longstaff argues that *TVM* is Porter's attempt at a comprehensive discussion for the Canadian case of the Hobbesian problem of order and an attempt to explain why, given the many divisive forces operating in Canada, it does not break apart. He also makes the point that an important part of the analysis is Porter's (unfortunately implicit) comparison of Canada's class and elite structures with those of the United States. The strong points of Porter's analysis, says Longstaff, are his macro-focus, his value commitment, and his excellent use of scanty evidence. Weak points include the ahistorical nature of the analysis, his failure to make explicit use of comparative data, his failure to discuss American domination, his failure to discuss developments in Quebec and his related tendency to overestimate the stability of the Canadian system and its brokerage politics.

1968   Resnick, P. "*The Vertical Mosaic* Revisited: The Dynamics of Power in Canada" in *Our Generation* 6(1,2) (Summer):134-51.

Resnick provides a succinct but relatively detailed account of Porter's findings regarding class, power, elites, ethnicity and education and a list of the theoretical traditions upon which Porter drew (often implicitly) in developing his analysis. He takes issue with a number of aspects of *TVM*. First, he says that Porter tends to substitute documentation for theory. As a result, his theorizing is often implicit. He criticizes Porter's adoption of a statistical definition of class and suggests that this leads him to adopt an ahistorical, static approach to the study of Canadian society. He is especially critical of Porter's failure to discuss the conservative ideological role played by liberal ideology and suggests that this is where a truly radical critique of the Canadian class system must start.

1971   Boldt, M. "Images of Canada's Future in John Porter's [The] *Vertical Mosaic*". Pp. 188-207 in *The Sociology of the Future* edited by W. Bell and J.Mau. New York: Russell Sage Foundation.

Boldt describes a number of the major themes and historical trends outlined by Porter in *TVM* and then outlines the implicit image of Canada's future suggested by this analysis. He argues that Porter's image of Canada's future is too deterministic and pessimistic and suggests that Porter's data are amenable to multiple interpretations. He contends that the trends toward bureaucratization, rationalization, the centralization of power, etc. that Porter stresses are not as inevitable as Porter seems to think and he argues that the potential exists for Canada to be more democratic than Porter's conclusions would suggest.

1972   Heap, J. "Conceptual and Theoretical Problems in *The Vertical Mosaic*" in *Canadian Review of Sociology and Anthropology* 9(2) (May):176-87.

      This is among the most extensive critiques of *TVM* yet to appear. Heap analyses what he sees as a number of "conceptual, theoretical, and ethical problems with Porter's work which make it unsatisfactory even in terms of the particular canons of science [which Porter] would recognize as applicable to his work". The basic issue which Heap addresses is Porter's failure to provide an adequate "definition" of class (one which would be relational and which would incorporate the phenomenon of class consciousness) and his failure to adhere to the statistical definition he does adopt. Among the other problems Heap examines are Porter's alleged value inconsistency, his adoption of a "muted radicalism" employed, in Heap's view, as a "strategy of respectability" within the academy, his functionalist conception of power (as authority), and his elitist conception of democracy. [See Porter's response, "Conceptual and Theoretical Problems in *The Vertical Mosaic*: A Rejoinder" (pp.188-9) in same issue.]

1974   Heap, J. (ed.) *Everybody's Canada: The Vertical Mosaic Reviewed and Re-Examined.* Toronto: Burns and MacEachern.

      This book contains reprints of a number of book reviews of *TVM* plus a reprint of Heap's (1972) article from the *Canadian Review of Sociology and Anthropology* (see above).

      Black, E.R. "The Fractured Mosaic: John Porter Revisited" in *Canadian Public Administration* 17(4) (Winter):640-53.

      This is a "harsh" and entirely negative assessment of *TVM* written by a political scientist. Black describes a number of "methodological" shortcomings of *TVM* (eg., inadequate definitions, argument by assertion rather than from evidence, drawing conclusions not warranted by the data) which, in his view, make it both inaccurate and simplistic as a description and analysis of power and politics in Canada.

1975   Clement, W. *The Canadian Corporate Elite: An Analysis of Economic Power.* Toronto: McClelland and Stewart.

      Clement's book is a partial 'update' of *TVM*. While it deals only

with the economic and media elites, it improves on Porter's analysis
by examining the role of foreign (particularly U.S.) corporations in
Canada and by providing an historical account of Canada's economic
development. Clement employs a method very similar to Porter's, but
comes to different conclusions. He uses more recent data than
Porter's to demonstrate that there has been a progressive increase in
the ethnic and class exclusiveness of the economic and media elites
since Porter wrote *TVM*. He concludes that the combination of
interlocking corporate directorships, shared lifestyles, common
social origins, etc. among the economic and media elites provides
sufficient evidence to challenge Porter's plural elite model of Canadian society. He makes the argument that this group constitutes a
"corporate elite" which comes very close to comprising a 'ruling
class' in Marx's sense of the term.

1976   Rich, H., "*The Vertical Mosaic* Revisited: Toward a Macro-sociology of Canada" in *Journal of Canadian Studies* 11(1)
(February):14-31.

Rich argues that *TVM* presented an inaccurate view of Canadian
society because of "faulty data presentation and interpretation . . .
[and] because Porter ignored or gave short shrift to . . . American
economic and cultural domination and . . . political and cultural
rejuvenation in Quebec"(15). He uses comparative data to suggest
that — contrary to Porter's view — Canada had a higher rate of social
mobility than other Western liberal democracies and a more open elite
structure than Porter claimed.

1977   Clement, W. *Continental Corporate Power: Economic Linkages
Between Canada and the United States*. Toronto: McClelland and
Stewart.

In *The Canadian Corporate Elite* Clement began to place Canadian
economic development within the framework of an economy closely
linked to and highly dependent upon dominant American multinational corporations. I have included this study in the bibliography
despite the fact he does not provide an extensive critique of Porter's
work because, as in *The Canadian Corporate Elite*, Clement is very
clearly using *TVM* as a point of departure. In fact, much of the
analysis in both books is inspired by Clement's desire to pursue issues
raised but not adequately dealt with in *TVM*; most notably, the impact
of American corporations and elites on Canadian society. In *Continental Corporate Power*, Clement extends the analysis of continental
corporate relations he began in *The Canadian Corporate Elite*. He
begins with a discussion of the historical development of the economic relations between the two countries and, then, having in the

process identified the dominant corporations involved in this continental economy, attempts to outline the impact on the Canadian economy of American dominance. Special attention is paid to the social origins and characteristics of the economic elites in each country. Data from questionnaires and interviews supplement the standard positional type of analysis used in the study.

Towards 2000 (1971)

1971   Hansen, B. and F. Ireland, in *The Business Quarterly* 36(1) (Spring):31-7.
   The authors offer a succinct summary of the major themes in *Towards 2000* and they provide a rationale for the report which emphasizes the importance of the post-secondary educational system in the context of the development of Canada as a 'post-industrial' society. The article is descriptive rather than critical and concludes with mention of a number of the specific policy recommendations made in the report.

Smith, D., "Where Angels Fear to Tread" in *Journal of Canadian Studies* 1(3) (August):1-2.
   Smith is very critical of the report because, he says, "the most basic questions about higher education and society are simply not faced"(2). The problem is that while many of the authors' policy recommendations are liberal and humane and "can be defended on the ground that they would encourage men freely to nurture their abilities and interests"(2), no attempt is made to consider the illiberal and inhumane context of the hierarchical, regimented and centralized "post-industrial society" within which the educational system exists and which it is being called upon to serve.

Gauthier, G. "Commentaires [on *Towards 2000*]" in *STOA: Canadian Journal for the Study of Higher Education* 1(1):55-8.
   While noting the overall merit of the study, Gauthier offers a number of comments and criticisms from the point of view of a Québecois. He discusses the authors' general philosophy regarding the role and structure of the university, their specific proposals for a general B.A. program and their view of the respective roles of the federal and provincial governments. He expresses reservations about a number of the authors' 'technical' recommendations and argues, in addition, that the university and its role is likely to change more than they foresee. He argues as well that recent developments in debates over the structure of education in Quebec could be instructive to the author and suggests in conclusion that some of the report's recommendations concerning the federal government's role do not satisfac-

torily address some issues (eg., provincial rights) that concern Quebec in particular.

Macpherson, C.B. "A Note [on *Towards 2000]*" in *STOA: Canadian Journal for the Study of Higher Education* 1(1):58-60.
The focus of Macpherson's critique is narrow. He addresses his remarks to two issues: the authors' view of the best way of retaining excellence of scholarship in the universities and their view of tenure. He disagrees with their view that the 'professor-scholar' must constitute a smaller proportion of the professoriat in the future and he contends that tenure should be retained.

1972   Livingstone, D., "Inventing the Future: Anti-Historicist Reflections on *Towards 2000*" in *Interchange* 3(4):111-119.
Livingstone accuses Porter (he makes little mention of the other authors) of ascribing to an historicist philosophy of history. In particular, he criticizes Porter for regarding the features of Canada's impending 'post-industrial' society as given rather than subject to change. He contends that developments in human knowledge and the pursuit of interventionist strategies by citizens could easily — and will likely — confound attempts by social scientists to predict the future. Further, he says that the historicist assumptions of Porter *et al* have prevented them from advocating alternative visions of a non 'post-industrial' society and he demonstrates how (with relation to education) one could go about constructing just such an alternative.[See Porter's "Reply" (pp.120-1) and Livingstone's "Rejoinder" (pp.122-3) in the same issue.]

Does Money Matter? Prospects for Education (1973)

1974   Axelrod, P., "Education for Inequality" in *Canadian Forum* 54 (November-December):29-30.
Axelrod notes that the authors demonstrate the class-biased distribution of educational opportunity but criticizes them for adopting a liberal, piecemeal 'solution' to the problem of equality of access to post-secondary education.

Pike, R. "Economic Inequality and Accessibility to Higher Education" in *STOA: Canadian Journal for the Study of Higher Education* 4(2) :97-101.
Pike provides a brief but thorough summary of the findings reported in *Does Money Matter?;* noting that the authors' overall aim is to challenge "cultural" explanations for low educational aspirations held by lower-class Ontario youth. He argues that the most valuable feature of the book is the data it provides rather than the

policy recommendations it makes. The only significant weakness he mentions is the relative lack of attention paid to the community colleges.

1976   Kristjanson, G.A. "Review" in *Canadian Review of Sociology and Anthropology* 13(1) (February):122-3.
        In this brief, mostly descriptive review, Kristjanson stresses the importance of the first chapter, which reviews the literature on educational costs and equality of opportunity, and the final chapter, which deals with means of realizing equality of opportunity. The middle section of the book he says offers nothing new, but does provide evidence to support earlier studies. The one problem with the book is the authors' use of an absolute rather than relative measure of educational aspirations.

1979   Gifford, T., "Book Review". Pp.311-2 in *Canadian Book Review Annual 1979*, Toronto: PMA Books.
        This is a basically descriptive, but complimentary review which suggests that the book retains a degree of relevance — despite the dated nature of its information — because of the important themes with which it deals.

The Measure of Canadian Society (1979)

1980   Pike, R., "Book Review" in *Queen's Quarterly* 87(4) (Winter):718-9.
        Pike's review uses the essays in *The Measure of Canadian Society* as a foil to provide a sensitive, thematic overview of the concerns — freedom, equality, rationality, and justice — that guided Porter's analysis of inequality, ethnicity, power and politics throughout his career. He notes the change in Porter's faith in the ameliorative, progressive, 'levelling' potential of education and his opposition to the growth of ethnic revivalism. He suggests that while Porter was a liberal, he was not a "tired old reformist" (719) but, rather, a "concerned left-liberal" (718); a reflective man of vision and intellect who remained throughout his life in "constant dynamic pursuit of a more just and equitable Canada through democratic social change" (719).

1981   Mann, W.E., "Book Review" in *Canadian Journal of Sociology* 6(3) (Summer):389-92.

        Mann's thoughtful review tends more to describe and assess Porter's intellectual approach and place in the landscape of Canadian sociology rather than examine the specific contents of *The Measure of*

Canadian Society. Mann argues that *The Measure of Canadian Society*, like Porter's other writings, reveals him to be among the most esteemed bearers of liberal Canadian sociology's "received wisdom"(389). He briefly discusses a number of the major themes in Porter's work — the importance of the university, the role of education in creating upward mobility, the possibility of 'egalitarianism', the movement toward increasing democratization in Canadian society, a belief in the compatibility of technological and human progress, and the necessity of a strong federal government — and concludes that, while flexible, Porter's overall political and sociological viewpoints demonstrated a considerable degree of resilience over time. The 'weakness' of Porter's work in *The Measure of Canadian Society* — as elsewhere — says Mann, is that it is insufficiently critical of the liberal faith in science, technology and the inevitability of progress. For this reason, he argues, some sociologists will find Porter's work "unimaginative and wanting" (391). He concludes by noting Porter's powerful, long-term and continuing impact on the development of Canadian sociology.

Stations and Callings: Making it Through the School System (1982)

1982   Thomson, A., "Book Review". P. 379 in *Canadian Book Review Annual 1982*, Toronto: PMA Books.

This is a brief, basically favourable account of the basic findings reported in *Stations and Callings*.

1983   Murphy, R. "Book Review" in *Canadian Review of Sociology and Anthropology* 20(3) (August):380-2.

Murphy argues that the authors use a test of mental ability which is "culturally biased" against cultural minorities and those of low socio-economic status. This mistakenly points to a lack of mental ability rather than to economic or economically-determined cultural factors as the causes of low aspiration among cultural minorities and those from lower socio-economic status groups. He questions the authors' conclusion that the school system itself is "reasonably meritocratic" (381; citing Porter *et al*, 1982:313) and criticizes them for failing to determine why students from privileged economic backgrounds have higher educational aspirations and attainment than the less fortunate students. He also takes them to task for having used path analysis as a substitute for theory and he disagrees with their argument that educational aspirations and expectations are reliable indicators of attainment.

Ellis, J.F., "Book Review" in *Queen's Quarterly* 90(4) (Winter):1163-5.

Ellis provides a brief summary of the investigators' findings but is critical of the dated nature of the information (collected 1971; reported 1982), their failure to review studies completed since 1971, and their weak and improper attempt (no data) to go beyond aspirations and explain educational achievement. He notes also the mistitling of the volume, which deals only with Ontario.

1984 Pomfret, A., "Book Review" in *Contemporary Sociology* 13(2) (March):186-7.

Pomfret's remarks are basically descriptive but he does suggest that he finds the study disappointing because of the "underdeveloped nature of the theory informing the data collection and analysis. . . . The explanations offered relied heavily on very general, and highly questionable, notions of class-and gender-specific socialization processes" (186). He suggests that more context-sensitive and situationally-specific concerns derived from ethnographic studies would have been useful.

Ascription and Achievement: Studies in Mobility and Status Attainment in Canada (1986)

1986 Conway, F., "Book Review" in *Canadian Review of Sociology and Anthropology* 23(4) (November): 593-5.

Conway's summary of the main findings of the 1973 Canadian Mobility Study describes it as a "very useful update on Porter's work in *TVM*" (593) vis-a-vis our understanding of the relationships between educational and occupational attainment, gender, social origins, ethnicity, immigrant status and migration on the one hand and individual social mobility on the other. In other ways, however, he finds the book a disappointment. The major reason is that it avoids discussion of "the most important aspects of inequality and mobility"; i.e., "the class location of the individual, the relations between classes, the role of the state, the structure of the educational system, and the structure of the economy" (592; citing Boyd *et al*, 1986:2). He also suggests that the volume suffers from a paucity of theoretical explanation. Most of what passes for theory is actually description.

II. ABOUT HIS WORK IN GENERAL

1976 Goldenberg, S., "Canadian Encouragement of Higher Educational Participation: An Empirical Assessment" in *International Journal of Comparative Sociology* 17(3,4) (September-December):284-99.

Goldenberg disputes the conventional 'culturalist' explanation of differential rates of university attendance in Canada and the United States. According to this view, one adopted by Porter, such differences are to be interpreted as a consequence of a lower cultural evaluation of the importance of education on the part of Canadians. Using interview data (1000 students at six matched universities in Canada and the United States), he makes the argument that it is structural variables — in particular, differences in educational costs to individuals and differences in the 'absorptive capacity' of the two economies (making for different outcomes in 'cost-benefit' analyses performed by individual Canadians and Americans) — that explain different rates of participation.

1978-9 Mellos, K. ''Critical Remarks on Critical Elite Theory'' in *Journal of Canadian Studies* 13(4) (Winter):72-88.

In this provocative and thoughtful essay, Mellos forges a different kind of analysis of Porter than has been offered by other students of his work [saving brief comments made by Heap (1972) and Hofley (1981)]. He makes his argument via a description and discussion of the differing ''critiques'' of liberalism and capitalism provided by Porter, C. Wright Mills and Wallace Clement — three well-known scholars who have worked within the ''elite studies'' tradition in North American sociology. Mellos argues that despite political, theoretical and methodological differences amongst them, each adheres to a common ''epistemological'' stance. This epistemological stance contains a number of ''liberal'' assumptions about human nature, social structure and knowledge that prevents them from offering the radical or fundamental sort of critique of capitalist society undertaken by Marx. Mellos outlines the details of his critique via an in-depth analysis of their respective views on inequality of condition and opportunity, power, representation, social mobility, the state, and class.

1979   Assheton-Smith, M. ''John Porter's Sociology: A Theoretical Basis for Canadian Education'' in *Canadian Journal of Education* 4(2):43-54.

Assheton-Smith describes the theory of education and the image of the relationship between knowledge and society that is contained in Porter's writings. She challenges the combined stratification-elite approach that he takes to the study of class and power, disputes the accuracy of the 'post-industrial' thesis that he adopts, and challenges his functionalist portrayal of the role of the educational system (i.e., as involved in the sorting and allocation of talent and the inculcation of dominant values). She also disputes his uncritical acceptance of a positivist and 'technicist' interpretation of knowledge. The alternative interpretation of the society-education-knowledge relation that she briefly outlines is heavily influenced by the work of Marxist theorists and the Frankfurt school.

Darroch, A.G., ''Another Look at Ethnicity, Stratification and Social Mobility in Canada'' in *Canadian Journal of Sociology* 4(1) (Winter):1-25.

Darroch combines his own re-analysis of the data which Porter used in *TVM* with a review of other studies of various aspects of Porter's data which have been done by other Canadian sociologists to develop the argument that neither ethnic group membership nor immigrant status had as great an influence on socio-economic status as Porter suggested. He also contends that there is little truth to the thesis of ''ethnically blocked mobility''; suggesting that neither ethnic affiliation nor immigrant status had as much influence on individual social mobility as the ''vertical mosaic'' hypothesis suggested. He does not, however, dispute Porter's argument that there were and are ethnic barriers to entrance into Canada's various elites.

1980   Clement, W. ''Searching for Equality: The Sociology of John Porter'' in *Canadian Journal of Political and Social Theory* 4(2) (Spring-Summer):97-114.

Clement provides an overview of Porter's scholarly contribution. He attributes the weaknesses in *TVM* to the lack of data available at the time of its writing and praises it as the first comprehensive analysis of Canadian society. He outlines and offers a critique of Porter's views on a broad range of sociological topics including the meritocracy, barriers to individual achievement, power, education, ethnicity, class. He stresses throughout that Porter was concerned in all of his research endeavours both to accurately describe existing social conditions and to try and discover the circumstances that would allow Canada to do away with the economic and political differentials that prevented it from becoming a fully rational, humane, and just society.

Olsen, D. *The State Elite*. Toronto, McClelland and Stewart.

Though Olsen's book does not contain a great deal of direct commentary, I have included it here because it is clearly inspired by Porter's *TVM*. Olsen examines the transformation in the structure and workings of the Canadian state 1953-73, updates some of Porter's findings from *TVM* regarding the social characteristics and backgrounds of the state elite, and performs an analysis of two major decisions taken by this group in the mid-1970s.

1981   Clement, W. ''John Porter and the Development of Sociology in Canada'' in *Canadian Review of Sociology and Anthropology* 18(5) (December):583-94.

Clement provides some biographical information about Porter, a brief listing of his major publications and an assessment of his contribution to the historical development of Canadian sociology. He notes the problems attendant Porter's reliance on education as a solution to the problems of 'post-industrial society' but remarks that Porter moved away from this position later in his career. In addition, he defends Porter against Heap's (1972) claim that by failing to adopt a more radical interpretation of the data in *TVM* he had pursued a self-serving "strategy of respectability" and he argues that Porter made more use of theory than is generally appreciated.

Hofley, J. "John Porter: His Analysis of Class and His Contribution to Canadian Sociology" in *Canadian Review of Sociology and Anthropology* 18(5) (December):595-606.

According to Hofley, Porter's views on class and power are those of a "liberal" and "Weberian", for he conceives of classes as distributive and nominalist groups rather than as relational and real ones and he thinks of power as an inevitable feature of society; particularly modern industrial ones. In an attempt to situate *TVM* in its historical context, he notes the relative lack of Marxist and/or critical literature available when Porter was preparing the manuscript. He remarks that Porter's relative lack of interest in theoretical issues led to the formation of a (partly implicit) eclectic theoretical position which was not particularly adequate and he concludes by suggesting Porter's long-term influence in a number of areas of contemporary Canadian sociological research.

Olsen, D. "Power, Elites and Society" in *Canadian Review of Sociology and Anthropology* 18(5) (December):607-14.

Olsen characterizes *TVM* as an outstanding example of the "power and stratification" approach to the study of inequality; an approach which had its roots in the work of Raymond Aron in the 1950s. It is one of a genre of such studies, e.g., Mills (U.S.A.), Encel (Australia), and Dahrendorf (Germany), which focusses on institutional and bureaucratic power in an attempt to find an alternative to the ruling class theory of the Marxists and the pluralism of the liberals. Olsen outlines his view of Porter's conception of power. He also notes that both his own work (*The State Elite*, 1980) and the work of W. Clement (*The Canadian Corporate Elite*, 1975; *Intercontinental Corporate Power*, 1977) demonstrate Porter's impact. He distinguishes their work from Porter's, noting that Porter was more influenced by liberalism than Marxism, and that his analysis of the structure of power focussed on equality of opportunity and individual mobility rather than on equality of condition and collective change. Olsen discusses some of the differences between Porter's study of elites and other period studies of elites and concludes with some remarks about recent developments in elite studies in Canada.

Pineo, P.C. "Prestige and Mobility: The Two National Surveys" in *Canadian Review of Sociology and Anthropology* 18(5) (December):615-26.

Pineo provides an historical sketch of Porter's major role in the completion of Canadian sociology's first two national surveys (i.e., the occupational prestige study of 1964 and the occupational mobility study of 1973) and argues that his involvement in and 'sponsorship' of survey research was crucial to accelerating the development of this type of research in Canada. He argues, in addition, that Porter's involvement in these surveys was sufficiently extensive that they must be seen as integral to the "main body of his intellectual work" (619). He concludes by arguing that Porter was interested in furthering the development of large-scale surveys because they would allow sociologists to deal with the larger issues that affect the whole of Canadian society.

Porter, M. "John Porter and Education: Technical Functionalist or Conflict Theorist" in *Canadian Review of Sociology and Anthropology* 18(5) (December):627-38.

Marion Porter reviews the historical changes in Porter's view of the role of education in modern, industrial society. She argues that, while early in his career his view corresponded closely to that of the 'technical functionalists', his later view, under the influence of important new empirical and theoretical work by liberal and Marxist critics of the system, came much closer to that of the conflict theorists.

Vallee, F. "The Sociology of John Porter: Ethnicity as Anachronism" in *Canadian Review of Sociology and Anthropology* 18(5) (December):639-50.

Vallee argues that Porter was against the maintenance of ethnic ties and against ethnic collectivism not because he believed in Anglo-Saxon cultural superiority but because he thought that both, by virtue of their stress on ascriptive and particularistic criteria of judgement, prevented the universal application of the principle of meritocratic individualism. If Porter was to choose between an ethnic "mosaic" and a "melting pot", Vallee says he would choose the melting pot because he didn't like the barriers to progress — measured in terms of individual mobility and social efficiency — which were created by the irrationality of ethnic prejudice. Vallee illustrates his point by analysing Porter's views on the independentist movement in Quebec, the native rights movement and the multicultural movement in Canada.

Forcese, D. "The Macro-sociology of John Porter" in *Canadian Review of Sociology and Anthropology* 18(5) (December):651-6.

In this wide-ranging and forceful essay, Forcese outlines his interpretation of Porter's views on both a number of substantive topics (e.g., inequality, power, ethnicity, meritocracy, education) and the nature and role of sociology more generally. According to Forcese, Porter saw inequality as inevitable. At the same time, though, he believed that it should be based on merit rather than property ownership. Furthermore, he regarded the educational system as the best — if imperfect — vehicle for developing a just, rational and efficient social order. Forcese suggests that Porter saw sociology as best practised when it was 'macro' in focus, informed but not distracted by theory, empirical in content, critical in approach, and morally engaged with the major issues and problems of society.

1985   Helmes-Hayes, R. ''John Porter'', Pp. 610-729 in *Images of Inequality in Early Canadian Sociology, 1922-1965*, unpublished Ph.D. dissertation, University of Toronto, Toronto.

This chapter contains a very detailed summary of *TVM* as well as a critical review of most of the major critiques of *TVM* that had appeared up to 1985.

1986   Helmes-Hayes, R. ''Images of Inequality in Pre-Porter Canadian Sociology'' a paper presented to the Plenary Session on John Porter at the Annual Meetings of the Ontario Anthropology and Sociology Association, Wilfrid Laurier University, Waterloo, October.

Through an analysis of the writings of Carl Dawson, Everett Hughes, Leonard Marsh and S.D. Clark, this paper demonstrates that early Canadian sociologists paid more theoretical and empirical attention to issues of inequality than has generally been recognized. Special attention is paid to the similarities between *TVM* and Leonard Marsh's *Canadians In and Out of Work* [Montreal: Oxford University Press, 1940].

IV. BIOGRAPHICAL INFORMATION

1979   Memorial Service for John Porter. Tributes by Bruce A. McFarlane, Hugh A, McRoberts, James Downey, A. Davidson Dunton, Carleton University, Ottawa, June 25.

Clement, W. ''Obituary: John Porter (1921-1979)'' in *Society* 3(3) (September):14.

Vallee, F. ''John Porter, 1921-1979'' in *Proceedings* of the Royal Society of Canada, Series IV, Volume XVII :92-6.

1980   Vallee, F. "Obituary: John Porter (1921-1979)" in *Society* 4(1) (January):14.

1985   Helmes-Hayes, R. "John Porter, 1921-1979". Pp. 99-104 in *Images of Inequality in Early Canadian Sociology, 1922-1965*, unpublished Ph.D. dissertation, University of Toronto, Toronto.

1986   Porter, M. "John Porter" a paper presented to the Plenary Session on John Porter at the Annual Meetings of the Ontario Anthropology and Sociology Association, Wilfrid Laurier University, Waterloo, October.

Index

Index

Industrialization; Mobility.
Labour party, 217; 1944 reforms in
English education and, 243
Lagacé, Michael D., 205n.
Leacock, Stephen, 34, 152
Leadership, 62, 210; importance
of, in Quebec, 108-9; inability of
Canadian political system to
provide, 166; role of, in
democracy, 232, 236. *See also*
Elites.
Liberal party supporters, 175ff.
Lipset, S.M., 42, 74-75, 80, 85n.,
99, 239n.
London School of Economics
(L.S.E.), 9-10

Macdonald Report, 203
Macpherson, C.B., 273-74
Marsden, Denis, 79
Marshall, T.H., 3, 128
Marx, Karl, 16, 212, 264
Mass media, elites and, 220; need
for control of, 231; politics and,
165-66
McDougall, Robert L., 96
McInnis, Edgar, 241
McKenzie, R.T., 239n.
McLuhan, Marshall, 67; global
village and, 187
McRoberts, Hugh A., 279n.
Means, G.C., 13-15
Merton, Robert K., 86n.
Métis, 53
Migration, American immigration,
141-42; Canadian immigration
and emigration, 35-36, 45-46, 93-
94, 131-32, 143-44, 154, 159;
immigration policy in Canada,
150; skilled and professional
worker, 37, 57, 60-61, 65, 68-70,
190, 241; stratification and, 32-
36, 122-25
Miller, S.M., 78, 87n.
Mills, C. Wright, 19-20
Minority groups. *See* Ethnicity.
Mobility, upward social, 57, 74-77,
82, 125-26, 147, 192; aspirations,
80-81; education and, 82, 241,

250, 269; erosion of traditional
culture and, 111; industrial, 213,
263; off-farm migration as
upward or downward, 266-67
Mosaic, ethnic, 49; melting pot
versus, 42-43, 116, 135, 139ff.
See also Ethnicity.
Mosca, G., 17, 18, 20, 174
Moynihan, Daniel Patrick, 103

Naegele, Kaspar, 99
New Democratic party, 207;
federal elections and, 175ff.;
founding of, 208; supporters,
175
Nisbet, Robert, 248
Noel, Donald L., 121
Nozick, Robert, and *Anarchy,
State and Utopia*, 1, 248-49;
entitlement theory, 249

O'Brien, Conor Cruise, 130
Occupations. *See* Labor force;
Industrialization; Mobility.
Official Languages Act, 118
Oliver, Michael, 208
Organization for Economic Co-
operation and Development
(OECD), 85n., 244

Pareto, V., 17-18
Parsons, Talcott, 12, 124, 128
Parti Quebecois, 48, 109, 163
Piaget, Jean, 249
Pickersgill, J.W., 97
Pineo, Peter C., 175, 279n.
Politics, Canadian political system
and, 5, 97-98, 166; journalists
and, 166; new conservatism in,
4; television, effects of, 165. *See
also* Federalism.
Popper, K.R., 10
Population, aboriginal, 52-53;
changing proportion of British
in, 92, 153; growth of, 43-44, 93-
94, 143
Power, 2, 207ff.; concentration in
banking, 227; concentration of
decision making, 275-76;